OTHER BOOKS BY STEPHEN PRICKETT

Do It Yourself Doom (Gollancz, 1962)

Coleridge and Wordsworth: the Poetry of Growth
(Cambridge University Press, 1970)

Wordsworth and Coleridge: the 'Lyrical Ballads',
in 'Studies in English Literature' series (Edward Arnold, 1975)

Romanticism and Religion

The Tradition of Coleridge and Wordsworth in the Victorian Church

STEPHEN PRICKETT

Lecturer in English
School of English and American Studies
University of Sussex

CAMBRIDGE UNIVERSITY PRESS

CAMBRIDGE

LONDON · NEW YORK · MELBOURNE

Published by the Syndics of the Cambridge University Press
The Pitt Building, Trumpington Street, Cambridge CB2 1RP
Bentley House, 200 Euston Road, London NW1 2DB
32 East 57th Street, New York, NY 10022, USA
296 Beaconsfield Parade, Middle Park, Melbourne 3206, Australia

Library of Congress catalogue card number: 75-22554

ISBN: 0 521 21072 0

First published 1976

Printed in Great Britain by
W & J Mackay Limited, Chatham

Contents

The influence of Plato tinges the British genius. Their minds loved analogy; were cognisant of resemblances, and climbers on the staircase of unity. 'Tis a very old strife between those who elect to see identity and those who elect to see discrepances [*sic*]; and it renews itself in Britain. The poets, of course, are of one part; the men of the world, of the other.

I can well believe what I have often heard, that there are two nations in England; but it is not the Poor and the Rich, nor is it the Normans and Saxons, nor the Celt and the Goth. These are each always becoming the other; for Robert Owen does not exaggerate the power of circumstance. But the two complexions, or two styles of mind, – the perceptive class, and the practical finality class, – are ever in counterpoise, interacting mutually, one in hopeless minorities; the other in huge masses; one studious, contemplative, experimenting; the other, the ungrateful pupil, scornful of the source whilst availing itself of the knowledge for gain; these two nations, of genius and of animal force, though the first consist of only a dozen souls and the second of twenty millions, forever by their discord and their accord yield the power of the English State.

Emerson, *English Traits* (Routledge, 1883), pp. 226, 246.

Acknowledgements

Part of chapter 1 was originally delivered as a paper (with the same title) to the Wordsworth Summer School at Charlotte Mason College, Ambleside, in 1972, and subsequently appeared in *The Wordsworth Circle* in Spring 1973. A shortened version of chapter 6 was published in *Theology* for July 1973. I am grateful to the editors of both journals for their permission to use the material involved. I am also grateful to Mr Alwyne Coleridge, as copyright owner, for giving me permission to quote from the unpublished Coleridge Notebooks.

It is a pleasure to record the personal debt I owe to the many friends and colleagues who have helped me with information, advice, and criticism during the five years I have been intermittently working on this book. Peter Burke will probably not remember the chance remark that launched me into reading Newman's *Essay on the Development of Doctrine*, any more than Kathleen Bliss will recall the conversation in a car on Tooting Broadway that first suggested to me the subtleties of Victorian prosopography, but it was in such moments that the idea of this book originated. For the consolidation of those first tentative ideas I owe an enormous debt to my former colleague at Smith College, Maurianne Adams, who allowed me to read her doctoral thesis, *Coleridge and the Victorians*. From Nicholas Lash, of St Edmund's House, Cambridge, and John Coulson, of Bristol University, I have received an immense amount of patient, detailed, and scholarly assistance – particularly with my studies of Newman. No less valuable was a paper on 'Objectivity' by Tony Palmer, of Southampton University, delivered at the University Teachers' Group Conference at Gregynog in September 1973; he has generously allowed me to make use of many of his ideas in that paper and another unpublished one, 'Belief and Will'. Dr Robert Burns, late of Princeton University, has kindly allowed me to refer to his unpublished thesis, *David Hume and Miracles in Historical Perspective*.

Many other friends have read the manuscript and made helpful comments or pointed out errors. I should like to express my gratitude to John Barrell, Duncan Forrester, George Mabbutt, Michael Moran, John Perry, Desmond Ryan, and Michael Wadsworth, as well as to my father, W. E. Prickett, for the time they have spent in this way. For the mistakes and inaccuracies from which I have been saved by these, and others, I am greatly indebted – for any that remain, I am solely responsible.

Sussex, 1975   S.P.

Introduction

'There are, I think,' wrote H. D. Traill in 1884, 'distinct traces of a Coleridgean legend which has only slowly died out.'

The actual truth I believe to be that Coleridge's position from 1818 or 1820 until his death, though one of the greatest eminence, was in no sense one of the highest, or even of any considerable influence... A few mystics of the type of Maurice, a few eager seekers after truth like Sterling, may have gathered, or fancied they gathered, distinct dogmatic instruction from the Highgate oracles; and, no doubt, to the extent of his influence over the former of these disciples, we may justly credit Coleridge's discourses with having exercised a real if only a transitory directive effect upon nineteenth century thought. But the terms in which his influence is sometimes spoken of appear, as far as one can judge of the matter at this distance of time, to be greatly exaggerated.[1]

To judge by the recent spate of books on Coleridge, even if we include only those that deal with his religious and metaphysical thought, Traill's obituary on the Coleridge legend was, perhaps, premature. Not all modern judgements have been favourable, it is true, but *odium theologicum* is the stuff of literary as well as theological legends.[2] Even were we to discount those studies which have largely concentrated on viewing Coleridge as conventional 'theologian', which possibly lay too much stress on his turning in old age towards conservatism and the safe haven of orthodox religious formulations to atone for a mis-spent Unitarian youth, it is still true to say that he is being more widely recognised than ever before as a major and seminal religious thinker.[3] The Coleridgean legend is alive and well.

[1] *Coleridge* (Macmillan, 1884), pp. 207, 205.
[2] See, most recently, Norman Fruman's *Coleridge: The Damaged Archangel* (Allen & Unwin, 1972).
[3] For instance, James D. Boulger, *Coleridge as Religious Thinker* (Yale, 1961). Robert Barth, *Coleridge and Christian Doctrine* (Harvard, 1969).

1

But there is a sense in which Traill himself is a part of that 'legend', for it has always been an equivocal one. It is hard to believe that Emerson did not have the tradition of Coleridge partly in mind when, in 1856, he made his observations about the 'two Englands'. Certainly, nowhere are his comments about 'the poets' and 'the men of the world' better illustrated. For the latter, Coleridge was what he seemed to be when Emerson actually made his tragi-comic visit to the Gillman's house in Highgate in August 1833: the ruined sage, corpulent, querulous, pompous, and all but unintelligible, 'too old and preoccupied...' to 'bend to a new companion and think with him'.[1] Carlyle's famous description[2] accords too closely with Emerson's and those of other visitors for this portrait not to carry conviction. Ostensibly his reputation as 'a poet' was unquestioned by his critics. It was Coleridge the philosopher, metaphysician, and theologian who drew such scorn; Coleridge the man who evoked such amazed contempt. For his critics, his religious thinking could either be 'explained' in terms of his own severe psychological problems, or assessed as a curious and even pathetic extension of his un-philosophical re-hash of contemporary German philosophy, mostly plagiarised, and put together without any insight into the 'essential incompatibility of different trends of thought'.[3] The view of Carlyle and De Quincey gained support from revelations about Coleridge's drug-addiction after his death, and by the time Traill produced his influential critical biography of Coleridge for Macmillan's 'English Men of Letters' series in 1884, the division between Coleridge the poet and Coleridge the theologian had hardened into a critical orthodoxy. Against this majority consensus there persisted a small number – never more than a tiny minority even within the Church of England – for whom Coleridge stood for much more: the possibility of unity between philosophy, theology, and aesthetics.

Classification [wrote F. J. A. Hort] is our pride and pleasure; and woe be to that which refuses to be classified. An author whose opinions will not range with those of any recognised party, or whose works never seem quite rightly lodged in any one division of a well-regulated library, occupies in general estimation what was once the place of a

---

[1] *English Traits*, p. 17.
[2] *Life of Sterling* (Chapman & Hall, 1893), ch. vii: and see pp. 34–6 below.
[3] Rene Wellek, *Immanuel Kant in England* (Princeton, 1931), p. 67.

zoophyte or a platypus, – an uncanny creature, possibly of demoniacal origin.

Such a divine monster was Coleridge.[1]

Hort's essay appeared in 1856 – the same year as Emerson's *English Traits* which displays this very perplexity over classifying Coleridge. Granted that much of what his detractors said about his propensity to plagiarism, the exaggeration of his claims, and the failure of his personal life, was only too true, it is the more surprising that many of this minority of admirers were in fact themselves professional philosophers, like John Stuart Mill, or, like Julius Hare and F. J. A. Hort, theologians and historians well-versed in the relevant German sources. Those who read Coleridge did not form a movement. 'I rejoice to think', wrote F. D. Maurice, 'that those who have most profited by what he has taught them, do not and cannot form a school.'[2] They included such men as Maurice himself, John Sterling, Julius Hare and his brother Augustus, F. C. Robertson, F. J. A. Hort, and George MacDonald; more cautiously, and with obligatory public reservations, members of the Oxford Movement like Keble and Newman; and, more surprisingly, men of totally different backgrounds and traditions, from Mill to Disraeli. Moreover, it is significant that even his enemies found themselves unable to leave Coleridge alone. They returned repeatedly to the attack as if the shambling Sage of Highgate still constituted some kind of threat that it was necessary to exorcise. As Maurice acidly observed about such detractors – probably with Carlyle specifically in mind – those who really wanted from him a justification of the status quo could find it better elsewhere – in de Maistre, for instance – but instead they returned to Coleridge, calling him always 'poor Coleridge',

And though this phrase is jointed, of course, with others about 'transcendental, mystical stuff' it is clear from the faces of the speakers, that they could well have endured what they did *not* understand in the discourse or his books; but that, now and then a phrase or passage made itself painfully intelligible to them, and produced a half-awakening in souls which preferred to be asleep.[3]

[1] 'Coleridge', *Cambridge Essays* (1856), p. 292.
[2] Dedication to *The Kingdom of Christ*, 4th. edn. (Macmillan, 1891), p. xi.
[3] Anonymous Introduction (by Maurice) to Julius Charles Hare's *Charges to the Clergy of the Archdeaconry of Lewes* (Macmillan, 1856), pp. xix–xx.

'There is something in Maurice, and his master Coleridge,' wrote Dean Church in one of his notebooks in 1828 at a time when he was fast falling under Newman's influence, 'which wakens thought in me more than any other writings almost: with all their imputed mysticism they seem to me to say plain things as often as most people.'[1]

Wordsworth's fate as a serious religious influence has been a kind of mirror-image of Coleridge's. Where Coleridge was held to be Mr Moly Mystic,[2] lost in the fogs of teutonic transcendentalism, his fellow poet and one-time closest collaborator was held to be too banal for serious attention as a moralist, too philosophically naive to be more than a reassuring guide to the landscape. 'We cannot do him justice,' declares Matthew Arnold, 'until we dismiss his formal philosophy.'[3] Whereas Coleridge had been reproached for his economic and emotional dependence on others, Wordsworth was held to be too indecently full of rectitude, respectability, and worldly success for a truly original mind.

The following chapters are about Coleridge and Wordsworth as religious thinkers, and about the minority tradition who found themselves, in various ways, 'awakened' by them. In our attempts to understand this awakening, it is important to notice at the outset that the debate about their metaphysics, philosophy, and theology cannot in fact – as many of their critics wished to claim – be entirely insulated from their poetry. This was an argument made superficially more plausible by the fact that Coleridge, in particular, had written his poetry at a different period of his life from his theology and metaphysics. Yet such a separation between form and content is not one that would have been critically acceptable for a moment to Wordsworth and Coleridge themselves, any more than it would have been to the poets and critics who preceded them, Milton, for instance, or Dryden, or Johnson – on whom the Romantics, in turn, had passed judgement. The notion of differentiating a poet's 'ideas' from his 'verse' would have seemed to be challenging the whole concept of poetry as the product of an organically unified sensibility. This kind of distinction put forward by both Carlyle and

---

[1] *Life and Letters of Dean Church*, ed. Mary C. Church (Macmillan, 1895), p. 17.
[2] Thomas Love Peacock, *Melincourt* (1817), ch. XXXI.
[3] 'Wordsworth', *Essays in Criticism: Second Series* (Macmillan, 1888), p. 149.

Arnold would have implied to them a lack of seriousness about the nature of poetry itself, and a fundamental devaluation of its status. Indeed, to maintain it with any stamina requires one of two positions. Either the doctrine of 'two truths' – the assumption that one may say as 'poetry' things that would be nonsense or lies said in prose – or the 'intentional fallacy' – the belief that what a poet actually says may be very different from what he intends to say. Now both these arguments have grave weaknesses when applied to Wordsworth or Coleridge. The idea of 'two truths', as advanced by John Stuart Mill,[1] is basically an attempt to defend poetry from the criticism of the hard-nosed Benthamite tradition of his father, who saw little more in it than a conglomeration of fanciful images of doubtful veracity. Against this view Mill argues that poetry is largely expressive of the feelings of the poet, and is not necessarily meant to tell us anything about the objects on to which that feeling is projected. It is the opposite of analysis, describing a different area of human experience. The truths of poetry are fundamentally different from the truths of science. Yet the essence of the Wordsworth/ Coleridge position (which Newman was to develop so brilliantly in the *Grammar of Assent*) was that religious experience, like sense experience, was *neither* 'internal' (subjective) *nor* 'external' (objective) but a balance or dialectic between the two. For them, poetry brought together the 'two worlds' in a bond that, like sense perception, was indivisible. Mill was only able to maintain his neo-Cartesian division simply because he was solely interested in the 'culture of the feelings'[2] and not in the fundamentally religious basis on which this depended. It is probably true, as Mill himself suggests, that he had almost no appreciation of what religious experience might mean.

Matthew Arnold, on the other hand, had. His case, that Wordsworth deceived himself about his true poetic qualities, is at first sight more plausible. Coleridge argues a very similar case about Wordsworth in *Biographia Literaria*.[3] To a limited extent, it is probably true. Yet to argue that we can ignore an author's 'intentions' in reading his poetry is as dangerous as the opposite approach: concluding that because a writer is a 'good' theologian

---

[1] 'Two Kinds of Poetry', *Essays on Literature and Society*, Ed. Schneewind (Collier-Macmillan, 1965).

[2] *Autobiography*, World's Classics (Oxford, 1924), p. 127.   [3] Ch. xiv.

or philosopher, his writing is therefore 'good' art. The relation-ship between an artist's beliefs and his work is never simple. In normal living we practice a modified behaviourism over people's 'intentions': we do not merely judge what a person intends by his ostensible beliefs or what he claims to be trying to do, but also by what he actually *does*.[1] In the case of Wordsworth, more than Coleridge, there *is* a discrepancy between poetic theory and practice, but most of us would not argue on account of this that, say, the poetic theory in the later books of *The Prelude* was *less* 'intentional' than the Prefaces of 1800/1802 or 1815. In the case of Coleridge, I have argued elsewhere, and will be arguing throughout this book, that the later theological speculation arises directly from his poetry, and cannot be understood without refer-ence to it. The influence of Wordsworth and Coleridge on their successors is neither simply theological, nor simply aesthetic, but in their sense of the word, 'poetic' – in other words, an indivisible union of the two. In the long run, the debate is not whether Coleridge and Wordsworth, two great poets, were in addition thinkers with something of importance to say, but whether they were major poets at all. Mill's claim that Coleridge was one of the two seminal minds of the nineteenth century[2] is not about his poetry, but it is not unconnected with the fact that he was a poet.

This book, then, is not a survey or summary of the develop-ment of nineteenth-century theology in relation to the work of Coleridge and Wordsworth. It has already been surveyed and summarised by better historians of theology than I:[3] my object is to question some of the assumptions on which the conventional judgements of 'influence' depend. It is more than thirty years since C. R. Sanders' *Coleridge and the Broad Church Movement*[4] was published and many of us today would wish to ask different kinds of questions from those answered by the conventional wisdom of a generation ago. Literature and theology still be-longed in separate compartments. We would be even more inclined now than then to doubt the value of describing as a 'movement' anything which included Whately, Matthew Arnold,

[1] See A. D. Nuttall's, 'Did Mersault Mean to Kill the Arab? – The Intentional Fallacy Fallacy', *The Critical Quarterly* (Spring, 1968).

[2] John Stuart Mill, *Bentham and Coleridge*, ed. F. R. Leavis (Chatto, 1950), p. 40.

[3] See, for instance, V. F. Storr, *The Development of English Theology in the Nine-teenth Century, 1800–1860* (Longman, 1913); or B. M. G. Reardon, *From Cole-ridge to Gore* (Longman, 1971).   [4] Duke University Press, 1942.

Jowett, Sterling, Kingsley, and Carlyle. The notion that Coleridge's influence is best studied in terms of 'movements' at all is
even more doubtful. What the following chapters attempt to do
is to re-interpret a whole theological tradition in the light of its
members' views on language and poetry, discussing certain key
works in some depth. One of the things the literary critic who
reads theology rapidly discovers is that modern theologians
often seem curiously unaware of the literary premises from
which such men as Hare, Maurice, Keble, and Newman begin.
Anyone who has read both literary criticism and theology in the
Victorian period soon comes to realise how deeply the two are
intertwined. The nature of literary criticism (and the kinds of
sensibility it implies) cannot be understood in the nineteenth
century without reference to contemporary theology, just as the
contemporary theology cannot be understood without reference
to the literary criticism of the period. The rest of this book tries
to give some substance to this thesis.

The idea of poetic 'creativity' developed by Coleridge, Wordsworth, and their successors in Victorian England, which is usually
seen in purely aesthetic terms, was in fact a re-discovery and a
re-application of a much older Judeo-Christian way of thinking
about religious experience. The Bible, St Augustine, and Dante
are among many major influences, but the result in early nineteenth-century England was that elusive and yet clearly recognisable phenomenon, a 'change in sensibility', which makes the
period characteristically different from all that had gone into
shaping it. We call that change in sensibility, loosely enough,
'Romanticism'. I shall be tracing, in particular, three distinct but
interwoven strands in the ideas of Coleridge and Wordsworth
and the minority tradition of writers influenced by them. Firstly,
that of the ambiguity of human experience: a sense of the continuing co-existence and conflict of the natural and secular 'outer'
world with the 'inner' world of religious experience, sacred and
felt as super-natural. Secondly, and growing from this, I shall be
tracing a linguistic tradition that saw language itself as *expressing*
this ambiguity. Language was seen as metaphorical, 'bi-focal', or
'stereoscopic', and in Coleridge's special sense of the word,
'symbolic'. Finally, we shall see how closely these two notions
became associated with ideas of creativity and development. It is
no accident that the writers who figure most prominently in this

minority tradition – which we may conveniently, and not unfairly, call 'the tradition of Coleridge' – people like Keble,
Newman, Maurice, and MacDonald, should be both what we
now call 'creative writers' (usually poets) *and* also theologians.

Some readers may feel that I do not pay sufficient attention to
Aids to Reflection in the opening chapters. This is because I have
already written on *Aids* at some length elsewhere.[1] In a very
real sense, this whole study arises from my growing interest in
what Coleridge was trying to do in that much-neglected little
book. As a result, observant readers may well perceive another,
more controversial, thesis on the nature of religious language in
general which is implicit, but not spelled out in the course of this
work. That is deliberate. Optimistically, it is intended to be the
subject of a further study which will deal with the topic on a
broader front than merely nineteenth-century England.

[1] See my *Coleridge and Wordsworth: The Poetry of Growth* (Cambridge, 1970),
ch. 7.

1

'The Living Educts of the Imagination': Coleridge on Religious Language

It is a commonplace that Coleridge's mind worked in wholes. He had to an extraordinary – and even exaggerated – degree the capacity to see whatever he was thinking about in simultaneous relation to all the rest of his ideas. To use a visual analogy: his mind was like a wide-angle lens. What De Quincey called 'the compass, and huge circuit of his illustrations' could open up surprising new horizons and panoramas – as well as, at times, disconcerting distortions. If on the one hand he had the ability to feel his intellectual processes with the immediacy and intensity of great poetry, on the other, that same ability enabled him to see his own poetic creativeness as but a part of a much wider metaphysical reality: a cosmic *natura naturans* whose fount was God's eternal and ever-present act of Creation. It was in the words of the *Biographia* but 'a repetition in the finite mind of the eternal act of creation in the infinite I AM'. To understand the parts it was first necessary to have a vision of the whole, and for him nothing less than the 'noumena' of Kant's 'Reason', the regulative Ideas of God, freedom, and immortality, could begin to suggest the magnitude of that 'whole'. In one of his late Notebooks we find the comment that 'we may be said to comprehend what we cannot properly be said to understand'.[1] Behind such a remark lies the full Latin force of the word 'comprehend': to 'grasp' and 'contain'. It contains the triumphant affirmation of St John's notion of the Logos: 'And the light shineth in darkness; and the darkness comprehended it not.' Coleridge's basic and fundamental effort of mind throughout his life was to *comprehend* – in both the ancient and modern senses of the word. And that, for him, meant that his political, poetic, aesthetic, critical, and philosophical speculations were in the last resort only to be fully explored in the light of his lifelong *religious* preoccupations.

[1] Notebook 38 (B.M. Ms. 47,533), p. 56.

There has in the last few years been an increasing recognition of this gigantic unifying drive behind Coleridge's multifarious and often fragmentary activities. Such diverse and distinguished critics as Basil Willey, Thomas McFarland, Owen Barfield, and John Coulson have all been at pains to emphasise Coleridge's rôle as an original theologian. Basil Willey's 'spiritual biography'[1] has shown, as never before, the close correlation between the events and failures of Coleridge's life and the development of his religious insights. Barfield and McFarland[2] have both demonstrated the fundamentally dialectical nature of these insights: his ideas of 'polarity', and the relationship between the irreconcilable worlds of nature ('it is') and self-awareness ('I am'). These are concerns essential to our theme. But we need to begin at the beginning – with Coleridge's conception of language. In the words of John Coulson, Coleridge's

... original concern was with religious language, and...his account of poetic language must always be interpreted as a derivative from a more fundamental enquiry. In the *Biographia Literaria* he speaks of the time *before* his active collaboration with Wordsworth as a period in which 'I retired to a cottage in Somersetshire at the foot of Quantock, and devoted my thoughts and studies to the foundations of religion and morals'. And we notice that the vocabulary Coleridge uses when he attempts to explain *what* the poetic use of language is concerned to communicate is insufficiently clear and determinate until we apply it to religion.[3]

There are two points here which I should like to consider with some care. The first is that Coleridge's continuing fascination with the possibilities and limitations of language begins with, and remains centred on his interest in *religious* language – how it works, and in what ways it can expose and transmit the inwardness and personalness of religious belief. The second point concerns Coulson's distinction between what he calls the 'poetic' use of language, and the 'religious' language which, he maintains, is 'a more fundamental enquiry'. This latter needs clarification. If Coulson is claiming that there are two different ways of using language one of which is 'poetic' and the other 'religious', then

[1] *Samuel Taylor Coleridge* (Chatto, 1972).
[2] Owen Barfield, *What Coleridge Thought* (Oxford, 1972). Thomas McFarland, *Coleridge and the Pantheist Tradition* (Clarendon, 1969).
[3] *Newman and the Common Tradition* (Clarendon, 1970), p. 22.

he appears to be the victim of an odd kind of category-mistake. As the words are normally employed, 'poetic' refers to a way of using language – a way of knowing – that is at once emotive and intellectual; the word 'religious', on the other hand, refers primarily to content: the experience or knowledge that is being communicated. If we then go on at once to add that such experience is inseparable from the way of knowing, in other words that religious experience is fundamentally 'poetic', we are saying no more than Coleridge himself said – as Coulson shows himself to be well aware in the rest of his book. We are left, therefore, with a second possibility, that the 'poetic' use of language, *by its very nature*, raises questions that are inescapably 'religious', and that for Coleridge, poetry, like all art, is essentially incomplete in that it points beyond itself to areas of experience not open to literary or aesthetic criticism. This seems to be a quality of what Coulson calls the 'Fiduciary Tradition' of language. We take language and its inseparable content of ideas 'on trust' because it can be accepted in no other way – any more than the mind itself can be defined from without. In contrast to Bentham and what we might call the 'empirico-positivist' school of thought, Coleridge believed that in dealing with language we cannot start with the kind of definitions or premises with which we might begin some abstract problem, but we conclude by *discovering* them. Language arises not from self-evident ideas, but from the life of a particular community and culture. Nowhere is this better illustrated than in the way Coleridge's ideas of religious language are formed.

'The Great Coleridgean Position', according to J. H. Green, can be described thus:

Christianity, rightly understood, is identical with the highest philosophy, and apart from all question of historical evidence, the essential doctrines of Christianity are necessary and eternal truths of reason – truths which man, by the vouchsafed light of Nature and without aid from documents or tradition, may always and anywhere discover from himself – an explanation for his own experience.[1]

This is a view that has been repeated, with variations, until it has become a critical orthodoxy.[2] To see how far it is true, and

---

[1] Quoted by Traill, p. 186; see also Robert Shafer, *Christianity and Naturalism* (Yale, 1926), p. 62.

[2] See for example Graham Hough: 'The aim of Coleridge's religious writing is

whether it adequately suggests the course and consistency of Coleridge's development, it is worth looking in detail at a number of examples of his religious writing. The first example is an early one, from the oddly-spelt 1798 text of the *Ancyent Marinere*:

> O sweeter than the Marriage-feast,
> 'Tis sweeter far to me,
> To walk together to the Kirk
> With a goodly company.
>
> To walk together to the Kirk
> And all together pray,
> While each to his great father bends,
> Old men, and babes, and loving friends,
> And Youths and Maidens gay.
>
> Farewel, farewell! but this I tell
> To thee, thou Wedding guest!
> He prayeth well, who loveth well
> Both man and bird and beast.
>
> He prayeth best, who loveth best
> All things both great and small:
> For the dear God who loveth us,
> He made and loveth all.

The overtones of *All Things Bright and Beautiful* are not, of course, entirely fortuitous. I think there is little doubt that Mrs Cecil Frances Alexander knew her Coleridge and had his 'moral' in mind when composing her great anti-Evolution hymn. But this seemingly unequivocal ending to the *Ancient Mariner* has failed to satisfy many other critics. Coleridge himself, when he was later challenged by the celebrated poetess Mrs Barbauld over its *lack* of a moral, replied that on the contrary it had too much of a moral:

... and that the only, or chief fault, if I might say so, was the obtrusion of the moral sentiment so openly on the reader as a principle or cause of action in a work of such pure imagination. It ought to have had no

to show that all the central doctrines or Christianity, all the sacraments and traditional devotional observances, are deducible, with the aid of revelation, from the constitution of the human mind itself.' 'Coleridge and the Victorians', *The English Mind* (Cambridge, 1964), p. 181.

more moral than the Arabian Nights' tale of the merchant's sitting down to eat dates by the side of a well, and throwing the shells aside, and lo! a genie starts up, and says he *must* kill the aforesaid merchant, *because* one of the date shells had, it seems, put out the eye of the genie's son.[1]

Coleridge's point is an important one – but, *is* he repudiating the ending of the *Ancient Mariner*? If the passage is indeed the moral, then it is surely a very curious one. Whatever the implications of the narrative may be, it is surely not *self-evident* that God loves us all! If we are looking for 'morals' we might as well follow the critic who said it was 'Don't shoot albatrosses!' Not surprisingly, some critics have chosen to see the ending much more pessimistic-ally. D. W. Harding for example, sees anything but a partial recovery as impossible: 'Creeping back defeated into the social convoy, the mariner is obviously not represented as having advanced through his sufferings to a fuller life; and he no more achieves a full rebirth than Coleridge ever could.'[2] Clearly, the great religious affirmation at the end of the *Ancient Mariner* is much more ambiguous in the light of the whole poem than its surface meaning might suggest. Is the Mariner's final state indeed one of irreparable damage where he can no longer take part in the simple ceremonies of innocence? – in which case the religious coda we have been discussing is not a statement of what he has found, but what he has *lost* for ever. Alternatively, does he achieve such insight through suffering that he is left isolated from his fellows by knowledge: 'no longer at ease here, in the old dispensation'? or, yet again, is he now able to re-join his fellows at the church just *because of* his new and terrible knowledge:

> . . . And the end of all our exploring,
> Will be to arrive where we started
> And know the place for the first time. ?

The ideal, 'to walk together to the kirk', that is celebrated in the final stanzas is one of organic communal harmony as an outward and visible expression of an inner psychic wholeness, yet, if what we are witnessing in the *Ancient Mariner* is spiritual growth towards an organic wholeness of the personality, it is, it seems, achieved by a bewildering variety of apparently arbitrary

---

[1] *Table Talk*, ed. H. N. Coleridge (Murray, 1852), p. 86, 31 May 1830.
[2] 'The Theme of the *Ancient Mariner*', *Scrutiny*, IX (1941), 341.

actions and events. The Mariner shoots the albatross for no good reason other than motiveless malignancy; his shipmates at first superstitiously repudiate the deed, and then, when the weather improves, endorse it on the same flimsy grounds. For this they are all condemned to die a lingering death from thirst. The Mariner's release and expiation occur with equal arbitrariness when he is least expecting it:

> Beyond the shadow of the ship,
> I watch'd the water-snakes:
> They mov'd in tracks of shining white;
> And when they rear'd, the elfish light
> Fell off in hoary flakes.

> Within the shadow of the ship
> I watch'd their rich attire:
> Blue, glossy green, and velvet black
> They coil'd and swam; and every track
> Was a flash of golden fire.

> O happy living things! no tongue
> Their beauty might declare:
> A spring of love gusht from my heart,
> And I blessed them unaware!
> Sure my kind saint took pity on me,
> And I bless'd them unaware.

> The self-same moment I could pray;
> And from my neck so free
> The Albatross fell off, and sank
> Like lead into the sea.

This is one of those climaxes peculiar to great Romantic art. One thinks of the last movement of Beethoven's Ninth Symphony, when after themes and variations from the earlier movements have been tried and found wanting, the amazing final theme that is to be taken up by the choir a few moments later bursts up, as it were, *through* the wreckage of discarded efforts to reshape and transform the whole symphony. The ingenious conscious strivings that have gone before are completely futile, and yet, they seem in some mysterious way necessary, since it is only through failure that the uprush of inspiration is able to take over. Even more explicit is stanza xxviii of Gerard Manley Hopkins' *Wreck of the Deutschland* where the poet's meditation on the dying nun's experience, theologically and poetically brilliant, is suddenly broken into and reduced to ragged unfinishable fragments by the real vision of Christ that is the moment of death:

> But how shall I...make me room there:
> Reach me a...Fancy, come faster –
> Strike you the sight of it? look at it loom there,
> Thing that she...there then! the Master,
> *Ipse*, the only one, Christ, King, Head:
> He was to cure the extremity where he had cast her;
> Do, deal, lord it with living and dead;
> Let him ride, her pride, in his triumph, dispatch and have done with his doom there.

This experience of disconfirmation where, in the moment of crisis, all the titanic strivings of artist or protagonist are weighed in the balance and found wanting is at once Biblical and Platonic.[1] But what in the Bible, or in a mediaeval poet like Dante, is fundamentally a mode of religious experience, becomes in the work of Coleridge, of Beethoven, or of Hopkins, simultaneously a mode of aesthetic climax in which the whole meaning and structure of the work of art is changed and transformed. Failure is not merely an essential for individual spiritual growth, it is simultaneously a psychological and aesthetic necessity.

What we are witnessing in the *Ancient Mariner* is clearly, at one level, a 'psychological' drama. At the crisis of the poem, the Mariner in blessing the water-snakes is blessing not just the representatives of all life, but is acknowledging and blessing in himself things which had previously disgusted and repelled him.[2] The spirit 'nine fathom deep' is, in that sense, a part of his own – or possibly in a Jungian sense, collective – unconscious which he offends at his peril. Within this schema the disconfirmation of the Mariner is no less significant. If we are to substitute for the mechanical and necessitarian analogy of mental growth held by Hartley and the other empiricists one of organic 'vegetable' development, as Coleridge seems to be doing in the *Ancient*

---

[1] See, for instance, the exchanges of Diotima and Socrates in *The Symposium*. As David Newsome puts it, 'When the discovery comes, the perception is sudden, but it would never come like a flash of inspiration without previous toil.' *Two Classes of Men* (Murray, 1974), p. 191.

[2] See L. C. Knights, 'Taming the Albatross', *New York Review of Books* (26 May 1966).

Mariner, we need to remember that there is still remaining a fundamental difference between organism and psyche. The growth of an organism is continuous, depending on a steady diet without violent shocks, while the growth of the mind depends on the ability to assimilate variety and discontinuity.[1] Not for nothing do we sometimes refer to those who have failed to develop mentally as 'cabbages'. Within the *Ancient Mariner* we find there is a continual tension between the organic wholeness of man and nature that is desired, and the series of catastrophic breakdowns of this relationship by which growth comes about. It is possible to account for this disconfirmation and even much of the supernatural drama that accompanies it in purely psychological terms; but such an account is, as we have seen, partial and finally unsatisfying. Lamb criticised the poem's 'unmeaning miracles', and even though many of these – such as the descriptions of Death, and burning arms of the spirits at the homecoming – were removed from the later drafts of the poem after 1800, most of us would probably agree that the seraph-bands and the zombie sailors do not contribute much to our understanding of the psychological crisis and questionable recovery we have been discussing. Either we must conclude that there are areas of the *Ancient Mariner* which are dead wood, and that for a great deal of the poem's nightmare atmosphere there is no objective correlative, or we are forced to suspect that there is something else going on over and above the psychological drama. And we have the best possible witness – that of many generations of sensitive readers – that the *Ancient Mariner* is not a partial failure with undigested elements, but a moving artistic whole, the perfection of whose structure may be tested in the reader's own response.[2]

The moment of blessing the water-snakes, we recall, is described unequivocally in religious terms:

> Sure my kind saint took pity on me,
> And I bless'd them unaware.

The Mariner's rehabilitation is not described to us as 'growth',

---

[1] See Dorothy Emmet's review of my *Coleridge and Wordsworth*, *Review of English Studies* (August 1971), pp. 358–60.

[2] The best discussion of the *Ancient Mariner* as an artistic whole is probably Robert Penn Warren's, 'A Poem of Pure Imagination', *Selected Essays* (Eyre & Spottiswoode, 1964).

but in simple uncompromising terms of good and evil, guilt and expiation:

> . . . the man hath penance done,
> And penance more will do.

The psychological element we have noted is everywhere present and everywhere contained by a further quality that is explicitly, if arbitrarily, moral, numinous, and religious. The Mariner's disconfirmation is not just psychological, but is also stressed as metaphysical. Whatever psychic wholeness is, or is not, achieved by the end is a by-product of the even more ambiguous and mysterious drama of Fall and Redemption through Grace that leaves the Mariner doomed to retell his 'ghastly tale' at 'uncertain hours' and sends the innocent wedding-guest forth the morrow morn a 'sadder and a wiser man'. Yet, as soon as we have reached this point, so coming full circle, we become aware as before of how arbitrary and unsatisfactory the 'Christian' affirmation at the end is. Indeed, as we have seen, it makes *more* sense as a psychological affirmation of unity and community than it does as a Christian declaration of the love of God for his creatures. We are left, it seems, with something that is both similar to, and very unlike Traill's account of Coleridge's religious position. There certainly is apparently a connection between the eternal truths of Christianity and the constitution of the human mind, but what that connection is seems to be highly ambiguous. The more we look at the psychological level the more it seems to demand a religious explanation, the more we look to the religious level the more we are forced back towards a psychological explanation. Neither seems satisfactory within its own terms without the other. This seems to me very different from Traill's formulation. Whereas he sees Coleridge striving for – and ultimately failing to create – a unity of psychology, philosophy, and revealed religion, what we actually find in the *Ancient Mariner* is a perpetually uncomfortable and disturbing dualism.

Some light may be shed on this problem if we turn now to *The Statesman's Manual*. Here Coleridge offers us one of his best (and most typically Coleridgean) descriptions of Biblical narrative. Having contemptuously dismissed modern histories which concentrate on political economy as the products of an 'unenlivened generalizing understanding', he contrasts them with what we find in the Scriptures where

> they are the living *educts* of the Imagination; of that reconciling and mediatory power, which incorporating the Reason in Images of the Sense, and organizing (as it were) the flux of the Senses by the permanence and self-circling energies of the Reason, gives birth to a system of symbols, harmonious in themselves, and consubstantial with the truths, of which they are the *conductors*...Hence...the Sacred Book is worthily intitled *the* WORD OF GOD. Hence too, its contents present to us the stream of time continuous as Life and a symbol of Eternity, inasmuch as the Past and the Future are virtually contained in the Present...In the Scriptures therefore both facts and persons must of necessity have a two-fold significance, a past and a future, a temporary and a perpetual, a particular and a universal application. They must be at once Portraits and Ideals.[1]

The scriptures are the medium of revelation and 'the living educts of the imagination' because they have 'a two-fold significance': by being particular and concrete they are symbolic of universal truths. As always, Coleridge the philosopher has not ceased to be Coleridge the poet. The fact that a person or an event is symbolic of wider truths does not detract from, but enhances its reality as particular and unique. A symbol, Coleridge continues,

> ...is characterized by a translucence of the Special in the Individual, or of the General in the Especial, or of the Universal in the General. Above all by the translucence of the Eternal through and in the Temporal. It always partakes of the Reality which it renders intelligible; and while it enunciates the whole, abides itself as a living part in that Unity, of which it is the representative.[2]

In Coleridgean terms, a 'symbol' is the opposite of a generalisation. The latter is a kind of lowest common denominator, deduced by the understanding from outward events according to the dead arrangement of a mechanical philosophy. Coleridge's thought is always basically Platonic, and for him a generalisation deduced from the shadow of events is like Plato's conception of art, at two removes from 'reality'. A symbol, in contrast, is 'true' art and the product of the Imagination, for it focusses *through the very*

[1] *The Statesman's Manual*, in *Lay Sermons*, ed. R. J. White (Routledge, 1972), pp. 28–30.
[2] Ibid. p. 30.

particularity of an event the light of the eternal truths which cast the shadows on the cave wall. Instead of a dead arrangement, it exhibits 'method' in its own dynamic of development.

The working of the Imagination is thus for Coleridge a *symbolising* activity. A symbol is only a part of the greater whole it reveals, but it *implies* the totality. He attempts to describe the way in which it does this by the concept of 'translucence'. In a symbol, he suggests, the material and temporal becomes as it were a lens whereby we can bring into focus for an instant the eternal abstraction of which it is a fractional and incomplete part. By insisting that a symbol was above all a living part of the unity it represents, Coleridge was able to combine Platonism with optics. His theory of perception depended on the primary imagination 'creating' its own world from visual stimuli: building up its 'reality' by an active balance between the projection of schemata, and the reception of sense-data.[1] When he talked of man and creation sharing 'One Life', what may at one level have started as a pantheistic affirmation at another described how he believed the mind worked:

> O Lady! we receive but what we give,
> And in our life alone does Nature live.

'Nature' was, for Coleridge, neither 'out there' objectively independent of the mind perceiving it, nor the mere subjective creation of the individual, but something that is simultaneously *both* objective *and* subjective – or, rather, the 'indifference' or meeting-point of the two, obeying the laws of science *and* symbolised by poetry. We shape our world in physics and art alike in metaphor and symbol.

Thus over and over again we find Coleridge describing the 'Imagination' in terms of the bringing into a single focus two separate levels of experience, and seeing them as a coherent whole. His concept of the Imagination is essentially 'stereoscopic'; it stands at the intersection of two different perspectives, and so enables us to see 'in depth'. In another metaphor, Coleridge describes the Imagination in terms of a polarised magnetic field: we cannot conceive the poles without also conceiving the special relationship that holds them in tension. Here, in *The Statesman's Manual* he sees the scriptural narratives as 'the living

[1] See my *Coleridge and Wordsworth*, ch. 3.

educts of the Imagination' because they impress upon the reader a sense of their polarity: their 'two-fold significance' as 'at once Portraits and Ideals'. In the *Biographia Literaria*, written at about the same time and published in the following year, we find that Coleridge has borrowed from Schelling the distinction between the 'Primary' (or 'unconscious') Imagination, and the 'Secondary' (or 'conscious') Imagination.[1]

The IMAGINATION then, I consider either as primary, or secondary. The primary IMAGINATION I hold to be the living Power and prime Agent of all human Perception, and as a repetition in the finite mind of the eternal act of creation in the infinite I AM. The secondary Imagination I consider as an echo of the former, co-existing with the conscious will, yet still as identical with the primary in the *kind* of its agency, and differing only in *degree*, and in the *mode* of its operation. It dissolves, diffuses, dissipates, in order to re-create; or where this process is rendered impossible, yet still at all events it struggles to idealize and to unify.[2]

Schelling's distinction between the two Imaginations is based on his view of Art as reconciling the conflict between the conscious and unconscious.[3] For him, the Imagination is 'the only faculty by which we are able to think and understand even the contradictory'[4] – a view which finds an echo in Coleridge, where in the next chapter of the *Biographia Literaria*, he tells us that the power of the Imagination 'reveals itself in the balance or reconciliation of opposite or discordant qualities'.[5]

Coleridge, however, has drawn on other sources apart from Schelling. Earlier in the *Biographia*, in chapter x, he quotes from *Paradise Lost*, book v, apparently with the aim of showing that Kant's distinction between 'Reason' and 'Understanding' is a development of ideas already to be found in the seventeenth century in the Cambridge Platonists and Milton. Though he refers to this notion on more than one occasion, it is (to say the least) disingenuous[6] – but the quotation does suggest fairly clearly from where he has borrowed his actual form of words:

---

[1] *Entwurf eines Systems der Naturphilosophie* (1799); see Shawcross's notes to *Biographia Literaria* (Oxford, 1907), I, 272.

[2] Ibid. p. 202.

[3] *System des transcendentalen Idealismus* (1800), III, 627; see G. N. G. Orsini, *Coleridge and German Idealism* (Southern Illinois University Press, 1969), p. 225.

[4] Ibid. p. 227.   [5] Vol. II, 12.

[6] See D. M. MacKinnon, 'Coleridge and Kant', *Coleridge's Variety*, ed. J. Beer (Macmillan, 1974), p. 191.

——both life, and sense,
Fancy, and *understanding*; whence the soul
Reason receives, and R E A S O N is her *being*,
D I S C U R S I V E or I N T U I T I V E : discourse
Is oftest your's, the latter most is our's,
Differing but in *degree*, in *kind* the same.[1]

'Discourse', as he hastens to explain in a footnote, refers here to the 'discursive' mode of philosophy: 'the process of generalization and subsumption, of deduction and conclusion. Thus, Philosophy has *hitherto* been DISCURSIVE; while Geometry is *always* and *essentially* INTUITIVE.' There are a number of levels in Coleridge's thought to be distinguished here. The first thing we notice is that there is a close parallel in his mind between 'Reason' (broadly to be taken in the German idealist sense) and 'Imagination' in Coleridge's own sense. The distinction between the Primary and Secondary Imaginations, however, which differ only 'in degree' and not 'in kind', is a verbal echo not of Schelling, but of Milton. Primary is to Secondary, it seems, as Discursive Reason is to Intuitive; the human mind, though it is largely discursive, is potentially capable of intuitive reasoning (as in geometry) – which, according to Milton, is the normal angelic mode. But that word *'hitherto'* is boldly italicised: something new is about to be born; we are about to be initiated into a philosophic process where the mind can apprehend truth intuitively rather than discursively.

Coleridge seems to have interpreted the Kantian distinction between 'Reason' and 'Understanding' to mean that it was possible, through the former, to perceive God absolutely and unconditionally. Moreover, as Professor MacKinnon has pointed out, he also apparently believed that Kant's *Inaugural Dissertation* of 1771 and the *Critique of Pure Reason* were in substantial agreement on this point – ignoring the fact that the later *Critique* explicitly rejects this 'Platonic dream' and erects as it were an iron curtain between the phenomenal world, where knowledge is possible, and the noumenal world, about which we must remain agnostic.[2] The noumena of the *Critique*, the famous ideas of God,

1 Book v, lines 485–90. The italics, capitals etc. are Coleridge's own, as is the misquotation of 'in' for 'of' in the last line.
2 'Coleridge and Kant', *Coleridge's Variety*; the phrase 'iron curtain' is Dorothy Emmett's from 'Coleridge on Powers in Mind and Nature' in the same volume.

21

Freedom, and Immortality are, Kant insisted, *regulative* only. That is, they offer principles by which we may order and explain phenomena; they do not necessarily describe what is presumed to be the case. They are not, as Coleridge wished, 'constitutive'; they do not themselves constitute an active shaping principle. Coleridge's footnote then, seems to suggest either that he thinks the whole nature of philosophy has suddenly been transformed by the new systems of Kant and Schelling, or that he himself is proposing a solution so radical that philosophy is about to be transformed. A remark in *The Statesman's Manual*, already noted as contemporary with the *Biographia*, implies that he knows perfectly well the difference between the notion of ideas as regulative and constitutive, and that Kant came down on the side of the former: 'Whether Ideas are regulative only, according to Aristotle and Kant; or likewise CONSTITUTIVE, and one with the power and Life of Nature, according to Plato and Plotinus. . . is the highest *problem* of philosophy, and not part of its nomenclature.'[1]

Is Coleridge simply being muddled in the *Biographia*? Or does he really believe that his conflation of Schelling and Milton to provide a new aesthetic theory has the potential to revolutionise philosophy, turning it from an imperfect discursive mode into one of apparently intuitive certainties? I suspect that he did – but the first point to notice, of course, is that what he is proposing is no longer 'philosophy' in the normally accepted sense. But for Coleridge, who had earlier urged Wordsworth on in his efforts to write 'the FIRST GENUINE PHILOSOPHIC POEM'[2], *The Recluse*, the word as often seems to imply the kind of insights given by poetry as it does those achieved by narrower more formal intellectual reasoning. This broad 'poetic' use of the word 'philosophy' was one that was to leave its mark on a whole strand of English thought[3], and, as here, its basis is explicitly theological.

Coleridge's formulation thus has a different weight of emphasis from Schelling's at the outset. If the two levels of Imagination somehow parallel Milton's distinction between discursive and intuitive Reason (now used, of course, in a non-Miltonic and loosely Kantian sense) we can see how far Coleridge

---

[1] *The Statesman's Manual*, p. 114.   [2] *Biographia Literaria*, II, 129.
[3] See ch. 9, pp. 258–9 below.

has moved from Kant's notion of 'Imagination'. For Kant, the 'Imagination' is 'reproductive' – that is, it operates in effect as something very close to memory. What he calls the 'speculative reason', however, is described as 'heuristic' in that it reaches out beyond the evidence to create and complete new wholes. It is, in this limited sense at any rate, 'creative'. For Coleridge, in contrast, it is clear that the 'Imagination' is the creative faculty. It seems, indeed, to be nothing less than the power by which Kant's regulative ideas are to be made constitutive. In other words, the Reason is seen as fundamentally 'poetic' in its mode of operation. As Coleridge saw, this aesthetic doctrine has immediate religious implications. Schelling seems to see in the conscious imagination that power of the artist, philosopher, or visionary which sets him aside from ordinary men. But Coleridge, by insisting that the Secondary Imagination differs from the Primary only in degree and not in kind, is (it seems to me) hinting at a relationship between artist and public that is simultaneously as élitist as that of Schelling or Goethe, *and* fundamentally egalitarian. The élitism, in one sense, is obvious: the artist is the man of genius, the creator of new wholes, reconciling opposite or discordant qualities. Yet in so being, he is also exemplifying a law of life that is to be found at every level of existence. In his 'Theory of Life' Coleridge argues that there is a correspondence between man's highest achievements in his various spheres of action:

In social and political life this acme is interdependence; in moral life it is independence; in intellectual life it is genius. Nor does the form of polarity, which has accompanied the law of individuation up its whole ascent, desert it here. As in the height, so the depth...As the ideal genius and the originality, in the same proportion must be the resignation to the real world, the sympathy and the intercommunion with Nature.[1]

The twin characteristics of 'life', he claims, are 'individuation' (or 'the power which unites a given *all* into a whole that is presupposed by all its parts')[2] and 'polarity'. In a sense apparently not unlike that of Hopkins' 'instress', the uniqueness of individual living things exists under *tension* between opposites. The originality of genius also gives wider sympathies with Nature, and with the ordinary world. The artist is not separated from his

[1] 'The Theory of Life', *Misc. Aesthetic and Literary* (Bohn/Bell, 1892), p. 423.
[2] Ibid. p. 385.

fellow men by his powers; he is more than ever involved with them.[1] He is not an isolate, but a sharer of open secrets. This is a theme we have already seen in the *Ancient Mariner*; and it underlies the whole conception of the *Lyrical Ballads*. Coleridge's criticisms of Wordsworth's theory of poetic diction in the *Biographia* that follow on from the definition of Imagination in chapter XIII need not be seen as attacking the aesthetic premises which they both shared in 1798. What he is now concerned to do is to show the relationship between poet and reader as itself a polarity.

Similarly, for Coleridge, the Primary Imagination is not merely 'the prime Agent of all human Perception' with its power of 'shaping into one' (a mis-translation of Schelling's *Einbildungs-kraft*) the manifold of sense-data, but it is, by the very act of perception, 'a repetition in the finite mind of the eternal act of creation in the infinite I A M'. This is one of the passages that Professor MacKinnon is thinking of when he sees in Coleridge's formulation 'frankly metaphysical implications of a deeply pan-theistic kind'.[2] Certainly there are here echoes of Schelling. In the works which Coleridge had so far encountered, Schelling had been heavily influenced by the pantheism of Spinoza, and in place of a personal God he had come to look for an idealistic absolute. But, clearly, this is not the only possible interpretation of the phrase. Though it was appropriated by certain pantheists, it was, we recall, first used by the very personal God of the Old Testa-ment in his self-revelation to Moses on Horeb. Coleridge had certainly felt the pull of Spinoza as well as Schelling,[3] and, as Dorothy Emmett argues, he was attracted to pantheism as part of a search for a 'ground of being' in Nature.[4] Yet by his own admission, it corresponded to only a part of his experience; for another part of Coleridge such a phrase invoked not a pantheistic

[1] 'All genius exists in a participation of a common spirit... In joy individuality is lost and it therefore is liveliest in youth, not from any principle in organization but simply from this that the hardships of life, that the circumstances that have forced a man in upon his little unthinking contemptible self, have lessened his power of existing universally; it is that only which brings about those passions. To have a genius is to live in the universal.' *Philosophical Lectures*, ed. K. Coburn (Routledge, 1949), p. 224. See also A. J. Harding's comments on this passage (to which I am indebted) in *Coleridge and the Idea of Love* (Cambridge, 1975), pp. 150–1.

[2] 'Coleridge and Kant', *Coleridge's Variety*, p. 190.

[3] McFarland, *Coleridge and the Pantheist Tradition*, ch. 3.

[4] 'Coleridge on Powers in Mind and Nature', *Coleridge's Variety*, pp. 178–80.

presence, but a transcendent Creator. Platonism is never very far beneath the surface of Coleridge's mind. Such a phrase as 'the repetition in the finite mind of the eternal act of creation...' may no less convincingly be applied to the Platonic theory of recollection, describing the process by which even in the simplest acts of perception the human mind is, as it were, echoing God's original act of creation and by its own unconscious creativeness thinking God's thoughts after him. To borrow the language of *The Prelude*, as 'an inmate of this *active* universe', it 'Creates, creator and receiver both,/Working but in alliance with the works/Which it beholds...' If we follow this argument, we can see how Schelling's pantheism might (however illegitimately) be incorporated into the framework of a wider Christian Platonism whose import is specifically incarnational. Even while he is apparently paraphrasing Schelling, Coleridge certainly seems to be moving in an altogether different direction. Thus Schelling describes his 'conscious imagination' as creating an 'ideal world';[1] Coleridge's expansion of this into his Secondary Imagination is characteristic: 'It dissolves, diffuses, dissipates, in order to re-create; or where this process is rendered impossible, yet still, at all events, it struggles to idealize and to unify.' Schelling's ideal view of art had already suggested a bifocal or stereoscopic reference: if on the one hand it 'idealises', on the other, it creates its own aesthetic structure and organisation, dissolving in order to re-create. Coleridge seems to have endowed this with new theological implications: the vision of the eternal is not divorced from this world, but embodies itself in a particular and concrete artistic structure. It is symbolic.

The theological paradigm of this 'dual vision' is Coleridge's idea of the 'Logos' – itself no less aptly described as 'the eternal act of creation in the infinite I A M'. In traditional Christian thought the 'Logos' had acquired a dual reference that seemed tailor-made for Coleridge's purposes. For the Greeks it was the Creative Word, or Word of God.[2] Heraclitus used it in the sense of universal Reason permeating the whole world. For Plato it was

---

[1] 'Intelligence,' writes Schelling in the opening words of his Introduction to *Entwurf eines Systems der Naturphilosophie*, 'is productive in twofold wise, either blindly and unconsciously, or with freedom and consciousness; unconsciously productive in the perception of the universe, consciously in the creation of an ideal world.' (*Biographia*, I, 272.)

[2] For this whole exposition of the history of the 'Logos' I am indebted to David

the archetypal 'idea' – or 'the idea of ideas'; in the *Republic*, in the discussion of the good, it is personified as the highest object of knowledge, but in the *Timaeus* it becomes the Creator or divine energy creating the world. What appears to be a latent ambiguity in Plato was made explicit by succeeding writers. Philo of Alexandria, for example, thought of the 'Logos' as not only the divine reason immanent in the world but also as the intermediary agent of God within the world and the act of creation itself. Thus St John's 'new' meaning of the 'Logos' as the Second Person of the Trinity becoming flesh in the Incarnation makes use of a paradox that had long been present by implication in the word. For Coleridge, the history and development of the word 'Logos' was an example of the imagination in action: the spirit incarnate in language: simultaneously a word, and the Word.

The description of the Bible stories as having a 'two-fold significance', therefore, makes it quite clear what Coleridge means by calling them 'the living *educts* of the Imagination'. Moreover, by means of his definition of a symbol as 'stereoscopic' he was able to use the idea of Revelation simultaneously in two senses: an 'outer', historical, revelation in the lives of the prophets and of Christ himself is matched by the 'inner' personal *consent* of the individual Christian. As a twentieth-century theologian has put it:

> Every symbol opens up a level of reality for which non-symbolic speaking is inadequate...But in order to do this, something else must be opened up – namely levels of the soul, levels of our interior reality. And they must correspond to the levels in exterior reality which are opened up by a symbol. So every symbol is two-edged. It opens up reality and it opens up the soul.[1]

For Coleridge, this personal assent is an essential part of the function of a symbol. The symbolic language of the Bible changes the way the reader thinks and feels. The human mind, by its very constitution, is not a closed organism, but points beyond itself – and it can only be ultimately understood in terms of that which it points to, not what it is.

As has become clear, the *Ancient Mariner* is supremely a poem

Newsome's *Two Classes of Men*, ch, 5, 'Plato and Incarnationalism', in particular pp. 79–80.
   [1] Paul Tillich, *Theology of Culture* (Oxford, New York, 1959), pp. 56–7.

of metaphorical or symbolic tension between incompatible yet interdependent worlds. So far from finding the truths of Christianity grounded independently in the mind of man, as Traill suggests, we have found that there is a constant, almost Biblical, progression in which the Mariner's expectations are broken down, disconfirmed, and transformed by something that is both arbitrary and mysterious, yet at the same time in some obscure sense undoubtedly moral. Like the wedding-guest, the reader is held in tension between unsatisfactory alternatives, which both demand and reject each other. The position Traill attributes to Coleridge – that the truths of Christianity may be discovered by reason from the constitution of the human mind – is, ironically, that of Hartley. In his monumental textbook on human psychology, *Observations on Man, his Frame, his Duties, and his Expectations*, David Hartley had attempted to show how, starting with the mind as a Lockeian *tabula rasa* at birth, we grow by a mechanical, necessary, and inevitable process from the first simple sensations of the new-born babe to the divine vision. For Hartley, our heavenly destiny was built into our developmental psychology. In contrast, it is not difficult to see the *Ancient Mariner* as Coleridge's break with his old world of necessity and Unitarianism, revealing instead his growing sense of the transcendent 'otherness' of a God of mystery, immanent in the world of nature and human psychology, but simultaneously standing over against that world in judgement. This is the unresolvable tension between the world of things – what Coleridge called 'It is' – and the world of our intuitive moral awareness – what Coleridge called 'I am'. As Thomas McFarland has argued in his book, *Coleridge and the Pantheist Tradition*, these are the only two possible starting-points for systematic philosophy, and *neither* is satisfactory. If there is one thing more ludicrous than the attempt to approach the world of science and art through a system of *a priori* moral values, it is the attempt of scientists or artists to create from their own fields a satisfactory ethical system. In the end, consciously or unconsciously, according to our individual temperaments and interests, we all of us either compromise or live in a divided world. Coleridge was, perhaps, unique in being *both* a major artist and a major religious thinker, and this was for him the shaping tension of his whole career. It is for this reason that what he has to say about religious language is of such importance. We can see more clearly both the development and the consistency of his thinking if we turn now from the *Ancient Mariner* to look at the last book published in his lifetime, *Church and State*.

It is in *Church and State* that he gives us his fullest account of what he means by an 'idea'. It differs from a 'conception', he tells us, in that while the latter is conscious, and therefore fully realised, the 'idea' of a thing can be neither generalised nor abstracted from particular concrete examples, but can only be grasped if we have a knowledge of its ultimate aim. The idea of a 'state', for instance, is not necessarily best discovered by look-ing at every example of a state there is. The form in which an idea is best expressed may not be a form in which it ever actually *does* find expression. Rather like the Marxist paradise, it may ever recede before us even as we seek it. It may sound as if this kind of Platonism enables Coleridge (like a certain variety of sectarian Marxist) to claim that he alone possess the true 'idea' of something, but there is no need for an 'idea' in this sense to be as unverifiable as this might suggest. For instance, while one cannot hope to re-assemble the shattered Portland vase without some prior 'idea' of what the whole was like – which cannot be deduced from the broken fragments – it is also true that in attempting it one would rapidly find out if the 'idea' of the whole was mistaken. Disconfirmation is always possible. What Cole-ridge is trying to do, in fact, is to put into some kind of philo-sophic form a quality of which he becomes increasingly conscious in thinking about language. Unlike the philosophers whom he so often pillaged for terminology, Coleridge's approach to words is not less poetic for being philosophical: he is always aware of the phenomenon that the language of great literature expresses *more* than we can know at any one time or place. Shakespeare speaks afresh to each generation with new insights; so do the creeds; so does the Bible. When, in *Confessions of an Inquiring Spirit*, Coleridge went on record with the scandalous assertion that he would approach the Bible as he would any other book, it was not widely appreciated how seriously and sensitively he read other books. He approaches Shakespeare with greater reverence than Paley approaches Holy Writ. Moreover, this reverence in-volves a recognition of symbolic tension. His actual words are as follows:

I take up this work with the purpose to read it for the first time as I should any other work, – as far at least as I can or dare. For I neither can, nor dare, throw off a strong and awful prepossession in its favour – certain as I am that a large part of the light and life, in and by which I see, love, and embrace the truths and the strengths co-organised into a living body of faith and knowledge...has been directly or indirectly derived to me from this sacred volume...[1]

Coleridge is not here, as some commentators have supposed, hedging his bets and trying to make radical views more accept-able to conventional readers; he is stating two contrary ex-periences. Firstly, that the Bible is indeed a book, and as such, it is open to the normal criteria of literary criticism and the historical method; but, secondly, it is also, for Christians, the Word of God mediating the transcendent in and through the temporal – and because of this tension the Bible is not less, but more than ever an artistic and organic unity.

For him, language is the key to self-knowledge; words are not counters to be used in barren scriptural crossword puzzles, where one verse wrenched from its context is matched with other de-racinated fragments. The parts are to be read in the spirit of the whole. It is no use clutching the odd phrase or little piece if in so doing we lose sight of the 'idea' of the whole – of which the pieces *are* but pieces. Again, the analogy of the broken vase is useful. The whole is greater than the parts, and it alone gives meaning to them. But an 'idea', of course, is more than simply the memory or notion of a particular thing: it is also a Platonic 'form'. Thus it is, for Coleridge, *both* an abstract absolute, never adequately conveyed in any given set of words, *and* simul-taneously bound up with the very life of the words themselves. Once again, at the centre of his thinking, we find this polarity – or stereoscopy. In *Biographia Literaria* he tells us that, 'An IDEA, in the *highest* sense of that word, cannot be conveyed but by a *symbol.*'[2] In other words, it can only be mediated to us in terms of a work of art. Given Coleridge's premises and preoccupations, we can see why this must be so. An 'idea' as it is normally thought of is linear and discursive: we can talk about it, argue over it, and in the process discover in it new meanings and possibilities. Thus, according to this view, 'Socialism' may be an idea which needs working out over many generations and

---

[1] *Confessions*, ed. H. N. Coleridge (1849), p. 9.　　[2] i, 100.

circumstances before its meaning and implications are fully understood.[1] But it must not only be discussed, it must also be *felt*. Until we have seen, say, a play like Brecht's *Caucasian Chalk Circle* we have not fully understood the emotional impact of socialism as a radical creed transforming our views on human relationships and property. The symbolism of art makes us grasp 'presentationally' the eternal truths of human nature through the particularity of an individual situation. What fascinates Coleridge is that this transcendence through the particular is not achieved in spite of language, but is itself a property of it.

We can see both Coleridge's difficulties in saying what he meant by an idea, and also why it was essential for him to make the attempt. He never lost the poet's sense of the full creative force of language. In *Aids to Reflection* he insisted 'For if words are not THINGS, they are LIVING POWERS, by which the things of most importance to mankind are actuated, combined, and humanized.'[2] Words do not come to us newly-defined and therefore empty-handed: they come carrying with them in their derivation and subsequent development the history of the development of human consciousness itself. As a Platonist and a philosopher, Coleridge desired an ideal existence for ideas independent of language, however, and so an idea for him comes to be something that by its nature exists under tension. So far from existing in timeless abstract perfection we find Coleridge in *Aids to Reflection* clearly thinking of ideas in terms of organic growth. Plato's ideas are made somehow *dynamic* – so that they are analogous to a seed that compounds within itself the whole history of its past and future growth. As early as *The Statesman's Manual* we can see how an idea for Coleridge has acquired its bi-focal tension: 'But every living principle is actuated by an idea; and every idea is living, productive, partaketh of infinity, and (as Bacon has sublimely observed) containeth an endless power of semination.'[3]

It is easy for this endless attempt at definition to seem tortuous and over-subtle if we lose sight of the practical concerns that lay behind these efforts. Coleridge's tensional theory of language is not something that he dreamed up from an innate love of complexity, or even something that he borrowed from German philosophy. It was an attempt to put into words complexities

---

[1] See ch. 6, p. 163 below.   [2] Ed. T. Fenby (Grant, 1905) p. xvii.   [3] P. 318.

that he had experienced. *Church and State* gives us an example.
The 'Church' and the 'State' are each concrete manifestations of
a living 'idea' that is in constant growth as we discover in it new
possibilities. On the 'Idea of a State' he writes:

The line of evolution, however sinuous, has still tended to this point,
sometimes with, sometimes without, not seldom, perhaps, against, the
intention of the individual actors, but always as if a power, greater and
better than the men themselves, had intended it for them. Nor let it be
forgotten that every new growth, every power and privilege, bought
or extorted, has uniformly been claimed by an antecedent right; not
acknowledged as a boon conferred, but both demanded and received as
what had always belonged to them.[1]

Each new development is not mere accretion. We may not know
in advance what the 'idea' of Church or State implies, but when
we are confronted by it we immediately *recognise* that it is part of
the original idea.

The Church of England is, in fact, not one, but *two* ideas. On
the one hand we have the National Church, existing within the
framework of a particular society in a particular time and place.
It is the servant of the State and of the society in which it finds
itself; it is not a 'contrary' to the civil and executive power of the
State, but a dialectical opposite, providing a balance of forces
within the nation – or 'State' in its widest sense. The clergy,
together with the other intellectual estates, the Universities and
the Schools, provide what Coleridge calls 'the Clerisy', to guide
and educate the nation, intellectually, morally, and spiritually.
On the other hand, it is also the Church of Christ, owing total
allegiance not to the monarch, the corpulent and worldly George
IV, but to Christ himself, and bearing witness through its teaching and sacraments in every town and village in the land to those
divine truths against which the State and the clerisy itself will
one day be judged and found wanting. These two ideas are
totally separate and distinct:

As the olive tree is said in its growth to fertilize the surrounding soil,
to invigorate the roots of the vines in its immediate neighbourhood,
and to improve the strength and flavour of the wines; such is the
relationship of the Christian and the National Church. But as the olive
is not the same plant with the vine...even so is Christianity...no

---

[1] *Church and State*, 2nd edn., ed. H. N. Coleridge (1839), p. 33.

essential part of the being of the National Church, however conducive or even indispensable it may be to its well being. And even so a National Church might exist, and has existed, without. . .the Christian Church.[1]

Yet in the Church of England the two ideas nonetheless co-exist in a single organic entity:

. . .two distinct functions do not necessarily imply or require two different functionaries: nay, the perfection of each may require the union of both in the same person. And in the instance now in question, great and grievous errors have arisen from confounding the functions; and fearfully great and grievous will be the evils from the success of an attempt to separate them. . .[2]

The Church of England is more than a strange historical accident. It is desirable that the contraries should co-exist and even co-inhere within the same organisation and even the same individuals. It may be a 'happy accident', as Coleridge calls it, that the Church of England should be Christian rather than Druidical or some other State religion, but it owes its stereoscopic quality to this accident of history. The teachers and writers of the clerisy are the better servants of the nation for also being Christians. Theirs is not a divided allegiance: they owe *total* commitment to each, just as Christ, whose Body the Church is, was wholly Man and wholly God without division or two sides to his nature. Coleridge's view of the Church of England rests in the most literal sense upon Trinitarian orthodoxy. What we mean by the Church of England is in fact an example of the particular dual vision that he finds characteristic of a symbol. Stereoscopic vision requires two separate points of view, but it gives not two images, but a single coherent view of the world 'in depth'. Existing under tension between two contrary ideas, the Church of England is itself a paradigm concrete example of what Coleridge had been struggling to say about the nature of religious language ever since the *Ancient Mariner*. The language of religious experience is not different in kind from any other form of language. As the Secondary Imagination differs from the Primary only in degree and in the mode of its operation, enabling us to understand consciously what in the Primary Imagination is unconscious, so religious language differs only from so-called 'ordinary' language

[1] *Church and State*, 2nd edn., ed. H. N. Coleridge (1839), p. 60.   [2] Ibid. p. 61.

in degree and mode. Openly symbolic, tensional, and stereoscopic, it reveals that this is also the condition of ordinary language. We come to understand poetic language via religious language, and not vice versa.

For Carlyle, this was a mystical and perverse dualism that enabled Coleridge to perform the impossible: to defend a corrupt, lax, and time-serving ecclesiastical establishment by seeing in its very degradation the seeds of eternal life. 'Can a thing be known for true, and known for false?...It was so Coleridge imagined it, the wisest of existing men!'[1] It was moral and intellectual treason, and he never forgave Coleridge for it. Yet even as Carlyle was pitying and denouncing Coleridge in alternate sentences of his *Life of John Sterling* the impossible *was* beginning to happen. The moribund Church of England was producing Julius Hare, Sterling's Cambridge tutor; F. D. Maurice, Sterling's fellow-student, founder of the Christian Socialists, and greatest of the new generation of Anglican theologians; Arnold of Rugby; and, above all, the Oxford Movement with Keble, Pusey, and Newman. Through Maurice's *Kingdom of Christ* Coleridge's vision became a challenge to the Church of England which it has neither been able to live with, or do without. Through Newman, Coleridge's Anglican heritage was carried right into the heart of the Church of Rome, where the *Essay on the Development of Doctrine* and the *Grammar of Assent* presented a challenge to the nature of that Church as radical as that presented by Coleridge and Maurice to their own.

It was Coleridge's great and lasting contribution to the nineteenth century, and no less to our own time, to have re-discovered and re-affirmed the complex symbolism that transforms the language of religious experience from easy platitude and comfortable doctrine to ambiguity and tension, to fear and trembling.

[1] *Life of Sterling*, p. 260.

2

'A Liberty of Speculation which no Christian can Tolerate' — the Later Coleridge

Carlyle's description of Coleridge's declining years at Highgate is well-known.

Coleridge sat on the brow of Highgate Hill, in those years, looking down on London and its smoke-tumult, like a sage escaped from the inanity of life's battle; attracting towards him the thoughts of innumerable brave souls still engaged there. His express contributions to poetry, philosophy, or any specific province of human literature or enlightenment, had been small and sadly intermittent; but he had, especially among young inquiring men, a higher than literary, a kind of prophetic or magician character. He was thought to hold, he alone in England, the key of German and other Transcendentalisms; knew the sublime secret of believing by 'the reason' what 'the understanding' had been obliged to fling out as incredible; and could still, after Hume and Voltaire had done their best and worst with him, profess himself an orthodox Christian, and say and print to the Church of England, with its singular old rubrics and surplices at Allhallowtide, *Esto perpetua.* A sublime man; who, alone in those dark days, had saved his crown of spiritual manhood; escaping from the black materialisms, and revolutionary deluges, with 'God, Freedom, Immortality' still his: a king of men. The practical intellects of the world did not much heed him, or carelessly reckoned him a metaphysical dreamer: but to the rising spirits of the young generation he had this dusky sublime character; and sat there as a kind of *Magnus*, girt in mystery and enigma; his Dodona oak-grove (Mr Gillman's house at Highgate) whispering strange things, uncertain whether oracles or jargon.[1]

It was there, at the Gilman's house, that the young James Sterling went during the years 1828–9 to hear the Sage of Highgate hold forth. Maurice went with him on at least one occasion, but he seems to have been so overcome by diffidence and awe

[1] *Life of Sterling*, pp. 230–1.

that at the last minute he could not face meeting his hero and remained outside. Perhaps it was as well for his opinion of Coleridge that he did, for some of those who met him were, like Carlyle, apt to be disillusioned.

The good man, he was now getting old, towards sixty perhaps; and gave you the idea of a life that had been full of sufferings; a life heavy-laden, half-vanquished, still swimming painfully in seas of manifold physical and other bewilderment. Brow and head were round, and of massive weight, but the face was flabby and irresolute. The deep eyes, of a light hazel, were as full of sorrow as of inspiration; confused pain looked mildly from them, as in a kind of mild astonishment. The whole figure and air, good and amiable otherwise, might be called flabby and irresolute; expressive of weakness under possibility of strength. He hung loosely on his limbs, with knees bent, and stooping attitude; in walking, he rather shuffled than decisively stept; and a lady once re-marked that he never could fix which side of the garden-walk would suit him best, but continually shifted, in corkscrew fashion, and kept trying both. A heavy-laden, high-aspiring and surely much suffering man. His voice, naturally soft and good, had contracted itself into a plaintive snuffle and singsong; he spoke as if preaching – you would have said, preaching earnestly and hopelessly the weightiest things. I still recollect his 'object' and 'subject', terms of continual recurrence in the Kantean province; and how he sung and snuffled them into 'om-m-mject' and 'sum-m-mject', with a kind of solemn shake or quaver, as he rolled along.[1]

Carlyle is a biased witness, but a memorable one. It is fair to add that others, Sterling among them, less fond of talking them-selves, have carried back a more favourable record,[2] but for many reverence was liable to be tempered with pity and even contempt. Yet accounts of what Coleridge actually *said* on these occasions – as distinct from the way he said it – are much less vivid. The *Table Talk* has flashes of fire, but hardly enough to set young ardent spirits alight. Perhaps, as Carlyle implies, his talk was mostly quite unintelligible to the majority of his hearers. It was not, however, unintelligible to Sterling, or to Maurice, or, for that matter to Carlyle himself, who, for all his mockery (half-impressed in spite of himself) knew very well what Coleridge was about.

[1] Ibid. p. 232.
[2] See R. W. Armour and R. F. Howes, *Coleridge the Talker* (Cornell, 1940).

The constant gist of his discourse was lamentation over the sunk condition of the world; which he recognised to be given up to Atheism and Materialism, full of mere sordid misbeliefs, mispursuits and misresults. All science had become mechanical; the science not of men, but of a kind of human beavers. Churches themselves had died away into a godless mechanical condition; and stood there as mere Cases of Articles, mere Forms of Churches; like the dried carcasses of once swift camels, which you find left withering in the thirst of the universal desert, – ghastly portents for the present, beneficent ships of the desert no more . . .

The remedy, though Coleridge professed to see it as in sunbeams, could not, except by processes unspeakably difficult, be described to you at all. On the whole, those dead Churches, this dead English Church especially, must be brought to life again. Why not? It was not dead; the soul of it, in this parched-up body, was tragically asleep only. Atheistic Philosophy was true on its side, and Hume and Voltaire could on their own ground speak irrefragably for themselves against any Church: but lift the Church and them into a higher sphere of argument, *they* died into inanition, the Church revivified itself into pristine florid vigour, – became once more a living ship of the desert, and invincibly bore you over stock and stone. But how! but how! By attending to the 'reason' of man, said Coleridge, and duly chaining up the 'understanding' of man: the *Vernunft* (Reason) and *Verstand* (Understanding) of the Germans, it all turned upon these, if you could well understand them, – which you couldn't. For the rest, Mr Coleridge had on the anvil various Books, especially was about to write one grand Book *On the Logos*, which would help to bridge the chasm for us. So much appeared, however: Churches, though proved false (as you had imagined), were still true (as you were to imagine): here was an Artist who could burn you up an old Church, root and branch; and then as the Alchymists professed to do with organic substances in general, distil you an 'Astral Spirit' from the ashes, which was the very image of the old burnt article, its airdrawn counterpart, – this you still had, or might get, and draw uses from, if you could . . . [1]

This, in short, is the material of *Church and State* which Coleridge was at work on in 1829–30. If the distinction between 'Reason' and 'Understanding' is freely adapted from Kant (as Carlyle suggests by the Kantian *Vernunft* and *Verstand*) there is in spite of Coleridge's avowed dislike of him more than a whiff of Hegel in the conceptual relationship of Church and State. None of it, Carlyle implies obliquely, is original, none of it properly digested and understood. In his view it was moonshine – an attempt at

[1] *Life of Sterling*, pp. 235–6.

once glorious and ignoble to pour new wine into wineskins so old and decaying as to be unrecognisable as vessels of anything but moral putrefaction. He takes it for granted that Coleridge's defence of the supernatural in religion was merely pusillanimous: a clinging to flotsam and driftwood when he should be striking out for the shore like a man. The book, *On the Logos*, could never be written, and for the absent Word Coleridge was substituting a torrent of words.

In later life Sterling seems to have come to share this view, and he hints that Coleridge's real opinions by this stage were a great deal more sceptical and heterodox than he was prepared to admit in print. 'I am not much surprised,' he wrote to his mother in December 1841, 'at Lady —'s views on Coleridge's little Book on Inspiration' (the *Confessions of an Inquiring Spirit* published posthumously in 1846):

Great part of the obscurity of the Letters arises from his anxiety to avoid the difficulties and absurdities of the common views, and his panic terror of saying anything that bishops and good people would disapprove. He paid a heavy price, viz. all his own candour and simplicity, in hope of gaining the favour of persons like Lady —; and you see what his reward is! A good lesson for us all.[1]

Similar suspicions of a lack of candour had evidently reached the ears of Emerson. 'Even in him, the traditional Englishman was too strong for the philosopher, and he fell into *accommodations*; and as Burke had striven to idealize the English State, so Coleridge "narrowed his mind" in the attempt to reconcile the Gothic rule and dogma of the Anglican Church, with eternal ideas.'[2] The basic ideas of *Church and State* and the *Confessions* were little better than an equivocating compromise – an 'accommodation' to a public that was not yet ready for the more radical speculations uttered 'oftener in private discourse'. From Emerson's account, Coleridge does not seem to have said anything radical or daring to him in person, and it is possible that the visiting American is simply echoing Carlyle. But the story of Coleridge's secret heterodoxy was widely enough in circulation for Newman – who disclaimed any close connections with Coleridge – to have heard it. It is his words that form the title of this chapter. In an article in the *British Critic* in April 1839 he

[1] Ibid. p. 364.   [2] *English Traits*, p. 236.

pays the following, slightly ambiguous, tribute to Coleridge:

While history in prose and verse was thus made the instrument of Church feelings and opinions, a philosophical basis for the same was laid in England by a very original thinker, who, while he indulged a liberty of speculation, which no Christian can tolerate, and advocated conclusions which were often heathen rather than Christian, yet after all instilled a higher philosophy into inquiring minds, than they had hitherto been accustomed to accept. In this way he made trial of his age, and succeeded in interesting its genius in the cause of Catholic truth.[1]

What are we to make of all this? If we are to believe Carlyle, Coleridge was a mere mystagogue and purveyor of transcendental moonlight; according to Traill, however, who, though he had no greater sympathy with Coleridge than Carlyle, was at least as well equipped to understand him philosophically, and had the added advantage of hindsight and J. H. Green,[2] Coleridge never really got beyond a pantheistic position.[3] On the other hand, Sterling and Newman believed, or perhaps had evidence, that Coleridge's speculations on scriptural inspiration had carried him to a scepticism and liberalism little removed from atheism. Even for the myriad-minded Sage of Highgate this is a theology of impressive contradictions. Is there any actual evidence behind this screen of dark hints and rumours, assertion and counter-assertion?

What written evidence we have in addition to the *Table Talk* from this period is scattered and imperfect. In a letter to Thomas Allsop written from Highgate in March 1820[4] Coleridge sets out his scheme of projected works under four headings. It is characteristically ambitious. The first is on Shakespeare and the Elizabethan dramatists: 'This work, with every art of compression, amounts to three Volumes Oct. of about 500 pages each.' Part II is a 'Philosophical Analysis' of Dante, Spenser, Milton, Cervantes, and Calderon – with some reference to Chaucer, Aristo, Donne, Rabelais, 'and others'. Reduced to reality, this is probably the material of his 1818 lectures which were finally published in fragmentary form in volumes I and II of the *Literary*

---

[1] *Apologia Pro Vita Sua*, ed. M. J. Svaglic (Oxford, 1967), p. 94.
[2] *Spiritual Philosophy: founded on the teaching of the late Samuel Taylor Coleridge* (1865).
[3] Traill, *Coleridge*, ch. XI.
[4] *Collected Letters*, ed. Griggs, vol. V (Oxford, 1971) no. 1228, pp. 25–7.

Remains, edited by his nephew, H. N. Coleridge, in 1836. Part III
was no less awe-inspiring, being nothing less than 'The History
of Philosophy, considered as a tendency of the Human Mind to
exhibit the powers of the Human Reason – to discover by its own
strength the origin & laws of Man and the world, from Pytha-
goras to Locke and Condillac – 2 Volumes.' The reality seems to
be the philosophical lectures of 1818, said by the long-suffering
Green to be 'wholly unfit for publication' in 1854, but finally
published by Professor Coburn as *The Philosophical Lectures of
Samuel Taylor Coleridge* in 1949. This philosophical excursus,
ambitious as it was in design, was not to be confused with
Coleridge's notorious GREAT WORK whose rainbowed
glories ever receded before him as he advanced.[1] Most important
for our purposes, however, was part IV of this grand scheme.
This was to consist of 'Letters on the Old and New Testament,
and on the doctrines and principles held in common by the
Fathers and Founders of the Reformation, addressed to a Candi-
date for Holy Orders – including advice on the plan and subjects
of Preaching, proper to a Minister of the Established Church.'
No trace of any theological work in this form appears to survive,
but some of the material may have found its way into volumes III
and IV of the *Literary Remains* which contain notes on such
divines as Hooker, Donne, and Jeremy Taylor, as well as the
short 'Essay on Faith'. In addition, both E. H. Coleridge and
J. D. Campbell, Coleridge's biographer, mention the manuscript
of 'a commentary on the Gospels and some of the Epistles'.[2] But
in his Preface to volume III of the *Remains* published in 1838
H. N. Coleridge betrays an uneasiness that has come to be
familiar to us as the keynote of those who examined the theology
of Coleridge's later years.

[1] In addition to Green's *Spiritual Philosophy*, descriptions and fragments of the
opus maximum are to be found in Alice Snyder's *Coleridge on Logic and Learning*,
(Yale, 1929), and J. H. Muirhead's *Coleridge as Philosopher* (Allen & Unwin,
1930) In the Coleridge collection at Victoria College, University of Toronto,
there is also an unpublished two-volume manuscript (Say Mss. II and III). It has no
title, but 'it consists of a philosophical demonstration of the truths of Christianity,
based on the sole assumption of the existence of a moral will in man'. This granted,
the existence of Conscience, the transcendence of God and the existence of the
Trinity are all made to follow.With the *Aids to Reflection* this manuscript seems to
cover a large part of Coleridge's projected philosophical defence of Christianity.
(Orsini, *Coleridge and German Idealism*, pp. 156–7.)

[2] *Letters*, II, 632 n., and J. D. Campbell *Samuel Taylor Coleridge* (1894), pp.
247 n. and 279 n.

Although the Author in his will contemplated the publication of some at least of the numerous notes left by him on the margins and blank spaces of books and pamphlets, he most certainly wrote the notes themselves without any purpose beyond that of delivering his mind of the thoughts and aspirations suggested by the text under perusal. His books, that is, any person's books – even those from a circulating library – were to him, whilst reading them, as dear friends; he conversed with them as with their authors, praising, or censuring, or qualifying, as the open page seemed to give him cause; little solicitous in so doing to draw summaries or to strike balances of literary merit, but seeking rather to detect and appreciate the moving principle or moral life, ever one and single, of the work in reference to absolute truth. Thus employed he had few reserves, but in general poured forth, as in a confessional, all his mind upon every subject – not keeping back any doubt or conjecture which at the time and for the purpose seemed worthy of consideration. In probing another's heart he laid his hand upon his own. He thought pious frauds the worst of all frauds, and the system of economizing truth too near akin to the corruption of it to be generally compatible with the Job-like integrity of a true Christian's conscience. Further, he distinguished so strongly between that internal faith which lies at the base of, and supports, the whole moral and religious being of man, and the belief, as historically true, of several incidents and relations found or supposed to be found in the text of the Scriptures, that he habitually exercised a liberty of criticism with respect to the latter, which will probably seem objectionable to many of his readers in this country.[1]

Objectionable his 'liberty of criticism' may have seemed to many readers, but there was little in the two volumes of the *Remains* to excite much scandal even then. We have the feeling, yet again, that H. N. Coleridge is glancing nervously over his shoulder, aware of something of which we are not.

It happens, however, that there is still one other, yet un-published and largely unexplored, source that gives us a clue to Coleridge's thinking during the late 1820s when he was in con-tact with John Sterling. With the bequest of the Ottery Manu-scripts to the British Museum, the complete run of Coleridge's unpublished notebooks has at last become easily available. It is now possible to match the hints and conjectures of Coleridge's editors, of Sterling, Hare, Carlyle, and Newman with the private record of Coleridge's theological speculations, and it is to these

[1] *Literary Remains*, ed. H. N. Coleridge, III (1838) ix–xi.

notebooks – and in particular those of 1828–9 – that the rest of this chapter will be devoted.

There seems little doubt that these notebooks contain what is at any rate one version of the 'commentary on the Gospels and some of the Epistles', though this description is an understatement, since there is also a detailed commentary on *Acts* and *Genesis* – evidently part of a scheme that was to embrace the whole Bible. Even a cursory examination of the contents suggests that H. N. Coleridge's disclaimers were somewhat disingenuous. However unselfconscious the jottings on the margins and fly-leaves of other people's books may have been, these notebooks, though disorganised and often apparently spontaneous in content, are always conscious of an audience. Here, at any rate, Coleridge is not communing with himself alone, but also with the reader. At one point the reader acquires a name, and we discover him to be none other than Joseph Henry Green, the London surgeon who was Coleridge's appointed literary executor and spiritual heir, the posthumous author of the already-mentioned *Spiritual Philosophy* which was eventually to fall stillborn from the presses in 1865. But beyond Green we are always conscious of Coleridge's awareness of a wider audience – eerily perhaps, the present author sitting in the Manuscripts Room of the British Museum and, you, the reader, as you read this book. At times Coleridge anxiously speaks over the head of Green to us directly:

Should these pages in their present state in consequence of death or disablement preventing me from arriving at a fuller and clear insight, meet the eye of an intelligent Reader, Let him know that he cannot be more sensible than I myself am of the turbidness and obscurity in the preceding imperfect exposition of the Thought . . . [1]

At times this consciousness of the reader over his shoulder draws Coleridge into parentheses and even double parentheses to assuage his fear of being misunderstood. Thus, commenting on the second chapter of *Acts*, he speculates whether verses 6–11 may be an interpolation 'tho' of very Ancient date' – perhaps contemporaneous with 'the latter half of the last Chapter of Mark'.

---

[1] But, he goes on, it has 'an importance extending far and reaching deep, even to . . . the foundation of right Judgement respecting Revelation generally, and the whole scheme of historic Evidences in particular'. Notebook 39 (B.M. Ms. 47, 534), p. 32.

At once, however, he feels that this is liable to misunderstanding, and he adds,

N.B. Instead of 'interpolation' I should have said, that it was one of the augmentations in an enlarged Edition or Revision of Luke's Memoir – a Church *Exemplum* – and I should say, edited at Rome (I use these Modernisms not that I am not aware of their inappropriateness but for want of a better).[1]

This is an extreme example, but it epitomises a quality that is, I think, *always* present in Coleridge's occasional writing. It is this continual *consciousness of an audience* that makes Coleridge's jottings and speculations so different in kind from similar 'private' writings of other authors, literary or religious – totally different in feel from, say, the notebooks of Gerard Manley Hopkins. Moreover, once we become aware of this quality in the notebooks it is very hard not to see it also as clearly in the 'confessional' material of the *Literary Remains*. The 'palpable design' upon his audience that Keats so disliked is a hallmark of Coleridge's style, even in soliloquy. It makes, incidentally, Carlyle's assertion of Coleridge's insensitivity to his audience when talking the harder to credit.[2] More significant from our point of view, it makes it relatively easy to follow the flow of Coleridge's ideas, for though he frequently relapses into shorthand, he never retreats into a private language.[3]

No less typical of Coleridge's mode of thinking is the arrangement of the notebooks. As in the *Remains* the entries are apparently fragmentary. Notebooks 37 and 38, for example, are written from both ends at once towards the middle. Number 37 is actually numbered three different ways: firstly in accordance

---

[1] His argument for this being an interpolation is on strictly literary criteria. Read 'aloud without pausing' it spoils the flow: 'in short (and this is the best test) read the first 18 verses omitting the six verses from the 5th to the 12th.' No. 37 (B.M. Ms. 47,532), p. 4.

[2] See Armour and Howes, *Coleridge the Talker*, Introduction.

[3] On several occasions he gives keys to his shorthand signs: e.g. on the fly-leaf of No. 37:

$=$ equivalent to, the same as
$+$ in addition to, and mark of the Positive
$-$ less by or mark of the Negative Pole
$\times$ multiplied with
$\mathpzc{x}$ distinct from – disparate
$\mathpzc{x}$ Opposite to, antithetic   Sweet $\mathpzc{x}$ Sour
$\mathpzc{x}$ Contrary to   Sweet $\mathpzc{x}$ Bitter

with an overall scheme for the set of 'theological' notebooks (of which it is number 5) it begins on page 351; secondly, it is numbered from the front in arabic numerals (beginning page 1, etc.); thirdly, and overlapping with this, it is numbered from the back by letters of the alphabet. Thus page 153 is simultaneously also page 503 and also page N! As with Alice falling to the centre of the earth, at the point of zero gravity in the middle strange juxtapositions and sequences occur. In the middle of the discussion of *Acts* there is inserted a series of speculations on the mechanism of sight and vision.[1] Though these are apparently unrelated to the Biblical commentary, and in any logical sense entirely irrelevant to it, the reader suddenly becomes aware how Coleridge's mind is shifting backwards and forwards from the theological problem of miracles and their 'meaning' to the parallel psychological question of the inseparability of perception from interpretation. Does, for instance, the perception of a miracle depend upon a particular kind of mental set arising from a specific culture? Later this hint is confirmed when we find him explicitly discussing this very question as an essential factor in his theory of miracles.[2] Similarly, at the beginning of a discussion of the *Epistle to the Romans* we find an apparently unrelated fragment that foreshadows *Church and State*. 'But Bishops of the Church by *Law* established, not a Christian nisi per accidens but a National Church, are Superintendents of tangible worldly professions... They are *Bishops* of the King's making: *Priests* of the Church's.'[3] It is as if we are looking into the deep well of Coleridge's unconscious. Only afterwards, and with hindsight, do we begin to wonder how fortuitous such abrupt juxtapositions may turn out to be.

An overall plan to these notebooks there certainly is. Indeed, at times, as so often with Coleridge, the reader begins to fear that there are too many plans in operation at once. A scheme at the end of number 38 outlines a series of three books in a plan whose credibility is enhanced by the fact that one was by this time actually published:

I

Aids to Reflection, in the discipline of the Understanding and in the Conduct of Life.

[1] No. 37 (B.M. Ms. 47,532), p. 18.   [2] No. 39 (B.M. Ms. 47,534), pp. 10, 17–35.
[3] No. 38 (B.M. Ms. 47,533), p. 38.

II

Aids to Discourse in Writing and Speaking: Practical Treatise on the power, use, and logical Management of WORDS, with an analysis of the Constitution and Limits of the *Human Understanding* – intended principally, as a preparation for the Senate, the Pulpit, and the Bar.

III

Aids to BELIEF for the attainment of stedfast (*sic*) Convictions from Insight, or the Faith & Philosophy of S.T.C. systematically evolved.

The first Work	COMMON SENSE
The Second	Logic
The Third	Faith & Reason[1]

But this is one of many such triads; it is not the scheme for these notebooks. Diverse and often fragmentary as they are, they make Coleridge's main purpose abundantly clear – and serve to confirm how closely this purpose was in fact related to the conversations he was having with Sterling and others during these years. As has been suggested, his grand design was for nothing less than a monumental Biblical commentary that would juxtapose first principles and detailed exempla from the text, showing scripture as a focus or 'symbol' of theological and philosophical meaning.

In December of 1828 we find Coleridge examining his feelings 'not as a Christian but as a Scholar, and in my *intellectual* calling as a Biblical Critic and Theologian, not in my spiritual Profession as a Believer in Jesus, Son of Man and Son of God'.[2] Such declared division between the critic and the believer would clearly reinforce contemporary uneasiness with the direction in which Coleridge's mind was moving. Less than a year later, sometime in the summer of 1829, we find him seeking to spell out the desired synthesis springing from this polarity. The miracles of the Pentateuch, he ponders, 'present a most interesting subject if those who were competent to treat it, dared talk about it. But we must first have a Religion of *Faith* not Fear; of Christians that are Philosophers and Philosophers that are sincere and undoubting Christians.'[3] He must be, therefore,

A Christian and a Philosopher who not only finds in his philosophy no obstacle to a belief in Miracles quoad Miracles, but a demonstration

---

[1] No. 38 (B.M. Ms. 47,533), p. 69.   [2] Ibid. pp. 22–3.
[3] No. 42 (B.M. Ms. 47,537), p. 48.

a priori of its necessity; but likewise the Cannons of Credibility as the conditions, under which Records of particular Miracles are capable of being positively established by testimony and thus raised from metaphysical to historical truth. . . Now, by what clew would this man follow the Truth thro' the Narration of the Deluge. . . ?[1]

But the gifts required for this kind of exegesis are formidable:

Great and wide Erudition, with curious research; a philosophic imagination quick to seize hold of analogies; an emancipation from prejudice, and a servile subjection to the prejudices of great names; a faith that shutteth out fear; a freedom from the superstition which assumed an absolute *sui generis* in every word of the O. and N. Testaments, and is for ever craving after the supernatural; a sound and profound Psychology – these are the principal requisites.[2]

Above all, Coleridge sees it as his duty to combat the evils and superstition of what would nowadays be called 'fundamentalism' – as he says here, a belief in the literal and unique inspiration of the actual *words* of scripture. Such a belief is only possible, Coleridge argues, through a timidity that excludes genuine faith, and a gross insensitivity to the nature and possibilities of language.

Earlier in that same year, in March 1828, we find Coleridge denouncing the 'gross inconsistencies and absurdities of the Superstitious Interpretations of the Cannonical Scriptures', where 'every sentence, nay, word [is] a Spider's Teat for an endless thread of Deduction – yea a System-web – to catch flies!'[3] Immediately following this entry is a memorandum on the kind of language necessary for 'a new translation of the Old Testament'. It would demand 'not only no word to be used of later date than Elizabeth's Reign; but for the character and genius of the Hebrew it would be most expedient to revive a number of pure Saxon words, make this proviso that they are such as to explain themselves'![4] This must be the only project on record for translating the Bible into language *more* archaic than the Authorized Version! How accurate were the assumed parallels between the 'character and genius' of Saxon and Hebrew may be open to question, what is more significant here is the movement of Coleridge's mind from the current abuses of Biblical exegesis to a consideration of an appropriate language to convey not

[1] No. 42 (B.M. Ms. 47,537), p. 55.   [2] No. 41 (B.M. Ms. 47,536), pp. 34–5.
[3] No. 37 (B.M. Ms. 47,532), pp. 46–7.   [4] Ibid. p. 47.

merely the formal literal sense of the text, but the poetic overtones and nuances of association that make up a particular
linguistic universe – qualities that he elsewhere calls 'the dramatic colour of style, the *life* of the language'.[1] What is required, he
argues, is a quite new approach to Biblical exegesis. On the one
hand it must take into account the developments and discoveries
of the German Historical Method – though such tools should
not be accepted or used uncritically, but always checked against
the overall 'life' of the passage or Book in question. On the other,
it requires what the Germans so often seemed to *lack*, a sense of
the poetic fire and imagination of Hebrew thought, the method
of which was allusive, metaphorical, and symbolic. This is a
quality of scripture Coleridge responds to with an almost Blake-
ian vehemence: even the dreams of the Old Testament, he says,
are *poetic*:

we need not suppose, that the Hebrew Nation set to work a cold-
blooded carpentry of Terrors like the Bard or the Vision of Judgement.
In those times and in that country men reasoned with the organ of
Imagination, and vivid Images supplied the place of words, and came
more readily than words in language so limited and scanty as the
Hebrew.[2]

In other words, if the divine power of scripture is to be allowed
to speak to men, the Bible must be set neither outside the canons
of historical scholarship,[3] nor those of literary criticism, for these
are the very *means* by which it speaks. The Bible is impoverished
if it is held to be literally inspired, because such a concentration
on the individual words denies the life and unity of the whole,
which is organically greater than the parts, and leads to a
myopic concentration on tiny fragments unrelated to their context. It is, on the contrary, immeasurably enriched if we see it as
a work of the Imagination, in which the various strands, his-

[1] No. 41 (B.M. Ms. 47,536), p. 30.
[2] No. 41 (B.M. Ms. 47,536), p. 34.
[3] If, for instance, Methuselah were a dynasty and not a single person, it would
bring such genealogies into line with Arabian and Persian Pedigrees: although the
tone of the Bible is quite different from their 'boastful, romancing, and eulogising
spirit'. In this instance, literary arguments outweigh historical, and after mature
consideration Coleridge, interestingly, concludes, 'On the whole, therefore, I
see not sufficient reason against the belief in the fact, and therefore none against the
literal understanding of the Document recording it.' No. 42 (B.M. Ms. 47, 537),
pp. 36–8.

torical, symbolic, and moral, take their place within a single artistic work.

Several times in the course of his commentaries Coleridge breaks off to attack literalists. 'Oh the deadening incubus of that notion of *dictation* by a Ghost,' he writes in the summer of 1829, ' – for such in fact is their notion of the Holy Spirit...'[1] 'It *should* be more than sufficient to ask these asserters of plenary inspiration (by which they mean *dictation*) – whether this fact had been *revealed* to them? For the Documents themselves make no such claim; but in twenty places imply the contrary.'[2]

It is in this context that we find full confirmation of the hints by Sterling, Hare, Newman, and others of Coleridge's feeling that he could not print many of his ideas and speculations. No one, declares Coleridge – as always addressing his invisible audience – no one has laboured more earnestly (and with greater belief in the confluence of the true and the good) to believe in the historical truth of *Genesis* and the Flood. But why is there no mention of it, for instance, in Homer?[3] He is forced to conclude that it sounds 'glyphic' and mythical. Similarly, we find him writing on *Acts* v early in 1828: 'Do I then doubt the historical truth of this Narrative of Ananias and his wife? No! That I cannot do, without making History of no avail – but I do think it probable that the event might have been in th' course thro' a number of reporters, *moralized*, and for that purpose compressed into a shorter space of time.'[4] At last, with his discussion of Stephen's speech before his accusers (*Acts* VII), Coleridge's bitter sense of the inadmissibility of what he is suggesting bursts out:

It reminds me of some of the rambling speeches of the first Quakers before the Magistrates – but this, I suppose, I must not acknowledge! & Why? O! because our [?] will not believe the Redeemer's words that by Babes & Sucklings (i.e. by rude and ignorant men) he would lay the foundations of his Church – and thanked his heavenly Father that he had so ordained it – no! but we must have these rude and ignorant men transmuted into consummate sages by miracle – as if this did not render our Lord's words a mere equivocation.[5]

Later, he continues in an even more sweeping vein:

[1] No. 41 (B.M. Ms. 47,536), p. 30.   [2] No. 42 (B.M. Ms. 47,537), p. 46.
[3] Ibid. pp. 64–5.   [4] No. 37 (B.M. Ms. 47,532), p. 23.
[5] Ibid. p. 26 The missing word is illegible.

A very useful article might be written on the History and Progress of the Vice of Lying on the Christian Church... I would begin with Justin Martyr, Irenaeus, & Tertullian, enumerating the lies that had been fabricated during the space of 90 years from the date of St. Paul's third year's residence at Rome – i.e. the concluding chapter of the Acts. The only objection to such a book is that it would comprize full half the contents of Ecclesiastic History.[1]

Can a man of mind, for whom *the Truth* on *all* subjects, & philosophic Freedom in the pursuit of it, are *good* per se... adopt the Church for a Profession?[2]

It would, I think, be easy to misunderstand Coleridge's problem here, and in similar passages. His outspoken anti-clericalism is nothing new. His opinion of the established clergy in general had not improved much since his revolutionary days in the 1790s. Even when he had emerged from his Unitarian phase, we find him as late as 1800 debating in these terms whether he should have his sons Hartley and Derwent baptised at all:

...Shall I suffer the Toad of Priesthood to spurt out his foul juice in this Babe's face? Shall I suffer him to see grave countenances and hear grave accents, while his face is sprinkled, and while the fat paw of a Parson crosses his Forehead.[3]

The 1790s were a far more dangerous ecclesiastical and political climate than the late 1820s. He had braved convention then; far less was seemingly at stake now. Mild iconoclasm was what the young turks like Sterling came out to Highgate to hear, and it was not Coleridge's ideas, but his refusal to state them *openly* that finally earned the contempt of many of them. There was nothing new in sceptical speculations. The utilitarian agnosticism of Bentham and the Mills was widely influential in sophisticated middle-class circles, and the question of the disestablishment of the Church of England was openly discussed, and to

[1] No. 39 (B.M. Ms. 47,534), p. 52.

[2] Surprisingly, the answer turns out to be 'Yes' – 'always presuming, that the Church of which he is to be a minister, is on the way of Truth, and with its face turned toward the interests of the Nation, or Unit of which the Church itself is a Member.' His reconciliation is that of *Church and State,* and here one can see how the 'Social Gospel' of Maurice or Ludlow is contained in embryo within the Coleridgean formulations. Ibid. p. 68.

[3] Letter to Godwin – with perhaps the rhetoric adjusted accordingly (Willey, *S.T.C.* p. 84) – *Letters,* I, 352.

some at one stage even seemed likely.[1] In Biblical criticism the Germans were a generation before Coleridge. As early as the 1790s the work of Eichorn and Herder was known in the English Unitarian circles where Coleridge was intimate. Some of his friends of that period had suffered considerably for their advanced political or theological views. William Frend had been expelled from Cambridge in 1793 for his Unitarian beliefs, and Thomas Beddoes from Oxford for his sympathy with the French Revolution. It was Beddoes who had persuaded Coleridge to go to Göttingen in 1798 where he read Eichorn and attended his lectures.[2] But after a false start in the last decade of the eighteenth century it was clear that by the 1820s the floodgates to German historical criticism were at last wide open. Pusey had begun to learn German; and Hare and Thirlwall were at work on their translation of Niebuhr.[3] Coleridge records in these notebooks that he began to read Niebuhr's History (of Rome) on 25 May 1828.[4] *His* problem, it seems to me, was that by the 1820s he was looking for a solution very different from either the historical radicalism of the German scholars, or the re-assertion of authority that was slowly building up in Oxford. It depended on unfettered enquiry and disinterested scholarship quite as much as the Germans or their liberal Anglican admirers, but it rested no less upon an ideal of 'faith' that was not just the personal construct of intellectuals and advanced thinkers, but which was the possession of the whole community *as a community*.

> To walk together to the kirk,
> And all together pray...

As we have seen, Coleridge's attachment to the Church of England was not based on any intrinsic admiration for its clergy or its institutions. In *Church and State*, whose germ is everywhere present in these notebooks, he wanted to reinvigorate the all-but vanished ideals of the Established Church, with its concomitant of the 'Clerisy', because it alone (in his view) was capable of providing the focus of a national and communal culture

---

[1] More a bogey than as a probability; some saw it as the logical consequence of Peel's Catholic Emancipation Acts, and the defeat of the Tories in 1830.

[2] Storr, *English Theology*, p. 193; Willey, *S.T.C.*, p. 245; E. S. Shaffer, '*Kubla Khan*' and '*The Fall of Jerusalem*' (Cambridge, 1975), p. 29.

[3] See below, p. 125 and pp. 256–7.

[4] No. 37 (B.M. Ms. 47,532) p. 75.

that lifted faith from the savage backbiting of sectarian politics and restored it to its place as part of the organic 'life' of society. It is the Word that draws together the dry bones and the breath that makes the nation 'come alive'.

Coleridge did not expect ecclesiastical corruption to vanish at the 'reformation' of the Established Church; what he did believe possible was a dialectic that could contain and balance the inevitable abuses by a re-spiritualising of the institutions themselves. For Grace to flow through earthly and human organisations it was not necessary to proclaim the millennium, but it was necessary, Coleridge saw, to keep clear the channels through which it might pour. It is the subject of one of his most brilliant and complex images:

The small Artery in the Finger or the thread-like Vein in the Foot witteth not of the Blood in the Chambers of the Flesh, and but a small portion thereof doth it need or can it contain – Yet by the never-resting Energy of the Heart, ever expanding to acquire, and contracting to communicate, is the distant vein fed, and its needful portion renewed, and the feeding Artery receives an aiding impulse in the performance of its humble ministry.[1]

Faith is the blood which flows throughout the Body Politic. By its *circulation* it renews both itself and the whole organism: if we interfere with that constant flow we damage not merely the life of the nation, but also the quality of the faith itself. The body is sick, perhaps mortally sick; the Church of England a feeble and diseased vessel; but while Church and State still hold together, and while the Church is yet more than a sect – the most corrupt because the most wealthy – the divine life-blood is still able to do its healing and redeeming work. The pulse still beats. If we incline to dismiss this essentially limited ideal as unrealistic metaphysics, we need to remember that from it grew the ideas of Hare and Maurice, of the Church as a pre-existing universal spiritual society for all men. It was primarily from this source, not from either the Evangelicals or the Oxford Movement, that the inspiration of the Christian Socialists was able to call into existence a social conscience in the English Church. Its descendents include George Bell, William Temple, and A. M. Ramsey.

Such an image illustrates too the sheer complexity of inter-

[1] No. 37 (B.M. Ms. 47,532), p. 60.

relations that characterise Coleridge's thought at its best. A single image of 'faith' links his social, political, and ecclesiastical concerns. Moreover, this analogy with the blood circulation is simultaneously symbolic of the unity of scripture on which the whole edifice is built. Amputate a verse or passage from the unity of the whole Bible and it dies in itself, while impoverishing the remainder. It is with images such as this in mind that we must, Coleridge argues, approach the Old and New Testament. We must do so not in the manner of a lawyer looking for contradictions, nor determined that isolated passages shall bear the whole weight of later doctrinal edifices, but, as he says of *Genesis*, comparing the apparent meaning of particular verses *'with the spirit and contents of the whole following document'*.[1] This follows the general approach of Lessing and the Schlegels. Coleridge can therefore describe the *collective* strength of the Bible as 'inspiration', even though it may not apply to every story or even every book.[2] Thus of *Genesis* II, verse 24,[3] he comments:

This very 'therefore' supplies a strong argument in support of the *symbolic* nature of verses 18–22. If these verses are to be understood literally and physically, the woman for the female Body, and the Rib for one of the male Vertebrae, the *logic* certainly would not be very obvious, or the conclusion promised by the *Therefore* easily cleared of a εἰς ἄλλο γένος not to speak of the whole narration being at variance with v. 27 of Chapter 1. But understand the narrative of the Institution of Marriage =the creation of the *Wife*, and of the cause and grounds of it in Man's rational, Moral, and yet finite, Being, and thence morally and rationally social – nothing can be more legitimate than the conclusion or more just and apposite than the causes and motives appearing in the law, enacting that 'Man shall live by'.[4]

Employing precisely the same methodology of reading the parts in the spirit of the whole, Coleridge weighs and dismisses traditional allegorical interpretations of Abraham's pleading with God (*Genesis* XVIII).[5]

The crux of this method of exegesis is, of course, the problem

---

[1] No. 42 (B.M. Ms. 47,537), p. 33.

[2] No. 37 (B.M. Ms. 47,532), p. 32.

[3] 'Therefore shall a man leave his father and mother, and cleave unto his wife: and they shall be one flesh.'

[4] No. 42 (B.M. Ms. 47,537), p. 39.

[5] E.g. that the 'three righteous men' represent the Trinity. Ibid. p. 79.

and status of miracles. Time and time again Coleridge finds himself turning back to this question. As always, he justifies himself before his audience:

> But on this and all similar occasions to set in the clearest light the folly of attributing my scepticism to a desire of discrediting the miracles of the O. and N. Testaments generally, or of supposing that I rejected a particular incident because it was miraculous. Surely Common Sense might shew these Metaphysicians that the man who believes in the conversion of Water to Wine at Cana, and the twice repeated Feeding of 3 and 4 Thousand with as few Loaves and Fishes; the Raising of Lazarus; and the Lord's Healing all manner of Diseases by the word of his Mouth [would?] sustain no increase of *Faith* in the Supernatural Character of our Saviour's Acts of Power and Mercy, tho' he had persuaded himself to believe all the additional wonders narrated in the Gospel of Nicodemus. – The opposite of Faith and its worst enemy is Credulity.[1]

His view of miracles is related directly to their moral or spiritual *purpose*.[2] Are they meaningless marvels, or can they be understood as 'acted parables', revealing Christ in the same way as does the rest of his teaching? The general principles of scriptural exegesis hold good. 'What I have said respecting the detection of spurious passages or books,' Coleridge explains, '...is founded on their diversity...from the other books of the Sacred Canon.' Doubtful areas 'cannot possibly affect the Belief in its Authenticity generally – for the very criteria of the spuriousness of the former imply the authenticity of the latter.' 'In short, Faith and Belief are different acts, and Credulity differs from both.'[3] What Coleridge is seeking is a twofold objective: to separate the genuine from the counterfeit, and, more important, to try and establish the principles by which such separations can be made.

What has been hitherto wanting and which if God grant me life, and the power of his grace I hope to supply is a Canon of Credibility a

---

[1] No. 37 (B.M. Ms. 47, 532), p. 6.

[2] 'Even respecting the far more awful and important Facts of the Gospel, the Miracles of our Lord himself, what more can the Believer be required to prove, than that the evidence is as great as it *ought to be*, and as great as it *can* be without destroying or cumbrancing the very objects & purposes of the Religion which the Miracles were worked to confirm?' No. 38 (B.M. Ms. 47,533), p. 8.

[3] No. 37 (B.M. Ms. 47,532), p. 6.

priori – a code of Principles determining what Evidences are *possible*, what reasonable, and what desirable, as means to the assumed end – and in this Code I hope to set forth every possible sense in which the term, Miracle, *can* be used – and not least to make men have a distinct knowledge of their own meaning and belief – which I am persuaded not one in a thousand does at present.[1]

If the establishment of these criteria causes him to have doubts about many of the miracles in the Bible, they also give added credence to some of the central events of the New Testament, such as the phenomena on Whit Sunday as recorded in *Acts* ii. The gift of tongues is not to be explained away – indeed, it gives us the clue to the 'method' that Coleridge is in the process of working out: 'And first let it be understood that the solution of the Phaenomena, and their true character, are not the points in question. Let them be effects or results of the Imagination – tho' here it may be fairly asked, what then *is* this Imagination capable of producing such effects... ?'[2] The Day of Pentecost is thus seen as a 'showing forth' – a miracle symbolic of the nature of miracles as a whole. It is, in some sense, an 'Imaginative event'. 'Question not to be even mentally answered without much discursion of thought, no less than stedfast meditation: ? May there not be a hidden contradiction in the Demand or Expectation, that a Miracle should be wholly *objective*?'[3] In so far as a miracle implies purpose and meaning, clearly criteria of 'objectivity' do not apply. For Coleridge, religious belief involves living in a universe implicit with hidden meaning which is 'revealed' in focal incidents almost akin to Wordsworth's 'spots of time'.

To every eye – Observe, I suppose myself to address Scholars, Men of Learning and of cultivated Intellects & and speak of *them* exclusively – to every eye not dim and red with the film of prejudices and the inflamation of professional Interests: the coincidence of the Providential with the Miraculous, and the existence of the former chiefly in the *Objective* portion of the Incident, must be apparently and seem a characteristic of the Miracles related in the last four books of the Pentateuch...

...collectively, we will not fail to remember that whatever this or that *Link* of the Chain may be the Chain itself is clearly Miraculous – i.e. a reduction of a whole too vast to have the relations of the component integral parts perceptible into a space capable of being comprehended

---

[1] No. 39 (B.M. Ms. 47,534), p. 49.   [2] No. 38 (B.M. Ms. 47,533), p. 4.
[3] No. 39 (B.M. Ms. 47,534), p. 10.

within a field of mental vision. What, were our knowledge & capacity adequate, would be found true of the whole History of the World viz: a pre-designing and pre-disposing Will (= Fate, Necessity, overriding Providence) in the contingency of the Particulars, so that the Events contemplated as a unity – i.e. the Chain as distinguished from the links – must be referred immediately to the divine Will – *this* is presented to us in the Series of Events resolved in the Bible in a size and compass proportionate to our faculties, and so as to supply the requisite knowledge. . . And is it possible, I confidently ask, to conceive a nobler definition of the Miraculous![1]

Miracles are, therefore, not breaks in nature, but *exempla* of the reality underlying its phenomena. It is merely a popular mistake, Coleridge argues, to suppose that a 'miracle' *necessarily* conflicts with the operation of natural laws. 'Nature is the Subject of a Law, not a Lawgiver.'[2] A miracle is only to be understood in terms of purpose, and in this it does not differ from the rest of the universe.

What other definition does the term, Miracle, require or admit than 'Acts, Incidents, Appearances calculated to excite awe and wonder.' And what more fitted to impress the mind with awe and wonder, than Law! The Effects are *always* admirable; but when they are such as to direct the Beholder's mind to the *Agent* while his attention is drawn to the Work – to make him recognize the presence of the Law itself shining thro' the effects – then do these most rightfully claim the name of signs and Wonders! S.T.C.[3]

Thus it is also a mistake to regard miracles as part of a static system – *natura naturata* rather than *natura naturans*. Central to Coleridge's idea of Biblical method is his sense of doctrine and belief as a living, changing, evolving process, constantly offering new perspectives and making new connections. The understanding of miracles is itself a part of a wider approach to scriptural interpretation in which there a progressive unfolding or discovery of meaning. Development of doctrine is the natural mode of Biblical thought. In an entry dated 26 August 1829 Coleridge begins portentously, 'I am about to put a question which will be (thank heaven) unintelligible to most, and startle the rest.'

Is not the true Meaning of the words of the Prophets, and of the Old

---

[1] No. 39 (B.M. Ms. 47,534), p. 27.   [2] Ibid. p. 17.   [3] Ibid. p. 18.

Testament generally, their applicability? Or – is not the meaner application of the words and sentences if not superseded yet over-built by the more important? Again: is not this importance to be measured by the permanence of the Truth expressed, by the *abiding* interest of the Fact? And this again by the Spirituality? And can the tenet of *Inspired* writings be otherwise made intelligible and vindicated, but on the assumption that as far as they are of the Holy Spirit, the sense must be spiritual? And does not the evidence of the over ruling In-presence of the Spirit in these writings consist in the immanence of the Spiritual, the *life* of the Letter, in the primary and temporary intention of the words – which *is* the Letter? May we only without any ecclesiastic or bibliolatrical evasion, assert that the Spirit, which prompted and [word illegible] the minds of the Prophets and Psalmists, provide by a series of providential events for the spiritual interpretation and application of their words – now by rendering the primary purpose obsolete, gone by, and now by the non fulfilment of the predictions in the sense first understood by the Contemporaries of the inspired Men – which yet their veneration and esteem of the writings themselves not only by this, but greatly, very greatly increased – /nay, the truer religious sense of value of these Books, the more than life-valuing of them, may be said to have commenced from the time that the *apparent* falsification of their promises, the failure of their *literal sense, became evident.*[1]

This is, of course, a very Catholic view of the scriptures, and we are reminded – as so often – of the curious parallels and affinities between Coleridge's patterns of thought and those of Newman. This idea of development is well illustrated by the concept of the Trinity, as it were 'latent' in the New Testament, but not yet brought to full consciousness. Referring to 2 *Corinthians* ii, 16–18, Coleridge writes:

Collated with the Gospel of John, does not this passage confirm the suggestion of my mind, that in the Apostolic *explicit* belief in the Spirit in the *personal* sense was not yet distinguished from the Word – but that as in the Church before Christ the Son was folded up, as it were, in the Spirit, so in the beginning of the Christian Church the Spirit was identified with the Word.[2]

But despite similarities to the concepts of development elaborated by Newman and Maurice in the 1840s,[3] Coleridge's idea of development is *not* primarily historical in basis, but still *a*

[1] No. 41 (B.M. Ms. 47,536), pp. 92 ff.   [2] Ibid. p. 49.
[3] See Ch. 6 below.

priori and metaphysical. The purpose of history is to illustrate metaphysical principles. His notion of the rôle of Prophecy in the development of doctrine clearly owes more to Plato than it does to the Old Testament.

the student able and inclined to follow me in the Maze by the clue... must have mastered the principle, that in the Sciences of Freedom, subsisting in intellectual Intuitions, the Idea contains its necessity in its actual presence. The *so it must be* is involved in the *so it is*. For all inferior knowledge, the knowledge of Generals presented to the Understanding...derive their ultimate intelligibility from Ideas...The Ideas, themselves, therefore, must needs have their evidence in their Being, first, each in itself a *Ray* of light...2nd. in the harmony of Ideas, 3rd. in the continuity of evolution, each fresh evolute throwing back light on the preceeding, as well as flashing at that which is to follow, and lastly in the involution & evolubility of all from the *Word* in the Beginning...[1]

This is difficult stuff to the modern reader, and it illustrates very clearly how remote we are from the *a priori* Platonic metaphysics that have enthralled many earlier generations. The similarity of the qualities evinced by 'continuity of evolution' to Newman's tests of development should not blind us to the fact that their basis is utterly different. Here, Coleridge stands for an older way of thinking.

What is much more genuinely similar to Newman's late thought is also to be found in Coleridge, however; that is the idea – stemming no doubt from Butler in both cases – that there is no break between the 'natural' and 'supernatural'. Though they stand in a dialectical relationship to one another, they are, nevertheless, the two ends of an unbroken continuum. In this example, Coleridge's expression is as lucid and concrete as before it was heavy and clumsy:

...as the lower part of the Coral consists of the same stuff with the Rock to which it is attached – so here what the Calcereous stem is to the Coral, the Body is to the Soul...This in the present life is to be continually loosening till finally it is transferred to a new ground... What Nature is to the Natural Man, in all its particularity[?] of Soil, Moisture, Air, Warmth, light, magnetic attraction etc., that Christ is to the Souls of the Redeemed.[2]

[1] No. 37 (B.M. Ms. 47,532), p. 84.   [2] No. 41 (B.M. Ms. 47,536), p. 51.

Yet in approaching all such themes as these in Coleridge's thinking it is necessary to proceed with extreme caution. The modern reader may find it all too easy to discern in Coleridge's metaphysical schemata preoccupations and concerns that appear modern and familiar. Those aspects of his thought that appear to lead directly towards the theology of Maurice or Newman, or even towards twentieth-century theologians such as Tillich, are the ones that stand out with hindsight. We need to remember how such a view of Coleridge may be anachronistic. Two recent studies have emphasised neglected and much more alien qualities in early nineteenth-century thought. Dr Robert Burns[1] has shown how the revived interest in miracles in eighteenth-century British theology was not part of a rearguard action by Biblical literalists, but, on the contrary, a relatively new approach by a theological 'avant-garde' who were seeking to find in miracles a kind of 'evidence' for Christianity that corresponded to the 'evidences' of natural science. As events proved it was doomed to failure in its own terms and to be overtaken by more fruitful movements on the Continent, but in looking at Coleridge's criticism of Paley and his followers it is as well to remember that as we have seen, his own interest in miracles is not purely negative. His concern with 'evidences' is not that of Paley, but neither is it that of Eichorn or Strauss. The attempt to sort out different categories of miracle according to certain principles of relevance owes much to the methods of those he is ostensibly opposing.

In his brilliant and provocative book, *What Coleridge Thought*, Owen Barfield focusses our attention on other aspects of Coleridge's world-picture that are usually ignored because they do not fit in with our own. His theories on the nature of Life, for example, are integral to his whole way of thinking. Barfield, himself a follower of Rudolf Steiner, is able to demonstrate very convincingly that Coleridge, like Steiner, was heavily influenced by a tradition of thought that comes from Goethe's biological speculations and German *Naturphilosophie*, and that Coleridge's notions had many similarities with modern Anthroposophy. This is a very salutary approach, and by it Barfield is able to explain areas of Coleridge's thinking that had previously been highly

[1] *David Hume and Miracles in Historical Perspective,* unpublished Ph.D. Thesis (University of Princeton, 1971).

obscure. But it needs careful qualification. We need to remember that in Coleridge's time natural science still attempted to span two different streams of thought that by the end of the century could clearly be seen as incompatible. These we may call the 'vitalist' and the 'mechanistic'. The former held that living matter must contain, or rather, be contained by some 'vital principle' or 'life-force' that differentiated it in kind from the mere 'dead' arrangement of matter in its inorganic form. Life must therefore be understood not merely in terms of structure, origins, and causes, but also in terms of purpose and goal – even in terms of immanent 'Will'. For thinkers like Coleridge such a teleological concept held numerous attractive corollaries. Yet, as so often, it is difficult to pigeon-hole Coleridge's ideas within the conventional divisions. From his *Theory of Life* (much of it a mosaic of unacknowledged borrowings from Schelling and his disciple Henrik Steffens)[1] it is clear that Coleridge did not believe that 'life' was something over and above mere complexity of organisation in the sense of being either an 'occult power'[2] or an added 'force' – like the steam in a steam-engine.[3] Dorothy Emmett, indeed, believes that he should not properly be called a 'vitalist' at all.[4] As she puts it, Coleridge was primarily interested in 'what it is to be a *living* creature'.[5] The teleological biology of Schelling and Steffens seemed to provide in natural science a direct equivalent of Coleridge's aesthetic distinction between 'Imagination' and 'Fancy'. The former was a living and vital principle of organisation where the whole transformed and modified the constituent parts; the latter was simple juxta-position, in which the parts themselves remained unchanged. In philosophical terms, similarly, 'vitalism' (however defined) seemed to correspond to the Kantian Reason, whereas Under-

[1] Fruman, *Coleridge*, pp. 121–34.

[2] *Theory of Life*, p. 377.

[3] Ibid. p. 406.

[4] 'I do not think that Coleridge should properly be called a Vitalist in the sense of one who believes that the life in an organism is not the whole organism in an active state, but depends on the existence of some distinct vital factor. Certainly Coleridge does sometimes talk about living principles in ways that suggest they are distinct existences. But we can recall the parallel with Ideas as living powers, when I suggested that in such talk an Idea is not a ghostly inhabitant of the mind, but the mind itself – indeed the whole thinking and feeling person – finding a form to express a theme...' In *Coleridge's Variety*, p. 176.

[5] Ibid.

standing could be held to refer to the material and mechanical. *Naturphilosophie*, as it was expounded by Schelling and his followers, held that it was possible to construct a single idealist philosophy of nature that would reveal *all* natural phenomena as deriving from a single unifying principle. New discoveries in electricity and galvanism seemed to show that both organic and inorganic material was subject to the same laws of polarity; parallel developments in physiology seemed to indicate a general law of 'irritability' in living tissue. The weakness of *Naturphilosophie*, unfortunately, was that it tended to remain pure speculation without being tied down to rigorous experiment and verification. But the very existence of such apparently impressive correspondences between science, aesthetics, and philosophy seemed to imply the possibility of a grand theological synthesis whereby the discerning Christian might point to a slow 'evolution' of consciousness from its primaeval roots latent in the inanimate world and ascending in an unbroken Chain of Being through plants and animals to Man himself. Such a Chain of Being could be either static and immutable hierarchy, or 'evolutionary' – and it seems to have been towards this latter developmental and progressive position that Coleridge increasingly inclined. 'Nature,' he says in *Aids to Reflection*, 'is a line in constant and continuous evolution.'[1] We should not, of course, confuse this kind of 'evolutionary' theory, based as it is on teleological, *a priori* metaphysical principles, with Darwinian evolution, which is in many ways its direct opposite. The vitalist position involves what has been rather grandly called the 'retrotensive fallacy'[2] that is, the argument that the qualities of the complex are, in some undetectable sense, 'implicit' in its simpler components. Thus a modern exponent of vitalism, Teilhard de Chardin, argues that the attributes of 'Mind' are already latent in the simplest molecules of matter. This kind of reasoning, in its various forms, can be traced right back to Aristotle.[3]

From the 'mechanistic' point of view, however, this approach simply lacks the possibility of experimental verification. Moreover Nature is demonstrably full of discontinuities. Sodium and chlorine are both poisonous; common salt, sodium chloride, has

[1] P. 232.　　[2] A. O. Lovejoy, *The Great Chain of Being* (Harvard, 1936).
[3] See, for instance, his concept of 'entelechy': the condition in which a potential has become actuality, thus (by extension) giving form and perfection to the thing

quite different properties from either, and is essential for life. Vitalism is an essentially unverifiable, and therefore redundant, hypothesis. 'Purpose' can be replaced by 'necessity' and 'chance'. The problem for many nineteenth-century thinkers was the inherent attractiveness of the purposive and teleological arguments as against the bleak universe of mechanism – epitomised in the popular notions of Newton. Kant's distinction between 'Reason' and 'Understanding' is one attempt to solve this dilemma.[1] At the level of 'Understanding' the laws of mechanistic science hold sway: the plant is determined by its seed; the stars and planets 'blindly run' according to immutable laws. It is only at the level of 'Reason' that we find purpose. Coleridge clearly hoped that his version of vitalism would provide a bridge between the two worlds. What better place for the meeting of two incompatible universes than Life itself, where we might find in natural science yet another paradigm for the two natures of Christ? Though, as usual, Coleridge has perverted Kant, such a hypothesis was still possible in respectable scientific circles without incongruity. This, it seems to me, is where Barfield's conclusions can be dangerous and misleading: it is a mistake to compare an early nineteenth-century figure like Coleridge with such late nineteenth-century vitalists as Rudolf Steiner or Teilhard de Chardin in the twentieth century without mentioning the intervening biological revolution that had reduced teleological arguments (for better or worse) to the stock-in-trade of the philosophical fringe.

The present experimental supremacy of 'mechanistic' biology – whether or not it lasts – is a reminder of how far our world-picture has departed from that of Coleridge and his immediate Victorian successors. It was still possible then for 'natural idealists' like Wordsworth who *felt* the 'unreality' of the material sense-world, and who desired to approach it from what they felt they knew to be the 'greater reality', to find confirmation of these intuitions in something that looked like science. By the time of Newman – who had similar boyhood intuitions to those of Wordsworth[2] – this was becoming increasingly difficult, and

[1] See A. O. Lovejoy, 'Coleridge and Kant's Two Worlds' for a slightly different approach to this problem. *Essays in the History of Ideas* (Johns Hopkins, 1948).

[2] For the similarity in childhood intuitions between Newman and Wordsworth, see ch. 7 below.

though in 1821 he could refer to Geology as 'most entertaining, and opens an amazing field to imagination and poetry'[1] later in his life he was to find himself in increasing opposition to the way in which scientific thought had developed in the intervening years.

However much Coleridge may have assumed the truth of vitalist theories of whatever kind, it is evident that his philosophical position is not dependent upon them. His reasons for holding them are primarily metaphysical, rather than experimental, but they seem to remain for him a convenient but incidental means of analogy. If the 'natural' and 'supernatural' are part of a continuum, it is a continuum between two poles whose relationship is essentially dialectical. Any teleological impetus in biological evolution is *illustration* of the fact that the whole universe is purposive; it is not *evidence* on which the argument rests. Speculating on the possibility that Paul's conversion coincided with a natural and therefore 'objective' event, Coleridge is quick to deny any simplistic relationship between the two. If it was a 'natural' electrical storm, for instance, was Christ there any the less? If it was 'miraculous', is it not like Hamlet able to see his father's ghost, when his mother could not? But who is impressed by either a 'natural' storm or a ghost that is only visible to one person?[2] The question of the 'reality' of miracles, Coleridge sees, is not to be settled in terms of 'objective' verifiable evidence at all. He is now moving towards a total integrating theory of miracles as an essential component of his Biblical commentary. The dialectic is essential:

The ultimate purpose of Science, Philosophy, and ordinary History, natural and political is to shew the Objectivity of the Supreme Mind (the *Word* or Law) – the purpose of Sacred History, or of Miracles, is to reveal the *Subjectivity*, the personal subsistence and life, of the supreme mind, to substitute an intuition of the *Law*, as God, in the Phaenomena for a *deduction* of the same from them.[3]

He returns immediately to his earlier question, 'May there not be a hidden contradiction in the Demand or Expectation, that a Miracle should be wholly objective?'

[1] Geoffrey Faber, *Oxford Apostles* (Faber, 1933), p. 60.
[2] No. 39 (B.M. Ms. 47, 534), p. 48.
[3] Ibid. pp. 29–30.

Well! and what conclusions do I draw from this . . . ? I draw no *conclusion* – I am only *commencing* . . . I am content to deduce a modest *suggestion* – whether the preceeding Exposition may not imply the necessity of a concurrent state of the Mind & Will in the Persons, who are to behold and in order to their beholding, the Will Divine in the Phaenomena? and whether, this concurrency not having place, these phaenomena must not necessarily be referred to the *Objectivity* of the Laws – i.e. to God as the Laws of Nature: in other but equivalent words, whether they must not be seen and interpreted as Natural?[1]

The essential *ambiguity* of miraculous events is part of a polarity that runs throughout all human experience – an extension into a further dimension of an ambiguity inherent even in ordinary sense-perception. He goes on: 'Where the habit, or at least the then mood of the Beholder's mind happens to be ir- or un-religious, and the *Light* or Reason is abstracted ex-clusively of the Life or personal Being, the phaenomena will be referred to God not as God but as Nature.'[2] The syntax may be elliptical, but the meaning is surely clear. Coleridge has here grasped the vital point about miracles, that – as with all paranormal events – perception and interpretation are not separable processes. The question 'did this or that miracle actually happen?' is a rainbow's end constantly receding before us as we try to follow it. A miracle is a symbolic event, showing to the believer 'in a size and compass proportionate to our faculties', the divine Will that is everywhere through its laws sustaining the universe. 'His mental Eye-sight purged and potenzialed by this celestial Euphrasy as he beholds the Sun in a fountain, so will he in the miracles of Religion behold the abbreviation of the Miracle of the Universe – Such at least is the anticipation of S. T. Coleridge'.[3] The quest for a 'reality' that is verifiable by objective scientific analysis is illusory, since the very qualities that make it 'real' to us are not accessible to this kind of enquiry. Thus Prophecy, says Coleridge, is *sui generis*. There is no need to assume that a prophet *is* 'dreaming' for the truth of what he sees to be established. Nor is the 'truth' of prophecy itself independent of the believing community. A note of 27 January 1829 reads:

Briefly – I would hold out the insight into the prophetic Spirit of the Old Testament, the spiritual treasures of the Bible, as the reward of the

[1] No. 39 (B.M. Ms. 47,534), pp. 30–1.   [2] Ibid p. 31.   [3] Ibid. p. 35.

Faith in Christ. Instead of attempting or even wanting to convert Jews or Infidels by the Hebrew Scriptures, it should be my *Boast*, that none but a Christian can understand them aright. For the Christian only reads them by the light of the same Spirit by which they were first dictated.[1]

Again, here as so often, we can see the overall unity of Coleridge's thinking. Faith, miracles, and prophecy are all ultimately related back to their roots in the idea of a Christian community – that is, not a sect, but a body co-extensive with the nation at large: something much more akin to Maurice's pre-existing universal spiritual society. The fact of its community is illustrated by its sharing of a common *language*. We do not either choose our language from a variety of possibilities, nor do we compose our own; we come to consciousness in the process of being initiated into language. Without understanding its history or growth, we accept it on trust and are shaped by it. It links us with people we have never met or heard of in a framework of common assumptions and ideas which have been carried forward from earlier generations of poets or theologians of whom the individual may know nothing. This is the reverse side of an argument Coleridge had already developed more than ten years before in his critique of Wordsworth's theory of poetic diction. In chapter xvii of *Biographia Literaria* he had attempted to counter Wordsworth's notion that rustic language is somehow more 'real' than the language of the educated by relating the language of the individual to his society at three levels.

Every man's language has, first, its *individualities*; secondly, the common properties of the *class* to which he belongs; and thirdly, words and phrases of *universal* use. The language of Hooker, Bacon, Bishop Taylor, and Burke differs from the common language of the learned class only by the superior number and novelty of the thoughts and relations which they had to convey.[2]

But this superiority of 'thoughts and relations' in turn affects not merely the language of the class, but even of the ordinary people. There is a collective process of coming to consciousness focussed at first in discrete individuals – poets or prophets – but affecting all in the end. Hooker, Bacon, and Bishop Taylor reveal, as it were, the potentialities of the language *to* itself. 'Anterior to

[1] No. 38 (B.M. Ms. 47,533), p. 26.   [2] II, p. 41.

cultivation, the lingua communis of every country, as Dante has well observed, exists everywhere in parts, and no where as a whole.'[1] But we are heirs through our language not merely of a collective consciousness – almost a collective entelechy – but also a collective spirituality. Here Coleridge the theologian is one with Coleridge the poet. Even miracles and prophecy are not isolated phenomena, but are part of the poetic or *mythological* structure of a whole society, and they cannot be seen apart from the linguistic community in which they are rooted.

The similarities with the German critics such as Niebuhr are obvious – but Coleridge has, as it were, stood German philological criticism on its head. Niebuhr's method consisted essentially of two operations: firstly, an analysis of sources into their components, distinguishing between earlier and later elements to assess their reliability; and secondly, by internal criticism of even the more reliable sections to show how the writer's viewpoint affected his account. For example, Niebuhr argues that much of the 'history' in Livy is later patriotic fiction, and that even the earliest stratum is not historical fact but analogous to ballad-literature – a 'national epic' of the ancient Roman people. Behind the epic was the historical reality of early Rome as a society of peasant-farmers.[2] Now Coleridge's overall method is not dissimilar to Niebuhr's, but his 'historical reality' is, as it were, facing the opposite way. Both are interested in what kind of a society thinks within a particular mythological framework, but whereas Niebuhr, uncommitted to Roman religion, is primarily analytic in approach, Coleridge is concerned with synthesis in a way that seems to distinguish him even from such Biblical critics as Eichorn. What he is doing, in effect, is working on a model drawn from aesthetics rather than history. In his *Shakespeare Criticism* he had described art as essentially progressive, working 'for itself new organs of power appropriate to the new sphere of its motion and activity'.[3] Each new work of art reveals all previous art in a new light. Similarly, he seems to be suggesting, we come to understand the more primitive religious phenomena such as miracles not in terms of their anthropological origins but through their highest manifestations. The Old

[1] II, p. 42.
[2] Collingwood, *The Idea of History*, p. 130.
[3] *Shakespeare Criticism*, ed. T. M. Raysor, 2nd Edn (Everyman, 1960), I, 174.

Testament is understood in the light of the New; the Resurrection gives meaning to all the other 'miracles'.

But this – as Coleridge saw very clearly – is a double-edged argument. If the scriptures are to be accepted as 'the living educts of the imagination', whose meaning is to be grasped not only through the disciplines of literary and philological criticism and historical enquiry, but also by the cumulative insight of a community whose language and mythology is grounded in belief, then the scriptures themselves are also part of the language and mythology of that nation. Such, for instance, is the rôle that the King James Bible has played in England. But in such cases the scriptures are not to be separated from the rest of the literature it has helped to shape. At the beginning of Notebook no. 42, as a kind of prolegomennon to his study of *Genesis*, Coleridge inserted a discussion of what he calls the 'phantasmagoric allegory'. Its 'prominent characters' are 'its breadth, or amplitude, and its rapid Aurora-borealis-like Shifting and thorough-flushing of its Cones & Pyramids – yet still within a loosely pre-determined Sphere and with a unity of direction'. 'The Allegoric does not exclude the Literal, nor the one Allegory another. The solution is given in the name, phantasmagoric –'[1] It is always rewarding to explore Coleridge's digressions in the light of the whole. His ostensible examples are taken from Rabelais and Swift, but within the overall context of his Biblical studies it is possible to discern further possibilities. If there is to be a fictional equivalent of the Biblical mixture of the miraculous and prophetic in the literatures of our Western Europe, it is to be found in the 'phantasmagoric allegory' of Rabelais and Swift rather than in more sober and realistic forms. The familiar may give us clue to the more alien. We should not forget that Coleridge was the author of the *Ancient Mariner*, *Kubla Khan*, and *Christabel*.

I believe that in these notebooks we can glimpse part of Coleridge's attempt to formulate an idea of myth within the context of its society as a vehicle of religious experience that, though it draws heavily on the German historical critics, is different in emphasis from them, or from their more direct English followers such as the Arnolds. If German antecedents are to be sought, we should look as much to Schlegel's *Lectures*

---

[1] B.M. Ms. 47,537, p. 14.

on *Dramatic Art and Literature*, with its 'organic' literary criticism, as to Niebuhr or Eichorn. For instance, in the light of what has been suggested about Coleridge drawing his models from aesthetics, the contrasts with Eichorn are revealing. In his *Einleitung in das Alte Testament* (1780–3) Eichorn is concerned to counter the deist argument that the Old Testament religious leaders were dishonest by the more 'historicist' but no less rationalist defence that they worked in the spirit of their age. They were not deliberately fraudulent, but simply credulous. He viewed the great prophets as conscious artists – a model which brilliantly spanned the gap between the traditional ideas of divine inspiration, and the Enlightenment charges of fraud. 'Yet,' says E. S. Shaffer, in a recent study of Eichorn and Coleridge, 'there is more than a trace of the notion of deliberate trickery left in Eichorn's conception of the artist. Ezekiel he praises as the greatest artist of the prophets – and therefore the least authentic visionary: "All these raptures and visions are in my judgement mere cover-up, mere poetical fancies."[1] Coleridge, in a marginal note, protested strongly against this division between artist and visionary:

It perplexes me to understand how a Man of Eichorn's Sense, Learning, and Acquaintance with Psychology could form, or attach belief to, so cold-blooded an hypothesis. That in Ezekiel's Visions Ideas or Spiritual Entities are presented in visual Symbols, I never doubted; but as little can I doubt that such Symbols did present themselves to Ezekiel in Visions – and by a Law closely connected with, if not contained in, that by which Sensations are organized into Images and Mental Sounds in our ordinary sleep.[2]

Eichorn's claim that Ezekiel's vision of God, 'so magnificent, varied, and great that the presentation can hardly be an impromptu, but must have been planned and worked out with much art', is similarly countered by Coleridge with an analogy from the complexity of dream-symbolism.[3] 'It is here,' says Shaffer, 'that the poet Coleridge soars out beyond the rationalist Eichorn.'[4]

[1] *'Kubla Khan' and the 'Fall of Jerusalem'*, p. 88.
[2] Ibid. p. 89. Coleridge, marginal note on *Einleitung A.T.*, III, 188–9.
[3] Ibid.
[4] Ibid. p. 88.

From wide evidence of Coleridge's notebooks and marginalia Shaffer concludes that his new apologetics were not merely 'more radical than Eichorn himself on several important issues'[1] but in general that his 'is one of the finest achievements of the new criticism, going beyond Schelling's *Philosophie der Mythologie* and beyond Strauss himself in his comprehension of the mythological bases of the leading ideas of his society, and it has still not been properly appreciated either in England or in Germany. At the end of the 1790s he had travelled with the higher criticism as far as it had gone, with Lessing, Herder, and Eichorn, and he was prepared to place Christianity in its mythological setting.'[2] But in entertaining such an enthusiastic claim as Shaffer's we need to define it very carefully. Coleridge's greatness was not as a Biblical scholar. We would do well to recall Julius Hare's words in the preface to his *Mission of the Comforter* (1846) – a book which was dedicated to Coleridge's memory. Hare acknowledges Coleridge as 'the great religious philosopher to whom the mind of our generation in England owes more than to any other man'. His life's work,

...was to spiritualize, not only our philosophy but our theology, to raise them both above the empiricism into which they had long been dwindling, and to set them free from the technical trammels of logical systems... [Coleridge had] a few opinions on points of Biblical criticism, likely to be very offensive to persons who knew nothing about the history of the Canon. Some of these opinions, to which Coleridge himself ascribed a good deal of importance, seem to me of little worth; some, to be decidedly erroneous. Philological criticism, indeed all matters requiring a laborious and accurate investigation of details, were alien from the bent and habits of his mind; and his exegetical studies, such as they were, took place when he had little better than the meagre Rationalism of Eickhorn and Bertholdt to help him.[3]

Hare's distinction is between Coleridge's grasp of textual minutiae and his vision of meaning in the whole. The difference between Coleridge and his German mentors is that Coleridge was a poet. It was as a poet that he was able to 'spiritualize' the theology of his age. As we have seen in a small section of his

[1] Ibid. p. 63.
[2] Ibid. p. 54.
[3] Reprinted in a 'Biographical Supplement' to *Biographia Literaria* vol. II, of 1847. Cited by Willey, *S.T.C.*, p. 253.

notebooks, his power lay not in speculative analysis, but in the ability to relate parts to the whole, and to demonstrate structure in terms of meaning: the coral on the reef, or the tiny blood-vessel in the finger. We have here, in brief, the paradox of Coleridge's influence on the nineteenth century.

In these notebooks is an idea of the Church, of Nature and Faith, and of the development of doctrine that was to foreshadow the debates and controversies of Keble, Maurice, and Newman. Yet none had direct access to Coleridge's papers or knew him personally; for two of the three his name was an object of the gravest suspicion. Nevertheless, as we shall see, all three use a language about the Church that has this in common: it draws its imagery in a very particular way from *aesthetic* criticism. It speaks of the Church in terms that are ultimately those of a work of art, and of the relationship between artist and public. One of the most puzzling aspects of nineteenth-century Anglican writing to the modern reader is the use of the word 'poetic', which, as we shall see, is used by Keble and Newman in contexts far removed from 'poetry'. We shall, I think, have great difficulty with this word until we see that it is used in a sense often very close to the modern meaning of 'myth'. As it is used by modern critics the word 'myth' is intended to convey no suggestion of being literally 'untrue' or of being anti-historical; it is simply the word for a *story* that contains for its teller and hearers many levels of meaning that are inseparable from the framework of the story itself, and which cannot, therefore, be put in any other way. Thus *Oedipus Rex* is a fictional myth which, as Freud has shown, may have a bearing on some of our sexual fantasies; Wordsworth's *Prelude* purports to be historical. The history of Israel in the Old Testament and of Christ's life and crucifixion in the New are, in this sense, foundation myths of the Christian world because they are believed to be true. A myth elicits from its participants a response that is both wider and deeper than the rational and propositional. It is the sharing of a common mythology in history, religion, literature, and art that differentiates one language-culture from another (or, as in the case of England and Scotland, or America, differentiates cultures within a language). When nineteenth-century theologians speak of the Church as 'poetic' they seem to be using the word to mean not merely that it has the unifying and emotional qualities of poetry, but also that it is 'mythological' rather than scientific in its mode of thought. This, of course, is something first seen by the German critics, but perhaps in a more reductionist sense than their English counterparts. If we use the word 'myth' to include poetry, we shall be stressing primarily the primitive qualities; if we use the word 'poetic' to include myth, we shall be stressing qualities of universality and complexity.

For reasons which can never be fully explained, the Anglican Church in the nineteenth century took the latter reading rather than the former – and Coleridge had something to do with it. One of the reasons why we can say this is that so many of the figures we shall be looking at in the course of this study themselves believed that he had. We shall probably never know for certain what Carlyle or Newman knew about Coleridge's work in 1828–9. But the rumours and hints persisted, and from them, if we balance our sources, the outlines of something not very far from the truth can be discerned. For Carlyle Coleridge was a highly intelligent and rational thinker who had abandoned rationality and retreated into Kantian mumbo-jumbo, choosing, like Pascal, to believe in the absurd and the impossible. For Newman, Coleridge was a religious and poetic genius whose speculative intellect had led him into barren wastes of liberal thought and infidelity. Both saw him as a ruined man, who had denied his own best gifts and to cover his nakedness had sewed himself a loin-cloth of incompatible heterodoxies. Even without the aid of the notebooks, an impartial observer might well wonder if this was not the description of a man trying simultaneously to achieve two things: on the one hand to preserve the possibility of rational belief in a God who was both supernatural and transcendent, and, on the other, to subject such a belief to the full investigation of the educated mind – not just in terms of rationality or logic, but in terms of history, philosophy, metaphysics, poetry, and myth. So it was to prove. The dark rumours were substantially correct. If Coleridge, writing often despondently in his notebook, believed his speculations were secret, it turns out that it was one of the worst-kept secrets of the century. But such an attempt to walk a razor-edge between opposing dangers has a long history behind it, and many comebacks to its credit. It also has a name. That name, as Chesterton, in the same tradition, was to re-assert nearly a hundred years later, is 'Orthodoxy'.

3

Wordsworth and the Language of Nature

Few poets can have been hailed as truly great with so many misgivings as Wordsworth has been. His 'greatness' was undeniable. His poetry showed men once again how to feel a kinship
with Nature. Many Victorians received from it what they most
wanted: a sense of *belonging* that could integrate head and heart.
That truth could be tested 'on the pulses' (in Keats' phrase)
mattered to them quite as much as that it could be intellectually
demonstrated. 'Feeling' provided its own 'inward witness' to
experience that was as much religious as poetic. Yet it is remarkable how many of those to whom Wordsworth's poetry had
meant most (Matthew Arnold, for instance, or John Stuart Mill)
in acknowledging that he had taught them 'how to feel', were
also among the quickest to deny the power of his philosophy and
the validity of the kinds of religious experience he was credited
with having opened up. The oddness of this is the more puzzling
the more we look at the characters involved. For instance, by his
own admission in the *Autobiography* it is clear that the nearest
J. S. Mill ever came to religious experience was in the autumn of
1828 when he began to read Wordsworth's poetry. But he also
says firmly that Shelley is a much greater poet because he is a
poet of purer feeling.[1] The trouble with Wordsworth, says the
philosopher, is that he thinks too much. His *Immortality Ode*, to
be sure, contains some 'grand imagery', but it remains no more
than 'bad philosophy'.[2] Matthew Arnold, who was much more
sympathetic to Christianity than Mill, is equally unsympathetic to
Wordsworth's Christianity and his philosophy: 'we cannot do
him justice until we dismiss his formal philosophy'.[3] 'However
true the doctrine may be, it has...none of the characters of

[1] 'Two Kinds of Poetry', *Essays on Literature and Society.*
[2] *Autobiography*, p. 126.
[3] 'Wordsworth', *Essays in Criticism, Second Series*, p. 149.

poetic truth, the kind of truth which we require from a poet, and in which Wordsworth is really strong.'[1] A cobbler should stick to his last.

Yet for many Victorians Wordsworth *was* pre-eminently a religious poet. If he spoke to Mill and Arnold, both in their own very different ways bystanders, outside the rigid dogmatic framework of institutionalised religion, he had also a profound and lasting effect on natural dissenters like Mark Rutherford and George MacDonald, on Evangelicals such as Kingsley and Hughes, determined non-party men like F. D. Maurice, and through Keble, perhaps the greatest Wordsworthian of them all, on the whole Oxford Movement including Pusey and Newman. While on the one hand Arnold assures us that Wordsworth's influence was on the wane by mid-century, on the other we find it repeatedly assumed in the second half of the century that his great affirmations of value in man's relationship to Nature reveal through divine immanence (by itself mere pantheism) a transcendent God who was loving, powerful, and moral. Thus we find George MacDonald, himself a mystic, and one of the most original of the Victorian Wordsworthians, has no hesitation about describing Wordsworth's crisis over the French Revolution and his subsequent recovery as a crisis of religious belief.

To the terrible disappointment that followed, we are indebted for the training of Wordsworth to the priesthood of Nature's temple. So was he possessed with the hope of a coming deliverance for the nations, that he spent many months in France during the Revolution. At length he was forced to seek safety at home. Dejected even to hopelessness for a time he believed in nothing. How could there be a God that ruled in the earth when such a rising sun of promise was permitted to set in such a sea!...But the power of God came upon Wordsworth – I cannot say as it had never done before, but with an added insight which made him recognize in the fresh gift all that he had felt of such in the past. To him, as to Cowper, the benignities of nature restored peace and calmness and hope – sufficient to enable him to look back and gather wisdom. He was first troubled, then quieted, then taught...The divine expressions of Nature, that is, the face of the Father therein visible, began to heal the plague which the worship of knowledge had bred. And the power of her teaching grew from comfort to prayer...[2]

It is difficult for us today to recapture this degree of confidence.

[1] Ibid. p. 150.　　[2] *England's Antiphon* (Macmillan, 1868), pp. 303–4.

The modern reader often finds nothing in the early Wordsworth that is specifically Christian, and very little that is overtly 'religious' at all. David Ferry[1] argues with brilliant perversity that Wordsworth's love of nature led not to the love of man, but to the rejection of him – towards a pessimism that some have seen as the only logical outcome of thoroughgoing 'Naturalism'. Wordsworth, it is darkly hinted, took refuge in the conventional pieties of Victorian Anglicanism only to avoid the more sombre path already trodden before him by the Marquis de Sade. Geoffrey Hartman,[2] arguing from an intrinsically similar standpoint, sees any movement towards transcendence in Wordsworth as being fundamentally *opposed* to Nature: not (as one might expect) the *via positiva*, the way of affirmation, but *via negativa*, or way of rejection. According to these views, Wordsworth does *not* find the solace he seeks in Nature, and finally flees *from* it to religious belief in disillusion and even terror.

The contrast between such interpretations and the vision of Wordsworth as the religious teacher and healer of men through Nature seems absolute. Yet as we have seen, a similar contradiction persists to a greater or less degree even among Wordsworth's Victorian admirers – MacDonald himself confesses a certain disquiet even in his praise.[3] Nor were Wordsworth's contemporaries immune. Keats' opinion is well known. Coleridge, who probably understood Wordsworth better than any other critic, often seems to be uneasily aware of a fundamental ambiguity in Wordsworth's attitude to Nature. Even more sharply contradictory is the attitude of another deeply religious romantic poet, William Blake. His comments on one of Wordsworth's most famous evocations of Nature are violently antagonistic. Wordsworth writes:

> Wisdom and Spirit of the universe!
> Thou Soul that art the eternity of thought,
> That giv'st to forms and images a breath
> And everlasting motion, not in vain
> By day or star-light thus from my first dawn
> Of childhood didst thou intertwine for me
> The passions that build up our human soul;

[1] *The Limits of Mortality* (Middletown, 1959).
[2] *Wordsworth's Poetry, 1787–1814* (Yale, 1964).
[3] See, 'Wordsworth's Poetry', *A Dish of Orts* (Sampson Low, 1893).

72

Not with the mean and vulgar works of man,
But with high objects, with enduring things –
With life and nature, purifying thus
The elements of feeling and of thought,
And sanctifying, by such discipline,
Both pain and fear, until we recognise
A grandeur in the beatings of the heart.
Nor was this fellowship vouchsafed to me
With stinted kindness. In November days,
When vapours rolling down the valleys made
A lonely scene more lonesome, among woods
At noon, and 'mid the calm of summer nights
When, by the margin of the trembling lake,
Beneath the gloomy hills I homeward went
In solitude, such intercourse was mine;
'Twas mine among the fields both day and night,
And by the waters, all the summer long.

(Prelude, 1805, book i, 427–51)

This passage from *The Prelude*, probably written as early as 1798, was first published by Coleridge in *The Friend* (28 December 1809), and finally appears as part of a separate lyric in Wordsworth's *Poems* of 1815 with the longwinded title of *The Influence of Natural Objects in calling forth and strengthening the Imagination in boyhood and early youth*. Blake first read it in 1826 and scribbled furiously in the margin of his edition, 'Natural Objects always did and now do weaken, deaden and obliterate Imagination in Me. Wordsworth must know that what he Writes Valuable is Not to be found in Nature...'[1] It was not the only time that Wordsworth's suggestions of 'Natural Religion' had caused a violent reaction in Blake. To Crabb Robinson he later declared that the Introduction to *The Excursion* had made him ill.[2] The literalness of his powerful gut-reaction did not prevent Blake from adding to Crabb Robinson that Wordsworth was, nevertheless, 'the greatest poet of the age'. Clearly, he finds Wordsworth something of a puzzle. Wordsworth seemed to him to be facing both ways – trying to eat his cake and have it with regard to 'Nature'. Blake concluded his note on the poem in question by trying to confound Wordsworth with

[1] *The Complete Writings of William Blake*, ed. G. Keynes (Oxford, 1966) p. 783.
[2] *Henry Crabb Robinson on Books and their Writers*, ed. E. J. Morely (Dent, 1938), i, p. 327.

his own words. He cites Wordsworth's translation of a Michael-angelo sonnet:

> Heaven-born, the Soul a heaven-ward course must hold;
> Beyond the visible world she soars to seek,
> (For what delights the sense is false and weak)
> Ideal Form, the universal mould.[1]

Elsewhere Blake had feared Wordsworth was no Christian, but a heathen Platonist;[2] now his fear is that Wordsworth is not being a Platonist at all, but a mere worshipper of Nature. For Blake, what should delight and strengthen the Imagination is not 'Nature', perceived by the senses, but the invisible and ideal world of Platonic Forms. His confusion on reading Wordsworth is understandable. Is Wordsworth a 'Naturalist', finding values inherent in nature itself, or is he a Platonist, perceiving *through* the fleeting appearances of nature the eternal values of which it offers us but insubstantial shadows? On page 1 of Wordsworth's *Poems* Blake had declared, 'I see in Wordsworth the Natural Man rising up against the Spiritual Man Continually, & then he is No Poet but a Heathen Philosopher at Enmity against all true Poetry or Inspiration.' By the time he reached Wordsworth's 1815 'Essay, Supplementary to the Preface' on page 341 his sense of a split in Wordsworth's poetic vision was so acute that he despairingly concludes, 'I do not know who wrote these Prefaces: they are very mischievous & direct contrary to Words-worth's own Practise.'

Blake's puzzlement is important. As we have seen, many critics after his time have noted a similar dichotomy apparent in Wordsworth, and have attempted either to reconcile the seeming contradictions, or to prove that he was hopelessly inconsistent, torn by inner doubts and driven by secret fears that vitiated his outward declarations of the grandeur and goodness of Nature. Yet it is worth noting that even the later 'orthodox' and con-ventional Wordsworth himself found no such inconsistency in the particular poem that troubled Blake: it is one of the few passages from the 1805 *Prelude* that appears word-for-word the same in the revised 1850 version. Blake, however, is not a critic

---

[1] 'No Mortal Object Did These Eyes Behold', *Poetical Works* III, 15, xxv. (Translated for R. Duppa's *Life of Michael Angelo*, 1808.)
[2] *Crabb Robinson on Books and their Writers*, p. 327.

to be disregarded lightly. He was not merely one of the most sensitive critics of his day, he was also one of the most perceptive theologians. His objections to what Wordsworth seems to be saying about the relationship of the Imagination to Nature become clearer if we see them, like his other strictures, as primarily *theological* rather than aesthetic in aim.

One of Blake's earliest pieces, written in 1788 – ten years before the publication of the *Lyrical Ballads* – is uncompromisingly entitled, *There is no Natural Religion*. For him, 'Nature', being in part the creation of the senses, is subject to the limits of sense-perception. It cannot, by definition, point beyond itself to anything greater: 'From a perception of only 3 senses or 3 elements none could deduce a fourth or fifth.' Touch, taste, and hearing would tell us nothing about sight if we were born blind. How much less, then, can Nature, the creature of sense, point to the 'infinite' which lies at the heart of man's religious awareness. On the contrary, it is the 'Poetic' or 'Prophetic', in Blake's terminology, which mediates revelation to man, showing him that his perceptions are *not* finally bounded by the limitations of sense, but as his desire is infinite (and ultimately *for* the infinite) so the possession of that desire and he himself, the possessor, are 'infinite'. Thus Blake came to see that quality he calls 'the Imagination' as analogous to an extra 'sense', but reaching *beyond* sense-experience. In this he appears to differ radically from both Wordsworth and Coleridge for whom 'Imagination' was both the creative power of the artist, and, simultaneously, the very ground of sense-experience itself without which sense-perception would be impossible.[1] Following Kant, they saw it as providing the basic schemata by which the manifold of random sense data was organised into a coherent 'reality'. Perception and interpretation were a single act. For Blake, however, the fundamental question was not concerning the mechanisms of perception, but the *source* of the values and judgements by which the interpretation is made. If these values ultimately control the world of sense, they cannot also be the product of it.

Blake has, in fact, detected in Wordsworth what seems like a crucial ambiguity. When Wordsworth writes of the 'Influence of Natural Objects in calling forth and strengthening the

---

[1] See *Biographia Literaria*, ch. XIII, and my *Coleridge and Wordsworth: The Poetry of Growth*, ch. 3.

Imagination. . .' does he see the 'Imagination' as being the *cause* of perceiving the 'natural objects' or the *product* ? Now it is possible to make too much of inconsistency in Blake and Wordsworth. Crabb Robinson, to whom we are indebted for much of our anecdotal knowledge of Blake, found him more inconsistent than Wordsworth. Nevertheless, Blake's question must be answered: what exactly *is* Wordsworth's relationship to 'Nature'? Wordsworth's concept of an 'ennobling interchange', a razor-edge balance between projection and receptivity by which we 'create' our landscape, does not answer here. 'Wordsworth must know that what he Writes Valuable is Not to be found in Nature.' In simple terms, Wordsworth appears to find in the contemplation of what he calls 'Nature' values that in fact belong *to him,* and which he seems to be reading into what he sees. Unless one holds that most pessimistic and anarchic creed, 'Whatever is, is right' – which Wordsworth certainly did not – one must accept that 'Naturalism' cannot affirm values. Values, as Blake so emphatically insisted, are the preconditions with which we approach the world, not things we find inherent in it. The problem is that we can be sure Wordsworth knew this as well as Blake.

His own long life (1770–1850) spans a crisis in religious belief that centred on this very question. What evidence we have from contemporaries and from booksellers' lists would suggest that in Wordsworth's youth in the second half of the eighteenth century most Anglicans who thought about the question at all would have been inclined to accept the view, implicit in Locke and explicit in Hartley, that the triumphant progress of physical science could only serve to strengthen and finally demonstrate the great truths of the Christian religion. Nature, properly understood, was implicit with value because it bodied forth for us the laws of the same Benevolent Deity already revealed in the Founder of Christianity. In Addison's words:

> The spacious firmament on high,
> With all the blue ethereal sky,
> And spangled heavens, a shining frame,
> Their great Original proclaim.

There *was* no conflict of science and religion. The two went hand in hand. Thus runs the message of Pope and Addison in the early years of the century; of Ray's *Wisdom of God in the Creation* (1701), Derham's *Physico-Theology* (1713) and his *Astro-Theology* (1715). The names speak for themselves. As late as 1802 this flourishing and continuing tradition of 'arguments from design' was to reach its climax with William Paley's best-seller, *Natural Theology*. It was, in effect, a popular summary of the *a posteriori* arguments of the previous hundred years, and it was to remain continuously in print until the 1850s – until after Wordsworth's death. Though it begins with the famous and classic analogy between the universe and a watch, it is important to remember that Paley, like his predecessors, was not tending towards deism, but specifically concerned to *refute* it. He was committed to disclosing in Nature the works of a personal and benevolent God, rather than the abstract motions of the 'Great Clockmaker' deduced by the deists.[1] Similarly, both Ray and Derham were devout and orthodox Anglicans, as well as being Fellows of the Royal Society. Derham and Paley were both clergymen and theologians of some pretensions.

Paley was, in fact, one of a powerful and important group of divines centred on Cambridge during the second half of the eighteenth century. His patron, Edmund Law, was master of Peterhouse from 1754–87, and for part of that time (1769–87) concurrently Bishop of Carlisle. In 1731 he had translated and published King's *Essay on the Origin of Evil*, prefacing it with John Gay's *On the Fundamental Principles of Virtue and Morality* as a 'Preliminary Dissertation'. This became one of the foundations of Hartley's *Observations on Man* which was to have such a profound influence on Wordsworth and Coleridge during the 1790s.[2] In 1777 Law edited Locke.[3] His protégés included John Hey, Norrisian Professor of Divinity at Cambridge during Wordsworth's undergraduate days, and Paley, who soon after resigning his fellowship at Christ's in 1775 became first prebendary and then Archdeacon of Carlisle. Also at Cambridge was Richard Watson, who exchanged his professorship of Chemistry for the Regius professorship of Divinity in 1771, and who finally,

[1] *Natural Theology*, ch. XXIII, p. 439, 'Of the Personality of the Deity'; ch. XXIV, p. 474, 'Of the Natural Attributes of the Deity'; etc.

[2] See my *Coleridge and Wordsworth*, ch. 2.

[3] In doing so he brings out the idea of 'progress' or development in religion, anticipating Lessing's notion that revelation is analogous to education. (See J. M. Creed, *The Divinity of Jesus Christ* (Cambridge, 1938), p. 14.)

in 1782, became Bishop of Llandaff.[1] The association of Locke and
Hartley with on the one hand experimental science, and on the
other, religious apologetic, is central to our understanding of
Wordsworth's Cambridge background. As a chemist, Watson's
work had led to the development of the black-bulb thermometer,
and his improvements in gunpowder technology after he became
bishop were said to have saved the British government the then
substantial sum of £100,000 a year. In a curious sense, the
same kind of pragmatism is typical too of the theology of these
Cambridge men. They had little respect for or interest in the
history and tradition of the Church, but they believed in divine
'revelation' as implicit in what was still, for them, a philosophically unified world-picture. The scriptures as the revealed Word
of God stood alongside God's great revelation of Himself in the
physical universe. The scientific divines like Bishop Watson,
embodied in their careers this confident faith.

Though there were always dissenters from this 'orthodoxy',
simple agnosticism was commoner than philosophical opposition;
Hume's scepticism or Blake's cloudy mythology were not such as
to attract widespread intellectual support.[2] The influences that
were eventually to achieve the transformation of the view of
'Nature' that we associate with Romanticism, the German
Idealists, *Naturphilosophers*, and above all, Kant and Schleiermacher, were virtually unknown until well on into the nineteenth
century. The attempts of the few scholars who could read German
– Coleridge, Carlyle, Hare, and Thirlwall – to spread Kantian

[1] Watson was unusual among bishops in being a Whig, and, for a very brief
period he seemed to favour the revolutionary cause in France. His subsequent re-
cantation of these supposedly 'liberal' views earned him the contempt and contumely
of nearly all the Romantic poets – giving him a curious literary immortality. See
Blake's annotations to Watson's 'An Apology for the Bible', *Complete Writings*, pp.
383–96; Wordsworth's 'A Letter to the Bishop of Llandaff' (1793), *The Prose
Works of William Wordsworth*, ed. Grosart (Moxon, 1876), I, 1–23.

Coleridge's unacknowledged use of Watson in his *Lectures* of 1796 may or may
not be a sign of approval, but by 1801 he referred to him in a letter to Poole as
'. . . that beastly Bishop, that blustering Fool' (July 1801: *Collected Letters*, II, 740).
When Coleridge issued his prospectus for *The Friend* Watson wrote urging him
'publickly' to disclaim those 'democratic' principles which general prejudice had –
the good bishop hoped unjustly – attributed to him. It is, perhaps, to Watson's
credit that he did in fact subscribe to *The Friend* in spite of his misgivings. (*The
Friend*, ed. B. Rooke (Routledge, 1969), II, 472.)

[2] Though Paley's *Evidences of Christianity* (1794) begins with a refutation of
Hume.

ideas met with the indifference of incomprehension.[1] The story of James Mill leafing through the *Critique of Pure Reason* and saying, 'I see clearly enough what poor Kant is about...'[2] may or may not be accurate, but it conveys vividly the patronising ignorance of the English intellectual establishment. In 1823, when Pusey went to Germany to study the German theologians it was said that there were only two men in the University of Oxford capable of reading German: Cardwell, Principal of St Alban Hall, and Mill of Magdalen.[3] But between the Cambridge divines of Wordsworth's youth and the new breed of German philosophers there lay not merely an almost impenetrable language barrier, but a shift in ideas that amounted to a change of sensibility. The difference can be seen over the change in attitude to history. Little as it would have gratified Bishop Watson to know it, his attitude to divine revelation was supported by the universal tradition of historic Christendom: we, like Schleiermacher and Coleridge, stand on the other side of a great divide from both him *and* the tradition he was prepared to reject.[4] For Watson or Paley the Bible was not a part of history – it *encircled* it. Christianity was its own evidence: a miracle different in kind from all other miracles.[5] Just as Holy Scripture did not need science to attest to its truth, but only as further and complementary revelation, so science did not need theological or ethical underpinning, but was for Watson or Paley redolent with values of a status tacitly assumed to be equal to those of scripture.[6] It is easy for a modern reader to find modern preoccupations in Paley, but this is to perpetrate an anachronism: though his *Natural Theology* may sound like a 'Fact and Faith' film, its

[1] See Wellek, *Immanuel Kant in England*; other typical examples of reactions are to be found in De Quincey, 'German Studies and Kant in Particular', *The Collected Writings of Thomas De Quincey*, ed. Masson (A. & C. Black, 1896), II, 81–109, and Dugald Stewart's *Philosophical Essays* (Edinburgh, 1810), pp. 97–100.

[2] Bertrand Russell, *Freedom and Organization 1814–1914* (Allen & Unwin, 1934), p. 115.

[3] David Newsome, *The Parting of Friends* (Murray, 1966), p. 78.

[4] Creed, *The Divinity of Jesus Christ*, p. 17.

[5] See Paley, *Evidences of Christianity*, in particular the 'Preparatory Considerations' (I, 1–15), which discusses Hume's 'Essay on Miracles', and his argument in part I, 'Of the Direct Historical Evidence of Christianity, and Wherein it is Distinguished from the Evidence Alledged for Other Miracles.'

[6] This, of course, was in origin a deistic position. See Tindal's *Christianity as Old as the Creation or The Gospel a Republication of the Religion of Nature* (1730); also Storr, *English Theology*, pp. 50–2.

presuppositions are in fact entirely different. He does not wish to demonstrate that the unverifiable assertions of scripture can be bolstered with 'proofs' from science,[1] but to show that Nature can lead us to the same conclusions of a loving God as the Bible.

Thus it is hardly surprising that Wordsworth and Coleridge both start their thinking about nature from what looks to us very much like a 'Naturalistic' position. To be on the side of Hartley and Paley is to be on the side of Christian orthodoxy against the massed legions of deism, scepticism, and atheism. Coleridge's painful disengagement from this tradition has been described as the great intellectual struggle of his life.[2] But where did Wordsworth stand?

Now it is possible to attribute to Wordsworth a struggle and development similar to that of Coleridge. By 1815 he could write Platonic sentiments like these lines from his poem, *Composed Upon an Evening of Extraordinary Beauty and Splendour* :

> No sound is uttered – but a deep
> And solemn harmony pervades
> The hollow vale from steep to steep,
> And penetrates the glades.
> Far distant images draw nigh,
> Called forth by wonderous potency
> Of beamy radiance, that imbues
> Whate'er it strikes with gem-like hues.
> In vision exquisitely clear,
> Herds range along the mountain side,
> And glistening antlers are descried,
> And gilded flocks appear,
> Thine is the tranquil hour, purpureal Eve!
> But long as godlike wish or hope divine
> Informs my spirit, ne'er can I believe
> That this magnificence is wholly thine!

[1] There is an interesting, if bizarre, example of the change in status of scientific and religious 'evidence' in an anonymous article in the *Contemporary Review* of 1870, called 'Nature Development and Theology'. The author thinks that geology could be used to support a revival of the doctrine of 'development' in Nature. He cites as examples of man's long history the fact that 'petrified ships have been dug up on the tops of Alps and Apennines', and 'keels and masts in the sands of Libya'. On a Swiss mountain, he informs us, 'there had been discovered the petrified bodies of sixty mariners who had been shipwrecked in a storm before the beginning of Egyptian chronology'. The famous story of the Peterhouse Mermaid is also re-told (May 1870, p. 176).

[2] Basil Willey, *Nineteenth Century Studies* (Chatto, 1949), p. 14.

> From worlds not quickened by the sun
> A portion of the gift is won;
> An intermingling of heaven's pomp is spread
> On ground which British shepherds tread.

George MacDonald draws from this poem assurance of Wordsworth's deep religious strength. 'Higher than all that Nature can do in the way of direct lessoning,' he writes, 'is the production of such holy moods as result in hope, conscience of duty, and supplication. Those who have never felt it need to be told that there is in her such a power.'[1] Philosophically we can see here what one critic has called the 'contemplative Platonist' side of Wordsworth.[2] Nature is not seen here as having values of itself, but as capturing the fleeting shadows of an invisible unchanging Platonic reality – even Heaven itself? – and it shares the values of that deeper reality precisely in so far as it is symbolic to the initiated eye of that hidden world. Without that invisible realm of absolutes its own changing phenomena would be meaningless. Nevertheless, since man is unable to perceive this other reality directly, nature, as its symbol, can still be for Wordsworth:

> The anchor of my purest thoughts, the nurse
> The guide, the guardian of my heart, and soul
> Of all my moral being.
>
> (*Tintern Abbey*, 109–11)

Yet the very fact that we can so directly relate the 'philosophy' of a poem of 1815 to *Tintern Abbey*, written seventeen years before in 1798, brings home something of Blake's dilemma. If it were simply that between the 1798 poem quoted earlier on *The Influence of Natural Objects in calling forth and strengthening the Imagination* and the 1815 poem Wordsworth had, in a movement parallel to his friend Coleridge's, come to reject Naturalism for a more idealist form of religion, the matter would be comparatively simple.[3] But *Tintern Abbey*, with its Platonic and idealist overtones is undoubtedly earlier than that passage from *The Prelude*, though probably written during the same year. In other words, the 'Platonist' and 'Naturalist' positions, as Blake suspected, were always present in Wordsworth *at the same time*.

---

[1] *England's Antiphon*, p. 304.

[2] Melvin Rader, *Wordsworth: A Philosophical Approach* (Oxford, 1967).

[3] Though not for Blake: the arrangement of the 1815 *Poems* would effectively have concealed such a progression, even had it existed.

A greater knowledge of Wordsworth's philosophical sources would not necessarily have been any help to him. Blake's theological difficulties, I think, do not concern Wordsworth's precise philosophic system at all. In *There is no Natural Religion* Blake sees 'poetry' not as a vehicle of 'philosophy' but as something directly opposed to it. The fact that 'philosophy' for him meant primarily the aridity of British eighteenth-century empiricism does not wholly explain this hostility: it is, to say the least, an open question whether a detailed knowledge of Kant would have softened Blake's opinion of philosophy. For him, 'poetry', though it may express and even influence philosophical ideas, is fundamentally different from 'philosophy' in that it is far *more* than a merely rational activity: it calls into action the whole man. It is, for Blake, the medium of revelation because it cleanses 'the doors of perception'. In poetry man is released from the 'mind forged manacles' of rationally compartmentalised thought (faculties, intellectual disciplines etc.) which are subject to 'the ratio of the senses'; instead he is able to think and feel *as a whole*. The parts find for the first time their true function in subordination to the living being that is organically greater than the sum of its constituents. Whatever their differences in terminology and belief, ironically enough this unifying and organic view of poetry is broadly common to Blake, Coleridge, and Wordsworth. It is, for instance, very similar to the view that Wordsworth expounds in his Preface to the *Lyrical Ballads*. Yet for Blake, reading Wordsworth's 1815 *Poems* and the Prefaces, it becomes increasingly clear that the fundamental problem is not that some of Wordsworth's philosophic ideas are repugnant to him, but rather that there appears to be in the very midst of the unity Wordsworth so successfully affirms, a no less fundamental dichotomy that lies so deep as to be apparently inseparable from the same qualities that make him the greatest poet of his age.

Coleridge, no less than Blake, was certain of Wordsworth's poetic stature, yet in his notebook for 26 October 1803 we find an account of a very curious argument:

A most unpleasant Dispute with W. & Hazlitt Wednesday afternoon . . . – I spoke, I fear too contemptuously – but they spoke so irreverently so malignantly of the Divine Wisdom, that it overset me. Hazlitt how easily roused to Rage & Hatred...Peace be with him! – But *thou*, dearest Wordsworth – and what if Ray, Durham, Paley, have

carried the observation of the aptitudes of Things too far, too habitually – into Pedantry? – O how many worse Pedantries! how few so
harmless with so much efficient Good! – Dear William, pardon
Pedantry in others & avoid it in yourself, instead of scoffing & Reviling
at Pedantry in good men in a good cause & *becoming* a Pedant yourself
in a bad cause – even by that very act becoming one! – But surely to
look at the superficies of Objects for the purpose of taking Delight in
their Beauty, & sympathy with their real or imagined Life, is as
deleterious to the Health & manhood of Intellect, as always to be
peering & unravelling Contrivances may be to the simplicity of the
affections, the grandeur & unity of the Imagination. – O dearest
William! Would Ray, or Durham, have spoken of God as you spoke
of Nature?[1]

Coleridge has come across something in Wordsworth's vision
of Nature that he finds deeply puzzling. Is Wordsworth's delight
in the beauty and sympathy with the 'real or imagined Life' of
objects the expression of an underlying Naturalism, or of its very
opposite – an underlying Platonism? The normal interpretation
of this 'unpleasant Dispute' is that Wordsworth and Hazlitt are
taking a Pantheist or Naturalist position, whereas Coleridge is
arguing that though one can deduce from the evidence of Nature
the existence of a God, Nature and God cannot be identified.
Wordsworth, it is assumed, believed Nature itself to be 'divine'.[2]
Paley, Ray, and Derham (whom Coleridge insists on calling
'Durham') by using Nature *merely* as the peg on which to hang
the argument from design are drawing too sharp a distinction
between Creator and creation. Yet is it as simple as this?

Coleridge, we notice, has taken up what looks like an oddly
uncharacteristic position. It comes as something of a shock to
those familiar with his later development to find that he is here
defending Paley, and it is Wordsworth who will apparently have
none of him. Coleridge had already read Kant and his fellow
Germans by 1803 and he must have known the weakness of the
argument from design. It is, however, typical of his eclecticism
that he seems willing to tolerate Paley's grand synthesis not on
philosophic grounds, but on *moral* ones: that it is 'harmless' and
capable of 'so much efficient good'. His really harsh judgements
on Paley come in *Aids to Reflection*[3] – written in the 1820s at a

---

[1] *Anima Poetae*, p. 35; *Notebooks*, 1, 1616.
[2] E.g. see Rader, *Wordsworth*, p. 35.   [3] P. 363.

much later stage of his development. Significantly, these are also based on primarily moral criteria.

Wordsworth's contempt for Paley owes nothing to Kant either. His argument is not that Paley, Ray, or Derham are guilty of any kind of philosophic error, but simply that they are a lot of 'pedants'. Wordsworth scorns their 'peering & unravelling Contrivances' as deleterious to 'the simplicity of the affections, the grandeur & unity of the Imagination'.[1] In other words, the conflict is *not* between natural and revealed religion, but between a fragmented pseudo-philosophic use of Nature, and a unified poetic appreciation of it by the whole man. For him, Nature is not a mechanism, but an involvement. Anyone who has read any of Ray, Derham, or Paley is likely to be struck almost at once by a peculiar characteristic of all three writers: their arguments are totally lacking in development. Though all three are full of learning and ingenuity, their organisation is purely encyclopedic. The argument, once stated, is hammered home by a cumulative weight of illustration. The index gives it all away: having read it, one knows exactly what the book has to say. There is no 'method'; no inner organic principle of progressive argument; nothing unfolds; the structure is mechanical, thorough, and exhaustive. It is perfectly clear what Wordsworth means by his charge of 'pedantry', and why he repudiates such an attempt to reduce the complexity of nature – and man's relationship with his evidence – to an inventory. His point is simple: 'we murder to dissect'.

Let us look again at *Tintern Abbey*:

> . . . For I have learned
> To look on nature, not as in the hour
> Of thoughtless youth; but hearing oftentimes
> The still, sad music of humanity,
> Nor harsh nor grating, though of ample power
> To chasten and subdue. And I have felt
> A presence that disturbs me with the joy
> Of elevated thoughts; a sense sublime
> Of something far more deeply interfused,
> Whose dwelling is the light of setting suns,
> And the round ocean and the living air,

---

[1] Copies of the works of Ray and Derham were in the library at Racedown where William and Dorothy were living from 1795–7. (Mary Moorman, *William Wordsworth, The Early Years 1770–1803* (Oxford, 1957), p. 285.)

And the blue sky, and in the mind of man:
A motion and a spirit, that impels
All thinking things, all objects of all thought,
And rolls through all things. Therefore am I still
A lover of the meadows and the woods,
And mountains; and of all that we behold
From this green earth; of all the mighty world
Of eye, and ear – both what they half create,
And what perceive; well pleased to recognize
In nature and the language of the sense
The anchor of my purest thoughts, the nurse,
The guide, the guardian of my heart, and soul
Of all my moral being.

It is difficulty to say which combination of Newton, Shaftesbury, Spinoza or Berkeley makes best sense here.[1] Wordsworth had read all four, but he is not a systematic thinker in the sense that he is aware of, or concerned with the incompatibility of their various systems. The tantalising ambiguity between Naturalism and Platonism seems, in part at any rate, to arise because Wordsworth is *consciously* seeking a *poetic* formulation which is neither. As we have suggested, there is reason to doubt if Wordsworth ever was a Naturalist in the sense that some modern critics have taken him to be, but the interesting thing to notice is that, as in this dispute and in many parts of *The Prelude*, when we encounter seemingly Naturalistic sentiments they are frequently coupled with other affirmations of a Platonic or Christian origin that directly contradict them. Coleridge's reaction is surprisingly similar to Blake's. Even while they remained convinced of his outstanding greatness as a poet, both Coleridge and Blake are dimly aware that Wordsworth's approach to Nature is profoundly different from either of theirs. Both are frankly puzzled and at times deeply critical of what they see as muddle or self-contradiction in Wordsworth.

Tintern Abbey is a good example. The fact is, as Blake saw, it is just not possible to produce the kind of fusion of Platonic and Naturalistic systems that Wordsworth seems to be putting forward in the passage just quoted. The evidence may be the same, but the two interpretations are mutually exclusive. *Either* Nature is merely a 'language' for a hidden unchanging reality, *or* Nature is

[1] See my *Coleridge and Wordsworth* pp. 95–7, and Rader, *Wordsworth*, pp. 41–8.

herself the 'soul' of all his moral being. It is like one of those well-known puzzle pictures: either the drawing is of a rabbit, or it is of a duck; either the figure is a vase, or it is two faces. We cannot, however hard we try, adopt both 'readings' at the same time.[1] Broadly speaking, the systems of Newton, Shaftesbury, and Berkeley can be resolved into the Platonist camp, that of Spinoza into the Naturalist: in philosophy, as in visual perception, there are no half-way houses. Or are there? One thinks, for instance, of the impossible three-dimensional worlds of M. C. Escher[2] – impossible, that is, in three dimensions, but 'possible' within the conventions of Western two-dimensional representations of perspective. Escher's purpose, of course, is to call attention to the very conventions that we normally take for granted. Are there, in fact, cases where our experience *can* only be described by a paradox so audacious as to break open the accepted logical and visual categories? Is Wordsworth simply muddled and naive, or is he concerned with a similar kind of paradox?

One Victorian critic who believed so was George MacDonald. He was as aware as Blake or Coleridge of a two-sidedness, an ambiguity in Wordsworth's experience of Nature, but for him this ambiguity assumed the profoundest *religious* significance. In his essay on 'Wordsworth's Poetry' he argued that Wordsworth exhibits better than any other poet the dialectic between God as transcendent creator, and God as omnipotent sustaining love. This is not a neat paradox, however, but an acute tension. 'The very element in which the mind of Wordsworth lived and moved,' writes MacDonald, 'was a Christian pantheism... This world is not merely a thing which God hath made, subjecting it to laws; but it is an expression of the thought, the feeling, the heart of God himself.'[3] He specifically contrasts the single focus of Paley's 'proofs of God' with the bi-focal reference of Wordsworth's poetry.[4] Poetry is, for MacDonald, a *theological* instrument: a means of vision whereby opposites may be held simultaneously

[1] See E. H. Gombrich, *Art and Illusion* (Phaidon, 1960), p. 4.

[2] *The Graphic Work of M. C. Escher* (Oldbourne Press, 1961). For a more extensive discussion of this point, see my article, 'Dante, Beatrice and M. C. Escher: Disconfirmation as a Metaphor', *Journal of European Studies* (1972), 2, 333–54.

[3] *A Dish of Orts*, pp. 245–6.

[4] On Paley, he merely comments 'What does it prove? A mechanical God, and nothing more.' Ibid. p. 246.

in focus. As we shall see, this is a view that is not uncommon among nineteenth-century churchmen. The ambiguity in Wordsworth's appreciation of Nature is never free from this theological tension. His sense of transcendence co-exists with its opposite, an ever-present possibility of Naturalism. The essence of Wordsworth's poetry, for MacDonald, is living dangerously:

> ...you will find that he sometimes *draws* a lesson from nature, seeming almost to force a meaning from her. I do not object to this, if he does not make too much of it as *existing* in nature. It is rather finding a meaning in nature that he brought to it. The meaning exists, if not *there*.[1]

This is very close to Blake's charge *against* Wordsworth. The difference, I think, is one of emphasis. For Blake this is at best muddle, at worst, falsehood. For MacDonald, the possibility or even the actual existence of Naturalism in Wordsworth is part of its opposite – and a necessary part. We make a mistake to think of his poetry as versified philosophy: the medium of poetry is different, it can reconcile opposite or discordant qualities. It is not merely thought, but *feeling*. Wordsworth, in his poetry, exemplifies the spontaneous overflow of immanence into its opposite – transcendence:

> ...whatever we feel in the highest moments of truth shining through beauty, whatever comes to our souls as a power of life, is meant to be seen and felt by us, and to be regarded not as the work of his [God's] hand, but as the flowing forth of his heart, the flowing forth of his love of us, making us blessed in the union of his heart and ours.
>
> Now Wordsworth is the high priest of nature thus regarded.[2]

The language is unfamiliar in its emotionalism, but it tells us why MacDonald the Victorian may have seen something in Wordsworth that it was much more difficult for Blake or Coleridge to see. MacDonald belonged to a different climate of *feeling*. He lived late enough to have read and studied *The Prelude* in its entirety, as his remarks about Wordsworth's crisis over the French Revolution indicate. Having looked at the whole, he could appreciate, in a way that Blake with only fragments at his disposal could not, the full dialectical complexity of *The Prelude*'s development. We can see with hindsight how much Wordsworth,

[1] Ibid. p. 252.   [2] Ibid. p. 247.

in contrast with Blake, owes his apparent difficulty to the fact that he does not seem to start with a conceptual idea so much as to *feel* his way towards one. He often appears to be struggling to understand his experience through the very attempt to articulate it as poetry. Now in many ways this is a much more typical Victorian sensibility than it is Romantic. It is this immense effort to articulate *feeling* that gives Wordsworth his appeal to Victorians so different from each other as Matthew Arnold and J. S. Mill:

> Others will strengthen us to bear –
> But who, ah who, will make us feel?[1]

Wordsworth, in effect, is attempting to find in Nature a language adequate to describe certain *new* kinds of experience – experiences that, as both Coleridge and Blake recognised, were very different from anything that had gone before and for which they had no existing categories. 'There have been in all history a few, a very few men,' wrote Hopkins, 'whom common repute, even where it did not trust them, has treated as having had something happen to them that does not happen to other men, as having *seen something*, whatever that really was.'

Plato is the most famous of these...human nature in these men saw something, got a shock; wavers in opinion, looking back, whether there was anything in it or no; but is in a tremble ever since. Now what Wordsworthians mean is, what would seem to be the growing mind of the English speaking world and may perhaps come to be that of the world at large/is that in Wordsworth when he wrote that [*Immortality*] ode human nature got another of those shocks, and the tremble from it is spreading. This opinion I do strongly share; I am, ever since I knew the ode, in that tremble. You know what happened to crazy Blake, himself a most poetically electrical subject both active and passive, at his first hearing: when the reader came to 'The pansy at my feet' he fell into a hysterical excitement.[2]

Hopkins' terms of reference for discussing the *Immortality Ode*, like MacDonald's, strike the modern reader as being curiously 'existentialist' in tone. And this, I think, provides us with a clue to Wordsworth's importance to the Victorians. If we are to make

---

[1] Matthew Arnold, *Memorial Verses* on the death of Wordsworth, April 1850.

[2] *The Correspondence of G. M. Hopkins and R. W. Dixon*, ed. Abbott (Oxford, 1935), pp. 147–8. I am indebted to John Perry for first calling my attention to this passage.

sense of him 'philosophically' we need to turn not to the philosophers most influential on Coleridge or Blake, the English empiricists or German idealists, but to a new *kind* of philosopher – for instance, to a younger thinker already in reaction against idealism whose work remained unknown in the English speaking world until the twentieth century: Søren Kierkegaard.[1]

That Wordsworth possessed a peculiar emotional and religious power for many Victorians is clear from a wide range of independent sources: from members of the Oxford Movement, from Arnold, Ruskin, George Eliot, and even Mill. Diverse testimonies witness to the way in which Wordsworth enabled his readers to feel in 'the language of Nature' an emotional unity and sense of wholeness in face of the ambiguities and doubts of an increasingly fragmented and complex intellectual climate. It is less often noticed that the *form* used by Wordsworth (like Kierkegaard) for affirming this unity in *The Prelude* and in the *Immortality Ode* – that of autobiography – is in fact the *traditional* Christian form for describing spiritual crises. The suggestion is often made, for instance, that in using himself as his model Wordsworth is being influenced by Rousseau's *Confessions*, but even the most cursory comparison shows that the narrative techniques of *The Prelude* are quite unlike the chatty, witty, candid flow of Rousseau's style. The elimination, concentration, and reticence that are part of Wordsworth's high seriousness hark back to a much earlier and more weighty source: the *Confessions* of St Augustine. It does not seem to be accidental that in Wordsworth's 1805 scheme his 'confessions' should be arranged, like Augustine's, in thirteen books.[2] But the similarity lies deeper than numerical ordering. The *Confessions* of Augustine, as has often been noticed, are not primarily about 'conversion' or 'spiritual crisis' *per se*; they are about the growth of Augustine's mind. Though it is ostensibly a 'spiritual' autobiography, the peculiar fascination and greatness of Augustine is that he could not separate the 'spiritual' from the whole of the rest of his mental development – any more than Wordsworth could separate the 'poetic'. Augustine, like Wordsworth, was in search of a

[1] For a detailed discussion of certain parallels between Kierkegaard and Wordsworth see Appendix below.

[2] How far this was conscious we cannot know; but the 1850 text with its fourteen books is strikingly less 'Augustinian' in its diminished interest in memory and the unconscious as shaping forces.

4

Keble's 'Two Worlds'

In 1839 Oxford University bestowed an honorary degree on
William Wordsworth. It was conferred at the annual Commemoration ceremony, and that year the Creweian Oration was
delivered by the professor of Poetry,[1] John Keble. J. T. Coleridge,
Keble's first biographer, tells us that the orator at Commemoration does not actually present the candidates for degrees himself,
and is not obliged to honour them in his speech, but Keble chose
to make it the occasion of a warm and lengthy tribute to the old
poet whom he had long admired.[2] The moment was a deeply
moving one for both poets and for the audience. 'Hearty and
general applause' greeted Keble's encomium, and at the mention
of Wordsworth's name there was a 'universal shout' of acclaim.[3]

For Keble the meeting was a momentous one, and the fulfilment of one of his greatest ambitions. He had first been introduced to the poems of Wordsworth and Coleridge in 1809 when
he made the acquaintance of John Taylor Coleridge, nephew of
the poet, at Corpus Christi College, Oxford. Keble was in his
third year, having come up as a scholar in 1806 at the precocious
age of fourteen. J. T. Coleridge, who was to become his lifelong
friend and later his biographer, was actually two years older,
having taken his scholarship at the more sober age of nineteen.
'This was a period', writes Coleridge,

. . . when the Lake Poets, as they were called, and especially Wordsworth and my uncle, had scarcely any place in the literature of the

[1] J. T. Coleridge, *Memoir of the Rev. John Keble* (1869), p. 247. The Oration
alternated between the public Orator and the Poetry Professor.

[2] J. T. Coleridge believed this was their first meeting (p. 248) but in fact they
had first met in 1815 (see Georgina Battiscombe, *John Keble* (Constable, 1963),
p. 41.).

[3] Coleridge, *Memoir of Keble*, p. 249. F.W. Robertson also seems to have been
present. He gives his own, deeply moved, account in his Lecture on Wordsworth
1853 (*Lectures on the Influence of Poetry and Wordsworth* (1906), pp. 155–7).

country, except as the mark for the satire of some real wits, and some mis-named critics of considerable repute. I possessed, the gift of my uncle, the *Lyrical Ballads*, and *Wordsworth's Poems*, (these last in the first edition). It is among the pleasant recollections of my life, that I first made the great poet known to Keble.[1]

The effect of this introduction to Wordsworth on Keble was profound and lasting. 'As might be expected', Coleridge continues,

he read him with avidity; the admiration for his poetry, which he conceived in youth, never waned in after life; indeed, when he came to know the man it was augmented, I may rather say completed, by the respect and regard which his character inspired. It was hardly possible for Keble to be a very enthusiastic admirer of any poetry, unless he had at least conceived a good opinion of the writer. I may say, in passing, that Wordsworth's admiration of the author of *The Christian Year*, and the volume itself, was in after life very warm.[2]

In fact, Wordsworth's praise of Keble's verse was more diplomatic than sincere. He admired Keble as a man and he approved of the content of *The Christian Year* – which, he said, was so good that he wished he had written it himself so that he could re-write it and make it even better.[3] But, as the back-handedness of the compliment implies, he was unimpressed by Keble's poetry which he considered inferior to Watts' and positively 'vicious in diction'.[4] Nevertheless, Wordsworth's was the inspiration behind the poetry (*The Christian Year* far outsold his own poems) and his tactful admiration could only strengthen Keble's sense of indebtedness to him. Keble's *Lectures on Poetry* are strongly marked by Wordsworth's influence, and when they were finally published in 1844 they were duly dedicated to the senior poet.

This impact of Wordsworth on Keble was to have a momentous effect on the development of the Oxford Movement and on English theology as a whole in the nineteenth century. Keble was a man of no less deep feeling than Wordsworth, but he had a totally different kind of intelligence and sensibility. In his hands Wordsworth's ideas undergo strange sea-changes and emerge sometimes in unexpected metamorphoses. His cast of mind was utterly unlike and yet sometimes strangely parallel to that of the

[1] Coleridge, *Memoir of Keble*, p. 17.   [2] Ibid. pp. 17–18.
[3] Battiscombe, *Keble*, p. 104.
[4] Mary Moorman, *William Wordsworth, The Later Years 1808–1850* (Oxford, 1965), pp. 479–80 and n. 1.

solitary single-mindedness of the Lake Poet. In contrast with Wordsworth's self-confessed idleness and disaffection at Cambridge, Keble at Oxford twenty years later had enjoyed a brilliant formal academic career – being one of two other men up to that time apart from Peel ever to have taken a double First.[1] In 1811, at the age of nineteen, he was elected a Fellow of Oriel – then the most academically distinguished college in Oxford – and the following year he took both the English and Latin Essay prizes. His reputation for academic brilliance and unostentatious piety drew high-minded young men to Oriel in search of both qualities – of which the contemporary Anglican Church was noticeably short. As has often been pointed out,[2] Keble had much in common with the temper and outlook of the old High Churchmen of the late seventeenth century, and before them with the reformed Catholicism of Donne, Herbert, Ferrar, and Andrewes – for whom he had a profound admiration. Yet the differences are as important as the similarities. Keble was very much a man of the early nineteenth century, and the value he placed upon visible moral 'seriousness'[3] and sound scholarship was within an *emotional* context that was quite new to the Established Church. He shunned with horror both the rationalism of Paley, with its defensive emphasis on 'evidences', and the fervour and aggressive individualism of the Evangelicals. 'Don't be original', he would solemnly advise his students; and to the best of his beliefs he practised what he preached. He published unwillingly: in the case of *The Christian Year* only after repeated urging. He did not want promotion or advancement, and he never received it: after resigning his Fellowship in 1823 to assist in his father's parish at Fairford in Gloucestershire as a curate, he eventually accepted (after several offers) the incumbency of Hursley, a country parish near Winchester, in 1836, and spent the rest of his life there. Even the Professorship of Poetry at Oxford in the 1830s was thrust upon him.

Yet the extraordinary growth and extent of his reputation and influence suggests that others found in this man so reserved and

[1] The other was a man named Bathurst who disappears thereafter from the pages of history. (Battiscombe, *Keble*, p. 23.)

[2] See, for instance, Owen Chadwick, *The Mind of the Oxford Movement* (Black, 1960), pp. 18 and 33.

[3] For the importance of the concept of 'seriousness' in the early nineteenth century see Newsome, *The Parting of Friends*, p. 49.

diffident something both original and unique. He was to the undergraduates of Oxford a living example of that quality of personal 'holiness' that for so many nineteenth-century men out-weighed the force of argument – and whose nearest equivalent in modern terms would be the attraction of a 'Guru'. After a visit to George Cornish's family at Sidmouth, one of the sisters wrote this description of Keble.

Sept. 8 1819. – Keble went away early. We are all very sorry to lose him, as he is a person not to be met with every day...His manners are singularly simple, shy, and unpolished, though without the least rude-ness or roughness, as he is the mildest and quietest person I almost ever saw. He speaks very little, but always seems interested in what is going on, and often says the cleverest and most witty things as if he was not the least aware of it. In his own family I should think he must be more missed when absent than any one else could possibly be; he seems formed for a domestic circle and all the feelings attendant on home. Without making any fuss about it, he seems so interested in every one, and has such a continual quiet cheerfulness about him, that I cannot imagine how his father and mother, brother and sisters, can do without him. But it is his religious character that has struck me more than anything else, as it is indeed that from which everything else proceeds. I never saw any one who came up so completely to my ideas of a religious man as Keble, and yet I never saw any one who made so little *display* of it (I use this word for want of a better at present); he seems to me a union of Hooker and George Herbert – the *humility* of the one with the feeling and *love* of the other. In short, altogether he is a man whom the more you see of and know, the less you must think of yourself.[1]

Not everyone found Keble's total union of thought and feeling quite so attractive. When Arnold disagreed with him, Keble terminated their friendship.[2] 'There was no getting on with Keble,' said Tom Mozley, 'without entire agreement, that is submission...He very soon lost his temper in discussion.'[3] J. A. Froude commented, 'If you did not agree with him, there was something morally wrong with you.' Nevertheless, what drew a

---

[1] Faber, *Oxford Apostles*, p. 97.

[2] This was done with typical scrupulousness. Though he would no longer receive Arnold in his home because of his theological views, Keble would not print anything against his old friend, and Matthew Arnold, Keble's godson, remained a welcome guest at Hursley.

[3] Thomas Mozley, *Reminiscences, Chiefly of Oriel College and the Oxford Move-ment* (Longman, 1882), I, 220.

growing band of adherents to Keble at Oriel – among them Richard Hurrell Froude, Isaac Williams, and Robert Wilberforce – was this very combination of qualities which amounted to a radically new kind of *academic* sensibility. Patristic scholarship and personal piety came together in Keble's feeling for the Church as a living organic tradition; history and dogma were pursued with rigour and even with rigidity, but in a context of mystery and reverence that re-opened a long-dormant sense of the numinous in religion. For many eighteenth-century students – as for many modern – this kind of approach would have immediately implied 'enthusiasm', with unpalatable associations of sentimentality, emotionalism, and a narrow pietism. But undergraduates such as the Wilberforce brothers coming up to Oriel to sit at the feet of a man whom they had been led to regard as one of the saints of the Church of England were repeatedly baffled and frustrated by Keble's refusal to talk to them of the Faith.[1] He avoided religious topics and eschewed the pious turns of phrase to which, if they came of Evangelical backgrounds, like Newman or the Wilberforces, they were habitually addicted. Anyone who has read the transactions of religious societies of the period, and even the ordinary correspondence of the members, will be all too familiar with the flow of pietistic commonplaces that seem to have been the unwritten condition of member-ship. For Keble, what a man felt most deeply in his heart was not often lightly to be spoken of, or made the counters of small-talk between comparative strangers. As he comments austerely in the *Lectures on Poetry*, 'do we not find that men of loftiest piety are reserved and reverent as regards holiest things; they bear themselves religiously in religious worship, and only in the nar-row circle of intimate friends ever speak of God's forgiveness or their hopes of heaven?'[2] What became called 'the Doctrine of Reserve'[3] had its theological foundations in Keble's distaste for the Evangelical preaching of 'cheap grace', but clearly for one of

[1] 'What a strange person Keble is! There is Law's *Serious Call*; instead of leaving it about to do people good, I see he reads it and puts it away, hiding it in a drawer.' Robert Wilberforce to Isaac Williams (Battiscombe, *Keble*, p. 73). See also Newsome, *The Parting of Friends*, pp. 73–6.

[2] *Lectures on Poetry*, trans. E. K. Francis (Oxford, 1912), I, 75.

[3] See Isaac Williams, Tracts *Eighty* and *Eighty-Seven*, 'On Reserve in Com-municating Religious Knowledge' (*The Oxford Movement*, ed. Fairweather (Oxford, 1964), pp. 260–70).

his sensitive and deeply emotional temperament reserve over matters of spiritual experience was very much an instinctive trait.

It is obviously dangerous to read too much into a man's choice of university, yet Keble's Oxford was at one of the rare periods when movements of the mind or changes in sensibility can, without too much distortion, be symbolised by the place. In the early nineteenth century university men received very little formal 'training' or teaching of any kind.[1] Preparation for ordination, for example, did not include much study of theology. Classics could equally well fit a man to become Archbishop of Canterbury *or* Prime Minister. Manning and Gladstone were both Balliol Firsts in Classics, and in 1829–30, when they were successively Presidents of the Oxford Union, it was commonly said that Manning was destined to be Prime Minister, and Gladstone, Archbishop. Yet Oxford saw itself as moulding its sons' characters, and it is striking to see how very different in temper and approach Oxford men like Keble, Manning, Gladstone, and Newman were from, say, Hare, Sterling, and Maurice, their approximate Cambridge contemporaries. The Oxford Movement *was* from Oxford: it could not have come out of Cambridge.

We have a clue to this difference in the idea of 'ethos' cherished by Keble and Thomas Arnold in the old unreformed Oxford. The word in this, its modern sense, was in fact coined by Keble. In 1869 it was still unfamiliar enough to the general public for J. T. Coleridge to need to offer a lengthy definition of the new word:

Some of my readers may ask what Keble meant by the quality which he so much valued, and called by a Greek name...It is a somewhat remarkable one. The same it is which denotes custom, or usage generally, differing only in this, that the first letter is then pronounced short, and is either doubled or pronounced long when it denotes, at least in Aristotle's mouth, not a custom, or usage generally, but one that is moral. With Keble it imported certainly no intellectual quality, scarcely even any distinct moral one, but an habitual toning, or colouring diffused over all a man's moral qualities, giving the exercise of them a peculiar gentleness and grace; it was not that the Oxford lad was more dutiful, more brave, more truthful, more punctual in his religious duties than any other, but that these qualities were habitually

---

[1] See Hugh Kearney, *Scholars and Gentlemen* (Faber, 1970), ch. IX; and Faber, *Oxford Apostles*, pp. 39–48.

exercised by him with more deference, and reverence towards his elders, more gentleness and loving-kindness to all.[1]

To speculate whether Keble or Arnold, having duly imbibed this Oxonian 'ethos', were or were not measurably more reverent, gentle, and loving than, say, Hare or Maurice is probably not profitable! But there is ample evidence that the word *did* serve to describe something very real, recognisable, and apparently peculiar to the experience of Oxford men of this period. To many the pervading 'ethos' of Oxford was embodied in Keble himself – even though he actually resigned his Fellowship in 1823, and his Poetry Professorship in the 1830s did not require residence. Newman's five-year agony over renouncing Oxford, and his subsequent crises over the twice-mooted question of the establishment of a Catholic college in Oxford[2] make it perfectly clear that 'Oxford' to him also was much more than a town, or even a university – it was a metaphysical reality; a platonic vision where holiness and learning met in eternal dialectic. It is this sense of a 'metaphysical' Oxford that Newman bears faithful witness to in his lectures on *The Idea of a University*, and for those Irish and other Catholics at large who had never known or shared this 'ethos' the lack of an 'objective correlative' in their own experience was sufficient to account for the lectures' incomprehensibility. An Oxford 'ethos' making the idea of a university an ideal at once academic *and* religious was something that came naturally and intuitively to Keble. It was an ideal that Newman was to learn from him, though, as we shall see in a later chapter, in his hands it was to become more conscious, more subtle, and more dialectical. Similarly, if Newman was later to think of the university as analogous with the Church, however personal might be his application of the idea he was, in essentials, also employing what he had learned from Keble.

The Creweian Oration with which we began this chapter uses this analogy in a peculiarly revealing way in relation to Wordsworth. 'The Oration commences,' J. T. Coleridge tells us, 'with pointing out a close analogy between the Church and the University as institutions, and after tracing this out in several particulars, notices a supposed and very important failure of the

---

[1] Coleridge, *Memoir of Keble*, pp. 384–5.
[2] Wilfred Ward, *The Life of John Henry Cardinal Newman* (Longman, 1912) ii, 51–5; 311–12.

analogy in respect to the poorer classes, to whom the gates of the latter are not practically open, nor instruction afforded. This failure the orator then proceeds to explain and neutralize so far as he is able. . .' In his concluding peroration Keble turned for the first time directly to Wordsworth.

But I judged, Gentlemen of the University, that I should satisfy, and more than satisfy, what this topic demands, if only I should recall to your recollection him, (specially now as in this honourable circle which surrounds me he is himself present,) who of all poets, and above all has exhibited the manners, the pursuits, and the feelings, religious and traditional, of the poor – I will not say in a favourable light merely, but in a light which glows with the rays of heaven. To his poetry, there-fore, they should, I think, be now referred, who sincerely desire to understand and feel that secret harmonious intimacy which exists between honourable Poverty, and the severer Muses, sublime Philo-sophy, yea, even our most holy Religion.[1]

It is interesting to notice that the influence of Wordsworth is here working at two very different levels in Keble's thought. At one level he is faced with the problem that in one way or another confronted all Wordsworth's most sensitive admirers during the nineteenth century: the failure of society to deal with poverty. Wordsworth was unmistakably the poet of 'the poor', and to try to dissociate his religious implications from his social message was simply to be a dishonest reader and critic. Keble was neither, and he takes the question squarely. Yet, basically, he has no answer, just as his Oxford 'ethos' had no answer, and he proves unable to grasp the nettle as Maurice and Ludlow were soon to do when faced by a similar challenge.[2] What is revealing about this tribute to Wordsworth, quoted with such evident approval and pride by his biographer, is that it is an *evasion*, a resort to the pious cliché which, however sincerely meant and felt, slides round the challenge of action implicit in all that Wordsworth stands for. Keble *was* genuinely concerned about the state of the poor, yet talk of 'honourable poverty' comes uneasily from the official spokesman of the most privileged corporation in the land.

The contrast between the Tractarians' social concerns and those of Maurice is well illustrated in a story from Thomas

[1] Coleridge, *Memoir of Keble*, p. 248.
[2] See Maurice B. Reckitt, *Maurice to Temple* (Faber, 1947), esp. chs. 1 and 2.

Mozley's *Reminiscences*. Oriel College owned an estate at Wadley, near Faringdon, which in 1830 had stood unoccupied for some years. A number of labourers from a hamlet on the estate asked permission to have cottage gardens for their own cultivation, but made the mistake of appealing in 'language which indicated a theoretical right rather than an appeal to benevolence'. 'This,' we are told, 'promised sport.' The Provost and senior Fellows (including, we must presume, some prominent Tractarians) rode out to confront these men. 'A labourer's best chance is wages,' they declared. 'His time and strength are due to his employer. Land above the scale of a garden is an encumbrance. Who is to pay rates and taxes upon it? What is to be done when the holders increase and multiply?' The discussion was predictably 'one-sided'. The poor labourers 'could only repeat that they would like some land to do what they pleased with, and that they had been told manors were for the poor as well as for the rich. Oriel College was a very great body...It could do anything.'[1] Anything, it seemed, except giving the men their gardens. A few years later one of the Fellows devoted himself to building a pretty little church there.

The Oriel men were, perhaps, no more than children of their time, but the *Lyrical Ballads*, containing such poems as *The Female Vagrant* and *Michael*, had appeared thirty years before. We recall the response of their contemporaries, Maurice, Kingsley, and Ludlow, when approached by London working men with a request for help in education. It was a significant irony of fortune that one of the senior Oriel Fellows in 1830 was Jelf – the man who was later, as principal of King's College, London, to preside over Maurice's dismissal from the College. Ostensibly the charge was heresy, but there seems little doubt, in view of the flimsy nature of the evidence, that the real question at issue was the social and political implications of Maurice's Christianity.

To return to Keble's Oration of 1839: the occasion was unique, but the evasion or failure to come to terms with this side of Wordsworth is characteristic. The explicitly 'Wordsworthian' qualities of *The Christian Year* and the *Lectures on Poetry* seem curiously partial and introverted ones to the modern reader. But there is a second level to Keble's tribute to Wordsworth which,

---

[1] *Reminiscences*, I, 200–1.

while it is linked with the former, seems to carry very much wider implications. The analogy between Church and university suggested by Keble in his Oration is based upon certain, unstated, premises about the nature of both institutions, and of man, which he has also inherited from Wordsworth. The possibility of drawing such an analogy between Church and university, for instance, itself depends on a belief in a universe of correspondencies, analogies, and sacramental significances. Such a belief has always been present in the tradition of the Church, and Keble was familiar with it from his study of the Fathers as well as in Butler, but the spirit in which he held this belief – his ability to *feel* this mystical correspondence between divine and human institutions, and to communicate this feeling to others – was a quality he had found re-discovered in the English Romantic poets, and, in particular, in Wordsworth and Coleridge.

What had been built up by the two Lake poets during the years of their closest collaboration – from the *Lyrical Ballads* in 1798 to the quarrel in 1810 – was not merely a new kind of poetry, but a new model of the human mind itself: as a thing whose characteristic activity was *creation*.[1] The poetry of Wordsworth and Coleridge was, as it were, a 'boiling point' of human consciousness, after which things could never be the same again. The elements that went into the new poetry and the new psychology were all present before, yet in the minds of the two poets they have undergone a change of state – an irreversible transformation that rendered them suddenly explosive and dynamic. In contrast with the psychology of the seventeenth- and eighteenth-century English empiricists, Locke or Hartley, who had assumed that the human mind was passive and cumulative in organisation, Wordsworth and Coleridge felt their own powers as active, unified, and organic. Instead of seeing the mind as a *tabula rasa*, passively awaiting external stimulation, it was held to be active and originating. Following and freely adapting Kant they came to believe that the imagination *created* perception from the raw-material of sense-data, thus ending at a stroke the old Cartesian dichotomy between the self and the external world. For Wordsworth and Coleridge, 'Nature' was living proof of a universe of correspondences where mind and matter interpenetrated in a living harmony that was neither 'internal'

---

[1] For a full discussion of this see my *Coleridge and Wordsworth*, chs. 1–4.

nor 'external'. As Wordsworth puts it in the Prospectus to *The Excursion*:

> . . .my voice proclaims
> How exquisitely the individual Mind
> (And the progressive powers perhaps no less
> Of the whole species) to the external World
> Is fitted – and how exquisitely, too –
> Theme this but little heard of among men –
> The external World is fitted to the Mind;
> And the creation (by no lower name
> Can it be called) which they with blended might
> Accomplish – this is our high argument.

(lines 62–71)

In place of the Hartleian idea of character as the cumulative legacy of past events, the personality was felt by Wordsworth and Coleridge to be an organic unity, integrated in such a way that to select a part in isolation was to distort it, and the rest. For them, poetry was the 'science' of the whole man – a being who *creates*. Similarly, the mind was held to be 'organic' in the sense that its growth was inner-determined like that of a plant: though outside forces may foster or inhibit that growth, and though the acorn in no way resembles the oak-tree, yet an oak it will become – not a daisy or a prickly pear.

For Keble, these were ideas that rapidly became part of his own basic way of thinking: unquestioned assumptions rather than tenets reached by intellectual and emotional struggle as they had been for the earlier generation. These 'Romantic' assumptions about the nature and growth of the mind were the premises from which he began to think about university and Church. In his thought we find it everywhere taken for granted that the Christian Church, 'Holy, Catholic, and Apostolic', answers in its nature to the needs of the human mind in its mode of development. The Church is 'Holy' in its activity: its divine ordinance is to change men's hearts and lives, not merely individually (as the Evangelicals would have said) but also communally, in the Church of England's office as the National Church. Its power was hidden, mysterious, and concealed in its working: a power in man, yet not under his control. Keble took from Wordsworth a theory of the unconscious that was to find detailed exposition in his discussion of poetry and religion in the

101

Lectures on Poetry. The Church was 'Catholic' in its universality and visible unity – adhering in its beliefs to the Vincentian canon, *quod ubique, quod semper, quod ab omnibus*.[1] Keble never wavered in his insistence that the Anglican Church and the Church of Rome were, with the Orthodox Churches, *parts* of the one Church: 'people do not realize,' he wrote, 'the fact that the three Churches are really one, though divided externally.'[2] Over points of doctrine he did not wish the Church of England to decide independently of the other sections of the Church, and he even proposed that another Ecumenical Council be called for this purpose in the wake of the Denison Case.[3]

We should keep in our own minds, and before all Christendom, the fact that we stand as Orthodox Catholics upon a constant virtual appeal to the Oecumenical voice of the Church, expressed by the Four Great Councils, and by general consent in all the ages during which she continued undivided...If that voice be disputed, is there any conceivable way of bringing the dispute to an issue, except only by another true Oecumenical Council when such by God's grace may be had.[4]

Finally, Keble saw the Church as 'organic' in the continuity of the Apostolic tradition. Prayer, the sacraments, the scriptures, the historic doctrinal authority of the Councils, the office of priesthood conferred by the laying-on of hands and through the Apostolic Succession of the bishops were all interwoven parts of the ongoing stream of the living Church. It was impossible to separate one aspect of this complex organic tradition from the rest without damaging it, and the whole – just as one organ cannot be separated from the rest of the living body. To elevate scripture into a position of authority by itself, as the Evangelicals and many nonconformists desired, was to endanger the balance and health of the whole by ignoring the interpretative tradition

[1] 'what [has been believed] everywhere, always, and by all'.

[2] Quoted by E. F. L. Wood, 'John Keble', *Leaders of the Church 1800–1900*, ed. G. W. E. Russell (Mowbray, 1909), pp. 53–4.

[3] George Anthony Denison (1805–96) was Archdeacon of Taunton and leader of the ritualists in the Lower House of the Convocation of Canterbury. Between 1854 and 1858 he fought a long series of legal actions largely brought on himself by his view of the Eucharist. He held that the Real Presence was received by all who partook of it, irrespective of their state of mind. This 'mechanical' view was suspiciously close to the Roman Catholic view of transubstantiation for many. See Owen Chadwick, *The Victorian Church* (Black, 1966), part I, pp. 491 ff.

[4] Coleridge, *Memoir of Keble*, p. 424.

of the Church. Equally, like Pusey and even Newman in his Tractarian days, Keble regarded the revival of Roman rituals in the Church of England – vestments, incense, altar lights, etc. – as an irrelevant and spurious affectation because it did not grow naturally out of the needs of the present situation in England.[1] Such a view of doctrine as an organic and living whole was the soil out of which Newman's *Essay on the Development of Christian Doctrine* was soon to emerge – as we shall see in the next chapter.

Like the Church, Keble saw the university also centred on the needs of the growing mind. It did not write 'knowledge' upon a *tabula rasa*, but actively fostered the personal development of the individuals within its care. It was the 'uni-versity' in its popular etymological sense:[2] its very 'ethos' was one of unity, demanding that all knowledge be shaped into one, given a single focus, and studied with a sense of its corporate wholeness. It was still possible in the early nineteenth century to pay lip-service to such an ideal: Keble's double First was in Classics and Mathematics; in 1821, the year after his spectacular crash in the Schools, Newman was studying mineralogy, chemistry, and music.[3] Behind such a vision of unity, of course, was an insistence on organic tradition and continuity almost as powerful as that of the Church. Classics embraced almost the whole learning of the Ancient World: language, literature, philosophy. For the Tractarians its study was inseparable from a view of society that was deeply conservative: implicitly hierarchical and élitist. The Oxford 'ethos' as envisaged by Keble, Arnold, and Newman (often, be it confessed, in the teeth of all evidence) was one of an organic Christian culture forming a commonwealth of intellectual and spiritual aristocrats and playing its leading part within the body of the nation, Church and State. This, in very broad outline, is the vision of organic unity that Keble felt that Wordsworth had made it possible to re-affirm, and to which he wished to recall Oxford.

[1] Faber, *Oxford Apostles*, p. 84. Ward, *Newman*, I, p. 64. Newman satirises ritualism in *Loss and Gain* (1848), Storr, *English Theology*, p. 267.

[2] The word 'university' meant originally something more like 'corporation', but the concept of universality, and the idea of bringing all knowledge into a single focus, though illusory, greatly influenced the word's later usage. See O.E.D. and Faber, *Oxford Apostles*, p. 191.

[3] Faber, *Oxford Apostles*, p. 61.

It is in this broad vision, not in any close following of poetic principles, that Keble is essentially Wordsworthian. *The Christian Year*, for all its echoes of the 'Platonism' of the *Immortality Ode*, is not very closely 'Wordsworthian' in style or content. The theory of poetic diction is only adhered to in the occasional banality; poverty and humility are given their due as Christian virtues, but there is no active belief that greater truth is to be found in the low or rustic portions of society; and Keble's idea of Nature has not the ambiguity of Wordsworth's. Nevertheless, it does share with Wordsworth the overwhelming sense of a universe that is essentially 'poetic' in Keble's special sense of the word: as not an inanimate order, but a living, active, organic whole charged with divine meaning inseparably binding man and Nature. The appeal of this to Keble's own time was staggering in its success. *The Christian Year* sold an average of 10,000 copies a year for fifty years.[1] It earned fulsome praise of fellow-poets from Wordsworth to Newman. Yet to the modern reader, whatever his religious persuasion, the verses seem mostly dull and above all insipid. It's 'Wordsworthian' echoes seem shallow:

> Mine eye unworthy seems to read
> One page of Nature's beauteous book;
> It lies before me, fair outspread –
> I only cast a wishful look.

> I cannot paint to Memory's eye
> The scene, the glance, I dearest love –
> Unchang'd themselves, in me they die,
> Or faint, or false, their shadows prove.[2]

The resolution of this poem, that for the Fourth Sunday in Advent, has none of the tension or ambiguity of the *Immortality Ode* which it so consciously draws upon,[3] but is straightforwardly other-worldly.

> The distant landscape draws not nigh
> For all our gazing; but the soul
> That upward looks, may still descry
> Nearer, each day, the brightening goal.

[1] J. S. Rowntree, 'Notes on *The Christian Year*', *Friends Quarterly Examiner* (reprint Bodley Library, 1927).

[2] *The Christian Year*, 43rd edn (Parker, 1851), pp. 22–5.

[3] For a detailed discussion of the resolution of the *Immortality Ode* see my *Coleridge and Wordsworth*, ch. 5.

How philosophically different this view of Nature is from that of Wordsworth can be seen at once if we turn to the famous passage from *Tintern Abbey* which we discussed in the last chapter. It was published in all the editions of the *Lyrical Ballads* and Keble must have known it well.

> And I have felt
> A presence that disturbs me with the joy
> Of elevated thoughts; a sense sublime
> Of something far more deeply interfused,
> Whose dwelling is the light of setting suns,
> And the round ocean and the living air,
> And the blue sky, and in the mind of man:
> A motion and a spirit, that impels
> All thinking things, all objects of all thought,
> And rolls through all things. Therefore am I still
> A lover of the meadows and the woods,
> And mountains; and of all that we behold
> From this green earth; of all the mighty world
> Of eye, and ear – both what they half create,
> And what perceive; well pleased to recognize
> In nature and the language of the sense
> The anchor of my purest thoughts, the nurse,
> The guide, the guardian of my heart, and soul
> Of all my moral being.
>
> (lines 94–112)

We have already seen something of the complexity of Wordsworth's vision: apparently contradictory in being at once both 'Naturalistic' and 'Platonic', and tending to hold in suspension opposite and conflicting points of view. 'Nature', for Wordsworth, is neither outside man, nor is it the creation purely of his own mind: it is rather an interact on, an 'ennobling interchange'. In contrast, Keble's attitude is much more narrowly within the mediaeval and early Church's tradition of allegorical correspondences. There is a hidden allegorical system implicit in the workings of the material universe which gives it meaning and value, and which only the initiated Christian may read with accuracy and understanding.

> There is a book, who runs may read,
> Which heavenly truth imparts,
> And all the lore its scholars need,
> Pure eyes and Christian hearts.

The works of God above, below,
Within us and around,
Are pages in that book, to show
How God Himself is found.

The glorious sky embracing all
Is like the Maker's love,
Wherewith encompass'd, great and small
In peace and order move.[1]

In *Tract Eighty-Nine* Keble goes into great detail over the mystical significance of the visible world. The sky, he tells us, represents 'a canopy spread over the tents and dwellings of the saints'; birds are tokens of 'Powers in heaven above who watch our proceedings in this lower world'; and waters flowing into the sea are 'people gathered into the Church of Christ'. The smell of flowers is the 'odour of sanctity'; trees and weeds are 'false principles'; the tamarisk, 'the double mind'; the palm 'eternal purity'. 'The Sun, the greater light, is our Lord; the Moon, the lesser light, the Church.' 'He appointed the moon for certain seasons, and the Sun knoweth his going down.'[2] Whatever Keble himself seemed to think, this is clearly a very un-Wordsworthian universe in its elaborate system of significations. Yet it is more complicated than it at first appears. Is Keble's vision of 'Nature' symbolic or sacramental, in that the natural objects *share* in the hidden reality they express, or are they mere allegorical counters of classical neo-Platonism, of no intrinsic importance beyond their function to point the initiated towards their hidden correspondents? The symbolism of sun and moon appears in the next verse of Septuagesima Sunday:

The Moon above, the Church below,
A wondrous race they run,
But all their radiance, all their glow,
Each borrows of its Sun.

However far Keble may be from Paley in feeling, there is here, and elsewhere, the suggestion that Nature, or Natural Theology, offers a way to God in some sense parallel to that of Revelation. He is enough of a classical theologian to see Nature as of *dual*

[1] *The Christian Year*, Septuagesima Sunday, p. 80.
[2] For an even more doubtful range of correspondences see Lytton Strachey, 'Life of Cardinal Manning', *Eminent Victorians* (Chatto, 1918), pp. 19–20.

significance: symbolic of a God who is at once both immanent and transcendent. Only Keble, however, would seem to be able to identify Nature with Natural Theology so effortlessly.

> Two worlds are ours: 'tis only Sin
> Forbids us to descry
> The mystic heaven and earth within,
> Plain as the sea and sky.

Keble had found rediscovered in the early Fathers, Augustine, Clement of Alexandria, and Origen, Plato's theory of 'two worlds' – though, as he says, 'in an incomparably higher sense'.[1] The idea that this was due to Platonic influence in the early Church he denied vigorously: 'the allegation implied...is about as correct as if one should say, the sun's light was borrowed from the reflection of the moon in the water'. What had happened was that the Fathers had brought to light a profound truth dimly glimpsed by the pagan Plato. For Keble, the two worlds are separate – indeed never to be confused – but the realm of Nature is not inferior or to be discarded, even if it is true that it takes its meaning ultimately from the 'mystic heaven and earth within'. Rather it is implicit in much of Keble's writing that the understanding of each level is to some extent dependent upon an initiation into the other. Keble never says (and hardly could say) that the Christian mystic *must* also be *ipso facto* a lover of Nature, but in *The Christian Year* he very much takes it for granted – just as he more explicitly assumes that a true appreciation of Nature only comes to someone who has also entered the inner world of the Spirit.

As immediate as any early Christian Platonism here is the influence of Butler's *Analogy* – a book still of such prestige that it was prescribed reading at both Oxford and Cambridge. 'Human creatures exist at present in two states of life and perception, greatly different from each other; each of which has its own peculiar laws, and its own peculiar enjoyments and sufferings.'[2] Just as (here) our physical and intellectual worlds co-exist as separate states, so, by analogy, can co-exist the natural and spiritual spheres. Keble drew from Butler the theory of analogy

---

[1] W. J. A. Beek, *John Keble's Literary and Religious Contribution to the Oxford Movement* (Nijmegen, 1959), p. 16; *Tract Eighty-Nine*, pp. 72–8.

[2] *The Analogy of Religion* (Everyman, 1906), p. 16.

and the idea of probability as a guide of life. Newman, like Keble, found the *Analogy* a major influence on his own thinking – and adds that the full force of Butler's doctrine of Probability was first brought home to him by *The Christian Year*.[1]

Keble was able to find in Wordsworth confirmation of Butler's theory of analogy – not merely in Wordsworth's Platonism (his version of the 'two worlds') but also in his aesthetics. Just as the poetic image itself worked by a process of analogy that could not be proved in any logical or philosophical sense, but strikes the reader (if it is to be successful at all) with an immediate sense of appropriateness – a conviction tested upon the pulses – so the Christian responds in faith to a universe of analogy and correspondence which can be immediately *felt*. As in reading poetry, questions of 'proof' are irrelevant. The Christian is drawn into a universe that is not fundamentally rational or logical so much as 'poetic'. Life lay not in powers of analysis, but in powers of response: 'We murder to dissect.'

The influence of this aspect of Wordsworth's poetics upon Keble has been widely recognised by recent critics.[2] What has received far less attention is the way in which Butler reinforces Wordsworth at another related point in Keble's thought. One of the recurring themes of the *Analogy* is that man is in a process of continual growth. For Butler, change and development are at every level characteristics of man's natural condition. 'Mankind,' says Butler, 'is left by nature an unformed, unfinished creature': 'But then, as nature has endued us with a power of supplying these deficiencies, by acquired knowledge, experience, and habits, so likewise we are placed in a condition, in infancy, childhood, and youth, fitted for it.'[3] Like children, we are not conscious of our development and change any more than we 'discern how food and sleep contribute to the growth of the body'.[4] Nor is growth seen by Butler as an individual separate process but, if we accept scripture, it must always take place within the framework of a community. We live in a world of 'reciprocal correspondences and mutual relations', by which 'everything which we see in the course of nature is actually brought about'.[5] For

[1] *Apologia*, pp. 23–29; Beek, *Keble's Literary and Religious Contribution*, p. 19.
[2] See M. H. Abrams, *The Mirror and the Lamp* (Oxford, 1953), pp. 144–8; or Beek, *Keble's Literary and Religious Contribution*, p. 85.
[3] Butler, *Analogy*, p. 69.   [4] Ibid. p. 71.   [5] Ibid. p. 101.

Keble this process of growth through mutual interdependence
was the essence of a 'poetic' universe. 'Instead of being a field of
activity, the world was to Keble a sphere of relationships. These
relations existed not only among people, but just as well between man and all inanimate objects. All communication of man
with the outer world was to spring from man's inner life, from
his desire of getting into contact with "the realities beyond the
visible world" through the intermediary of the visible world.'[1]

The most complete exposition of Keble's vision of the relationship between poetry and religion occurs in his *Lectures on Poetry*
which he had given, as Professor of Poetry at Oxford, between
the years 1832 and 1841. They appeared in 1844 under the title
De Poeticae vi Medica, but their impact on the public at large was
less than it might have been since Keble, following the accepted
custom, published as he lectured – in Latin.[2] Though John
Taylor Coleridge had offered to translate them into English
when they first appeared,[3] they were not in fact translated into
English until 1912. For good measure, Burns' poem beginning

> I look to the West when I gae to rest,
> That happy my dreams and my slumbers may be:
> For far in the West, is he I lo'e best,
> The lad that is dear to my baby and me.

is even translated into Theocritan Greek.[4] The fact that Keble
dedicated the *Lectures* to Wordsworth is more than a gesture of
respect. It runs as follows:

> TO WILLIAM WORDSWORTH
> TRUE PHILOSOPHER AND INSPIRED POET
> WHO BY THE SPECIAL GIFT AND CALLING OF ALMIGHTY GOD
> WHETHER HE SANG OF MAN OR OF NATURE
> FAILED NOT TO LIFT UP MEN'S HEARTS TO HOLY THINGS
> NOR EVER CEASED TO CHAMPION THE CAUSE
> OF THE POOR AND SIMPLE
> AND SO IN PERILOUS TIMES WAS RAISED UP
> TO BE A CHIEF MINISTER
> NOT ONLY OF SWEETEST POETRY
> BUT ALSO OF HIGH AND SACRED TRUTH...

[1] Beek, *Keble's Literary and Religious Contribution*, p. 11.
[2] Matthew Arnold (Keble's godson) was the first Poetry Professor to lecture in
English in 1855.
[3] Coleridge, *Memoir of Keble*, pp. 204–5.
[4] Which happily the translator, E. K. Francis, leaves intact as Greek.

While Keble's emphases are in many ways quite alien to the spirit of the early Wordsworth, the *Lectures* advance what is certainly the most thoroughgoing exposition ever devised of poetry as the spontaneous overflow of powerful feelings. But whereas, for Wordsworth, the image behind that phrase seems quite consistently to be that of a spring or natural fountain, for Keble publishing in the railway boom the metaphor appears to suggest a safety-valve of a steam boiler. Writing to J. T. Coleridge in February 1832 he outlines the scheme of his lectures like this: 'My notion is to consider poetry as a vent for overcharged feelings, or a full imagination, and so account for the various classes into which Poets naturally fall, by reference to the various objects which are apt to fill and overpower the mind, so as to require a sort of relief.'[1]

For Keble, poetry depends on tension or repression. The man who under emotional stress utters his feelings easily and without reserve is no poet.[2] As he puts it in his 1828 review of Lockhart's *Life of Scott*: 'Poetry is the indirect expression in words, most appropriately in metrical words, of some overpowering emotion, or ruling taste, or feeling, the direct indulgence whereof is somehow repressed.'[3] Repression or reserve – a tension between what is felt and what finally finds expression – is the essential factor in what he calls the 'poetic'. Though the form of expression is normally verbal, words are not absolutely necessary. Keble suspects that the 'ejaculative cries of savages', for instance, may well be one of the origins of poetry. Moreover, the 'poetic' is not a quality peculiar to poetry. All the various art forms, including music, sculpture, painting, and architecture have a 'poetical' element in them. 'What is called the poetry of painting,' says Keble, 'simply consists in the apt expression of the artist's own feeling.'[4] The traditional genres of poetic criticism which had held sway since Aristotle are found meaningless within this new 'expressionistic' framework: clearly, 'there will be as many kinds of poems as there are emotions of the human mind'.[5]

Keble divides poets into two main classes: Primary and

---

[1] Coleridge, *Memoir of Keble*, p. 199.   [2] *Lectures on Poetry*, I, 36.

[3] Abrams, *The Mirror and the Lamp*, p. 145; Review of *Life of Scott* (1838) in *Occasional Papers and Reviews* (Oxford, 1877), p. 6.

[4] *Lectures on Poetry*, I, 38.   [5] I, 88.

Secondary. The Primary consist in 'those who, spontaneously moved by impulse, resort to composition for relief and solace of a burdened or over-wrought mind'; the Secondary are 'those, who, for one reason or another, imitate the ideas, the expression, and the measures of the former'.[1] The list of Primary poets is strictly classical, ending properly with Virgil – though Dante appears to be permitted as an afterthought.[2] Tactfully, perhaps, Wordsworth is not mentioned in this context: there would appear to be an unresolved clash of criteria here, since Wordsworth, as a poet, seems clearly to belong to the Primary category, but suffers as a man from the grave disadvantage of being neither an ancient Greek, nor a Roman. A clue to the way in which Keble intended to rectify this unnecessarily classical bias is to be found in a letter to J. T. Coleridge of 5 July 1844, where, in connection with the question of an English translation, he adds that if it were not for the time he would like 'to substitute modern examples for the Greek and Latin'.[3] Byron and Shelley, however, are allowed in as examples of poets who are mentally affected by the intolerable tensions of their art.[4] For all the fact that, according to Keble, the test of a Primary poet is truth, sincerity, and modesty,[5] the demands of modesty or reserve mean that the truth often is veiled. Primary poets rarely dwell minutely on the real objects of their enthusiasm, and if they do, it is with unexpected emphases and a strange delight in socratic irony.[6]

This, then, is the aesthetic theory that Keble advances – apparently (or ostensibly) in the belief that he is doing no more than re-state and draw out what is latent in Wordsworth's poetics. In place of the classic post-Aristotelian criticism based on 'kinds' of poetry, the tendency to look instead at the *poet*, begun by Wordsworth in his Preface to the *Lyrical Ballads*, is carried to its logical conclusion, and the poetry is classified by the emotions of the writer, who seeks relief and health by disguised utterance. Poetry is, *par excellence*, the healing art. Long neglected, there has been a sharp revival of interest in Keble as an aesthetician since the publication of M. H. Abrams' book on Romantic critical theory, *The Mirror and the Lamp*, in 1953. He describes Keble's *Lectures on Poetry* 'as, under their pious and

---

[1] I, 53–4.   [2] II, 471.   [3] Coleridge, *Memoir of Keble*, p. 205.   [4] II, 339.
[5] I, 68.   [6] I, 77.

diffident surface, the most sensationally radical criticism of their time.'[1] This theory of poetry as 'relief for the over-burdened mind', argues Abrams, is a 'radical, proto-Freudian theory, which conceives literature as disguised wish-fulfilment, serving the artist as a way back from incipient neurosis'.[2]

Such an emphasis certainly goes a long way to explain certain qualities in Keble's own poetry. Wordsworth, in the *Immortality Ode*, had delighted in the 'soothing thoughts that spring/Out of human suffering', and in so doing touched a chord in nineteenth-century sensibilities that continued to reverberate in a host of lesser poets – Keble prominent among them. It is to the 'soothing' power of poetry that Keble tries to lead us with what the modern reader often feels is quite indecent haste. In his 1827 Advertisement to *The Christian Year* he calls our attention to the poems concerning the Occasional Services of the Prayer Book which he had added at the end of his collection (including one on the Commination Service!). These, he tells us, 'constitute, from their personal and domestic nature, the most perfect instance of that *soothing* tendency in the Prayer Book, which it is the chief purpose of these pages to exhibit'. Nor is it merely the prime purpose of *The Christian Year* to 'soothe' the jaded reader: the title of the poem for the Fourth Sunday after Epiphany gives us explicitly the full strength of this word for Keble – and presumably also for his readers. It is entitled, *The World is for Excitement, the Gospel for Soothing*. Clearly there is in the appeal of this kind of religious sentiment a good deal of that incipient Victorian desire to praise a cloister'd virtue: to find 'rest' and 'peace' 'safe upon the Saviour's bosom', or in 'the arms of mother Church' – according to taste. Too many Victorian poets *were* in search of an infantile dream-world. Keble, like Newman and many of the Tractarians, was not immune to this kind of feeling – and it is a salutary reminder of how emotionally alien much of the Oxford Movement would be to corresponding sensibilities today. Nevertheless, Keble was too good a theologian not to be aware of the force of such a statement about the Gospel. Clearly the power of 'soothing' is absolutely central to Keble's understanding of religious experience. Some of the strength of the word clearly comes from its older meaning: 'to prove or show to be true; to assert or uphold a truth'; or 'to give support', 'encourage', or

[1] *Memoir of Keble*, p. 145.   [2] P. 157.

'confirm' – by which it reaches its weaker modern sense of 'to calm' or even 'tranquillise'. Yet the weaker sense had come to co-exist with the stronger by the seventeenth century, and there is no doubt that by Keble's time it was the primary meaning. For further explanation of the importance of the word for Keble we need to refer to his aesthetic theory.

'Each several one of the so-called liberal arts,' says Keble, 'contains a certain poetic quality of its own, and. . . this lies in its power to heal and relieve the human mind when agitated by care, passion, or ambition.'[1] This argument contains such a bold and unexpected inversion of normal Romantic aesthetics that it is easy to miss what Keble is actually saying. He does not believe that one of the powers of 'the poetic' is that it can heal or give relief to the person under strain, he believes that we *define* 'the poetic' by this healing power. *Ibi ars medica, ubi poesis.* Where there is healing, there is the poetic. It is, apparently, as simple as that. Moreover it is perfectly clear, both in this passage, and in other similar ones, that 'soothing' and 'healing' are very closely related in Keble's thought. We can recognise the 'poetic' by its powers of soothing the agitated mind – even if we do not necessarily claim that *all* things that soothe are therefore poetic. Thus what he means by the power of 'soothing' is not simply a calming or tranquillising effect, but something much closer to the Aristotelian notion of 'catharsis' – the release of tension in tragedy through the emotions of pity and terror. It is, I think, quite clear that Keble actually has the idea of catharsis at the back of his mind. The 'poetic' involves the building up of an unresolved tension between private emotion and the restraints of public expression which finally finds utterance in some veiled or even ironic form whose release brings with it a healing and soothing effect for both poet and audience. But the mind of the poet is healed and set at rest not in any mere anodyne sense: it rests on the much more profound process of 'asserting and upholding the truth' even in the hidden symbolic forms of poetry. The Prayer Book and the Gospel are essentially 'poetic' because they compellingly assert the truth. By implication, we notice, 'feeling' itself becomes a means of verification, or a condition of assent to the truth. We can see here, in Keble's aesthetics, the link between Wordsworth's Preface and Newman's *Grammar of Assent.*

---

[1] *Lectures on Poetry,* I, 53.

What, then, *is* the relationship between poetry and religion? Keble seems to think of it at two levels. Historically, and perhaps in the development of the individual, poetry prepares the way for theology. The classic poets, philosophers, and historians 'may all be considered poets, so far as they are wont to elevate the mind by the clear light either of memory or lofty speculation'.[1] Poetry leads on the sensitive and enquiring soul from the first of the two worlds to the second. 'Men come to realize that the various images and similies of things, and all the poetic charms, are not merely the play of a keen and clever mind, nor to be put down as empty fancies: but rather they guide us by gentle hints and no uncertain signs, to the very utterances of Nature, or we may more truly say, of the Author of Nature.'[2] The age-old dream of man that his imaginative longings should, somehow, be found to be more 'true' than the world that denied those dreams is claimed as coming true for the Christian. We are closely reminded of Keats' Platonism: 'The Imagination may be compared to Adam's dream – he awoke and found it truth.'[3] 'It would be hard to believe,' declares Keble, that poetry and theology 'would have proved such true allies unless there was a hidden tie of kinship between them.'[4] If the images of poetry point towards another world of greater reality, it is also true that the hidden tie of kinship binds religion to poetry in the very structure of the language by which those images are created. If religion is the 'tenor', then poetry is the 'vehicle'. 'Poetry...supplies a rich wealth of similies whereby a pious mind may supply and remedy, in some sort, its powerlessness of speech.'[5] Poetry makes religion live in men's imagination, just as religion makes the imagination live in another world. It is interesting to notice how this argument is indebted not so much to Wordsworth, as to Coleridge. Poetry, Keble affirms, is the true medium or vehicle of religious experience, revealing its contents not so much by direct statement (which would be impossible, given the limitations of language) but through the very organic creativity of its form. Its concealed symbolism is an expression of the hidden inwardness of religious feeling. In Keble's reference to 'symbols' the

---

[1] *Lectures on Poetry*, II, 477.   [2] II, 481.
[3] Letter to Benjamin Bailey, 22 November 1817. *The Letters of John Keats*, ed. M. Buxton Forman. 4th edn (Oxford, 1952), p. 67.
[4] *Lectures on Poetry*, II, 479–80.   [5] II, 481.

verbal echoes of *The Statesman's Manual* are quite unmistakable:

In short, Poetry lends Religion her wealth of symbols and similies: Religion restores these again to Poetry, clothed with so splendid a radiance that they appear to be no longer merely symbols, but to partake (I might almost say) of the nature of sacraments.[1]

The hint of Coleridge behind Keble's concept of a symbolic and sacramental universe hardly comes as a surprise, but it does give us a pointer towards the solution of one of the most difficult problems in Keble's aesthetics: the meaning he attaches to the much-overworked word 'poetic'. On the one hand the word serves narrowly and conventionally as an adjective from 'poetry'; on the other, it is – as we have seen – applied with reckless abandon to the entire range of liberal arts, before being some-what ambiguously defined in terms of its healing power. Abrams offers us a tentative explanation of the 'proto-Freudian' theory that makes possible this wide-ranging use of the term:

...the very fact that Keble was more a theologian than a critic goes far to explain the nature of his poetics. Ideas, which in theology have become matter of course and inert, may become alive and drastically innovative when transferred – as Keble patently transferred them – into the alien soil of aesthetics.[2]

There is obviously a lot of truth in this, yet explanations in terms of the sacramental mysteries of the Church, of confession, and 'evidence of the extent to which psychoanalysis is a secularised version of religious doctrine and ritual', seem an anti-climax to anyone who has borne thus far with the intricacies of Keble's complex but always fascinating thought-processes. The explanation explains nothing. No one could be in any doubt of the amount Keble's aesthetics owe to theology – but it does not explain why Keble wishes to give such width to the word 'poetic', any more than it would have explained to us the force of the word 'soothing'. Yet Abrams' suggestion that ideas transferred from one field to another take on a new vitality is surely correct. The key, I suspect, is Coleridge.

Keble, we notice, consistently talks of 'poetry' as if it is a *mode* of mental activity. Reduced to the individual metaphors of langu-age we find it related less to any particular art form or artifact

---

[1] II, 480.   [2] Abrams, *The Mirror and the Lamp*, p. 147.

than to the process of creation itself. It seems, indeed, to serve
for Keble a very similar function to that of the word 'Imagination'
in Coleridge's vocabulary. Both are words used to describe a
particular kind of tension – a 'union of opposite or discordant
qualities'; both refer to processes rather than artifacts; both,
curiously enough, are sub-divided into Primary and Secondary
categories – and there is a marked, though not exact, parallel
between Keble's and Coleridge's categories. Coleridge's Primary
Imagination is the 'instrument of all human perception', the
power, common to all men, of shaping the inchoate mass of
sense-data into intelligible sense-experience. It is an instinctive
and unconscious activity below the threshold of sense: we do not
use our eyes, we *see*. His Secondary Imagination is the peculiar
possession of the creative artist. It shapes and re-forms sense-
experience in new ways, changing the way in which the rest of
mankind sees and feels. Keble's Primary poets similarly work
from spontaneous impulse, it is true, rather than by design and
imitation as do the Secondary, who, in a sense, dissolve and
dissipate in order to re-create – but there the similarity ends.
For Coleridge, it is the Secondary or creative Imagination which
is the higher faculty, whereas for Keble there is no question that
the Primary poets are the more important. If Keble had his
categories suggested to him by Coleridge, his use of them is not
primarily Coleridgean. But it is not difficult to see where he did
get them from: Keble marks his trail from theology so clearly
that Abrams' hint is scarcely necessary to us. Both Coleridge and
Keble suggest that the processes of poetic creation and religious
experience are not merely analogous, but, in Coleridge's sense
of the word, 'symbolic' of one another. The poet, in creating a
poem, allows the translucence of the eternal in and through the
temporal; his work is a part of the whole which it describes.
Similarly, the Christian's experience of God is essentially
'poetic', revealing to us the poetic nature of the whole universe –
in which he shares. Poetry makes us aware of the sacramental
nature of all human experience. For Keble, therefore, the
Primary poets are analogous to the founders of the Church – the
prophets, Apostles, and early Fathers who have shaped the
development of our religious sensibility through the tradition of
the Church; like the Fathers, they bring catharsis and soothing
out of the intolerable tensions of the human predicament. The

Secondary poets are, as it were, the army of saints and ecclesi-
astics who have kept pure the tradition of the Church, cleansing
and reforming it so that it is fresh and new to every age and
society. In one sense, such a structure can be no more than a dim
analogy, yet Keble constantly seems to argue that it is more than
analogous: the saints and Fathers *are* true poets, making the unseen world perceptible to man.

It is not difficult to see why Keble needs Coleridge's concept of
the Imagination as a creative process, common to all men and
pre-eminent in some, yet has to use some other, for him,
stronger, term to describe it. By and large, his critical vocabulary
comes from Wordsworth, not from Coleridge, and by the time
of his 1815 Preface to his *Poems* we find that Wordsworth has
slipped out of the 'strong', Coleridgean, use of the word 'imagination' and has returned to something much more like the common and 'weak' meaning, using it to describe the power of
drawing attention to hidden likenesses by means of metaphor
and simile. When Keble uses the word 'imagination' in his
Lectures on Poetry it is invariably in this 'weak' later Wordsworthian sense. The 'chief aim' of poetry, he informs us, is to

recall, to renew, and bring vividly before us pictures of absent objects:
partly it has to draw out and bring to light things cognate or similar
to each object it represents, however slight the connexion may be;
partly it has to systematize and explain the connexion between them:
in a word, it is the handmaid to Imagination and Fancy.[1]

It is 'poetry' in Keble's critical vocabulary, not 'Imagination'
which 'recalls', brings to light hidden similarities, 'systematizes'
and 'explains' connections. In Wordsworth's own work there is
a similar tendency to substitute the words 'poetry' or 'poetic'
where Coleridge would have said 'Imagination'. The passage in
book II of *The Prelude* where he describes the development of the
growing child, 'an inmate of this *active* universe', whose mind
learns 'through the growing faculties of sense' to 'create',
'Working but in alliance with the works/Which it beholds' is
astonishingly close in spirit to Coleridge's description of the
Imagination in chapter XIII of the *Biographia Literaria*. Nevertheless, the passage concludes, 'Such, verily, is the first/*Poetic*
spirit of our human life. . .'[2]

[1] I, 21.   [2] Lines 264–76, 1805 text. The italics are mine.

117

This is in line with a general tendency throughout the first half of the nineteenth century. By and large, Coleridge's pseudo-Kantian use of the word 'Imagination' is ignored or forgotten, and the word is appropriated to describe the dream-worlds of Victorian poetry. In its place the word 'poetic' tends to rise in status, taking to it many of the qualities Coleridge had attributed to the Imagination. In this shift there is no doubt that Keble plays an important rôle. In 1852, for instance, we find F. W. Robertson delivering a series of lectures on 'The Influence of Poetry' and on 'Wordsworth' to the working men of Brighton. Robertson, though greatly influenced by both Wordsworth and Coleridge, was in general of 'broad Church' persuasion and no friend to the Tractarians who, he felt, sought 'to reproduce the piety of the past by the forms of the past',[1] but he was nevertheless an avowed admirer of Keble as a man. What he is less quick to acknowledge is his evident debt to Keble's aesthetics. Robertson's whole theory of poetry follows very closely that of Keble's *Lectures*. He recapitulates the notion of Primary and Secondary poets, but takes up Keble's hint that modern poets might be substituted for ancient as examples, and breaking away from any temporal ordering, he names Tennyson as a Primary poet, Pope as a Secondary.[2] Similarly, Keble's theory of poetry as catharsis is retained: from reading Byron's poetry... 'Exhaustion follows – then health. For it is a mistake to think that Poetry is only good to nurse feeling. It is good for enabling us to *get rid* of feeling for which there is no available field of action. It is the safety-valve of the heart.'[3] For Robertson *feeling* is the prime quality of poetry: 'the office of Poetry is not to make us think accurately but feel truly'.[4] With this stress on 'feeling' comes that same shift of attention from 'imagination' to 'poetry' that we see in Keble. The 'imagination' is not 'esemplastic' as in Coleridge, the shaping process which reveals the 'leading idea' and its organic unity is a quality of 'poetry' itself. 'Poetry is not imagination, but imagination shaped. Not feeling; but feeling expressed symbolically: the formless suggested indirectly through form.'[5] Once again, the concept of the 'poetic' emerges as paramount.

To take another example, Newman's essay on Keble was written in 1846, just after the publication of his *Essay on Develop-*

---

[1] *Lectures on the Influence of Poetry and Wordsworth*, p. 104.
[2] P. 57.   [3] P. 93.   [4] P. 59.   [5] P. 68.

ment and his reception into the Roman Catholic Church. In it he pays tribute to what he sees as Keble's greatest achievement: 'He did that for the Church of England which none but a poet could do: he made it poetical.'[1] It might be more true to say that he did it for the Oxford Movement rather than for the Church as a whole, but Newman's praise for the Church of England in 1846 is like that of a cat praising a mouse for its uncommonly fine feline whiskers.

It is sometimes asked whether poets are not more commonly found external to the Church than among her children; and it would not surprise us to find the question answered in the affirmative. Poetry is the refuge of those who have not the Catholic Church to flee to and repose upon, for the Church herself is the most sacred and august of poets. Poetry, as Mr Keble lays it down in his University Lectures on the subject, is a method of relieving the overburdened mind: it is a channel through which emotion finds expression, and that a safe regulated expression. Now what is the Catholic Church, viewed in her human aspect, but a discipline of the affections and passions?[2]

It is always instructive to watch how Newman handles Keble's ideas. Assumptions which are embedded in the foundations of Keble's world-view are delicately prized loose and held up for scrutiny, as if by accident, to prove the strength of the mortar. One reason why Keble was never a good poet is that, for his naturally Platonic and unconcrete cast of mind, the 'poetic' was always somehow more *real* as a quality than any actual poetry. Newman has deftly picked it up and finding it loose put it back where (in one sense) it had always belonged – in the Church. The Catholic Church is more 'poetic' than poetry itself, since poetry is only a symbol of that greater reality. She is the true catharsis.

Newman has seized with unerring skill on Keble's achievement – in both its strength and its weakness. In struggling to make the Church of England 'poetic' in his terms, Keble helped to prevent it from becoming imaginative in Coleridge's. It was left not to the Oxford Movement, for all its intellectualism and emotional appeal, but to Frederick Denison Maurice to try and re-build within the Anglican Church the dual vision of the first Romantics.

[1] *Essays Critical and Historical* (9th edn, Longman, 1890), vol. II, 'Keble', p. 442.   [2] Ibid.

5

F. D. Maurice: The Kingdom of Christ

Judgements on F. D. Maurice, both contemporaneous and modern, have tended to suggest that he was a saintly man with a second-class intellect. For Matthew Arnold, Maurice was 'that pure and devout spirit – of whom, however, the truth must at last be told, that in theology he passed his life beating the bush with deep emotion and never starting the hare...'[1] Carlyle's faintly patronising admiration is similar in tone: 'Maurice has come twice athwart me: a man I like always for his delicacy, his ingenuity and earnestness: he is wonderfully patient of me, I often think; and I ought to esteem his way of thought at its full worth, and let it *live* in me, if I could. Hitherto, I regret to confess, it is mainly moonshine and *Spitzfindigkeit*, and will not live. But the man is good, and does live in me.'[2] John Stuart Mill sadly comments that 'there was more intellectual power wasted in Maurice than in any other of my contemporaries'.

Great powers of generalization, rare ingenuity and subtlety, and a wide perception of important and unobvious truths, served him not for putting something better into the place of the worthless heap of received opinions on the great subjects of thought, but for proving to his own mind that the Church of England had known everything from the first, and that all the truths on the ground of which the Church and orthodoxy have been attacked (many of which he saw as clearly as anyone) are not only consistent with the Thirty-nine Articles, but are better understood and expressed in those Articles than by anyone who rejects them.[3]

Nor has Maurice's reputation fared much better with his modern admirers, who have confessed that in the last resort he was a

[1] *Literature and Dogma*, popular edn (Smith, Elder, 1895), p. 200.
[2] *New Letters of Thomas Carlyle*, ed. Alexander Carlyle (Bodley Head, 1904), p. 29.
[3] *Autobiography*, p. 130.

'muddled thinker'[1] severely handicapped by his lack of training in the German Historical Method.[2] His avowed hatred of intellectual 'systems' has been noted as an example of his moral integrity, but assumed to be a fatally debilitating intellectual flaw. Yet, if by narrow definition of 'theologian' we exclude Coleridge, there is a good case for regarding Maurice as the greatest Anglican theologian of the nineteenth century – certainly he was the Church of England's greatest Victorian one. Though he was by no means Coleridge's closest disciple,[3] there are, as Mill saw, many ways in which Maurice is of all the Victorian thinkers the most similar to Coleridge. Like Coleridge he was a peculiarly *difficult* thinker, and like Coleridge he was widely misunderstood for this very reason. The conversion of James Martineau to Maurice is very revealing. At first sight he was not impressed.

I am reading Maurice's 'Theological Essays' and find them notwithstanding a good deal of interest in parts, on the whole shadowy and unimpressive. I hardly think a man has any business to write till he has brought his thoughts into distincter shapes and better defined relations than I find in Maurice. He seems to me to have a mere presentiment of thinking, a tentative process in that direction that never fairly succeeds in getting home. But I have thus far read only some half-dozen of the essays.[4]

But on closer acquaintance his turn-round of opinion is dramatic. In his *Essays and Reviews* he writes, 'for consistency and completeness of thought, and precision in the use of language, it would be difficult to find his superior among living theologians'.[5] To link the 'completeness' and unity of Maurice's thought with his 'precision in the use of language' suggests that he has found cause to change his mind over the very faults which at first seemed to him the most glaring. It is this minority view of

[1] A quotation from Alec Vidler at the Maurice Centenary Conference, Trinity Hall, Cambridge, March 1972. The Conference in general, with honourable exceptions, demonstrated how ingrained is the Church of England's habit of damning Maurice with faint patronage.
[2] A. M. Ramsey, *F. D. Maurice and the Conflicts of Modern Theology* (Cambridge, 1951), p. 35. An unfair quotation this – since Ramsey is, in fact, one of Maurice's greatest admirers in the twentieth century.
[3] This honour must go to J. H. Green. See ch. 2 above.
[4] Letter to R. H. Hutton, 1853. H. G. Wood, *Frederick Denison Maurice* (Cambridge, 1950), pp. 5–6.
[5] *Essays, Reviews and Addresses* (Longman, 1890), I, 253.

Martineau's that I intend to try and explore in this chapter.

Frederick Denison Maurice was only thirty-three when he published the first version of *The Kingdom of Christ* in 1838. It is a remarkable book by any standard – threatening an apotheosis of the Church of England so radical that (to invert Arnold's aphorism) ever since Anglicans have neither been able to live with it, nor live without it. It is the more remarkable since Maurice was not even brought up in the Church of England. He was born and raised a Unitarian. For a time in adolescence he was strongly influenced by his mother's growing Calvinism.[1] Though both Unitarianism and Calvinism were passing phases, rapidly transcended, there is a sense in which the two positions remain as constant lifelong poles in his thought. *The Kingdom of Christ* stems from, on the one hand, an extreme theological liberalism and openness (following Coleridge's principle that men are more usually right in what they affirm, than in what they deny), and on the other, an extremely exalted view of the Church as the means of personal salvation. Maurice's movement from Unitarianism to the Church of England is, indeed, not unlike Coleridge's. But his idea of the Church has all the freshness and originality of a man who has come into the tradition in which he is writing from the outside. In 1854, some sixteen years after the publication of *The Kingdom of Christ*, he describes 'originality' like this:

An original man is not one who invents – not one who refuses to learn from others. I say, boldly, no original man ever did that. But he is one who does not take words and phrases at second hand; who asks what they signify; who does not feel that they are his, or that he has a right to use them until he knows what they signify. The original man is fighting for his life; he must know whether he has any ground to stand upon...[2]

'He must know whether he has any ground to stand upon' – the matter is an important one for anyone who, like Maurice, is concerned to embrace the Church of England not merely as a fact, but as an 'idea'.

At Trinity College, Cambridge, Maurice was to meet on coming up as an undergraduate in 1823 the two men who were

[1] *The Life of F. D. Maurice*, ed. Frederick Maurice, 4th edn (Macmillan, 1885), I, 28–31.
[2] *The Doctrine of Sacrifice*, 1854, pp. xi–xii.

to become his closest friends and greatest influences on his early thought. One was John Sterling, a fellow undergraduate who, with Maurice, was one of the leading members of the Apostles' Club. The other was their young tutor, Julius Hare. By a curious quirk of fate, both men were to be successively his brothers-in-law.[1] Though for his final year Maurice with Sterling moved to Trinity Hall to read Law, and though his Unitarian scruples were still then powerful enough to make him unable to accept a Cambridge degree (then, as now, bestowed in the name of the Father, Son, and Holy Ghost) there is no doubt that Hare was, increasingly, the dominant influence on his intellectual and theological development.

This was fortunate. In 1823 the Reverend Julius Hare was a unique figure in the English universities. He was a Coleridgean at a time when Coleridge as a philosopher and theologian was neither well-known nor intellectually respectable. Maurice later referred to Coleridge at this time as 'a man whose name was ordinarily tabooed in literary as well as in religious circles'. In 1823, the year in which Hare himself first came to Trinity as a tutor, Coleridge's *Aids to Reflection* was published. Maurice and Sterling were immediately introduced to it, and Coleridge's intended manual for university students fell instantly into fertile ground. In 1848, in his 'Memoir of the Life of Sterling', Hare recalled:

At that time it was beginning to be acknowledged by more than a few that Coleridge is the true sovereign of modern English thought. The *Aids to Reflection* had recently been published, and were doing the work for which they are so admirably fitted; that book, to which many, as has been said by one of Sterling's chief friends, 'owe even their own selves'. Few felt this obligation more deeply than Sterling. 'To Coleridge (he wrote to me in 1836) I owe *education*. He taught me to believe that an empirical philosophy is none, that Faith is the highest Reason, that all criticism, whether of literature, laws or manners, is blind, without the power of discerning the organic unity of the object.'[2]

To Hare Maurice owed not merely his introduction to Coleridge, but to the whole tradition of English Platonists of which Coleridge

[1] In 1837 Maurice married Sterling's wife's sister, whom he met at Hare's house in Hurstmonceaux; in 1849 after her death he married Hare's sister, Georgiana.

[2] *Essays and Tales of John Sterling* (1848), pp. xiii–xiv. Sterling's 'chief friend' is, of course, Maurice – to whom, Hare adds, Sterling 'owed more than to any other man except Coleridge'.

was the latest and, for him, most illustrious example. It is not too much to say that his appreciation of Coleridge was rooted in Plato. From Hare's lectures on Plato's *Gorgias* he tells us how he came to see that 'there was a way out of party opinions, which is not a compromise between them, but which is implied in both, and of which each is bearing witness'. He continues, 'Hare did not tell us this... Plato himself does not say it; he makes us feel it.'[1] The conclusion is important for our understanding of Maurice's Coleridgeanism, but as important is the *way* in which he apprehends Plato's teaching. For Maurice, Plato's method of teaching is essentially 'poetic' in that he tells us only a part of what makes us 'feel'. As we shall see throughout Maurice's thinking, he takes it for granted that articulate knowledge is rooted in certainties and modes of awareness that extend far beneath consciousness to layers that are accessible to aesthetic rather than discursive forms of apprehension. Maurice's Platonism gave him a new gloss to Christ's sayings about the need for a childlike mind. Edward Strachey, writing to his aunt in 1836, recorded how he had consulted Maurice about the choice of a university:

Maurice says it is the great evil of everything at Oxford that there is nothing but Aristotelianism. And I find it was the superiority of Cambridge in this respect that made him think it so much better for me to go to the latter University. Maurice says all little children are Platonists, and it is their education which makes them Aristotelians.[2]

Lastly, and no less significantly, Hare was a good historian and first-class German scholar – of his day, possibly the best in England. When he moved from Trinity to the rectory at Hurstmonceaux in 1833 it was said that the removers had to transport over 2,000 volumes in German alone. His library[3] at Hurst-

---

[1] *Life*, I, 54–6.

[2] Letter of Edward Strachey to his aunt, Lady Louis, 27 October 1836, cited by Newsome, *Two Classes of Men. Life*, I, 206–7.

[3] 'You entered, and found the whole house was one huge library – books overflowing in all corners, into hall, on landing-places, in bedrooms, and in dressing-rooms. Their number was roughly estimated at 14,000 volumes, and, though it would be too much to say that their owner had read them all, yet he had at least bought them all with a special purpose, knew where they were, and what to find in them, and often, in the midst of discussion, he would dart off to some remote corner, and return in a few minutes with the passage which was wanted as an authority or illustration.' 'Memoir' of J. C. Hare, *Guesses at Truth*, 3rd edn (Macmillan, 1866), p. xlv.

monceaux was estimated to contain 14,000 volumes. At a period when the Schlegels were still almost unheard of in the English universities, Hare's students were reading August Schlegel's dramatic criticism. He himself had published an essay on Schlegel in 1820. Hare was also responsible for introducing into England the work of the German historian Georg Barthold Niebuhr, and in 1827 he and Connop Thirlwall began their translation of Niebuhr's most famous book, the *History of Rome*. It was to change the course of English historical scholarship.[1]

It is important to notice that Hare was familiar with many of Coleridge's German sources before he came to Coleridge, and that he was singularly unaffected by the dark hints of plagiarism which, then as now, accompanied discussion of Coleridge's ideas in many quarters.[2] As he repeatedly stressed, he had come to value Coleridge not for his popularisation of German thought, but because Coleridge had something to say that was very *different* from the Germans. According to Maurice, Hare owed to Coleridge 'probably more than to any other man, that he was able to trace the path which connects human learning with the divine, the faith of one age with the faith of another, the sense of man's grandeur with the sense of his pettiness and sinfulness'.[3] All these, too, were the paths of Maurice's own development which were to lead him into controversy with Mansel on the value of human learning, with Newman on the doctrine of development, and with utilitarians and simple-minded believers in 'progress' over the paradoxical nature of man.

Maurice's introduction to Coleridge, then, was one that kept in perspective the problems of German influence, and which, without undervaluing the poetry and criticism, taught him to value the originality of the late Coleridge – the *Lay Sermons, Aids to Reflection, Confessions of an Inquiring Spirit*, and *Church and State*.[4] It is against this background that we should try to understand his oft-cited hatred of 'systems', and his distinction between 'system' and 'method'. What Hare had taught him to

[1] Duncan Forbes, *The Liberal Anglican Idea of History* (Cambridge, 1952), pp. 15–16.
[2] See Maurice's (anonymous) 'Introduction' to Hare's *Charges to the Clergy of the Archdeaconry of Lewes*, passim – but in particular p. xviii.
[3] Ibid. p. xxiii.
[4] For the value Maurice placed on these works see his Introduction to *The Kingdom of Christ*.

value in the later Coleridge was not a particular philosophical 'system' (the existence of an original 'system' in Coleridge is, in any case, very doubtful) but a particular *mode* of thinking: a quality of response in many ways more literary than strictly philosophical, more poetic than theological. He was happy to abandon, for instance, most of Coleridge's elaborate terminology of the Imagination without wavering in his sense of it as an active assimilating power in which the reader is not a spectator but a participant. For Maurice himself, the opposite of a 'system' is not *lack* of system – the modern conception of 'creative confusion' based on a falsely magical notion of creativity – but 'method' in Coleridge's sense of the word.

When once a man begins to build a system, the very gifts and qualities which might serve in the investigation of truth, become the greatest hinderances to it. He must make the different parts of the scheme fit into each other; his dexterity is shown not in detecting facts, but in cutting them square.[1]

For Maurice, a 'system', and its outward political and ecclesiastical expression, a 'party', is a mental and spiritual straightjacket, permitting only pre-determined gestures towards predefined goals. It is the vehicle of the second-hand; it holds at bay the new and the possibility of change; it is the enemy of the creative. 'Method', in contrast, is the essential pre-condition of *all* first-hand experience. Without it, our impressions and intuitions alike are random and disorganised. 'To me,' he writes in *The Kingdom of Christ*, 'these words seem not only not synonymous, but the greatest contraries imaginable: the one indicating that which is most opposed to life, freedom, variety; and the other that without which they cannot exist.'[2] The Bible affords the perfect example of this contrast. The systematiser 'is tormented every page he reads with a sense of the refractory and hopeless materials he has to deal with', whereas the disinterested reader who does not approach it with rigid pre-conceptions finds a unity and meaning in the very diversity of its contents. 'Method' is – in the Coleridgean terminology that Maurice here was happy to use – 'organic' in its operation. We only understand

[1] *Lectures in Ecclesiastical History of the First and Second Centuries* (Macmillan, 1854), p. 222. Cited by Alec Vidler, *F. D. Maurice and Company* (S.C.M. 1966), p. 22.
[2] I, 272–3.

the parts of the Bible in relation to the whole. 'Method' is a 'principle of progression' by which we move from the known to the unknown, and without which the infinite possibilities of the new remain unexplored because inaccessible. We can see how in Maurice's thought the outworking of this distinction is both consistent and lucid, but at the same time leads to a complexity in his *way* of thinking that was to prove peculiarly irritating to a different and blunter kind of mind.

The Kingdom of Christ offers a very good example of this complexity: to some it has seemed to epitomise Maurice's lack of clarity and organisation. His thinking is consistently 'organic' in the sense that it works from level to level by a series of analogies, parallels, and correspondences – the parts constantly being referred to the whole, and vice versa. In this he, like Newman, reaches back beyond Coleridge to Butler's *Analogy*. Man's experience of God is of a piece with the rest of his experience. Neither sense-perception nor language are given as *a priori* starting-points to the individual as Benthamite thought assumed. They are conditioned by the particular world-picture of a particular time and society and are to be understood as essentially *collective* phenomena. The Church cannot (and should not) be separated from society. Now this can and does sound like an argument from the German Historical Method, but, in fact, it is based not so much on a historical as a literary position – as Maurice makes abundantly clear. He does not wish to relativise the Church, but to particularise it – just as the eternal truths mediated by poetry are not less but more transcendent for being inseparable from its concrete metaphorical structure and the language of a particular time and place. Growth and development are essential qualities of life. Poetry is one of the deepest expressions of national life, revealing the mental development of a people;[1] the Bible is just such a progressive record, showing the spiritual growth of a particular people. Thus Revelation is not to be thought of as something breaking in from the outside, but rather as the discovery of the in-dwelling of the supernatural growing up and out of the particular, the concrete, and the ordinary. It is not divine light shining on a darkened world, nor yet 'evidence' for a miraculous design in Creation, but (to continue the metaphor of light) a *translucence* of the mundane to

[1] See Hare's essay on the course of poetry in *Guesses at Truth*, pp. 38–58.

produce a symbolic and sacramental universe. Even miracles are not seen as intervention, breaks in the natural order, but as visible symbols of the dependence of Nature on a greater, hidden order which they affirm.[1] They are acted metaphors. The underlying image, often explicit, and always implicit, is that of a work of art – and like Keble and so many Romantics, Maurice instinctively takes poetry to be the archetypal art form. For this reason we do best to approach Maurice's view of the Church in *The Kingdom of Christ* by way of his views on poetry, and on language in general, and their effect on the way he sees scripture.

In a talk delivered to the students of Guy's Hospital in 1838 – the same year as the first version of *The Kingdom of Christ* – Maurice distinguishes between two different approaches to language. The first, of which he takes Dr Johnson as representative, he calls the 'Lexicographical'; the second, exemplified by Horne Tooke, the 'Derivative' or 'Etymological'. The former approach offers the enquirer a variety of current usages of a word, just as a dictionary might. This, for better or worse, it implies, is how the word is used. The problem for the enquirer is to see any connection between one meaning of the word and the next. He lacks a derivation, any organising idea to link the multitude of separate meanings and show them for what they are: the fruits of a single stem. What, for example, *is* the link between the word 'property' as used by a surveyor, and the same word in the mouth of a naturalist?[2] Are they the 'same' word, or are they two entirely different ones that happen to be spelt and pronounced in the same way? Horne Tooke, in contrast, falls into the opposite vice. He goes straight for the root, and reduces all subsequent developments of the word to their common origin. Thus, according to Tooke's method the word 'property' simply means 'that which was a man's own'.

All those higher meanings of the word, which we found expressed in so many beautiful passages in old English authors, would have been brought down till they intimated nothing more than is intimated by the word in every bill of sale, or at any auction mart; and we should have been told, what is certainly true, that this is a much simpler method, and is a great saving of trouble. But the mischief is, that in this way, just as much as in the other, we get rid of facts.[3]

[1] *Three Lectures on the Epistle to the Hebrews* (1846), Preface, p. xxxiv.
[2] 'On Words', *The Friendship of Books*, 2nd edn (Macmillan, 1874), p. 44.
[3] Ibid. p. 52.

Both methods, in fact, are defective, and their fault, though it results in two opposite positions, is a common one:

...their common error is, that they both alike deny the living, germinating power of words. Horne Tooke, who ties a word down to its lowest sense, Johnson, who bandages each word in a separate definition, alike disbelieve in that principle which, had they acknowledged it, would have brought their methods into coincidence. If they would have stooped to the strong and irresistible evidence which the workings of our own minds, which all history, furnishes, that there is as much vital principle in a word as in a tree or a flower, they would have understood how it was possible that the root should be a small ugly thing, and that yet it should contain in itself the whole power and principle of the leaves, and buds, and flowers, into which it afterwards expands... They would have understood, too, how the peculiar circumstances of any age, moral or political, like the influence of sun and air, of spring breezes, of mildew and blight, may modify the form and colour of a word, may stint or quicken its growth, may give it a full-blown, coarse, material look, cause it to sicken into a pale and drooping abstraction, or strengthen it in all its spiritual sap and juices.[1]

This approach to language as a living, organic, and yet 'ideal' entity is central to any understanding of Maurice's *mode* of thought. He himself is fully aware of its implications. He continues:

In using this language I am far from intending to be metaphorical. I use that language which I believe does most literally and exactly convey my meaning. The point in debate is, whether words are endued with this principle of life, the manifestations of which it is impossible in any way so truly to express as in the language of outward nature. Whether it be so or not, I repeat, is the question. To call this language metaphorical is to beg the question.[2]

For Maurice, there is no break between ordinary everyday language, and 'poetic' language. The language of poetry exhibits qualities already to be found in every colloquial phrase. In claiming that words are 'endued' with 'life' Maurice is echoing Coleridge's well-known affirmation in *Aids to Reflection*: 'For if words are not THINGS, they are LIVING POWERS, by which the things of most importance to mankind are actuated, combined, and humanized.'[3] This is not some kind of magical

[1] Ibid. p. 53.   [2] Ibid. p. 54.   [3] P. xvii.

attribution, but rather what, at another level H. H. Milman called the capacity of 'accommodation':[1] words like institutions are progressive in their development, constantly adapting and changing to fit new situations, yet always laden with their past history; simultaneously, they reach out from their immediate context towards something that is other and transcendent. The ambiguity of language is not a hinderance, but a help towards greater clarity, given the complexity and richness of real thinking compared with the artificial simplicities of philosophers and theologians. In this context Maurice compares 'the flesh, so far as it is identical with the body', with 'the flesh so far as it is identical with the corruption into which man has fallen'.

Neither of these senses of the word flesh can be exclusively adopted or rejected; something of the idea would perish if the ambiguity were removed from the expression; a consideration perpetually lost sight of by commentators and theologians in their eagerness to nail a word to one dead, invariable use, but most important for the clearness, the honesty and the vitality of our thoughts, really helping not hindering us to arrive at as simple a view of the case as the case itself permits.[2]

In a letter of 1863 Maurice distinguishes three different ways in which the eighteenth century looked at the Old Testament:

(1) The purely orthodox. The divine history is in its essence miraculous – i.e., it is an exception from the law of other histories.
(2) The purely naturalistic. All the so-called miracles of Scripture may be explained into ordinary phenomena.
(3) The spiritualistic (either in the Romanist or Methodist form). Miracles have not ceased. There are interferences now as there were of old.[3]

Turning to the nineteenth century, Maurice observes that 'Strauss and the Mythical School' had had the effect of subverting the second of these schemes. They had demonstrated 'that *no* records of human life can be content with merely naturalistic phenomena. There is always the dream of something transcendent.' But this, he points out, is a two-edged weapon. Followed in one direction, granted, it implies that all history is based on falsehood. But

[1] Forbes, *The Liberal Anglican Idea of History*, p. 75.
[2] Ms. letter to Sarah Coleridge, Autumn 1843. Quoted by F. McClain, *Maurice: Man and Moralist* (S.P.C.K., 1972), p. 34.
[3] *Life*, II, 454.

'follow it to its extreme in the other direction and you come to the true supernatural origin of history'. In other words the transcendent yearnings of everyday language are not part of the perpetual process of 'projection' by which man endows his universe with his own values – as Feuerbach and Strauss believed – but are a proper part of the sacramental nature of language. The three theories of scriptural interpretation, which in the hands of eighteenth-century expositors had reached stalemate, each unable to sustain itself unaided, and yet incompatible with the alternatives which it nevertheless needed, are now seen as part of a perpetual conflict about the nature of language itself. It is, of its nature, incomplete: possessing 'method' but denying 'systems' that would provide a total explanation. Language is *never* wholly to be accounted for by language, but points beyond itself. 'Miracles are not exceptions,' writes Maurice, 'but manifestations.' They are visible and tangible epiphanies of laws that are always latent in a God-centred universe.

For Maurice, the special property of scripture is not that it itself possesses this 'bi-focal' ambiguous quality of standing between two worlds – which it does – but that it progressively reveals similar tendencies in the everyday world of the reader's own experience. History – and supremely Biblical history – shapes and conditions the way we interpret the present; language is simultaneously vehicle and symbol of this process. Thus, if the language of religion most clearly exemplifies the transcendent yearnings of all language, it is the *more*, not less, rooted in the historical consciousness of a particular period. Maurice seems much more aware of German Historical Method than many of his modern commentators have allowed. Here he seems to be taking up the new German ideas and using them in a typically original way. The Historical Method and the rise of a historical consciousness – a sense of the difference rather than the sameness of the past – he sees as being a part of the wider phenomenon we now loosely call 'Romanticism'. There has, he observes, been a philosophical revolution since the middle of the eighteenth century.[1] Its beginnings can be seen in such movements as Methodism, though the Methodists themselves did not subscribe intellectually to the beliefs to which their own distinctive religious experience pointed, and so, in this sense, cannot be counted part

[1] *The Kingdom of Christ*, I, 172.

of the new movement.[1] They, however, like their Romantic successors saw man as a 'spiritual being'. He was no longer to be treated as merely a mechanism, or as a creature dominated by 'reason' in its narrow empiricist sense of 'logic'. For the Romantics, man is not an assemblage of separate faculties, but an organic unity in which the parts are subordinated to a whole that is beyond the measurement of empirical mechanism or logic. He is a being with values and purpose. Feeling and thought are not separate activities, and neither can they be divorced from the total spiritual life of the personality. For long the Romantics had been a beleaguered minority. But now, concludes Maurice, the idea of man as a spiritual being has suddenly 'arrived', and is passing into popular modes of thought almost before the professional theologians in England are aware of it. From being the unconscious possession of English enthusiasts, or part of the philosophical speculations of Germany – 'a country of recluse students' – it has become 'the common talk and profession of the lecturers and coteries of France'.[2]

How does this 'philosophical revolution' affect our approach to religious experience? English theology of the eighteenth century, and, indeed, with the exception of the Coleridgean and Liberal Anglican tradition, almost up until the time when Maurice was writing, was obsessed with the clash between empiricism and the belief in the literal inspiration of the Bible. Christianity had to stand or fall by its 'evidences'; difficulties, such as contradictions between gospels, had to be ironed out or argued away. Above all, miracles must either be explained away, or shown – in spite of appearances – as not inconsistent with a scientific world-picture, unless one wished to take the extremist ('orthodox') position that miracles were direct and arbitrary interference by the Almighty in the natural scheme of things – a position that was becoming increasingly untenable. Scripture, as the received Word of God, was still not open to the normal techniques of criticism. Since they were the sacred and inspired Word, texts could be wrenched from context and re-arranged eclectically to suit any particular argument. Maurice, however, had encountered Lessing, Herder, and Niebuhr through Hare. As we have seen, he was well aware of the strength of the Historical Method, in contrast with English Biblical criticism, in that it

---

[1] *The Kingdom of Christ*, I, p. 171.   [2] Ibid. p. 172.

accepted man's experience of the divine as part of a cultural whole. In J. M. Creed's words:

The books of Scripture were seen to be not merely pictures of a discredited world-view, but literary monuments of great religious personalities...These personalities take their place as the fine flowering of the growth which is 'history of religion'. The Bible may be treated as a text-book for the study of this organic growth.[1]

It is easy to see how far this kind of approach chimes in with Maurice's own feelings. Theology cannot be separated from literature without weakening it *as* theology; the theologian must also be an expert literary critic, fully conversant with all the critical apparatus involved. It is no accident that the great tradition of nineteenth-century religious thinkers, men like Coleridge, Maurice, Keble, Newman, Arnold, and even Hort, were part of a literary tradition as much as a theological one. Any attempt to understand them in narrow theological terms alone is doomed to distortion and failure.

Nevertheless, Maurice has no intention of going all the way with the German critics. Their weakness is that they, themselves, are not sufficiently literary in their approach. In the last resort, he claims, they remain systematisers.

A considerable number of persons in Germany, in France, and in England believe that they have found an explanation for most or all of the facts which readers of the Bible attribute to the power and the Spirit of God. They believe that the last age had no such explanation, and that its attempts to interpret or deny these facts were ridiculous. Treating human beings, they say, merely as material mechanical creatures, you will always be puzzled with what pious people tell you they have felt, and with what they have actually done; treat them as spiritual beings, and the difficulty ceases. You can account for everything; their divine interventions, spiritual illuminations, and miracles, were not mere inventions of priestcraft, though priestcraft has much to do with the continued belief of them; they are all to be traced to man's spiritual nature; by observing what theory prevailed in each age on such matters you form a notion of its character, and of its relation to that which succeeded it. This is a language which perfectly satisfies some persons who can put all these subjects at a distance from them, and speculate about them with entire calmness.[2]

[1] *The Divinity of Jesus Christ*, p. 107.   [2] *The Kingdom of Christ*, I, 174–5.

The very apparent success of such an approach contains its greatest danger: 'you can account for everything'. All facts can be made to fit – *provided* the theoretician remains the true Cartesian observer, assuming a total detachment from what is being observed. But *is* this in fact a satisfactory standpoint? Does it take into account the realities of the situation as it is actually experienced? Does it not itself rest on certain hidden presuppositions about the nature of religious experience which ignores the evidence of many of those who have written or spoken about it? Religion is not an activity in which the spectator sees most of the game. To use Peter Berger's neat phrase, Maurice now proceeds to relativise the relativisers.[1]

There are others, on the contrary, whose phrases will be very like these – nay, the very same – but in whom they are indications of an entirely different state of mind. These are men who do not consider it their duty or vocation to explain away facts, or to philosophise upon them; they cannot look at anything as apart from themselves; when they talk of sufferings and conflicts, they are not expounding a scheme of metaphysics, they are speaking of what they have known and what they can therefore sympathize with in others.[2]

In one sense this is no more than a re-statement of Coleridge,[3] but used as a critique of certain aspects of the Historical Method it opens up such striking new possibilities that it is fair to wonder if the term 'existentialist' is not more appropriate than 'Coleridgean' in this context. In one sense there is no clearly definable transition between Romanticism and Existentialism – they can be represented as a continuum, with the latter as one of the philosophical possibilities latent in the former. In the Appendix I suggest some possible parallels between Wordsworth and Kierkegaard. Yet here Maurice is not merely declaring that religious belief can only be described from the inside, he is using this argument to reach a further, much more complex, philosophical position about the nature of religious language.

Such persons cannot adopt the old religious language, because it seems to set aside facts which they feel to be certain; it seems to deny that a man is anything in himself; that he has an eye wherewith to receive

---

[1] *A Rumour of Angels* (Pelican 1971), chapter 2.

[2] *The Kingdom of Christ*, I, 175.

[3] *Aids to Reflection*, p. 178: 'Christianity is not a Theory, or a Speculation, but a *Life*. Not a *Philosophy* of Life, but a Life and a Living Process...TRY IT.'

light. But neither can they wholly reject this old religious language; they feel inwardly that the philosophical is no substitute for it; they feel that the words about gifts and inspirations did mean something more than that a man has all powers within him; they feel that an abdication of powers, a denial of self, is the characteristic of all really honest men; they feel that humility, and not exaltation, the acknowledgement of receiving, not the boast of possessing, ought to be the criterion of spiritual excellence. They therefore hover between the two forms of language, using either as the feeling of the weakness or falsehood of the other predominates, often comitting the grossest inconsistencies, often uttering the most absurd extravagancies, but proving the honesty of their intentions more by these inconsistencies and extravagancies than by much which seems to their admirers coherent and reasonable... [1]

There is a deceptive semi-ironic underplaying in that last sentence that, taken out of context, could imply an anti-intellectualism that is quite foreign to Maurice. The whole passage, however, makes his position clear. He is not praising pious incoherence as a proof of honesty and sincerity; he *does* believe that there is a fundamental polarity in man's experience of the divine, and that this polarity, this sense of fundamental contradictions held in tension, is of the very essence of religious experience. We find it enshrined at every level of Christian dogma. The systematisers who wish to iron out this tension and, all too often in the eighteenth and nineteenth centuries, reduce faith to a series of rational unambiguous propositions are flying in the face of seventeen hundred years of developing Christian tradition and threatening the very springs of religious awareness in modern man.

What we have already seen in Maurice's secular thinking as a fundamental ambiguity in all language now finds expression, at another turn of the spiral, in the condition of received orthodox religious language. Steeped on the one hand in the organic traditionalism of Burke and Coleridge, and, on the other, becoming increasingly involved in the social radicalism that was to lead to the Christian Socialist movement, Maurice himself feels the tensions within the Church of England strained almost to breaking-point. How does the traditional language of Christianity speak to the rapidly changing urban world of nineteenth-century England, and its accompanying intellectual climate? For such

[1] *The Kingdom of Christ*, I, 175–6.

people as Carlyle, Mill, George Eliot, Matthew Arnold, or T. H. Huxley it clearly meant less and less as the middle years of the century rolled by. More personally, John Sterling's own crisis of faith in 1835 had brought the question home to Maurice with a new urgency as he began writing *The Kingdom of Christ*. His answer anticipates Arnold, but is unironic: men can neither live with it, nor live without it. Our religious language is that of another age, and of a different world-view, resting on different and outmoded cultural assumptions, yet it is, partly for that very reason, the vehicle of a different kind and *quality* of consciousness without which the sophistication of philology and Historical Method is drained of meaning and becomes lost in a sterile relativity.

It should now be apparent why, for so many thinkers and even theologians, Maurice should have seemed to be unclear or muddled. That language could be seen as Janus-faced was incomprehensible enough to Victorians not reared in the minority tradition of Coleridge; but that religious experience could be seen as essentially and of its very nature ambiguous and contradictory was inconceivable and needlessly perverse to most of Maurice's contemporaries who were of the household of faith. To an Evangelical temper such as Rigg's or Candlish's this kind of complexity was dangerous intellectual moonshine.[1] To a spiritually-minded agnostic such as Carlyle who (I suspect) had some idea of what Maurice was getting at, and whose ideas were in certain respects similar, it was no less intolerable that Maurice should be using the dual focus of language as an analogy of faith rather than scepticism. To anyone who had grasped the basis of Maurice's argument in *The Kingdom of Christ*, however, his subsequent attack on Mansel's Bampton Lectures of 1859 should have come as no surprise.

Entitled *The Limits of Religious Thought*, Mansel's lectures began from the thesis that the problems posed by the central Christian doctrines were paralleled by the philosophical problems we encounter in investigating the nature of God. All human knowledge, he insists, is conditioned and relative. God, as infinite and absolute, is unknowable to human minds. In the last resort, metaphysics is impossible and absurd. We are utterly dependent on Faith and Revelation for our knowledge of God, even if they

---

[1] Storr, *English Theology*, pp. 344–6.

seem to offer us nothing but contradictions. 'It is our duty to think of God as personal; and it is our duty to believe that He is infinite.'[1] That we cannot imagine how a Being can be both infinite *and* personal need not trouble us – indeed, by an extension of this argument, it is our *duty* not to be troubled! Faith is above Reason; it cannot be questioned. The Christian Revelation can be safely defended from all onslaughts if we only bear in mind the puny inadequacy of the human intellect. Mansel seemed to be offering the English Church – always, and notoriously disinclined to hard theological thinking – a safe stronghold.

The vehemence of Maurice's attack on Mansel in fact took many of Maurice's contemporaries by surprise.[2] To an early twentieth-century Church historian such as Storr, Maurice's position contra Mansel is clear-cut:

Mansel's position was a denial of all that Maurice held most dear, and for which he most earnestly contended. For him the knowledge of God was not only possible, but was the root and condition of all other knowledge. As his biographer points out, he had himself, in his early days, experienced all the difficulties about the Infinite, of which Mansel made so much; but had been saved from doubt by his conviction that in the Incarnation God had revealed himself in His essential character.[3]

Yet such an answer begs the very questions with which Maurice and Mansel were embroiled. As we have seen Maurice is as concerned as Mansel with the fundamental contradictions of Christian belief; he has not so much ceased to doubt, as incorporated doubt into the structure of his belief. If Maurice's position had really appeared so very different from that of Mansel one would need to believe very strongly in the intellectual torpor of the Anglican Church to explain *why* Maurice's critique aroused so much astonishment. The whole point is that there was a much greater superficial *similarity* between Maurice's position and Mansel's than Storr is willing to allow – and just as there was sufficient similarity between Maurice's position and Carlyle's to ensure the latter's implacable scorn, so this apparent similarity

1 *The Limits of Religious Thought*, 2nd edn (1858), p. 72.
2 *What is Revelation?* (1859). Mansel replied the same year with *An Examination of the Rev. F. D. Maurice's Strictures on the Bampton Lectures of 1858.* Maurice returned to the attack in 1860 in his *Sequel to the Inquiry, 'What is Revelation?'*
3 Storr, *English Theology*, p. 421.

with Mansel was to drive Maurice to attack him with a fervour unusual even for himself in controversy. Mansel's position is far too close for comfort: it is like a heavy-footed parody of the very subtle structure that Maurice was struggling to expound in *The Kingdom of Christ*.[1]

Mansel was no more interested in Paleyite evidences of Christianity than Maurice. He believed, on the contrary, that there is a fundamental difference between the nature of scientific evidence and the evidence of Revelation or religious experience. The former is 'objective', pertains to a world of verifiable physical realities independent of the observer or his state of mind. The latter is 'subjective' – our evidence *is* the state of mind of the experiencer. This kind of distinction has a superficial empirical commonsense about it, and, in Mansel's case, there is no suggestion that the latter kind of evidence is of inferior status – it is merely different, and not open to the same kind of rational enquiry. But, as we have seen, this is the very distinction that Maurice is not prepared to accept under any pretext. His emphasis on the complexity and dual-focus of language was to show the *unity* of human experience. All human affairs are, to a greater or less degree, subject to the kind of problems exposed and highlighted by religious language. A central section of *The Kingdom of Christ* is devoted to an examination of how the Romantic movement in poetry has altered the consciousness of nineteenth-century man. To make it clear that this is not just a

---

[1] In a letter of 12 February 1832, the twenty-six year-old Maurice writing to his father shortly after becoming an Anglican describes the very tension under discussion with Mansel here. To see God, he writes,

...was the desire of Abraham, of Moses, of Job, of David, of Solomon, of Isaiah; they were practical men, and they wanted a practical revelation; a revelation which they could understand and grapple. God, they knew, must be for ever the Unsearchable, the Mysterious. They would not for worlds He should be anything else; for it was the glory of Judaism that their God was not a visible, intelligible idol, but an incomprehensible Spirit. Yet they longed to behold Him, and to behold Him so as they could understand Him. I would beseech you to observe attentively whether nearly every verse in the old Testament does not exhibit these two apparently opposite and most contradictory feelings; an acknowledgement of God as incomprehensible and infinite; a desire to see, to understand, to comprehend that same God.

Life, i, 135–6.

It is clear that Maurice's vision of religious language as one of tension between incompatible and irreconcilable opposites is closely associated in his mind with the decision to leave the Unitarians and join the Church of England – to leave an unambiguous rational faith for one of tension and contradiction.

matter of poetic or subjective consciousness, Maurice specifically includes the natural sciences:

... above all, nature itself has been, to a very great extent, conquered from the natural philosopher. Sympathies have been discovered between the beholder and the objects which are presented to him, and attempts to express these sympathies or investigate the conditions and laws under which they exist, have become the favourite, are threatening to become the exclusive, occupation of the more thoughtful and abstracted men in this time.[1]

The full impact of Romanticism on the physical sciences has yet to be studied.[2] Wordsworth had helped to stand eighteenth-century science on its head by showing how Newtonian optics implied not a Cartesian duality between observer and observed, but an *interaction*. His heart leaped up at the beholding of a rainbow not because it illustrated the laws of refraction of light, but because those same laws assured him of his own part in nature: there can be no rainbow without an observer.[3] What we mean by 'nature' pre-supposes the active participation of the naturalist. In other words, the state of emotion, of conditioning, and of ultimate uncertainty in which Mansel seemed to wish to retreat religious experience in order to safeguard it by special pleading, is for Maurice, in *The Kingdom of Christ*, the normal ground of all our endeavour. Science and poetry describe the same complex and inconsistent universe.

From about the middle of the last century, we may trace the commencement of a poetry which had a much more direct and substantive reference to the outward universe than that of earlier periods. The doings of men, as well as the songs in which they were celebrated, had become artificial and conventional: those whom domestic habits had inspired with a dislike of the hollowness of general society, or whom their early cultivation had taught to desire something more living and permanent than the modes of a particular generation, took refuge in nature.[4]

Poetry, claims Maurice, has led to a new way of seeing the

[1] I, 177.
[2] Among others, see Marjorie Hope Nicolson, *Newton Demands the Muse* (Archon Books, 1963) and E. A. Burtt, *Metaphysical Foundations of Modern Science* (Routledge, 1932), as well as the 'Introduction' to my own *Coleridge and Wordsworth*.
[3] Prickett, *Coleridge and Wordsworth*, pp. 10–11.
[4] I, 177–8.

outward material world. The work of Wordsworth, Coleridge, and Scott has helped to break down the old distinction between 'external' and 'internal' worlds and has shown how far each is dependent upon the other. The ambiguities now revealed in human perception reveal corresponding ambiguities in our notions of creativity and of science alike. When we speak of 'laws' in literature, in philosophy, or in nature, are we referring to qualities inherent in the objects themselves, or to constructs of the human mind? 'Is the man of genius the author of them, or does he merely perceive them, and adapt himself to them?'[1] The question is itself a product of the outmoded empiricist habit of mind: it is no longer meaningful.

It has been found impossible to affirm either position, to adopt either form of language as the sufficient and exclusive one. Those who endeavour to do so, are soon seen to contradict themselves; some unconscious phrase asserts in one sentence that which was denied in the previous one. It seems to follow, that the law of the imagination is a law of fellowship or intercommunion with nature; you cannot describe it in any terms which do not imply this to be the case; you cannot go deeper than to say, that it creates only so far as it sees, and that it sees only so far as it has the faculty of creating; just as sight and sound can neither be predicated solely of the eye nor of the thing beheld, of the ear nor of the thing heard, but are the product of both.[2]

To ask such questions and reject them is to begin to look at the world in a new way. Our attempts to describe man's relationship with his environment[3] are distinguished by a necessary and truthful inconsistency.[4] This profound and perpetual dualism, or, rather, tension, must be recognised as one of the foundations of human experience. At the simplest level this tension is present in the literal absurdity of every metaphor; at the opposite pole, it is to be found in the mystery of the Incarnation itself.

The development of a single metaphor illustrates how inseparable this tension is from our thinking about the nature of the Church:

. . . the Lord is throughout presented in the character of the *husband* of the nation; . . . acts of apostasy and false worship are constantly

[1] *The Kingdom of Christ*, I, p. 181.   [2] Ibid.

[3] The word 'environment' is a neologism of Carlyle's in *Sartor Resartus* (1831) and illustrates very well the new way of looking at the world which Maurice is describing.

[4] *The Kingdom of Christ*, I, 183.

referred to as adulteries;...the greatest pains are taken to convince us, that these are no poetical flourishes or terms of art, by connecting the actual human relation and human offence with the properly spiritual one. Oftentimes the verbal commentator is at fault, from the apparent confusion of the two. He cannot make up his mind whether it is the infidelity of the nation to her God, or of actual wives to their actual husbands, which the holy man is denouncing. And such perplexity there needs must be in the thoughts of all persons who are determined to separate these two ideas – who do not see that it is the main object of the prophet to shew their bearing upon one another, – who will not enter into his mind, by feeling that human relationships are not artificial types of something divine, but are actually the means and the only means, through which man ascends to any knowledge of the divine;[1]

A metaphor is a two-way process, and not a mere analogy. Behind the metaphor of adultery there lies another, even more important, metaphor: that of the *family*. It is this that binds together the members of the Kingdom – for Israel was unique among political entities in seeing itself simultaneously as an extended family. Here at the centre of Maurice's thinking about the Church we can see how his ideas of metaphor shape, and are shaped by his religious insights. For Israel the 'family' is both fact and image; for Christianity to lose this ambiguity, and to start to stress kinship as a simile or analogy only is to break this tension that it inherited from the Jewish faith. The sense of family gives to the Bible a 'pervasive unity' that transcends the differences between individual books.[2] The Children of Israel were not a 'gathered' sect, linked by common affirmations of belief, they were – as their name reminded them – born into it. The Patriarchs were first and foremost relatives. Jacob, says Maurice, stands a witness to the fact that God's people were founded on family relationship and not on choice.[3] It is against this background that we must understand both Hosea's metaphors of adultery and Jesus's description of God as 'father'.

Such an argument exhibits another strand in the complex web of Maurice's thought about the Church. Throughout *The Kingdom of Christ* Maurice follows the Old Testament typological pattern by which history is charged with a dual meaning. It exists both as an end in itself at every stage, and, simultaneously, points

---

[1] I, 280–1.   [2] I, 274.   [3] I, 275.

always beyond itself. The Kingdom of Christ is both utterly transcendent and a part of the historical process. Thus the Kingdom of David was, compared with what preceded it, both a good in itself, being based on moral principles unlike those of any other empire, and, by this very uniqueness, it foreshadows and reveals typologically the coming kingdom of which it fell so far short.[1] It is one more step along the path.

For Coleridge, the model for *Church and State* evolved simultaneously from his picture of Biblical history on the one hand,[2] and from his critical notions of an 'Idea' and 'Symbol'. Similarly, for Maurice, far more deeply rooted in Biblical and historical modes of thought than Coleridge, the concept of the Church as a universal spiritual society grows both from Coleridge[3] and from the new canons of literary and historical criticism that the German theologians were applying to scripture. Yet the differences are as important as the similarities. Coleridge's dualism between two separate ideas in the Church of England seems to be thought of as perpetual and unresolvable; for Maurice, possessed by a vision of history as change and fulfilment, this polarity becomes a dynamic dialectic.[4] An institution may indeed – as Coleridge and Newman recognised – be both corrupt and God-filled, but these cannot be eternal polarities – otherwise history would be meaningless. The indwelling Spirit of Christ shapes and uses the corrupt form, but is not shaped by it. Everywhere man is subject to the divine dialectic: he cannot be content with a spiritual society that is not universal, or with a universal society that is not spiritual.[5]

Maurice's later Christian Socialism springs directly from this conviction. Unlike both the Tractarians and the Evangelicals, his concern for poverty and its accompanying educational deprivation was not an extension of the old idea of 'charity', but a principle of social theology. A universal spiritual society ultimately implied a redistribution of wealth. His foundation of the London Working Men's College was not an offshoot of Christian Socialism, it was fundamental to it – an expression of his vision of man as a whole being. Social justice meant nothing without education – by

---

[1] *The Kingdom of Christ*, I, 288–9.

[2] Not a very accurate picture. Coleridge's historical weakness was that he scanned the past for illustrations of general metaphysical principle rather than looking at detail or for the stubbornly intransigent exception.

[3] *Life*, I, 178.   [4] *The Kingdom of Christ*, I, 296–300.   [5] I, 252.

which he meant not the 3 Rs of the Dickensian ragged school, but an ideal of learning and articulate reasoning that he had learnt in tutorials with Hare at Trinity. If the Working Men's Colleges were to embody the ideals of the Kingdom of Christ there was no place in them for either snobbery or the intellectually second-rate. Anyone who reads the lectures of Maurice or Robertson to Working Men's Associations is left in no doubt as to how much they demanded – and presumably received – from their audiences.

The paradox of Maurice's vision of the Church is that his emphasis on its 'openness' and universal inclusiveness is based on a sense of its historical tradition far stronger than Coleridge's and more akin to that of Newman and the Oxford Movement. His account of the growth of the idea of the Church as a universal and spiritual society is one of slow and painful evolution, with 'truth...working itself out into clearness for many centuries' through a 'strange and painful process'.[1] Christianity is not a sect professing certain clear-cut notions. It would, for instance, be 'hard to establish in a court of law the identity of the dogmas of the New Testament with those which prevailed in Scotland and Germany during the eighteenth century.[2] Indeed, the vigour of this unique universal spiritual society depends on the dialectic of tensions within it. Just as at a linguistic level scripture is charged with a metaphorical tension by which the concepts of family, adultery, and fatherhood acquire themselves a new meaning from the use to which they are put, so the perpetual tension between the Church as an outward physical organisation and as an inner spiritual society re-shapes our ideas of what it means both to be an organisation, and a spiritual society. Maurice's chosen title illustrates this tension.[3] The ideas of the kingship of God and the fatherhood of God are inseparable poles of Christian experience. The 'Kingdom' of Christ *is* a 'family'. 'The deepest writings of the New Testament, instead of being digests of doctrine, are epistles, explaining to those who had been admitted into the Church of Christ their own position.'[4] Epistles are personal, concrete and particular in reference, and sent within a family. The tension between organisation and spirit is present in

---

[1] II, 75.   [2] I, 159. For an expansion of this point see next chapter.

[3] The stress on Christ's Church as a 'Kingdom' seems to have come to Maurice from the Rev. J. A. Stephenson of Lympsham. *Life*, I, 167.

[4] *The Kingdom of Christ*, I, 296.

the Old Testament, and helps to create the peculiar paradox of Jewish history, but from the time of Christ and the universalising of the Kingdom this tension has been central to the experience of God's people. It is, for Maurice, the necessary dual focus of a universal spiritual society. If one forgets this dual focus, one can slip into the assumption that the spirit is good and the organisation bad – a kind of unconscious Manicheism. Maurice, in fact, believes that each is a good – but only in so far as it exists in tension with the other. Each needs the other if it is to be properly itself. Hence his interest in examining, among others, the Quakers and the Roman Catholics who seem to represent the two extremes of thought about the nature of the Church. The subtitle of *The Kingdom of Christ* is 'Hints to a Quaker Respecting the Principles, Constitution, and Ordinances of the Catholic Church', and the first version (1838) is arranged in the form of a series of letters to a Quaker. The Quakers, Maurice maintains, have laid such one-sided stress on 'inner light' that they have come to see organisation as, at best, a necessary evil. Lacking a sense of polarity, they confuse one pole with the other.

The mere spiritual faculty, which is awakened in him by the voice of the Spirit of God, will be confounded with that Spirit himself; His personality will be forgotten in His operations; there will be a fearful confusion between the human speaker and the invisible power which speaks in him, alternating with a continual attempt to separate them; the intellectual faculties and endowments will first be despised because they have no connexion with the Spirit; and then will be confounded with the faculty which is truly Divine and spiritual in man, when both are found to proceed from the same source, and the former to be the means of evoking the latter.[1]

In a very deep sense they have failed to grasp the meaning of the Incarnation, and what they have created is the religion of the Old Testament. The Quaker is 'the reviver of the old economy while he is professing to assert the glory of the Gospel'.[2]

The Church of Rome, in contrast, rests upon an essentially 'vicarial' system: the power of the priest – and ultimately that of the Pope – depends upon the assumption that he is acting for someone (i.e. Christ) who is absent and who 'only at certain times and under certain conditions, presents himself to men'.[3] In other words, for the Roman Catholic, 'the veil between us and

---

[1] *The Kingdom of Christ*, ii, 142.   [2] ii, 136.   [3] ii, 172.

the invisible world is not yet withdrawn; . . . offices and ordinances are not the organs through which men converse with their Lord and He with them, but are mere outward things, which He has stamped with a certain authority and virtue, or mere pictures which exhibit Him to the imagination'.[1] The result of denying the inner light is to devalue the outward ordinances. The papal system is not therefore a 'corruption' of the idea of the Church, such as might arise from excessive emphasis of one aspect at the expense of others, but a 'counterfeit' that, in denying one aspect, violates *both* the idea *and* the organisation.[2]

As with the polarity within the Church, so with the polarity between Church and State. Here Maurice's debt to Coleridge is generously acknowledged,[3] but, as always, he is never interested in merely paraphrasing Coleridge: he develops him. The tension between Church and State is not fortuitous (a 'happy accident' in Coleridge's phrase) but necessary to the true meaning of each.

What I have been endeavouring to maintain is, that a nation just so far as it is a nation, is anti-secular in one way, just as much as the Church is anti-secular in another. Both are God's appointed instruments for resisting the evil, rebellious, disorderly principles which make up the scriptural notion of 'this world'. . . The Church has become secular when she has attempted to realise herself as a separate body; the Nation has become secular when it has tried to realise itself as a separate body. But each does so, by violating the law of its existence, by refusing to be that which the Scriptures affirm and history proves that it was meant to be.[4]

Maurice's vision of the spiritual value of the nation (in its true rôle in polarity with the Church) is not merely the nineteenth-century English liberal's assumption of the self-evident virtues of nationalism – though he undoubtedly shared those assumptions. National, for him, is not the antithesis of universal; it is rather the necessary condition of universality. To belong to a universal society, a man must have roots in one particular place.

---

[1] Ibid.   [2] II, 177.

[3] The little book upon Church and State you will suppose, from the title and character of these volumes, that I am likely to have studied still more attentively. And, indeed, if you watch me closely, you will discover, I doubt not, many more thoughts which I have stolen from it than I am at all aware of, though I think I am conscious of superabundant obligations. . .

The Kingdom of Christ, Dedication to 2nd edn (1842) to the Rev. Derwent Coleridge, p. xx.

[4] II, 297.

The man who is at home everywhere, is at home nowhere. In embryo a Coleridgean position, this is an argument we find restated in the twentieth century by both T. S. Eliot and Simone Weil.[1]

Where the *State* professes to *be* the Church we get one kind of tyranny; where the Church professes to *be* the State we get another – similar to the first, and no less repugnant. In the former case, the State can only command spiritual obedience by the same means that it can command civil obedience: namely, the law. But the spirit is moved not by law, but by love, and so, as the Romans found, the result is self-defeating. In the latter case – that, say, of the Scottish Covenanters – there results the same kind of counter-productive attempt at coercion from the opposite motives.[2] The new dispensation brought by Christ is a liberation from the old dispensation of Jewish theocracy. Similarly, Maurice argues, a State *without* a Church is bound to become a tyranny, for it is forced eventually to try and suppress whoever stands in judgement on it. The preservation of liberty does not depend on the virtue – or otherwise – of the rulers and politicians who constitute the civil power. In a unitary or monolithic state Christian rulers will be subject to the same pressures as any other leaders to move against the opinions and ideas that threaten to divide the community deeply. Toleration, he claims, is only possible where there is another power, separate from that of the State, to command spiritual allegiance and defend the fundamental values of the society.[3]

The outward polarity of Church and State rests on the inner polarity between the conflicting demands of love and law. Maurice's belief that the Church is an open, all-embracing, universal spiritual society does not mean that he sees love as replacing law,[4] any more than law can replace love. The problem is rather to preserve their polarity:

How can these two sets of duties, apparently so opposite, be fulfilled? Clearly, there is the greatest danger in omitting either; there is the greatest danger in confusing them. What weak, ineffectual lovers we

---

[1] T. S. Eliot, *Notes Towards a Definition of Culture* (Faber, 1947), and Introduction to Simone Weil's *The Need for Roots* (Routledge, 1952).

[2] *The Kingdom of Christ*, ii, 294.

[3] Maurice would, no doubt, have seen much of the history of liberty in the twentieth century as vindication of this view.

[4] *The Kingdom of Christ*, ii, 283.

are, when love is separated from law, we have hinted at already; what monstrous perverters of the Divine law when we set up law against love, it requires no words to explain. But do we fare much better if we try to keep up a balancing system in our minds? Not too much love, lest you should grow lax – not too much law, lest you should become cruel. Will this kind of see-saw satisfy any man who wishes to be honest to himself and his fellow creatures? Not too much love! How can there be too much, if dying for love was not too much? Not too much law! How can there be too much, if the destruction of cities and empires, yea, of a world, for the sake of it was not too much? Then, I say, if it be so, there must be some distinct Divine scheme for asserting the dignity and glory of each; for upholding love in its fulness lest law should perish; for upholding law in its fulness lest love should perish.[1]

What, then, is this 'Divine scheme'? How does it operate? Maurice's answer is cryptic to the point of being startling:

By acting in concert with each of them, a man shall find that the feeling of God's universal love in himself does not clash with the feeling of God's eternal and unchangeable law; that his perception of his own duties, inward and external, and of the perfect compatibleness of those which seem most opposed, waxes clearer and clearer; and, by refusing to act in concert with each of these schemes, he shall find one set of duties continually interfering with another, the peculiar temper of his mind determining which he shall prefer, which neglect.[2]

Here, if anywhere, it would seem that the criticisms made by Arnold, Mill, Carlyle, and Maurice's other antagonists have most substance. Maurice has promised us a key to polarity, a 'Divine scheme' that enables the Kingdom of Christ to reconcile opposite and discordant qualities without making those qualities any the less themselves – and what does he offer us? A pious hope that all things work together for the best for those who love the Lord? Somehow, it will all be all right in the end? It is a pardonable interpretation – but, I think, a mistaken one. When Maurice is being pious, he is also often being at his most complex. Again we need to be reminded of the strongly existentialist strand in his thought. He is one of those who 'must know whether he has any ground to stand upon'; he is one of those who 'cannot look at anything as apart from themselves'. There are in his solution, we notice, two distinct elements: the first is *obedience*, the second is *feeling*. By acting in obedience in given situations

---

[1] *The Kingdom of Christ*, II, 283–4.   [2] II, 284.

as they arise, the Christian finds he feels the incompatibles compatible; by failing to act, he feels their philosophical incompatibility, and is left adrift to be guided by his own arbitrary preferences. There is here a paradox about 'feeling' of which Maurice is keenly aware. 'Feeling' is the product not merely of obedience, but of action – rather than, as one might expect, vice versa. It is not to be confused with mere preference. In other words, feeling is not a guide to behaviour, but an end product to which Maurice seems to be according something of the status of a value.

Theologically, this significance given to feeling may have parallels with Schleiermacher – but I do not think that theology proper is the source of Maurice's use of the word here. It is interesting to notice that the word is very widely used in the first half of the nineteenth century in this sense of being almost a value in itself. It is the key to Teufelsdrockh's 'conversion' and salvation in *Sartor Resartus*; even more important it is a word that occurs over and over again in chapter V of Mill's *Autobiography* as he describes his own spiritual crisis and recovery through reading the poetry of Wordsworth. For Arnold, too, 'feeling' is a word of immense significance, conveying most vividly what Wordsworth's poetry has meant to Europe:

But who, ah who, will make us feel?[1]

Yet in spite of his acknowledged influence on Keble and Newman, it is still all too easy to overlook the enormous influence Wordsworth had on the development of English theology in these years. To some extent this is a matter of *kinds* of influence. The contrast with Coleridge is instructive. The Coleridge who was important to nineteenth-century thought was Coleridge the metaphysician and theologian,[2] not Coleridge the poet – even though it would be true to say that Coleridge could only have been the massive theological influence he was because he remained first and foremost a poet.[3] Wordsworth's influence, in contrast, is not theoretical at all. His achievement was that he transformed the whole *climate* of feeling in the first half of the nineteenth century in England. He was not a source of ideas, but he had a very great

---

[1] *Memorial Verses* (On the Death of Wordsworth), April 1850.

[2] See, for instance, Mill's essay *Bentham and Coleridge*, or F. J. A. Hort's essay, 'Coleridge', *Cambridge Essays*.

[3] Prickett, *Coleridge and Wordsworth*, ch. 7.

effect on the emotional structure which produced and nourished those ideas. His influence is pervasive and diffuse rather than concentrated and specific, but the testimony of such temperamental opposites as Mill and Keble is strong evidence of his power over the emotional development of a whole generation. What Wordsworth offered sensitive minds in the 1820s and 30s (in a way that not even Coleridge could) was the affirmation that man was more than a mere biological mechanism: he was a creature of profound and subtle feelings. 'Feelings' became for many Wordsworthians a touchstone of their humanity – a proof of Being. It is easy for the modern reader, outside this emotional climate, to misunderstand the impact of a poem like *Simon Lee*, which is a poem about feeling. Wordsworth not merely asserted the value of feeling – he showed it as an artist, as a poet. His readers could *feel* the value of feeling. In a vulgarised strain a similar spirit had entered the novel – responsible, alas!, for some of Dickens' weepiest writing, which dates from this period.

The influence of Wordsworth on Maurice has not received the same attention as that of Coleridge, partly for the reasons suggested above. Nevertheless, the degree to which Maurice's theology shares this climate of feeling is self-evident. More specifically, the debt to Wordsworth is very clearly marked in chapter IV of part I of *The Kingdom of Christ* where Maurice describes the progress of the idea of man as a spiritual being. Without giving names, he writes of a poetry which 'was the calm utterance of a calm mind, which had sought to discover what bonds of fellowship existed between it and men of all different orders and degrees. Nature was evidently a common thing in which lord and peasant might participate, from which no prescriptions and formalities could exclude.'[1] Wordsworth, for Maurice, is not merely responsible for a new vision of the relationship between man and nature – a relationship in which the feelings of the observer are themselves a part of what we mean by nature –[2] but he is also the poet of universal inclusiveness. This, for the author of the book proclaiming the universal spiritual society as including all mankind, is clearly of central importance. The idea of the 'Imagination' evolved over a decade

[1] I, 179.
[2] There is a striking similarity between Maurice's view and that of Mill in his 'Wordsworthian' argument with Roebuck. *Autobiography*, pp. 128–9.

of close poetic and philosophic collaboration between Coleridge and Wordsworth involves, for them,[1] a belief in a fundamental spiritual nature common to all mankind. The mark of this spiritual nature is a feeling of communion. Maurice writes:

> I cannot but think that those who have detected this law of the imagination – this law of sympathy and communion between themselves and that which is distinct from them, have been assailed by a conviction which they cannot resist or part with, that *some* such law of communion is the law of their whole life; that life is an unintelligible blank without it; that here must be the key to its deepest mysteries.[2]

The fundamental law of polarity to which the Church bears witness at every level of its activity is based, for Maurice, not on a dialectical system of thought, but on a feeling – which the honest man must acknowledge. 'The sincere minds who have given currency to this tone of thought and speech, or to whom it conveys a real meaning, will exhibit their difference from the rest by their inconsistency.'[3] Maurice in fact wishes to assert the primacy of feeling over systematic thought even when it is not necessary to do so, for to do otherwise would be to invert his scale of values. Wordsworth has taught Maurice to live in a universe informed by feeling: not in a mechanism, but a divinely ordered communion – a coinherence of man and nature. It is the ultimate safeguard and guarantee of man as a spiritual being. It bears witness to the divine nature of the imagination.

This, indeed, is what the Kingdom of Christ is all about. It is, for Maurice, the paradigm of the inescapable and irresolvable polarity of all human experience. The universal spiritual society, as yet existing in potential rather than actuality, is of a piece with the rest of our existence, but immanent in it, shaping and organising it into an organic whole. Wholeness is the prerogative of the Church. In an autobiographical fragment he writes: 'The desire for *Unity* has haunted me all my life through; I have never been able to substitute any desire for that, or to accept any of the different schemes for satisfying it which men have devised.'[4] What men cannot devise, God can. He continues, 'I not only believe in the Trinity in Unity, but I find in it the centre of all

---

[1] This is not true of all the Romantics. Schelling's view of the Imagination, for example, is strictly elitist. See Shawcross' notes to *Biographia Literaria*, vol. I, ch. XIII.

[2] *The Kingdom of Christ*, I, 182.   [3] I, 183.   [4] *Life*, I, 41.

my beliefs.' As in the Trinity, the 'wholeness' that Maurice finds in the Church is not a synthesis, but rather sense or *feeling* of unity-in-tension: an affirmation that the universe is not dead mechanism, but Life. The Incarnation of Christ, whose body is the Church, is the revelation of ultimate meaning in the historical process of growth and development for which the 'family' exists.

6

Newman versus Maurice: Development of Doctrine and the Growth of the Mind

At Oxford, the Long Vacation of 1839 began early. On 13 June, the day after the Commemoration at which Keble paid his moving tribute to Wordsworth, another chain of events of far more dramatic long-term significance was set in motion. John Henry Newman, Fellow of Oriel and Vicar of St Mary's, began reading about the Monophysites.

There had been a great many visitors to Oxford from Easter to Commemoration; and Dr. Pusey and myself had attracted attention, more, I think, than in any former year. I had put away the controversy with Rome for more than two years... I was returning, for the Vacation, to a course of reading which I had many years before chosen as especially my own. I have no reason to suppose that the thoughts of Rome came across my mind at all. About the middle of June I began to study and master the history of the Monophysites. I was absorbed in the doctrinal question. This was from about June 13 to August 30. It was during the course of this reading that for the first time a doubt came upon me of the tenableness of Anglicanism.[1]

As he read, he tells us, 'I saw my face in that mirror, and I was a Monophysite.' The position and claims of the Anglican *via media* in relation to Rome could be closely compared with those of the Monophysite heresy of the fifth century. 'There was an awful similitude, more awful because silent and unimpassioned, between the dead records of the past and the feverish chronicle of the present.' Ranged against the Anglicans and the Monophysites alike was the awful *authority* of Rome. An article of Cardinal Wiseman's in the *Dublin Review* was put into his hands which quoted an ambiguous phrase of St Augustine: '*Securus judicat orbis terrarum*'.[2] In these words, which struck him with a power

[1] *Apologia*, p. 108.
[2] An almost untranslatable sentence. Faber suggests as a 'paraphrase': 'The judgement of the whole world cannot be shaken' (p. 415). It is interesting to

which he had never felt from any words before,[1] Newman felt concentrated the judgement of eighteen hundred years of the Catholic Church upon his own Communion. But Newman's feelings were as complicated as his intellect. His movement towards Rome was agonisingly slow – for himself, and for the devoted band of disciples who accompanied him. In the end, most of them were to break ranks and be received before their leader. *Tract Ninety*, in which he tried to show how every one of the Thirty-Nine Articles could be interpreted in a 'Catholic' sense, was not published until 21 February 1841 – his fortieth birthday. The storm that then broke was clearly the beginning of the end – clearly to everyone except Newman, who still held back. Even the Bishop of Oxford's condemnation of the Tract in his charge of May 1842 still did not speed the death-throes of Newman's Anglican existence. It was not until September 1843 that he preached his last sermon as an Anglican at Littlemore. Just over two years later, on 9 October 1845, he was finally received into the arms of Mother Church who had been so long awaiting him.

During this interval, between March 1844 and September 1845 he wrote his *Essay on the Development of Christian Doctrine*. In effect, it punctuates with peculiar emphasis the gap between the two halves of Newman's life: it was written in limbo, defending the claims of a Church he did not belong to with the weapons of the Church that had abandoned him. It starts from the conviction, based on his study of the Fathers, that 'one thing at least is certain, whatever history teaches, whatever it omits, whatever it exaggerates or extenuates, whatever it says and unsays, at least the Christianity of history is not Protestantism'.[2] When it was finished, Newman offered it to his new Roman Catholic superior. Bishop Baggs with due caution referred it, and its author, to Cardinal Wiseman, who, after some hesitation, declined to look at the book at all before publication – on the ground that it was a fact which 'all his seeing could not alter'. When it was finally published in November 1845, Newman inserted a Preface absolving the Roman Catholic Church from all responsibility for its

compare Wiseman's own translation, '...the entire world judges with security', with Newman's, 'The universal Church is in its judgements secure of truth' (*Apologia*, p. 543).

[1] *Apologia*, p. 110.
[2] *Essay on the Development of Doctrine* (Sheed & Ward, 1960), p. 6.

contents, and declaring complete submission 'to the judgement of the Church with whose doctrines . . .' he wished 'all his thoughts to be coincident'. A week later it went into a second printing.

The *Essay* is, he tells us, 'a hypothesis to account for a difficulty'.[1] Historical research could show beyond reasonable doubt that every contemporary version of Christianity revealed marked differences in doctrine and practice from the early Church. Newman believed that one contemporary Church – the Church of Rome – was more like its ancestor than any other. But did age alone account for the changes? The essence of Newman's answer was apparently simple, even if its applications were less so. Christianity, he tells us, is to be considered as a single organic 'idea'. In spite of seeming diversity and contradiction its unity is clear *provided* we look at it from the right standpoint – that is, not as something immutable and rock-like, but rather as a living organic unity. Thus it has no 'leading idea' which dominates the rest, or which can be separated from the whole. No one aspect of Revelation can be 'allowed to exclude or obscure another; . . . Christianity is dogmatical, devotional, practical all at once; it is esoteric and exoteric; it is indulgent and strict; it is light and dark; it is love and it is fear.'[2] This organic unity is demonstrated simply by the fact that the 'idea' is *alive*. It is not received passively by men, 'but it becomes an active principle within them, leading them to an ever-new contemplation of itself, to an application of it in various directions, and a propagation of it on every side'.[3] In short, it displays the common characteristic of all living organisms: it is in a continual process of growth and change. Developments of doctrine are, therefore, not difficulties to be accounted for, but what we should expect:

If Christianity is a fact, and impresses an idea of itself on our minds and is a subject matter of exercises of the reason, that idea will in course of time expand into a multitude of ideas, and aspects of ideas, connected and harmonious with one another, and in themselves determinate and immutable, as is the objective fact itself which is thus represented.[4]

Indeed, the true test of Catholicity is not just which Church is most like the supposed primitive form, but also which has shown the greatest power of organic development. Bossuet had declared

---

[1] *Essay on the Development of Doctrine*, p. 22.
[2] Ibid. p. 27.   [3] Ibid. p. 27.   [4] Ibid. p. 41.

a simple test of heresy: change. If it was new, it *must* by that very fact be false.[1] Newman now argues that only by change can true doctrine be preserved. What is unchanging is untrue because it does not live in men's hearts and minds. 'The more claim an idea has to be considered living,' he declares, 'the more various will be its aspects; and the more social and political its nature, the more complicated and subtle will be its issues, and the longer and more eventful will be its course.'[2]

Unfortunately, however, not all changes are good changes. There is, for instance, Protestantism. In a situation of progressive change, how are we to distinguish between 'growth' – what he calls 'genuine development' – and decay or 'corruption'? Newman's answer is a series of seven tests of 'organic growth': 1. Preservation of Type; 2. Continuity of Principles; 3. Assimilative Power; 4. Logical Sequence; 5. Anticipation of its Future; 6. Conservative Action on its Past; and 7. Chronic Vigour. Nearly all branches of Christendom will satisfy one or more of these conditions, but only the Church of Rome displays them all. Newman does not, be it noticed, believe in 'Progress'.

The *Essay* was widely read and widely reviewed with equally varying degrees of incomprehension. Reactions of Anglican critics ranged from anger to amusement. Few possessed the scholarly apparatus to meet him on his own ground. Gladstone was deeply disturbed by its possible effects, and cast around for a promising Anglican champion to match the reluctant but formidable renegade. At first he favoured Robert Wilberforce, son of William Wilberforce the reformer, and brother of Samuel, the new Bishop of Oxford,[3] but more and more he came to pin his hopes for an effective counterblast on the Wilberforces' brother-in-law, Henry Manning, Archdeacon of Chichester.[4] Manning was a rising young man in the Church of England, and as a scholar he was, perhaps, most nearly Newman's equal. In the event, Manning, the future Cardinal and Archbishop of Westminster, defected to Rome in April 1851,[5] whereas Robert needed the combined persuasion of Newman, Manning, and his recently converted

---

[1] See Owen Chadwick, *From Bossuet to Newman* (Cambridge, 1957), ch. 1.

[2] *Essay on the Development of Doctrine*, p. 41.

[3] 'Soapy Sam'.

[4] Newsome, *The Parting of Friends*, chs. 6–8, pp. 255–397.

[5] Newman's *Essay* was not the principal cause of Manning's conversion, but it certainly seems to have been a contributory factor.

brother, Henry, before finally capitulating to Rome in October 1854.[1]

On the whole, however, Catholic critics, as distinct from Anglican converts, found Newman's reasons for submitting to Holy Mother Church as tortuous and eccentric as many found his reasons for leaving the *Via Media*. In America the *Essay* was flung at a scandalised Catholic community by the Unitarians, who used it as evidence to argue that the Doctrine of the Trinity was not primitive, but a development of the third century.[2] One Catholic theologian, to whom Newman presented a copy of the *Essay* wrote, no doubt hoping to encourage him, 'Allow me to say that as you advance in the sweet participation of Catholic Communion, your mind will happily develop, and you will understand as a man, and think as a man, and speak as a man . . .'[3] Catholic theology in the 1840s was still scholastic and even syllogistic in emphasis, and the Jesuit theologians who dominated the Roman colleges at this time found Newman's historical and philosophical approach so far outside their academic tradition as to be almost unintelligible. Aquinas and even Aristotle were honoured without being read,[4] and the tradition of the British empiricists was, of course, totally unfamiliar to them. Oxford men are not noted for their humility, and Newman was not one to take kindly to being patronised by his intellectual inferiors, whether former colleagues or those who represented the judgement of the Church to whose doctrines he had just announced his total submission. Though he knew little of the new movements in Germany at first hand (he had a tendency to avoid reading things that might weaken his faith), through Pusey he knew more than Rome did; he had read the Fathers in depth; he had also read Hume at the age of fourteen, and Bentham only a little later; he was, moreover, reared in the English literary and linguistic tradition of Wordsworth, Coleridge, and Keble.

As a result, few authors can ever have been less inclined to give ground to critics. Since the *Essay* contained his reasons, on historical grounds, for quitting the Anglican fold, it was hardly likely that he would easily be prepared to modify his position in

[1] Newsome, *The Parting of Friends*, pp. 361–97.
[2] Ward, *Life of Newman*, I, 159–60.
[3] F. C. Husenbeth. See Chadwick, *From Bossuet to Newman*, p. 165, and n. 236.
[4] Ward, *Life of Newman*, I, 472.

response to criticism from his former co-religionists. In five agonising years he had thought through their position already. But from the quarter where he most earnestly desired serious criticism there was simply no meeting of minds. Owen Chadwick, having made a detailed study of Newman's notes for the revised third edition of the *Essay* in 1878,[1] concludes that most of the alterations are mere tinkering. There is, he argues, no substantial change in Newman's thinking between 1845 and 1878. There is no evidence of concessions to Roman scholasticism, and none that he altered a single line in response to any of his Anglican critics.[2]

Evidence, however, depends in part on the questions we ask of our data – and upon the expectations those questions imply. If we concentrate solely on direct evidence, the letters, notes, and other writings, where we are apparently on safest ground, we may get a clearer picture of a writer's *intentions* than of his actual results. Among his Anglican reviews was one by F. D. Maurice. It has not attracted the same kind of critical attention that, say, James Mozley's has – and it is easy to see why. It appeared as the Preface to Maurice's *Lectures on the Epistle to the Hebrews* in 1846 and is well over 100 pages in length – about the same as the three lectures put together. A rambling, if patchily brilliant critique, it is difficult to summarise because of the apparent diffuseness of the central argument. Yet there is strong circumstantial evidence to suggest that Newman (consciously or unconsciously) was peculiarly sensitive to parts of Maurice's criticism in a way that he was not to others. If we compare the first and third editions of Newman's *Essay* we find some of his most important changes concern points raised by Maurice; others pass totally unheeded. But to see these alterations as significant rather than coincidental we need to look outside the confines of theology as such – and to examine more closely Maurice's approach.

Maurice's tone is unexpected. He makes it clear that this review is part of his discussion of *Hebrews*, and not mere publishing opportunism, for *Hebrews*, he tells us, contains the 'true doctrine of development'. In other words he is not challenging Newman's

---

[1] The second edition appeared in 1846, too close after the first for reviews to have had any influence on Newman.

[2] Chadwick, *From Bossuet to Newman*, p. 165.

central thesis at all: that there is development he has no doubt, and he believes development, moreover, to be an essentially Biblical doctrine. He agrees wholeheartedly with Newman's main contention that Christianity is an 'idea' living and growing organically in men's minds:

Nothing, I think, can be more just and striking than his description of a strong conviction upon a mind which has become possessed with it; how it must work and cannot be let; how it must grow and cannot remain in its first seed; how it must communicate itself to other minds, and be affected by all it finds in them; how spiritual conflicts, and conflicts in the world, the one always answering the other, must prove its soundness and strength.[1]

His praise for Newman runs throughout the review. Where he disagrees, he is at pains to be fair, quoting at inordinate length in order not to distort or seem to be carping at snippets wrenched from context. Though the review follows Newman's order, its criticism can be divided roughly into two kinds: first, of his historical logic, and, second, of his philosophic and linguistic approach – especially over the meaning of such key concepts as 'idea' and 'method'.

To the casual reader, the first line of argument appears to be the most damning. Newman's argument, Maurice points out, is circular. He has defined 'Fidelity to Type' in terms of the Roman Church, and then lucidly demonstrates that only the Roman Church has this 'fidelity' so defined. This 'monstrous contradiction'[2] in logic leads him into errors of fact. Thus Newman's assumption of the self-evident perversion of Protestantism leads him to statements like: 'Lutheranism, as is well-known, has by this time become simple heresy or infidelity.' Maurice replies bluntly: 'This fact is not well-known; Mr. Newman does not know it himself; if he believes that Dr. Pusey's work on Germany is the work of an honest eye-witness, he knows the contrary.'[3] Newman, however, remained sublimely untroubled by this kind of refutation. His intense intellectualism was matched by a no less intense scepticism about the powers of the intellect – especially the intellect unguided by faith. The *Essay* describes what is, to him, self-evident and unassailable, and denials on the ground of logical circularity simply miss the point. It is 'a hypothesis to

[1] Preface to *Lectures on the Epistle to the Hebrews*, p. xii.
[2] Ibid. p. xvii.   [3] Ibid. lxxxvii.

account for a difficulty', and the testing of all hypotheses must, in this sense, be circular. We do not decide on the true Church by logic or even argument: we *recognise* it. When we meet it, we are left in no doubt about just what is we have encountered:

There is a religious communion claiming a divine commission, and holding all other bodies around it heretical or infidel; it is a well-organized well-disciplined body; it is a sort of secret society, binding together its members by influences and by engagements which it is difficult for strangers to ascertain. It is spread over the known world; it may be weak or insignificant locally, but it is strong on the whole from its continuity; it may be smaller than all other religious bodies together, but it is larger than each separately. It is a natural enemy to governments external to itself; it is intolerant and engrossing, and tends to a new modelling of society; it breaks laws, it divides families. It is a gross superstition: it is charged with the foulest crimes; it is despised by the intellect of the day; it is frightful to the imagination of many. And there is but one communion such.[1]

Anyone, pagan or Protestant, who stubs his toe on this rock, knows it for what it is. 'Place this description before Pliny or Julian; place it before Frederick the Second or Guizot...Each knows at once, without asking a question, who is meant by it.'

Though in the re-arranged 1878 edition this passage appears at the beginning of chapter VI instead of chapter IV, it remains word-for-word the same. However, the passage immediately preceding it in chapter IV of the first edition is completely omitted in the course of this re-shuffling. It read as follows:

It was said, then, that a true development retains the *essential idea* of the subject from which it has proceeded, and a corruption loses it. What then is the true idea of Christianity? and is it preserved in the developments commonly called Catholic, and the Church which embodies and teaches them?[2]

Maurice's attack on this looks at first sight like an extension of his general charge of 'circularity', but this proves to be merely a mask for what turns out to be his second line of criticism – which is couched in a very different set of terms. Maurice is concerned with the meaning Newman has attached to the word 'idea'. Newman, he points out, has been very careful up to this point never to say that Christianity *is* an 'idea'. It is a 'fact' which excites an

[1] *Essay on the Development of Doctrine*, p. 150.
[2] *Essay on the Development of Doctrine*, 1st edn (1845), p. 204.

'idea' in the mind. The idea, we recall, varies according to the sensibilities and predispositions of those who happen to hold it. Such is the organic unity of Christianity that it can have no 'leading idea', according to Newman, since the whole is greater than the parts. Whence, then, comes this phrase *'essential idea'* at the beginning of chapter IV? Doesn't it sound suspiciously like the notion of a 'leading idea' that Newman rejected at the outset? What is Newman up to? Is he playing with a misleading tactical definition of terms? There seems to have been a shift in the meaning of the word 'idea'. At the outset Newman uses the word in connection with the impossibility of imposing one particular pattern upon the multiplicity and richness of Christian experience; now he redeploys it to discover the unity of the emerging Catholic Church. In the former case the word suggests rigid mechanical organisation; in the latter it is invoked as a unifier of diversity, so that just as a painter portrays different aspects of a man within a single portrait and yet harmonises them, so the 'leading idea' does not dominate but creates and reveals the essential unity of all the constituents. Isn't this latter use of the word, asks Maurice, the normal one? Certainly it is the meaning Newman himself adopts later in the *Essay*. Under 'Logical Sequence' we find him declaring that 'knowledge of the essential idea, the type of Christianity, is necessary...for the purpose of studying the actual history of Christianity'. Here, Maurice observes, Newman has modified the meaning of 'essential idea' to something much closer to the ordinary meaning. In one sense the ostensible weight of the attack falls on *what* Newman is saying, in other words that his arrangement is dishonest and 'circular', but Maurice presses the charge well beyond the immediate needs of the case – into *how* Newman is saying it. He seems deeply disturbed by the contradictions he suspects lurk inside Newman's concept of the 'organic'. The word 'idea', as Newman attempts to define it, retains an eighteenth-century empiricist flavour[1] that contrasts uneasily with the far more organic and Romantic connotations it acquires in the heat of composition.

In the light of this criticism of Maurice's, Newman's revisions of the text in 1878 are striking. He is impervious to the general charge of circularity, and there is no change in the main structure

---

[1] See, for instance, the definition of an 'idea' in Hume's *Treatise of Human Nature*, part I.

of his argument. On the other hand, references to 'essential ideas' are systematically omitted – including *both* the passages cited by Maurice we have just quoted. The lines at the beginning of chapter IV which Maurice fastened on, we recall, went as follows:

It was said, then, that a true development retains the *essential idea* of the subject from which it has proceeded, and a corruption loses it. What then is the true idea of Christianity? and is it preserved in the developments commonly called Catholic, and in the Church which embodies and teaches them?

In the third edition we find this:

How does this apply to Christianity? What is its original type? and has that type been preserved in the developments commonly called Catholic, which have followed, and in the Church which embodies and teaches them?[1]

Instead of 'essential idea' Newman has put 'original type' – changing the argument to a question of 'preservation of type'. The word is used now in the sense of 'species': the rose continues to breed true, without degenerating into the wild briars of infidelity.

I wish to suggest two things from this. Firstly, that Newman was much more sensitive to criticism of the way in which he used certain concepts than he was to attacks on the logic of the whole. Secondly, following from this, that Maurice's criticism of Newman takes its weight not so much from the actual context of the debate, important as the main issue was for both, but from the sense both still have of working within a *common tradition* of language and feeling that was accustomed to thinking of 'ideas' as, active, organic, and creative. The apparent shadow-boxing of Maurice's distinction is concerned specifically with the difference between the empiricist and mechanical use of the word 'idea' and its fundamentally opposed use by the Romantic poets in terms of creativity. Both Newman and Maurice seem to accept a common tradition which saw words not as mere 'Things' but as 'living powers, by which the things of most importance to mankind are actuated, combined, and humanized.'[2] The literary and linguistic tradition, in short, of Coleridge.

---

[1] P. 150.

[2] *Aids to Reflection*, Preface, p. xvii. The phrase 'common tradition' is, of course, John Coulson's (*Newman and the Common Tradition*).

I believe it is in the light of this common tradition that a large part of Maurice's criticism of Newman must be understood. Newman, Maurice implies, for all his brandishing of an 'organic' terminology, is not really prepared to treat ideas as if they *were* 'alive' – in that they could create *new* ideas. However he *uses* such words, when he attempts to define them with any rigour the result often sounds more like Bentham than Coleridge. Newman, for his part, shows no sign of giving way to Maurice in his revisions. It is unlikely that he had Maurice actually before him as he sat down in 1878 to revise his text, and whether or not he was conscious that the criticisms he was responding to came from Maurice is immaterial. What is significant is the way in which his mind had moved. He finds himself compelled to clarify his position within the tradition of 'organic' terminology. Only in *some* of the changes found in Christian doctrine is he prepared to recognise 'growth' (or 'true development') – and the quality of those changes is judged on strictly external *a priori* criteria, those of the Catholic Church. He makes it clear that he is writing about *individuation* of species[1] – the process by which an organism strives to become ever more fully itself – not the *evolution* of species, which appears to be Maurice's model of the 'esemplastic' activity of the Divine Imagination ever shaping new combinations of disparate elements into ever-evolving ever-richer coherence. Both models, we notice, are possible variations within the same tradition; both owe as much to literary criticism as they do to

[1] The question in exactly what sense, in 1845, Newman believed that genuinely 'new' doctrines could be 'true development' seems almost impossible to answer. Certainly the *Essay* could be construed in that light. V. F. Storr declares, 'Nothing is more certain than that Newman at this time believed in a real development of doctrine, in the emergence of new truth which was not there before' (p. 302). This is also what Perrone, Professor of Dogmatic Theology at the Collegio Romano, clearly suspected. In his comments on the *Essay* he insists,

(1) that the Church was always conscious of the whole *depositum* committed to her of all the truths of faith, (2) that this *depositum* was committed to her as it were in a block and as one revelation, (3) that the truths of faith are not capable of increase in themselves but only of more explicit exposition, (4) that therefore these truths do not grow materially... and in themselves, but only in relation to our fuller comprehension of them and more distinct knowledge by definition of the Church... Ward, *Life of Newman*, I, 185.

Clearly, this looks like an attack on Newman's whole thesis – until we discover that the doctrine of the Immaculate Conception was held by Perrone to be part of the original *depositum*. With this in mind Newman held 'that this criticism substantially left his position untouched'.

philosophy or theology. Neither appears to owe anything to contemporary biology.[1]

The analogy between an 'idea' and a complex living organic structure lies at the heart of Newman's whole conception of the development of doctrine. Chadwick likens this meaning of 'idea' to the modern sense of 'ideology' – as in, say, 'socialism.'

The meaning of this general and influential idea is not immediately evident, and its understanding varies between man and man. Though based upon *some* concrete information, it is at first a vague impression, yet an impression which influences a man's behaviour, his vote, his sympathies. Only as this general idea is brought into concrete relationship with particular problems, can it be comprehended in its different aspects – the consequences of nationalization, the union between capital and labour, the meaning of 'classes', the question of how when you guarantee employment to everyone you can prevent the value of money from continuously falling – in a series of concrete relations and changing historical circumstances the meaning of the idea is brought out and understood, you become aware what the original proposition meant throughout its ramifications. You may say that these ramifications are 'implicit' – but not implicit in the logical sense. New knowledge, new awareness is gained.[2]

Newman, Chadwick thinks, would not have repudiated this analogy. Certainly it effectively highlights the problem involved in saying what is 'implicit' and what is 'added'. The trouble is that like most analogies it is incomplete, and, in particular, it leaves one important question open. Socialism is *not* a divine revelation. For all its apparent dogmatic controversies it is ultimately pragmatic: there does not *need* to be an absolute truth to be distinguished from deviation and corruption. Socialism is not in essence Platonic. Christianity, as Newman seems to conceive it, must be. Somewhere, he believed, there is a core of revealed truth which is absolute and final and which must be protected from error. Now most theologians, like Storr among the Protestants or Perrone among Catholics, have assumed that there is a fundamental confusion in Newman's mind between logical and biological development. But Maurice never suggests this. By

[1] For the dearth of contemporary biological models of evolution see John Burrow, *Evolution and Society* (Cambridge, 1966) – but Coleridge actually defines 'life' as a principle of individuation. (Muirhead, *Coleridge as Philosopher*, p. 127; *Theory of Life*, p. 385.')
[2] Chadwick, p. 150.

taking what amounts to a Platonic idea and treating it as if it were not static and immutable, but alive, growing, and changing, Newman is following a line of thought we first find in Coleridge's *Aids to Reflection* (which we know Newman had read). If his initial neo-empirical distinction between 'Christianity', which is a 'fact', and what he calls the 'idea' of Christianity, which is the impression that fact makes upon the minds of men, is designed to anticipate objections to this 'dynamic Platonism' it fails. According to Newman an 'idea' develops not merely by a process of explication and elucidation, but also through actual assimilation of foreign material: incense, ecclesiastical vestments, the ring in marriage, and the tonsure are all incorporations from the pagan world – as he well knew. What he means by the 'fact' of Christianity is not what is given but the total changing historical phenomenon. It cannot remain fixed and immutable in the mind of God while Christianity here below alters and assimilates to itself new characteristics. Indeed, this idea of what we may call a 'dynamically evolving absolute' is central to Newman's vision of the Church. All his seven tests of true development, including, as we have seen, 'Assimilative Power', hinge on it. Even 'Logical Sequence' turns out not to resemble the syllogistic logic of Jesuit theology, but to mean something more like 'in harmony with' – a usage which, incidentally, is thoroughly Coleridgean. One recent theologian, following this line, has suggested that the image of a musical fugue is appropriate to Newman's argument. The various models he uses serve as basic structures for the fugue: historical, philosophical, and christological. The tendency to hypostatise the 'idea', to treat it as if it were a person, which we find in some passages, he suggests, is partly due to the fact that one of the themes of the fugue is an explicit identification of the 'idea' with the person of the living Christ striding, as it were, through history.[1]

Maurice's doubts, however, continue to centre around Newman's ability adequately to distinguish the mechanical from the organic – not in the personification of an 'idea' in Christ, with which he would have heartily agreed, but in the *mode* of its operation. Mr Newman, he says,

...finds an established system not indeed a dead system, but a living one...a system of generative powers, vital energies, in unceasing

---

[1] I am indebted for this suggestion to Dr Nicholas Lash in a letter.

movement and operating with a correcting power...gradually evolving itself in the course of these workings, and, no doubt, contemplated from the first by the great Demiurgus. This is his hypothesis to explain, not the physical world, but the life and history of man; not of man only considered as dwelling in some outward circle, but of man brought within the family of God![1]

The concept of 'organic' development contains itself an important ambiguity: is it an entirely self-regulating process fulfilling patterns already predetermined? or does it involve constant adaptation and change in response to new circumstances? Put in theological terms, Maurice's questions concern Newman's doctrine of the Holy Spirit. Newman's idea of Christianity seems to grow according to an 'organic' principle so inflexible as to exclude the spontaneity we associate with human growth. The rose of the true Church unfolds unmistakably as a rose amidst brambles and wild sports of Gnosticism, Pelagianism, Arianism, and a whole host of other heresies right down to Lutheranism and the Church of England. There can be no surprises.

Maurice's problem is one that had occupied Coleridge before him: the growth of an organism demands a steady diet without too many shocks; the growth of the mind depends on the mastery of variety.[2] Human growth cannot be adequately described in 'organic' terms without confusing the higher with the lower, the more complex with the less complex. Is the development of doctrine *less* complex than the minds in which it grows, or will it be subject to the same laws of growth and development? Once again, Maurice is applying principles of literary criticism to theology. For Coleridge, in the development of literary tradition the principle of organic development came to be balanced by a second principle – that of dialectic. Not merely does tradition make the writer, but also, the writer, by being new, *re-makes* the tradition. What we mean by 'tradition' is this constant interaction of history and the individual who creates, even as he is created by it. In his *Lectures on Shakespeare* Coleridge writes:

...few there have been among critics, who have followed with the eye of the imagination the imperishable, yet ever-wandering, spirit of poetry through its various metempsychoses, and consequent metamorphoses; – or who have rejoiced in the light of clear perception at

1 Preface to *Lectures on the Epistle to the Hebrews*, p. lxvii.
2 See ch. 1, p. 16, n. 1 above.

beholding with each new birth, with each rare *avatar*, the human race frame to itself a new body, by assimilating materials of nourishment out of its new circumstances, and work for itself new organs or power appropriate to the new sphere of its motion and activity.[1]

It is this interaction between the organic development of an 'idea' and its constant dialectical modification by the new and unpredictable that Maurice finds so characteristic of human growth – and so apparently lacking in Newman's model. For Maurice, this failure is to misunderstand the element of disconfirmation that is inseparable from Biblical revelation.

Here is the link between Maurice's review and his *Lectures on Hebrews*. 'In the second of these lectures,' he writes, '. . . I have maintained . . . that the *Epistle to the Hebrews* sets forth not only the essential *idea* of Scripture, but the method of it; in other words the method of divine education by which men in the old time were enabled to enter into this idea, to see how it must be realized.'[2] *Hebrews* is the great exemplum of 'method' in the development of an idea. As Coleridge expounds his concept of 'method' in his Preface to the *Encyclopædia Metropolitana* (later to form part of the 1818 text of *The Friend*) the word is used exclusively to describe a sequence of development where there is an internal self-generating principle of progression.[3] For Coleridge once again the word is primarily one from literary criticism. Maurice has made it into a self-conscious principle of divine education, by which the development of doctrine is simultaneously a growth in human spiritual capacity. He goes on:

By referring to acknowledged instances of the allegorical method, I have endeavoured to show that the method which the Epistle traces out is not *that*, but one altogether unlike it – one which does fullest, completest justice to the words of Scripture, and to the circumstances in which they were uttered; that it is however in the strictest sense a spiritual method, one which does not deal with letters only, but with the heart and conscience, and inward conflicts of those who were subjected to it; one lastly, which was pointing at every step to this end, the discovery or Revelation of a Lord who must be perfectly one with men and one with God; in whom there must be two natures; in whom there could not be double personality; whose manifestations must

---

[1] *Shakespeare Criticism*, I. 174. See also T. S. Eliot's reworking of this idea in 'Tradition and the Individual Talent', *Selected Essays*, 3rd edn (Faber, 1951).

[2] Preface to *Lectures on the Epistle to the Hebrews*, p. lxvii.

[3] See *The Friend*, I, 448–524.

destroy the cultus or homage of inferior creatures, at the same time must exalt the creation as it had never been exalted before.[1]

The 'method' Maurice discovers in the Bible is precisely that interaction of continuous organic growth and its dialectical modification by disconfirmation that he finds lacking in Newman.

Thus, for Maurice, the infallible guide is not the Church, but the scriptures. This sounds as if he is re-stating, in rather a peculiar context, a common extreme Protestant position, but in fact he seems to be doing no such thing. His position, which he is here, in his *Lectures on Hebrews* attempting to define in contradistinction to Newman, is unique almost to himself. Newman is led by Butler's argument for 'antecedent probability' towards the external authority of the Church. Maurice rests on the 'antecedent probability' of the authority of the scriptures, whose language, he declares, is the 'truest and simplest and most reasonable language of all that has ever been uttered'. This extraordinary 'Mauricism' illustrates the degree to which he has pushed his view of the Bible *as poetry* to its logical conclusion. Just as a poem should not be didactic and moralising, but inward, allusive, symbolic and dialectical if it is to arouse the mind to active assimilation and response, so the 'method' of the scriptures suggested by antecedent probability and the living organic nature of an idea is similarly symbolic and dialectical. Human experience of good and evil is not dogmatic, but poetic. 'It was probable, therefore,' writes Maurice of the Church, that, as in Israel of old, 'there would be a clearer unfolding of some great truth, and at the same time a greater darkening and enveloping of this same truth under the shadows of the earth, and the corruptions of the flesh.' As in the macrocosm, so in the microcosm: 'It was probable that this same process would go on in the minds of individual men – that they would bring out the truth and darken it, seize hold of one portion of it with wonderful power, and almost lose sight of another; that they would beget sects and heresies, and sustain them by the holiness of their lives and the truths which they had been permitted to testify for.'[2] If Butler's antecedent probability was to be invoked, it pointed not towards that phenomenon totally unknown in the rest of human experience, infallible authority, but towards the inextricable mixture of good

[1] Preface to *Lectures on the Epistle to the Hebrews*, p. lxviii.   [2] P. xxxix.

and evil, order and confusion everywhere apparent in the development of Christianity. The *Epistle to the Hebrews*, with its sense
of the past and its stress on organic continuity, emphasises the
way in which Christianity has grown out of the tradition of
prophecy and revelation begun in the Old Testament. Against
the historically doubtful authority of the Bishop of Rome must be
set the *artistic* and *poetic* authority of the Bible whose symbolic
method compels an inner personal assent.

The influence of Coleridge in Maurice's argument is indicated
by his very choice of phrases and individual words. Thus in his
first lecture Maurice writes of the prophets:

We wrong them grievously when we deal with their words as if they
were oracles uttered in some moment of wild inspiration; with their
books as if they were a collection of Sibylline Leaves. The power
which they possess of announcing that which must be, seems to be
involved in their divine gift of perceiving the eternal under the
temporary – the substance through the shadow: for they are certain
the counsel of the Lord will stand...[1]

The presence of Coleridge here is worthy of a Freudian analysis.
His first book of poems to be published after the *Lyrical Ballads*
was entitled *Sibylline Leaves*. This apparently irrelevant coincidence is immediately followed in the next sentence by a near
paraphrase of Coleridge's definition of a symbol: 'the eternal
under the temporary...'

But if Maurice is right, as I think he is, in suspecting that
Newman's theory of development has bound him to a concept of
organic 'life' more appropriate to a vegetable than to a human
being, many would feel that over the question of authority Newman is the more plausible. Newman would not have attempted
to gainsay Maurice's emphasis on the sheer complexity of
human spiritual development: Jesus himself told the parable of
the wheat and the tares. But this very complexity points to the
difficulty of understanding the Bible unaided. Beyond the complexity, Maurice seems to hint, lies something in essence very
simple that can be reached by all men. The analogy at the back
of his mind is with a work of art. A poem may be highly subtle
and complex, yet speak to its readers at many levels because its
method is symbolic rather than direct. Newman, no less than
Maurice, wishes to use this analogy – and it is this common

[1] Preface to *Lectures on the Epistle to the Hebrews*, p. 4.

framework of ideas that makes their debate so interesting. But that a thing was 'symbolic' for Newman was not necessarily proof that it was true, whereas the implicit Platonism of Coleridge and Maurice sometimes seem to make them assume just that. Newman was more sceptical, less tolerant of this kind of ambiguity. His external criteria of judgement do not consist primarily in the 'seven tests', as Maurice seems to suppose, but in the authority and tradition of the Church. This is a point that will be dealt with in some detail in the next chapter. Suffice it here to say that Newman seems to be more aware than Maurice of how far our assumptions of interpretation about a work of art are themselves culturally induced, and therefore culturally variable.

Where he stands with Maurice is in his sense of language as a living creative *poetic* medium whose words and ideas are not defined in advance, but are forged, tempered, and hardened into meaning by the literature from which they are inseparable – and by the needs of the society of which that literature is both product and creator. The meaning of an 'idea' is understood in retrospect. This is once again the 'fiduciary' tradition of language.[1] We take it on trust, Coleridge believed, because we cannot stand outside it: it is the vehicle of our very consciousness and imagination. It is the vehicle of activity by which our minds develop.

Newman's considerable debts to Coleridge, though less explicitly acknowledged than those of Maurice, have been conclusively demonstrated by Coulson.[2] There is nothing new in suggesting such a debt: Martineau, Brémond, and Ward all noticed similarities and drew specific comparisons. But Newman was never a 'Coleridgean' in the sense that Maurice openly claimed to be. There are many other strands of influence – even that of Bentham – that lead his development in other directions. We are not discussing membership of a club – whether, for instance, Newman did or did not know the password to the kind of secret society that Disraeli in one of his novels pictures the Coleridgeans as forming. Newman's own comments on Coleridge have already been quoted.[3] Somewhat confusingly in extreme old age he seems to have told Ward that he had 'never read a line of Coleridge' – but Ward merely cites this as an example of

[1] Coulson, *Newman and the Common Tradition*, ch. 1.
[2] Ibid. Appendix, 'How much of Coleridge had Newman read?' pp. 254–5.
[3] See ch. 2, p. 38 above.

how badly the old Cardinal's memory was failing.[1] In fact he makes direct references in his published work to Coleridge's *Treatise on Method*, *Biographia Literaria*, and *Aids to Reflection*. More surprising was the discovery, comparatively recently, of nine letters from Coleridge to H. J. Rose among Newman's private papers.[2] They deal with philosophy, theology, the *Lay Sermons*, and the *Treatise on Method*. Coulson himself concludes:

The evidence does not so much establish that Coleridge had a direct influence on the formation of Newman's ideas as the existence of a common way of seeing the Church and of setting up the problem. It amounts more to a shared tradition and common vocabulary than to the influence directly of one mind upon the other.[3]

Perhaps more important, from our point of view, is the evidence of Maurice's review itself. In spite of his deep differences with Newman, Maurice clearly believed that a particular background of assumptions, as much literary and linguistic as theological, was common to them both. It is a background that includes not merely Coleridge, but Butler, Wordsworth, and above all, Keble.

It is little wonder that Newman found his *Essay* was even less understood by his new brethren than by his old. The Oxford Movement was a religious flowering of the English Romantic movement: as we have seen, an inheritor of the 'poetic' tension of head and heart so typical of Wordsworth and Coleridge. The Roman Catholics of England, barred still from the two ancient universities, understood little of this, and felt it less.[4] In contrast to Manning after his conversion, Newman remained emotionally and aesthetically within the tradition which had brought him *to* Catholicism – the world embraced by the Anglican sensibility of Coleridge and Keble. He remained within a way of feeling that separated him even from many of his fellow converts.[5] F. W. Faber, a man with in many ways a very different kind of poetic sensibility from Newman, belonged nevertheless to the same ethos. In May 1843 he wrote home to a friend from Rome about his Anglican doubts, 'Of course I could not make any use of a *feeling* as an argument, yet I confess that sometimes when I am hard pressed I feel that there is a little fortress in the background

---

[1] *Life of Newman*, i, 58.
[2] Coulson, *Newman and the Common Tradition*, pp. 254–5.
[3] Ibid. p. 58.   [4] Ward, *Life of Newman*, i, 248.   [5] Ibid. p. 577.

quite unsuspected by the enemy, namely recollections of Oxford...'[1] That unsuspected fortress was to make the eventual Catholicism of Newman and Faber, for all their differences, a Catholicism of a new kind. In part at any rate, it helps to account for the four agonising years at Littlemore between Newman's retreat from Oxford and his reception into the Roman Church. The *Essay on Development* is an expression not only of Newman's reasons for going over to Rome, but also of the tradition of literary sensibility that formed those reasons and made them so compelling – reasons which, in the last resort, and however unsatisfactory a term it may be, we have to call 'poetic'.

There was nothing very original about the idea of development of doctrine in 1845. The liberal Anglicans such as Hare, Thomas Arnold, Milman, and Stanley, under the influence of the German theologians, had already evolved a far more historically sophisticated theory of development which was opposed to both the Victorian notion of 'progress' and to crude analogies between the growth of individuals and the race.[2] They, too, looked to Coleridge.[3] Hare treated Newman's *Essay* with withering contempt: its arbitrary selection of evidence to suit its convenience was typical of the essentially *unhistorical* nature of the Oxford Movement.[4] He contrasts Newman's piecemeal approach with the *method* of the Germans, 'ever seeking to behold all things in their connections, as parts or members of a great organic whole ...while the Eclectic is content if he can string together a number of generalizations'.[5] Newman cannot discriminate between a 'hypothesis' and a 'theory'.[6] The liberal Anglican idea of development is based on what Milman called 'accommodation', that is, 'the power of a religion to adapt itself and progress'.[7] 'The Everlasting Gospel,' said Milman, 'is everlasting, not because it remains stationary, but because being the same, it can

---

[1] *Faber: Poet and Priest*, Selected Letters by Frederick William Faber, 1833–1863, ed. Raleigh Addington (D. Brown & Sons, 1974), p. 98.

[2] See Forbes, *The Liberal Anglican Idea of History*, pp. 6; 85.

[3] 'Coleridge had defined the Church (in its universal aspect) as the sustaining, correcting, befriending, opposite of the world. The response of the Oxford Movement to the crisis of civilization was to lay stress on opposition and correction as the special work and glory of the Church; the Liberal Anglicans emphasised the sustaining and befriending aspects of religion. The one was moved by the spirit of dogma, the other by the spirit of history.' Forbes, *The Liberal Anglican Idea of History*, p. 102.

[4] Ibid. p. 103.   [5] Ibid. p. 105.   [6] Ibid. p. 106.   [7] Ibid. p. 75.

adapt itself to the constant change of society, of civilization, of humanity itself.'[1] This was a view to which Newman was implacably hostile. He reviewed Milman's *History of Christianity* in the *British Critic* in 1841 and attacked very specifically the notion that Christianity was 'an idea which had developed itself' in response to circumstances – the very notion that was to form part of his own theory of development only four years later.[2]

One can perhaps see why. Ideas transplanted into alien soil can cause ecological transformations. Newman is undoubtedly borrowing ideas from contemporary philosophy of history, just as he is making use of theological dogmas with a similar eclecticism. Once again the image of a fugue comes to mind. For Newman, Church history is no longer an outward sequence of events and ideas, but part of a process inseparable from the growth of the minds that assimilated and nurtured those ideas. The development of Christian doctrine is indeed the story of the mental and spiritual growth of mankind, but in terms very different from those of the liberal Anglican historians. He did not believe in a *moral* improvement any more than did Milman or Hare: the grown man is not morally superior to the child, but he *is* more mature, experienced, and self-conscious. By drawing out the essentially literary and poetic implications of organic growth Newman is suggesting a quite new way of apprehending Christianity: that is, *as a work of art*.[3] In Coleridge's criticism it is assumed that the response to great literature brings into being a complex ordering activity of the mind. 'To know,' says Coleridge 'is a verb *active*.' The scriptures, we recall, are for him the 'living educts of the imagination' because they bring into play 'the self-circling energies of the reason'. Seen in this light, the growth and development of an idea is not necessarily the closed

[1] *Sermons on Special Occasions*, p. 46; Forbes, *The Liberal Anglican Idea of History*, p. 76.

[2] Chadwick, *From Bossuet to Newman*, p. 100. He comments, 'Though he [Newman] repudiated the historical methods and principles which he thus found in the Germans and the liberal Anglicans, it is undeniable that (by 1845, even by 1839) his mind had been influenced by their methods and insights...The theologian in Newman vehemently distrusted the new school of historians, the historian in him could not help learning from them.'

[3] The analogy is, of course, implicit in Coleridge, and employed in specific instances by both Keble and Hare. What is new is the close parallel Newman seems to assume between aesthetic and religious experience, and consequently the way in which he uses an aesthetic model to shape his philosophy of history.

'mechanical' process that Maurice accused Newman of believing. If we want an artistic analogy for Newman's organic 'philosophy of history' we should turn to Wordsworth's *Prelude*. In so doing, we see too Newman's vision of the rôle the *Essay on Development* has played in his own personal development. Up to the point where the theory of development was propounded by Newman, that development had been latent within the Roman Church: implicit rather than explicit. Now, in explaining to itself how it has changed, and how it must interpret for itself that change, the Church has reached a new threshold of consciousness. Similarly, in writing the *Essay* Newman has himself reached a new stage of self-awareness. The whole course of his life is re-interpreted as pointing inexorably towards Rome. His Anglican stage was not a 'mistake', it was a necessary part of what he now has become; but only now is he in a position to understand it. In submitting to the Church of Rome, Newman is bringing with him his own version of *The Prelude*: the history of the growth of the mind of Holy Mother Church herself, and, indirectly, the history of his own.

In so doing, with his idea of 'development' Newman has re-solved a major ambiguity in Coleridge and Wordsworth's con-cepts of 'growth', viewing it not merely as an internal organic process, but also as something which can only be explained and evaluated by value-judgements external to itself. By his review of Newman, Maurice achieved something no less important. In returning to and re-stating Coleridge's conviction that *neither* organic *nor* dialectical models of the mind are satisfactory in isolation from each other if we are to describe its growth, he reasserted the importance of disconfirmation, and defended the complexity and unpredictableness of mental development. Though the form in which we have been examining this debate and the personalities of Newman and Maurice tend to make these principles look like polarities, this may not in fact be so. The criticisms that Maurice makes of Newman's thesis need not be seen as external. We have enough evidence to suggest that they existed as contraries in Newman's own mind – as part of the progression towards the resolution of a complex of problems on 'growth' that Coleridge had bequeathed to Victorian England.

7

Newman: Imagination and Assent

It is to the living mind that we must look for the means of using correctly principles of whatever kind.[1]

Newman always wants to tell us the story of Newman. What is probably unique about his perennial fascination with the growth and development of his own mind is the way in which it combines two characteristics normally found in very different kinds of people. On the one hand, he never loses sight of the *emotional* unity of his own nature; on the other, he is constantly apprehending his own emotional processes in terms of philosophical first-principles. A peculiarly intense capacity for feeling is transformed into a peculiarly intense capacity for analysing that feeling in intellectual terms. Many of his contemporaries were struck by this fusion of apparently opposite qualities. His biographer quotes a Dr Irons who, reviewing the *Apologia* in 1864, observed:

As a specimen of mental analysis, extended over a whole lifetime the 'Apologia' is probably without a rival. St. Augustine's Confessions are a purely religious retrospect; Rousseau's are philosophical; Dr. Newman's psychological. One might almost attribute to him a double personality. The mental power, the strange self-anatomy, the almost cold, patient review of past affections, anxieties, and hopes, are alike astonishing. The examination is not a *post-mortem*, for there appear colour, light, and consciousness in the subject; it is not a vivisection, for there is no quivering, even of a nerve.[2]

Augustine and Rousseau had something of the same self-absorbed detachment necessary to a first-class intellectual autobiography. Another, recent, critic has pointed out similarities between Newman's childhood difficulties in believing in the

---

[1] *A Grammar of Assent*, ed. C. F. Harrold, new edn (Longman, 1957), p. 274.
[2] Ward, *Life of Newman*, II, 34.

reality of the external world, and those of Tolstoy and Words-worth.[1] In the *Apologia* Newman tells us how he thought life might be a dream, and he an angel, and 'all this world a decep-tion, my fellow-angels by a playful device concealing themselves from me, and deceiving me with the semblance of a material world'.[2] This was a fantasy not unlike that of the boy Words-worth, who, as an old man, told the assiduously note-taking Miss Fenwick, that

. . . it was not so much from [feelings] of animal vivacity that *my* difficulty came as from a sense of the indomitableness of the Spirit within me. I used to brood over the stories of Enoch and Elijah, and al-most to persuade myself that, whatever might become of others, I should be translated, in something of the same way, to heaven. With a feeling congenial to this, I was often unable to think of external things as having external existence, and I communed with all that I saw as some-thing not apart from, but inherent in, my own immaterial nature.[3]

Newman, his biographer tells us, was 'devoted' to Wordsworth's *Immortality Ode*.[4] We have other hints, too, that Newman shared with Wordsworth to some degree the qualities of a 'childhood visionary'. The house at Ham, in Surrey, where he was brought up always occupied a peculiarly vivid place in his imagination. In 1861, at one of the darkest points in his career, we find him writing to a friend, 'I have been looking at the windows of our house at Ham near Richmond, where I lay aged 5 looking at the candles stuck in them in celebration of the victory at Trafalgar. I have never seen the house since September 1807 – I know more about it than any house I have been in since, and could pass an examination in it. It has ever been in my dreams.'[5] Memories of that 'paradise of delight' continued to haunt him. It is the setting for the imaginary friend who lives in absolute worldly contentment in Newman's essay on 'Discipline and Influence'.[6] Ham was the place where, in the words of his most moving personal poem, the 'angel faces smile/Which I have loved long since, and lost awhile.'

Such peculiarly vivid childhood memories are not all that un-common. What *is* extremely uncommon, and what makes New-

---

[1] Thomas Vargish, *Newman: The Contemplation of Mind* (Oxford, 1970), p. 1.
[2] *Apologia*, p. 16.   [3] *Poetical Works*, iv, 463.
[4] Ward, *Life of Newman*, ii, 336.   [5] Ibid. i, 607.
[6] *Historical Sketches*, iii, 62, in Ward, *Life of Newman*, ii, 336–8.

man in this respect similar to Wordsworth, is the way in which these childhood memories and visions give Newman an irresistible and all-inclusive autobiographical impulse, at once intensely particular and personal, and, simultaneously, philosophic and cosmic in its implications. Nothing happened in Newman's world that did not have an immediate and personal meaning for him; nothing held a meaning for him that did not also have a direct bearing on the rest of creation. At its crudest, this could result in naive and not very edifying superstitions, such as his disconcertingly literal and slightly Manichean belief in daemons of the middle air; his view of the divine significance of Bishop Shuttleworth's untimely death at the beginning of 1842, just before he could deliver his attack on Newman's *Tract Ninety*;[1] or his belief in a special providence that struck him down with fever in Sicily in 1833, and then preserved him by a hair's breadth from death.[2] At its finest, the same impulse produced, under the stimulus of Kingsley's charge of indifference to truth, the *Apologia pro Vita Sua*. In spite of their vast differences, what Newman shares with Wordsworth (and in a slightly different way, with Coleridge) is a sense of personal individuality so great as to need a universal philosophic system to make sense of it. His ideas of growth and development are central to his understanding of himself, and consequently to his vision of man as a whole. The writing of the *Apologia* as a declared autobiography should not blind us to the existence of the same ideas, repeated in varying keys, in nearly all his works.

As we have already seen, the *Essay on the Development of Christian Doctrine* applies the principle of 'life' as a test of truth in doctrine. Precisely the same test is applied by Newman in a much more knockabout polemical vein to the Church of England in the *Lectures on Certain Difficulties felt by Anglicans*. For Newman, the Anglican Church counterfeited life. If it ever had the powers of growth, they had dried up; it had ceased to manifest itself 'in activity of principle' and so it no longer lived. It was openly 'no body politic of any kind', but 'a department of government.'[3] Newman had chosen unmistakably to deliver

---

[1] Faber, *Oxford Apostles*, p. 429.

[2] Ibid. pp. 315–34.

[3] *Lectures on Certain Difficulties felt by Anglicans in Submitting to the Catholic Church*, 2nd edn (1850), p. 7.

the main weight of his attack against Coleridge's *Church and State* because with the semi-collapse of his own doctrine of the *via media* it represented both the weakest and the strongest point in the Anglican defences. The weakest, because of the obvious inherent difficulty of defending the Church establishment, with its naked use of political patronage at every level, culminating in the appointment of its bishops by the Crown. The strongest, because Coleridge had managed, with brilliant ingenuity, to turn this weakness into an argument of strength whereby one thought not of a subservient and Erastian Church, but of a single entity, the nation, composed of Church and political establishment held in tension. To destroy the theory of the *via media* Newman has a devastating historical weapon to hand: the Monophysites. Coleridge's defence however rests not on historical evidence, but on the very principle of 'life' so dear to Newman himself. For Coleridge, Maurice, and Gladstone Church and State were organic parts of the life of the nation. Of course the Church of England *by itself* lacked coherence: any organ so separated would do so. One must ask instead the Coleridgean question, 'What is the meaning of it?' What purpose does it serve in context? It is this very principle of 'life' therefore that Newman must wrest from Coleridge and turn against him. He must make the principle of organic unity his own. The Roman Catholic Church comes not to destroy the Coleridgean principles, but to fulfil them.

Above all, Newman argues, the 'life' of the Church of England is false because it lacks that basic condition of intelligent life, self-awareness. In the process of doctrinal development the final position may not always be clearly apparent from the premises, but it is not reached by blind evolution. It develops by a conscious dialectical movement; the Holy Spirit works through, and not against human reason. Within Christ's Body, the Catholic Church, there is not merely a development of doctrine, but parallel with that development a growing understanding of the very principles by which it comes about. The primacy of the Bishop of Rome, for instance, or the defining rôle of the Councils, is at first implicit and then progressively more and more explicit. Development of doctrine is always a growth of consciousness, a development of theological insight. But the Church of England has no such centre of consciousness.

Nor can it in consequence be said to have any antecedents, or any future; or to live, except in the passing moment. As a thing without a soul, it does not contemplate itself, define its intrinsic constitution, or ascertain its position. It has no traditions; it cannot be said to think; it does not know what it holds and what it does not; it is not even conscious of its own existence.[1]

Without the basic condition of self-knowledge the other accoutrements of life are vain. Its properties are a theatrical sham; its robes borrowed; its splendours a trick.

Thus it is that students of the Fathers, antiquarians, and poets, begin by assuming that the body to which they belong is that of which they read in time past, and then proceed to decorate it with that majesty and beauty of which history tells, or which their genius creates...But at length, either the force of circumstances or some unexpected accident dissipates it; and, as in fairy tales, the magic castle vanishes when the spell is broken, and nothing is seen but the wild heath, the barren rock, and the forlorn sheep-walk: so it is with us as regards the Church of England, when we look in amazement on that which we thought so unearthly, and find so common-place or worthless.[2]

Newman's extended conceit is carefully chosen. It is, of course, familiar to us from Keats' *La Belle Dame Sans Merci* – and the echoes are deliberate. Which 'poets' have decorated the English Church with the beauty created by their own genius? Is Coleridge one? Who are those erstwhile enchanted by the dream of the Church of England that now has turned to dust and ashes? Who are those left 'alone and palely loitering'? They are surely the remnants of the Oxford Movement, repudiated by the Church which they had loved, and for whose authority they had claimed such high status. It is to these that Newman is now very specifically addressing himself in these lectures. They must now seek life not in semblance, but in reality within the Catholic fold. Rome is not an enchantment, but, demonstrably, a release from enchantment. One does not discover 'life' by abstruse theological debate; it is not created by ingenious dialectical theories. The chronic vigour of the true Church is to be seen, felt, and lived.

But there is a further echo in Newman's imagery that would be familiar to many of his hearers. It is from Addison musing on the apparent paradox of sense-perception in an essay on 'The Pleasures of the Imagination' (*Spectator*, 413 (1712)).

---

[1] *Anglican Difficulties*, p. 8.   [2] Ibid. pp. 6–7.

Things would make but a poor appearance to the eye, if we saw them only in their proper figures and motions... We are everywhere entertained with pleasing shows and apparitions, we discover imaginary glories in the heavens, and in the earth, and see some of this visionary beauty poured out over the whole creation; but what a rough and unsightly sketch of Nature should we be entertained with, did all her colouring disappear, and the several distinctions of light and shade vanish? In short, our souls are at present delightfully lost and bewildered in a pleasing delusion, and we walk about like the enchanted hero of a romance, who sees beautiful castles, woods, and meadows; and at the same time hears the warbling of birds, and the purling of streams; but upon the finishing of some secret spell, the fantastic scene breaks up, and the disconsolate knight finds himself on a barren heath, or in a solitary desert.

For Addison, in the passage quoted above, the revelations of Newton's *Opticks* seemed to confirm the world-picture presented by Locke. We are sealed off from the world of 'real' objects by the manifest unreliability of our senses. Colour is but a trick of the light: a way of making our prisons bearable, perhaps, but nevertheless a reminder that we are imprisoned in an illusion. It was left to Wordsworth and the Romantics to show the way out – or rather to declare that the prison itself was an illusion. 'Reality', the Romantics affirmed, is what we *see*. Light and colour are among the given premises of our world. We cannot consider them in detachment, nor can we in the proper sense of the word be deceived by them because they are part of the very framework of our experience – what constitutes and differentiates our particular form of life. We can postulate theoretically, but we cannot experience any other.

Newman is a great prose writer, not a great poet. But it is a mark of the quality of his prose that one can treat his images as one might the complex imagery of a Shakespearean play. To understand what he is doing in applying this familiar image to the Church of England we need to see that he stands with Wordsworth against Addison and the Lockeians. Our world is 'real', concrete, and particular. We experience and even 'part create' it because we have the necessary first condition of life. It is, he argues in the *Grammar of Assent*, 'unphilosophical to speak of trusting ourselves.'

We are what we are, and we use, not trust our faculties. To debate about trusting in a case like this, is parallel to the confusion implied in wishing I had a choice if I would be created or no, or speculating what I should be like, if I were born of other parents... We are as little able to accept or reject our mental constitution as our being... We do not confront or bargain with ourselves.[1]

The idea that living within a particular set of conditions in some way cramps our style and limits us is a fundamental philosophic error, Newman argues. It perpetuates the Lockeian fallacy of supposing a 'sensorium', or, crudely, a 'watcher' inside the head who is somehow separate from the senses which feed him with partial and imperfect data. This simply puts off the problem of consciousness within the machine in a kind of infinite regress. But in fact we do not 'use' our eyes as we might a pair of spectacles or a telescope, we *see*. Ironically, Locke's model is not that of a conscious living organism, but of a machine. Nevertheless, the Church of England is right to be dominated by such a model since the division between senses and sensorium is, in its case, only too true. Search for its conscious life and you *will* find yourself caught in an infinite regress. It is precisely because the English Church is not a form of life but part of the mechanism of State that the Englishman finds himself abandoned upon the barren heath. In his *Lectures on Certain Difficulties felt by Anglicans* Newman specifically contrasts the destructive and sceptical rationality of Locke and his successors which, he says, characterise Protestant thought, with the all-embracing unity of thought and feeling which are the premises of Catholic culture. The one murders to dissect, the other is a living organic consciousness. Why do Catholics blaspheme more than Protestants, he asks?[2] Blasphemy is a mark of the believer. The Italian or Spanish Catholic in a state of sin knows without doubt where he stands – even if he does not choose to repent. The Englishman in a state of sin has no such collective consciousness. He can simply ignore the existence of God as an unproved hypothesis. Religion has never been, in this sense, since the Reformation, an instinctive part of his culture. If we need 'evidences' for the existence of light, then we are already blind.

The attack on Locke and the English empirical tradition is characteristic of the 'fiduciary' position – in which Newman

---

[1] *Grammar of Assent*, p. 47.   [2] *Anglican Difficulties*, ch. IX.

stands squarely in the tradition of Coleridge. But there is another element constantly present in Newman's thinking that while it can look like an aspect of the 'fiduciary' approach and flourishes in the same hedgerow, is, in fact, diametrically opposed to it. Wilfred Ward, his greatest biographer, notes right at the beginning of his study two opposite tendencies in Newman: a belief in the self-evident existence of God, and a strong intellectual tendency towards scepticism.[1] But it seems to me that Ward does not sufficiently allow for the way in which these tendencies, under certain circumstances, can actually reinforce one another. Such a tendency had been noted as early as the sixteenth century by a man who had become preoccupied by certain problems in this respect very similar to those of Newman: Michel de Montaigne. Scepticism, he observes, can so undermine reason that 'faith' is the inevitable result. Such arguments render a man's mind

...naked and empty, recognising his natural weakness, ready to receive some strange power from on high, unstripped of human knowledge and so much more apt to have laid in it the Divine, destroying his own judgement in order to make way for faith, neither misbelieving nor establishing a single dogma against custom. Humble, obedient, disciplined, studious; the sworn enemy of heresy, and consequently being free from vain and irreligious opinions introduced by false sects. It is a carte blanche ready to receive from the finger of God whatever forms it pleases him to engrave thereon.[2]

Faith is the outcome of despair of intellectual certainty. Now there are times when Newman seems to come very close to such a position. Many of his contemporaries – certainly Kingsley, and possibly Maurice as well – would have recognised in the Montaigne quotation a tolerably accurate reflection of Newman's post-1845 position. There are, so the argument runs, only two tenable alternatives: either 'faith' is based on 'reason' (in its broad sense, not the Kantian or Coleridgean meaning), or reason must be seen as an effective instrument only when it starts from the totally committed standpoint of faith. One way lies deism and liberalism, the other way lies Catholicism. As Newman himself had so aptly demonstrated, there can be no *via media*. He

[1] *Life of Newman*, I, 31.
[2] 'Apologie de Raimond Sebond', *Les Essais de Michel de Montaigne*, ed. Pierre Villey, II, (Paris, 1922), 238–9.

was fully prepared to accept and make use of Hume's jibe 'Our most holy Religion is founded on Faith, not on Reason.'[1] His persistent attacks on the evils of liberalism made it abundantly clear that once he had faced these two alternatives, he would unhesitatingly choose Catholicism. 'Liberalism', Newman defined as 'the exercise of thought on subjects on which, from the constitution of the human mind, thought cannot be brought to a successful conclusion.'[2] In one of the last great speeches of his life, his 'Biglietto Speech', made at the presentation of his Cardinal's hat in 1879, he attacked yet again the dangers of liberalism in religion.

[It]...is the doctrine that there is no positive truth in religion, but that one creed is as good as another, and this is the teaching which is gaining force daily. It teaches that all are to be tolerated, for all are matters of opinion. Revealed religion is not a truth, but a sentiment and a taste; not an objective fact, not miraculous; and it is the right of each individual to make it say just what strikes his fancy. Devotion is not necessarily founded on faith. Men may go to Protestant Churches and to Catholic, may get good from both and belong to neither. They may fraternise together in spiritual thoughts and feelings, without having any views at all of doctrines in common, or seeing the need of them. Since, then, religion is so personal a peculiarity and so private a possession, we must of necessity ignore it in the intercourse of man with man. If a man puts on a new religion every morning, what is that to you? It is as impertinent to think about a man's religion as about his sources of income or his management of his family. Religion is in no sense the bond of society.[3]

Enough has been quoted – from a wealth of material available – to make Newman's position apparently clear and unequivocal. Yet to polarise the problem in the way that Montaigne (for instance) implies, and Newman (it was widely believed) wished to do, is to beg the very question that so exercised them both. It was because Kingsley thought Newman really believed 'commitment is all', that he made his notorious charge that 'Truth for its own sake has never been a virtue with the Roman clergy. Father Newman informs us that it need not be, and on the whole ought not to be...'[4] The ins and outs, smears and innuendoes, retractions and evasions that dogged the actual dispute need not

---

[1] Chadwick, *From Bossuet to Newman*, p. 131.
[2] Ward, *Life of Newman*, I, 413.   [3] Ibid. II, 460.   [4] Ibid. I, 1.

concern us here. Kingsley had boobed. What is significant is
Newman's response: an *Apologia pro Vita Sua*. When challenged
to define the basis of religious commitment (the question of
Newman's own integrity really arose with Kingsley's later
'retraction'), Newman answers by telling the story of his own
life. Ostensibly this is to clear him of the accusation that he
advocated lying, but the defence is not wholly to the point. Few
by that stage really supposed he had. In fact the *Apologia* is not
so much 'a history of his religious opinions' as a personal account
of the nature of religious belief. For Newman, if not for Kingsley,
the two things were as different as chalk from cheese; both may
be edible, at a pinch, but only the latter nourishes. The distinction between 'opinion' and 'belief' (or 'notional' and 'real
assent') was to become the basis of his *Grammar of Assent*. It is
safe to say that if Newman had really accepted the position on
commitment that Kingsley ascribed to him, he would never have
written the *Grammar*. What interests him, from his own experience, is the felt tension between the two apparently exclusive
extremes. Is the alternative to reason (in human terms) simply
an act of the will, or is it the case that the kind of religious assent
that we loosely call 'faith' is not best accounted for by this kind
of model at all? Newman, like Coleridge, had a dialectical cast of
mind. Wilfred Ward was one among many to have noticed that
in the *University Lectures* there are two opposite lines of thought
'maintained with equal insistence':

One was that, although reason rightly exercised would in the long run
justify belief in Theism and Catholic Christianity in the face of all
difficulties, still in man as he exists, with his passions and with the
constant presence of the visible world to bring forgetfulness of the
invisible, a force stronger than his unaided intellect is needed to keep
alive and vivid those first principles on which religious belief depends.
And that force is supplied by the living Catholic Church. Secondly,
while free discussion is essential in order to clear the issues, in the
complicated structure of human knowledge, the intellect of man has
actually and historically a constant tendency to exceed its lawful limits
and arrive at unbelief, by reason of its failure in an impossible attempt.[1]

Newman is always acutely, often painfully, aware of the difficulties of enquiry into religious assent. His dialectic of opposites
is the product of a tenacious determination not to simplify or

[1] *Life of Newman*, I, 412–13.

evade material facts, or to produce paper answers to problems of the human heart. Running through all these quotations has been his sense of the life of the individual mind that is not to be contained by simple either/or logic. Speaking of Paley's arguments he comments 'I do not want to be converted by a smart syllogism; if I am asked to convert others by it, I say plainly I do not care to overcome their reason without touching their hearts.'[1] Elsewhere he adds, 'I think it is the fact that many of our most obstinate and most reasonable certitudes depend on proofs which are informal and personal, which baffle our powers of analysis, and cannot be brought under logical rule, because they cannot be submitted to logical statistics. If we must speak of law, this recognition of a correlation between certitude and implicit proof seems to me a law of our minds.'[2]

About the same time as he was writing the *Grammar of Assent*, Newman was in correspondence with a 'doubter':

You must begin all thought about religion by mastering what is the fact, that anyhow the question has an inherent, ineradicable difficulty in it. As in tuning a piano, you may throw the fault here or there, but no theory can anyone take up without that difficulty remaining. It will come up in one shape or other. If we say, 'Well, I will not believe anything,' there is a difficulty in believing nothing, an intellectual difficulty. There is a difficulty in doubting; a difficulty in determining there is no truth; in saying that there is a truth, but that no one can find it out; in saying that all religious opinions are true, or one as good as another; a difficulty in saying there is no God; that there is a God but that He has not revealed Himself except in the way of nature; and there is doubtless a difficulty in Christianity. The question is, whether on the whole our reason does not tell us that it is a duty to accept the arguments commonly urged for its truth as sufficient, and a duty in consequence to believe heartily in Scripture and the Church.[3]

Written to a Victorian 'doubter' it is easy to read that last sentence as a rhetorical exhortation: 'One thing thou needest to be saved: go, pull thyself together, and do thy Duty.' But knowing the way in which Newman's mind had been moving for more than thirty years, it is clear that he means exactly what he says. The burning *question* is just that, for him and the doubter alike.

[1] *Grammar of Assent*, p. 323.   [2] Ibid. p. 229.

[3] Ward, *Life of Newman*, p. 330. The 'doubter' was Louisa Simeon (*Letters and Diaries*, ed. C. S. Dessain (Oxford, 1961–) XXIV, 274–5).

Part of the 'inherent, ineradicable difficulty' lies in the complexity of the relationship between reason and will: a relationship which is neither random, nor reducible to a formula, but *personal*.

What establishes Newman so clearly as belonging to the tradition of Coleridge is this sense of an over-riding 'life' in ideas that runs counter to, or makes irrelevant, the precision of conventional logic, without undervaluing their intellectual force or blurring distinctions. Our ideas do not float free in the pure aether of reason. They are part of our whole framework of life, and cannot be separated from it. Newman's chosen motto as a Cardinal, *Cor ad cor loquitur*, summarises his lifelong preoccupation. 'Instead of presenting his readers,' writes Ward, 'with a logical formula which says equivalently "accept my position on pain of being convicted of an absurdity" – a treatment for which most Englishmen in the region of metaphysic have not sufficient logical nerve – he would seem to say, "take pains to understand my language, stand where I stand and see if you do not feel as I am feeling".'[1] Early in the *Grammar of Assent* he notes with interest the paradox that 'when Inference is clearest, Assent may be least forcible, and when Assent is most intense, Inference may be least distinct'.[2] Belief, it is true, will tend to be grounded in logical inference, but the strength with which we hold a belief is *not* in fact directly proportional to the strength of the evidence. Are we here up against human irrationality so cross-grained that this kind of enquiry into the human mind and its processes is simply impossible without explaining all 'belief' away as manifestations of deep unconscious psychic needs, peculiar to the individual, and largely inaccessible to rational study, or is this rather evidence that we are using simply the wrong conceptual framework for dealing with the problem? Must we choose between Locke and Montaigne? – or does the Romantic tradition of Coleridge offer a different set of conceptual possibilities? In the *Grammar of Assent* Newman is concerned with what he sees as the fundamental distinction between personal knowledge ('real assent') and second-hand ('notional assent'). Now these are categories that cut right across the faith/reason dichotomy in which the problem had previously been cast, and to which he himself was to some extent still conceptually bound. I think we

---

[1] *Life of Newman*, II, 357.   [2] P. 32.

fail to grasp what is going on in the *Grammar of Assent* if we try to read it as 'an hypothesis to account for a difficulty' in the sense that the *Essay on the Development of Christian Doctrine* was. As Newman grew older his interests changed in a number of ways, not least in that he became progressively less interested in providing answers to problems, and more interested in trying to understand the nature of the problems themselves. The *Grammar of Assent* grows out of the *Essay on the Development of Christian Doctrine* in the sense that it is now trying to formulate a different kind of problem. In a letter of 1868 to Henry Wilberforce Newman makes it clear that he saw his *Grammar* as 'a first map'.[1]

'My Essay on Assent', he wrote to Aubrey de Vere in 1870, immediately after its publication,'. . . is on a subject which has teazed me for these twenty or thirty years. I felt I had something to say upon it, yet, whenever I attempted, the sight I saw vanished, plunged into a thicket, curled itself up like a hedgehog, or changed colours like a chameleon. I have a succession of commencements, perhaps a dozen, each different from the other, and, in a different year, which came to nothing.'[2] It was at Glion on the Lake of Geneva in 1866 that what he called the 'Open Sesame' finally came to him. He realised, he tells us, that certitude is a form of assent, and that to treat the psychology of assent as distinguished from inference was the key.[3]

In book 4 of the *Essay Concerning Human Understanding*, chapter xv, Locke states that

. . . most of the propositions we think, reason, discourse, nay, act upon, are such as we cannot have undoubted knowledge of their truth; yet some of them border so near upon certainty that we make no doubt about them, but assent to them as firmly and act accordingly to that assent as resolutely as if they were infallibly demonstrated, and that our knowledge of them was perfect and certain. But there being degrees herein, from the very neighbourhood of certainty and demonstration quite down to improbability and unlikeness, even to the confines of impossibility, and also degrees of assent from full assurance and confidence, quite down to conjecture, doubt, and distrust. . .[4]

This idea that there are degrees of assent is made the cornerstone of Locke's ethics of belief.[5] We can only believe in some-

[1] Ward, *Life of Newman*, II, 248. [2] Ibid. p. 245. [3] Ibid. pp. 245–6.
[4] Ed. J. W. Yolton (Everyman, 1961), section 2.
[5] Here, as frequently in this chapter, I am indebted to Tony Palmer of the

thing in proportion to the evidence available. We ought not to accept any proposition 'with greater assurance than the proofs it is built upon will warrant'. To Newman this was nonsense. It just didn't happen like that. 'Locke's theory of the duty of assenting more or less according to degrees of evidence, is invalidated by the testimony of high and low, young and old, ancient and modern, as continually given in their ordinary sayings and doings.'[1] His attack on Locke is not a vindication of faith as a refuge from scepticism, but an onslaught on what he saw as the crude fallacy of supposing that we can treat relations between beliefs in the same way that we treat relations between propositions. Such was not Newman's own experience. The contrast between his conversion to Rome and that of his Oxford contemporary, W. G. Ward,[2] illustrates the difference, even when retold by Lytton Strachey:

'The thing that was utterly abhorrent to him', said one of his friends, 'was to stop short.' Given the premises he would follow out their implications with the mercilessness of a medieval monk, and when he had reached the last limits of argument be ready to maintain whatever propositions he found there with his dying breath...Captivated by the glittering eye of Newman, he swallowed whole the supernatural conception of the universe which Newman had evolved, accepted it as a fundamental premise and began at once to deduce from it whatsoever there might be to be deduced.[3]

In contrast, it took Newman six years from the beginning of his doubts in 1839 to be received into the Roman Church. Of Ward, he wrote to Pusey, 'As to my being entirely with Ward, I do not know the limits of my own opinions. If Ward says that this or that is a development from what I have said, I cannot say Yes or No...It is plausible and it may be true; but I cannot, with that keen perception which some people have, appropriate it. It is a nuisance to me to be forced beyond what I can fairly accept.'[4] There is, for Newman, all the difference in the world between changing one's mind, and one's mind changing. In the *Grammar*

Department of Philosophy, Southampton University both for remarks made in conversation, and for permission to quote from his unpublished paper, *Belief and Will*.

[1] *Grammar of Assent*, p. 133.
[2] Father of Wilfred Ward, Newman's biographer.
[3] 'Life of Cardinal Manning', *Eminent Victorians*, p. 33.   [4] *Apologia*, p. 157.

of Assent he is trying to map largely unexplored territory: the movement of his own belief. A modern philosopher has pointed out Newman as standing in the minority tradition of those who see 'that belief and will might be so related that it is neither the case that belief is voluntary nor the case that it is involuntary any more than willing itself can be voluntary or involuntary'.[1] What wills the will? One only has to ask the question to see that it is either absurd, or entangles one in an infinite regress of voluntary causes. For Newman, the first two parts of a syllogism might be demonstrably true, yet intellectual honesty and integrity (not cowardice and muddled thinking) could compel him to deny that the conclusion necessarily followed. Similarly it was not the case that belief rested on inference, nor was it, he saw, the case that belief was unconnected with inference. What makes Newman a philosopher of stature is that instead of dismissing such areas as atypical and unhelpful, he chooses to try and understand them in relation to the whole.

The basic distinction between 'real' and 'notional' assents is to be found in Paul and Augustine, and is part of a continuous tradition of Christian thought from earliest times. It was in this tradition that John Wesley preached his famous sermon 'The Almost Christian' from the pulpit of Newman's own church, St Mary the Virgin, before the University of Oxford in 1741.[2] He cites as his authority the Anglican homily, 'On the Salvation of Man', thus drawing on the much rarer Anglican tradition of Cranmer and Luther, rather than that of Calvin. The way in which Newman uses the distinction, however, suggests that it owes more to Coleridge than to either Wesley or Augustine. As we have seen, he was prepared to discard the distinctions concerning 'evidences' and 'will' that still obsessed Evangelicals and High Church alike. Newman's is a psychological problem: the active 'life and force' possessed by a 'real' assent as against the mere passive acquiescence of a 'notional' assent. The distinction is not a new one to Newman. It underlies his views on the nature of an 'idea' in the *Essay on the Development of Christian Doctrine*, and again in his *Lectures on Certain Difficulties felt by Anglicans*, and it is the basis of his conception of a liberal education in *The*

[1] Palmer, *Belief and Will*.
[2] *Sermons on Several Occasions*, first series, consisting of 44 discourses, 4th edn (1787), no. 2.

Idea of a University. For Coleridge, the distinction between 'active' and 'passive' states of mind was a turning-point in his philosophical career. It meant the rejection of Locke and Hartley and their associated psychological systems in favour of those of Kant and Schelling; it paved the way for the distinction between 'Imagination' and 'Fancy', and again between 'Reason' and 'Understanding'. Possibly even more important for Newman, it enabled him from personal experience to distinguish between 'thinking that was dynamic, imaginative, and fertile, and the relatively passive thing that often went by its name'.[1] This was probably the central stimulus for Coleridge in developing his theories of the growth of the mind.

> O Lady! we receive but what we give,
> And in our life alone does Nature live.[2]

I. A. Richards argues that Coleridge had to 'extricatè himself from the Locke tradition' of the mind as a passive receptor 'not because it was "false", but because for himself, at some hours, it was too painfully true'.[3] In what is possibly the best short study that has been written on this aspect of Coleridge, Professor Dorothy Emmet comments,

I believe that Coleridge was concerned to explore not only a source of the creative power of the imagination shown in genius but also more generally the liberation of the mind from deadness and dereliction, a liberation on which growth depends... Coleridge's 'empirico-religious' philosophy was concerned with exploring the conditions which made possible, and the conditions which frustrate this joy which underlies the creative growth of the mind.[4]

For Coleridge, the active, creative power of the imagination manifest typically in genius, and available to all through the symbolism of art, poetry, and above all the scriptures as 'the living *educts* of the Imagination', is also the characteristic expression of religious response. It is not possible, he believed, to separate religious *experience* from religious *development*. For this he has Christ's authority: 'I am come that ye might have life,

---

[1] Snyder, *Coleridge on Logic and Learning*, p. 12.

[2] *Dejection; An Ode*, lines 47–8.

[3] *Coleridge on Imagination* (Kegan Paul, 1934), p. 60.

[4] 'Coleridge on the Growth of the Mind', *Bulletin of the John Rylands Library*, vol. 34, no. 2 (Manchester, March 1952), p. 292.

and have it more abundantly.' 'Christianity is not a Theory, or a speculation, but a *Life*. Not a *Philosophy* of Life, but a Life and a Living Process...TRY IT.'[1]

Newman's distinction, however, though it starts from a similar point to Coleridge's, is not quite the same. It is not simply a distinction between first-hand and second-hand knowledge. He clearly sees the dichotomy between 'notional' and 'real' at work inside both the former categories. It is, rather, that between the *kind* of grasp we can have of concrete imaginatively realised facts, and those that remain abstract and essentially 'un-realised'. His problem is, as it were, at one step from Coleridge's. It is concerned with the nature of the imagination – and therefore with the nature of the symbols and myths by which we give shape to our experience.

By his own admission – which was not always to be trusted – Newman first began to read Coleridge in the spring of 1835,[2] and he confessed himself 'surprised how much I thought was mine, is to be found there'. For those who suspect that he had come across Coleridge earlier, the admission is an ambiguous one. Certainly many contemporaries felt the hand of Coleridge in the whole Newmanite ethos. Mark Pattison, writing in bleak old age of the fact that Newman had supported him for an Oriel fellowship, records:

It will appear strange that I could have satisfied Newman on the questions of morals and logic...But...early in 1837 I had fallen under the influence of Coleridge. I got all his books that I could; they had not then been reprinted, and were difficult to procure. The *Aids to Reflection* especially dominated me. The vague mysticism in which he loves to veil himself had a peculiar charm for me. Led on by Coleridge I had read Augustus Schlegel, and I certainly had fallen away from Baconian principles, and passed under the first influences of a realistic philosophy. It so happened that I could not have handled the Oriel philosophy paper in a way to meet the views of the examiners, but for this strong infusion of Coleridgean metaphysics.[3]

The evidence for a 'common tradition' is beyond question. As for evidence of *direct* influence, one normally assumes that the effect one writer has on another will be greatest when the works are

[1] *Aids to Reflection*, p. 178.
[2] At the instigation of the Acland family, who had known Coleridge in Somerset.
[3] *Memoirs* (Macmillan, 1885), pp. 164–5.

first read, and when the reader is relatively young and impressionable. Now Newman, it seems to me, is a curious exception to this rule. As I hope to show in the rest of this chapter, there is evidence to show that as Newman grows older and as his interests as a Catholic become less formally dogmatic and more concerned with the nature of ideas, imagination, and belief, so the parallels with Coleridge (and the apparent borrowings) become strikingly more marked. He becomes progressively more 'Coleridgean' with age – or, to put it no less fairly, if we wish to understand the implications of many of Coleridge's philosophical and religious insights, it is to the writing of Newman, the old Roman Catholic theologian, more than to any other thinker that we must look.

As we have seen, in focussing his attention not on logic, or metaphysics as the cornerstone of belief, but on 'the living mind', Newman stands in the common tradition of Coleridge and Wordsworth. He is as wary of 'systems' as Maurice himself. He is not, he warns us, trying to invent a 'psychological' theory, but merely to look at the way in which the mind actually moves, 'by whatever hidden mechanism'. The enquiry is, in this sense, 'empirical'. 'A locomotive engine could not move without steam, but still, under whatever number of forces, it certainly does start from Birmingham and does arrive in London.'[1] In appealing to the strength of common observation and intuitive feeling, Newman is criticising Locke from the same standpoint as Coleridge does in chapter XII of *Biographia Literaria*. As his Romantic opponents came increasingly to realise, the real effect of Locke's psychology is to blur the boundaries between physiology and epistemology. The individual became trapped inside his own skull fed only on 'ideas' conveyed through the nerves which were demonstrably unreliable links with a 'real' world outside. In a curious way, Locke out-Platos Plato, since at least Plato's 'real' world of ideal forms *is* ultimately knowable to the initiated, whereas Locke's 'reality' can *never* be.[2] Coleridge in *Biographia Literaria* sees very clearly where Locke is leading us, and is not impressed.

[1] It is significant to notice which way the journey is being undertaken, in view of the parallel with Newman's own spiritual journey from a 'provincial' to a 'metropolitan' faith.

[2] See A. D. Nuttall's *A Common Sky* (Chatto, 1974), ch. I, 'The Sealing of the Doors'.

The realism common to all mankind is far elder and lies infinitely deeper than this hypothetical explanation of perceptions, an explanation skimmed from the mere surface of mechanical philosophy. It is the table itself, which the man of common sense believes himself to see, not the phantom of a table, from which he may argumentatively deduce the reality of a table, which he does not see. If to destroy the reality of all, that we actually behold,[1] be idealism, what can be more egregiously so, than the system of modern metaphysics, which banishes us to a land of shadows, surrounds us with apparitions, and distinguishes truth from illusion only by the majority of those who dream the same dream? '*I* asserted that the world was mad,' exclaimed poor Lee, 'and the world said, that I was mad, and confound them, they outvoted me.'[2]

The danger, as Coleridge sees, is for a covert *a priori* reasoning to take over under the impeccable guise of 'common-sense'. Newman elaborates this point carefully when he comes to introduce what he calls the 'Illative' sense:

There are those, who, arguing *à priori*, maintain, that, since experience leads by syllogism only to probabilities, certitude is ever a mistake. There are others, who, while they deny this conclusion, grant the *à priori* principle assumed in the argument, and in consequence are obliged, in order to vindicate the certainty of our knowledge, to have recourse to the hypothesis of intuitions, intellectual forms, and the like, which belong to us by nature, and may be considered to elevate our experience into something more than it is in itself. Earnestly maintaining, as I would, with this latter school of philosophers, the certainty of knowledge, I think it enough to appeal to the common voice of mankind in proof of it.[3]

Platonism, Kantian Idealism, and all other such metaphysical systems – be they true or false – are supported by hypotheses which, however much they may claim their own 'proofs', ultimately rest on the same kind of *a priori* reasoning as does Locke. Newman wants to break away from all such, and claim instead a truly empirical base: the common testimony of mankind. 'It is to be accounted a normal operation of our nature, which men in general do actually instance.' Here is the authentic echo of Coleridge. The illative sense, as Newman explains it, is nothing less than the deep-seated human capacity to draw certainties from evidence that is only probable. Certainty

---

[1] See *Tintern Abbey*, line 104.   [2] *Biographia Literaria*, I, 179.
[3] *Grammar of Assent*, p. 261.

...is the cumulation of probabilities, independent of each other, arising out of the nature and circumstances of the particular case which is under review; probabilities too fine to avail separately, too subtle and circuituous to be convertible into syllogisms, too numerous and various for such conversion, even were they convertible. As a man's portrait differs from a sketch of him, in having, not merely a continuous outline, but all its details filled in, and shades and colours laid on and harmonized together, such is the multiform and intricate process of ratiocination, necessary for our reaching him as a concrete fact, compared with the rude operation of syllogistic logic.[1]

Here Newman draws, as he so often does, on Butler, but he adds to Butler's force of probability the *active* and assimilating nature of our mental powers. Thought is not analogous to the image on the retina of the eye (this is the essence of Locke's error), but it has the capacity to step beyond evidence and create for itself wholes that are greater than the constituents, individually assessed.[2] 'Such a living *organon* is a personal gift, and not a mere method of calculus.' We can verify this by simple observation. Thus certitude is 'an *action* more subtle and more comprehensive than the mere appreciation of a syllogistic logic'.[3] It 'is not a *passive* impression made upon the mind from without by argumentative compulsion, but...an *active* recognition of propositions as true...'.[4]

'There is,' says Newman, 'no ultimate test of truth besides the testimony borne to truth by the mind itself.' Man's 'progress is a living growth, not a mechanism'.[5] This 'active' and self-authenticating recognition of truth, is, we notice, directly linked by Newman with 'real ratiocination' and 'present imagination'. I have described the *Grammar of Assent* in Newman's words as an attempt to draw a 'map', but the map-image is in fact too static a one for the way in which Newman develops and works out his ideas in the course of his argument. Take, for instance, his use of this word 'imagination'.

Vargish and Coulson are at loggerheads over Newman's use of it. 'Newman,' Vargish tells us, 'usually employs the word to mean approximately what Coleridge meant by "Fancy"' – but with something too of the eighteenth century's idea that it can be dangerous and misleading.[6] Coulson, on the contrary, finds

[1] Ibid. p. 219.   [2] Ibid. p. 240.   [3] Ibid. p. 241.   [4] Ibid. p. 262. My italics.
[5] Ibid. p. 266.   [6] Vargish, *Newman*, pp. 48–9.

Newman's use of 'imagination' very close to Coleridge's.[1] Both are, in fact, right. Newman's use of the word changes dramatically in the course of his life, moving from the eighteenth-century sense when he was a young man to a sense that is similar to, and perhaps goes beyond that of Coleridge by the time he came to write the *Grammar of Assent*. In his early essay on *Poetry, with Reference to Aristotle's Poetics* in 1829 we can see how very similar Newman's use of the word is to Keble's. 'Poetry,' he says, 'recreates the imagination by the superhuman loveliness of its views, it provides a solace for the mind broken by the disappointments and sufferings of actual life.'[2] Since this pre-dates Keble's Lectures by some five years it is even possible that Newman here is an influence on the older man, rather than vice versa. Yet while Newman is ostensibly discussing Aristotle, he is more Platonic than Keble ever was. 'The metrical garb' and 'metaphorical language' of poetry are 'but the outward development of the music and harmony within'. The poetical mind 'is called imaginative or creative, from the originality and independence of its modes of thinking'. Now it is not clear from this kind of context how far 'imagination' is concerned solely with organising the 'metrical garb', and how far it is the power by which the poet perceives 'the music and harmony within'. The former sense would be akin to Coleridge's 'fancy'; the latter would be more similar to Keats' use of the word 'imagination'. In either case it does not seem to resemble Coleridge's since it does not appear to be a 'strong' word, and it lacks the characteristic bi-focal quality that is the hallmark of his conception. Forty years later, in 1869, when Newman came to write the *Grammar of Assent*, we find a striking change. Nowhere does he use 'imagination' to suggest powers of ornament or aggregation. Writing on 'the apprehension of propositions' he describes by elaborate circumlocutions 'an inventive faculty, or as I may call it, the faculty of composition...'[3] without ever once employing the obvious word. The reason for this abstinence becomes clear as his argument unfolds. 'Imagination' is for Newman now the active power of the illative sense, making the abstract concrete, and the notional real. 'The question before me,' he writes of the doctrine of the Trinity, 'is whether in any sense it can become

---

[1] 'Belief and Imagination', *Downside Review*, vol. 90, no. 298 (January 1972).
[2] *Essays Critical and Historical*, I, p. 10.   [3] *Grammar of Assent*, p. 22.

the object of real apprehension, that is, whether any portion of it may be considered as addressed to the imagination, and is able to exert that living mastery over the mind...'[1] The illative imagination is the 'principle which rightly interprets the riddle, and...converts a chaos into an orderly and luminous whole'.[2]

The similarity to Coleridge here is significantly close in its bi-focal suggestions. 'Imagination' is an organising power, but its powers of organisation are directly associated with a very different transcendent quality reminiscent of Plato's 'recognition' theory of knowledge. The creative power of the illative imagination leaps boldly from inference and probability to certainty, as if thinking God's thoughts after him. The key difference from Coleridge lies in that word 'rightly'. For Coleridge the bi-focal symbolising power of the imagination had always seemed to carry with it some kind of self-authenticating guarantee of truth. For Newman, this was plainly not so in all cases. The problem of the truth or falsity of the imagination was one that became very important to him. Though he himself seems to come very near to Coleridge's assumption of self-authentication in the *Essay on the Development of Christian Doctrine*, the guarantee is in fact given here not by the symbolising process itself (as it often appears to be with Coleridge) but by the special subject-matter: an infallibly guided Church. To interpret rightly is not a gift of the illative imagination working by itself: 'such aspects are often unreal, as being mere exhibitions of ingenuity, not of true originality of mind'.[3] 'This is especially the case in what are called philosophical views of history,' Newman adds darkly, singling out Warburton and Gibbon as examples of error. Indeed, there is no suggestion that the illative imagination is not as fallible and prone to misapprehension as any other faculty. Knowledge is ambiguous and relative in great things, as in little.[4]

Newman's conclusion is not that there is no objective truth, but rather that 'there is something deeper in our differences than the accident of external circumstances; and that we need the interposition of a Power greater than human teaching and human argument to make our beliefs true and our minds one'.[5] It comes as no surprise to us to learn that this 'Power' is that of the Roman Catholic Church. However, Newman soon makes it

[1] *Grammar of Assent*, p. 95.   [2] Ibid. p. 283.   [3] Ibid. p. 283.
[4] Ibid. p. 284.   [5] Ibid. p. 285.

clear that he is *not* thinking of the dogmatic power of the papacy or even of the great Councils. The pressure for the official declaration of papal infallibility from certain vocal sections of the Roman Church in the years leading up to 1870 was intense, and Newman's argument here can be read as an implicit refutation of Ultramontane extremism:[1] to which he was, in fact, opposed. The establishment of 'truth' by dogmatic ruling, however unexceptionable it might be doctrinally, damages the very principle of the 'life' of the mind which he has been at such pains to describe. In his own terms, it would produce a 'notional' assent, a mere passive acceptance, rather than an active 'real' assent. It would not engage the imagination. For Newman, the objective truth of Catholic belief is infallibly safeguarded by something far stronger than historically dubious explanations of Pope Honorius' support for the heretical Patriarch Sergius.[2] It is safeguarded by its own inner life as a whole.

Earlier in this chapter I used the phrase 'a form of life' to describe the total unity of our sense-world envisaged by the Romantics in contradistinction to Locke's model of man imprisoned by his senses. In using the phrase I wished to emphasise the paradox that the *means* by which we perceive cannot be separated from our mode of consciousness:

> Why has not man a microscopic eye?
> For this plain reason, man is not a fly.[3]

The senses cannot be understood as separate faculties, but as part of the living system of a conscious and volitional being. The Cumberland beggar sees a different world from the boy Wordsworth. The botanist sees a different hedge from the farmer. The religious man will perceive a different universe from the irreligious one. There is, however, another reason why the phrase 'a form of life' is peculiarly apposite to Newman's argument. The phrase comes not from Newman but from Wittgenstein:

240. Disputes do not break out (among mathematicians, say) over the question of whether a rule has been disobeyed or not. People don't come to blows over it, for example. That is part of the framework on which the working of our language is based (for example, in giving descriptions).

---

[1] Ward, *Life of Newman*, vol. II, ch. XXVII.   [2] Ibid. pp. 235–7.
[3] Alexander Pope, *Essay on Man* (1733), lines 193–4.

241. So you are saying that human agreement decides what is true and what is false? – It is what human beings *say* that is true and false; and they agree in the language they use. That is not agreement in opinions but in form of life.

What has to be accepted, the given, is – so one could say – *forms of life*.[1]

Now Wittgenstein himself was not entirely happy with his phrase, and there remains considerable disagreement between philosophers as to his exact meaning. Nevertheless, it does seem to me a helpful analogy in trying to describe what Newman seems to mean by 'life' as a collective quality within the community of the Catholic Church. Wittgenstein makes two points about the phenomenon of belief which seem to echo and shed light on Newman. The first is that certitude constitutes an enclosed world which one cannot step outside. 'I say of someone else,' Wittgenstein observes, '"He seems to believe..."' and others rightly say it of me. Now why do I never say it of myself, not even when others rightly say it of me?' A 'form of life', for him, as for Newman, is not analogous to a 'language game' in the sense that we can be aware of other language games. Newman comments that it is a characteristic of certitude that we also believe that if our acceptance of it (for some reason) should fail, it would nevertheless be still true.[2] We can describe our 'form of life' as resting upon a network of interlocking certitudes which are analogous to our perceptions in that we reason with them rather than about them: they are, as it were, the groundwork on which our consciousness itself is based. As do the senses, which are among these certainties, they both create and provide the limits of our experience. If a 'form of life' is thought of in this way as the 'ground of our being', it is obvious that other alternatives, like other languages we do not speak, do not make sense to us. Thus – and this is the second point – there comes a moment at which questions about the justification of beliefs make no more sense. Describing how we obey a rule, Wittgenstein says, 'If I have exhausted the justifications I have reached bedrock, and my spade is turned. Then I am inclined to say: "This is simply what I do".'

For Newman, the metaphorical frame of reference of any language cannot be understood apart from the communal life

---

[1] *Philosophical Investigations* (Blackwell, 1953), part ii, section xi.
[2] *Grammar of Assent*, p. 151.

from which it springs – and of which it is itself a part.[1] The price of speaking and thinking in a particular language is that we are also bound by 'the framework on which the working of our language is based'.[2] Religious language is no exception. Newman's increasing distrust of formal syllogistic logic turned him more and more towards an interest in analogy, metaphor, and symbol as the appropriate vehicles of the living ideas of a community. It is the very purpose of formal logic to *lose* the richness and vitality of actual experience in the interests of artificial clarity. Similarly, he notes that language itself undergoes an impoverishment at the hands of logicians.

The concrete matter of propositions is a constant source of trouble to syllogistic reasoning, as marring the simplicity and perfection of its process. Words, which denote things, have innumerable implications, but in inferential exercises it is the very triumph of that clearness and hardness of head, which is the characteristic talent for the art, to have stripped them of all these connatural senses, to have drained them of that depth and breadth of associations which constitute their poetry, their rhetoric, and their historical life, to have starved each term down till it has become the ghost of itself...[3]

[1] The fullest exposition of this view is in the *Idea of a University*, but see also Ward, *Life of Newman*, I, ch. XII; and Coulson, p. 174.

[2] There is an interesting parallel between Newman and Wittgenstein here. Neither was a particularly good linguist, though both often found themselves forced to try and express their ideas in a second language. Both assume that we have a *basic* language-knowledge which enables us to learn others, and explore different linguistic possibilities. We need to move out, as it were, from a fixed point. Neither seems to envisage the possibility of being truly bilingual. Such an idea lies behind Wittgenstein's conception of a 'form of life':

> We say of some people that they are transparent to us. It is, however, important as regards this observation that one human being can be a complete enigma to another. We learn this when we come into a strange country with entirely strange traditions; and what is more, even given a mastery of the country's language, we do not understand the people. (And not because of not knowing what they are saying to themselves.) We cannot find our feet with them. *Investigations*, Part II, section XI.

Clearly, this is most revealing of Wittgenstein's own predicament as a native German-speaker living unhappily in England. But his wider point is very close to that of Newman: it is possible to understand apparently every word of a language and still 'not understand the people'. What the foreigner does not share with the people, is the form of life. Clearly, such a position is very close to Newman's view of religious language.

[3] *Grammar of Assent*, p. 203. Notice the similarity of sentiment with that of Coleridge:

> ...accustom yourself to reflect on the words you use, hear, or read, their birth, derivation and history. For if words are not THINGS, they are LIVING

In short, Newman seems to suggest, the Catholic Church is ultimately safeguarded from error not by pronouncements of Pope or Council (essential as these are) but by the *living* organic structure of the whole body. How should we describe the richness of historical tradition, of language, of emotional association that we feel in the organic life of the Catholic Church? Newman repeats the answer he had already given in his 1846 essay on Keble: the life of the Church is *poetic*. 'The Church herself is the most sacred and august of poets...'[1] Dogmatic formulations are a necessary part of the total poetic nature of the Church – analogous, perhaps, to the conscious cerebration of the poet – yet it can only be a putting into philosophic language of what is inarticulately felt by the whole body. If the intellect is dissociated from the instinctive unconscious life of the whole, be it never so clever, it will tend to seek not the truth, but tactical advantage – as in the case of Pope Honorius.[2] The head, separated from the heart, will move towards notional and not real assent. Christianity is a form of life. Its evidence rests not on the cumulative weight of presumptives and probabilities, but on the fact that these in turn are a part of the ongoing life of the Church: in her life they acquire their proper meaning. 'The very idea of Christianity' is a 'Revelatio revelata', bearing witness to its own truth.[3]

This essentially 'poetic' view of assent as an imaginative act involving the life of the whole person serves to explain a curious paradox in Newman's thinking in the *Grammar of Assent*. On the one hand, he believes that assent is not separable from the Church as a 'form of life' and a living community of belief with its own metaphorical and symbolic structure; on the other, he holds no less strongly to the intuitively observed fact that whereas notional assent can easily be shared and communicated, real assent 'is proper to the individual, and as such, thwarts rather than promotes the intercourse of man with man'.[4] It is of the nature of real assent that it is *both* deeply personal to the point of incommunicability, *and* simultaneously arises from a linguistic

POWERS, by which the things of most importance to mankind are actuated, combined, and humanized. *Aids to Reflection*, p. xvii.

1 *Essays Critical and Historical*, ii, 442.
2 Ward, *Life of Newman*, i, 504; ii, 235–7, 556–7, 562–3.
3 *Grammar of Assent*, p. 294.   4 Ibid. p. 64.

and metaphorical community. We sense at once the closeness of this to Keble's idea of the poet as a man speaking to men, but *necessarily* under tension, and by disguise, hiding his own feelings even as he arouses feelings in others. But Newman has moved beyond Keble, just as he has moved beyond Coleridge. This paradox he sees as central to the life of the individual within the Church. From his conversion in 1845 onwards Newman never ceased to bewail the demise of the great theological schools of Catholic christendom, without which, he believed, the intellectual life of the Church was in danger of becoming unbalanced and impoverished. It should be the theological schools, not populist pressure groups, that should weigh, sift, and debate the arguments for papal infallibility. As usual, this has a personal reference. Newman as an Anglican was part of a movement, which was potentially, and to some extent actually a great power-house of piety and scholarship to renew the English tradition. By 1845 Hurrell Froude, perhaps his closest friend in the Oxford Movement, was already dead. Those who went to Rome during the late 30s, 40s, and early 50s were either men of inferior intellectual calibre to Newman, like Dalgairns and Ambrose St John, or men of very different intellectual outlook, like W. G. Ward, and Manning.[1] Keble and Pusey remained Anglicans. As a Roman Catholic Newman had many friends but never ceased to feel emotionally isolated. He saw himself in the tradition of bold innovating theologians who had in times past seized on the philosophical weapons of the Church's opponents and used them in her service – men like Albertus Magnus, Aquinas, and Alexander of Hales.[2] To some extent he had done so in his *Essay on the Development of Christian Doctrine*, the *Lectures on Certain Difficulties felt by Anglicans* and the *University Lectures*. Yet his attempts had passed largely unnoticed and undebated in the Catholic world. Ironically, it was the Anglicans, not the Catholics, who read and debated his new theology: there was no Roman Maurice to engage him in dialectic within the Coleridgean tradition. He had to stand unsupported by any school such as a Catholic university might have provided, and knowing that there were no similar schools elsewhere who could

[1] By a nice irony one such convert in 1846 was Frederick Apthorp Paley, grandson of the author of the *Evidences*.
[2] Ward, *Life of Newman*, I, 396.

study and criticise his work with informed skill. Though the Catholic hierarchy realised they had acquired a 'formidable engine of war' on their side, they were very unsure which way it might go off, or what it might do. They had no Roman Oxford in which they might put him. Instead, his ideas were met with suspicion rather than argument, his proposals (for instance, for a true Catholic university) were neither implemented nor rejected, they were quietly dropped in a conspiracy of silence.

It is small wonder that Newman returned again and again to the rôle of the individual theologian within the Catholic Church. 'It is individuals,' he decided, 'and not the Holy See that have given the lead to the Catholic mind in theological enquiry.' 'Religion is never in greater danger than when in consequence of national or international troubles the schools of theology have broken up or ceased to be.'[1] The individual theologian was analogous to the poet (whom he often so closely resembled) and helped to strengthen and purify the 'dialect of the tribe' – the 'poetic' tradition of the whole. Nor is originality out of place in such an analogy. For Newman, 'patristic and scholastic theology' each involved a 'creative act of the intellect...There is no greater mistake surely than to suppose that revealed truth precludes originality in the treatment of it.'[2] The basic image in his mind is the 'poetic' nature of revelation itself, shaping our awareness of the world in new and totally unexpected ways. 'Strangeness is the characteristic of revelation if made.'[3] We are changed by it.

But the idea of the Church as 'poetic' is far stronger than an analogy to Newman. It often seems, indeed, that for him the aesthetic unity of poetry is analogous to the divine unity of the Church, rather than vice versa – an inversion we find hinted at in Keble. Similarly, 'imagination' is, as we have seen, a 'strong' word in Newman's vocabulary by the time of the *Grammar of Assent* because it is the prime instrument of religious perception.[4] Propositions are useful in religion just as formal logic is useful in language, but neither produces more than notional assent. 'Religion has to do with the real, and the real is the particular; theology has to do with what is notional, and the notional is the

---

[1] Ward, *Life of Newman*, I, 250.   [2] Ibid. I, 436.
[3] Ibid. I, 424.
[4] Or of religious infidelity, as the reverse side of the coin. *Ibid.* II, 478.

general and systematic.'[1] Real apprehension of the being and attributes of God is the product of the imagination,[2] which, paradoxically seizes on the finite and the particular. Hence the Church actually *lives* not through its theology, but in its symbols and sacraments. The Catholic Church, the scriptures, the sacraments, and even the crucifix 'in every house and chamber', ensure that Christ 'lives, to our imaginations, by His visible symbols'.[3] Thus the doctrine of the Trinity is clearly 'notional' at the level of a proposition. Can it, asks Newman, *also* be real? 'The question before me is whether in any sense it can become the object of real apprehension, that is, whether any portion of it may be considered as addressed to the imagination, and is able to exert that living mastery over the mind. . .'[4] There must always be, in his view, a tension between a propositional knowledge of the Trinity and the experiential real knowledge of the individual believer. A real assent to the whole doctrine of the Trinity is impossible, since the 'whole' must be finally a mystery,[5] but without a real imaginative grasp of this mystery the whole doctrine is lifeless and without meaning. For Newman, this is illustrated by the first part of chapter i of St John's Gospel, which shows us a real assent to the notional proposition, 'The Son is God.'[6] The scriptures have the concreteness and inwardness of real assent, rather than the generalisation and abstraction of theological propositions – just 'as true poetry is a spontaneous outpouring of thought, whereas no one becomes a poet merely by the canons of criticism'.[7] As 'poetry' the scriptures appeal not to man's intellect alone, but to his imagination as well. In effect, Newman is at last both endorsing and elaborating Coleridge's view of the scriptures as the 'living *educts* of the Imagination'.

At every level, indeed, Coleridgean principles are being applied and simultaneously transformed in the *Grammar*. For Newman, as for Coleridge, there is no clear break psychologically and empirically between natural and supernatural: they may pull in opposite directions, but they are no less mutually dependent. His whole approach has been with the aim of showing that we live our natural lives by depending on certainties for which we lack evidence. Such certainties are not merely notional assents, but also real – in the sense that they are not just ideas, but beliefs

[1] *Grammar of Assent*, p. 106.   [2] Ibid. pp. 92–3.   [3] Ibid. p. 372.
[4] Ibid. p. 95.   [5] Ibid. p. 97.   [6] Ibid. p. 105.   [7] Ibid. p. 251.

to which we are totally committed; they constitute the media and the boundaries of our form of life. Religious beliefs differ in their subject, but psychologically do not differ in kind or in the mode of operation from these 'natural' beliefs. We are able to entertain religious belief because we have already depended upon natural belief. 'Instead of saying that the truths of Revelation depend on those of Natural Religion,' argues Newman, 'it is more pertinent to say that belief in revealed truths depends on belief in natural.'[1] In each case, the processes that lead us from inference and probability to certainty are essentially the same. 'The habits of thought and the reasonings which lead us on to a higher state of belief than our present, are the very same which we already possess in connexion with the lower state.'[2]

The parallel with Coleridge's two imaginations appears too exact and calculated for Newman not to have been aware of what he was doing. For Coleridge, we recall, the Primary Imagination is 'the prime instrument of all human perception'; it is the active power of the mind by which we create coherent wholes from the inchoate pattern of sense-data. The Secondary Imagination is the creative power of the artist, which changes the way in which we think and feel – and ultimately, in which we perceive. As we have seen, Coleridge's formulation differs from that of Schelling in that it is fundamentally egalitarian in concept. The artist is not a lonely isolated figure, cut off by his gift, but one who shares his powers with mankind as a whole. His creativity differs not in kind, but merely in degree from that which makes us all human. Newman's argument is closely analogous, both in purpose and method. 'Belief', as a religious act, is conscious and involves intellectual assent as a *sine qua non*, but it is much more than an act of will or even an act of the conscious mind. We recall that it took Newman six years from the time he began to read of the Monophysite heresy to his reception into the Roman Church. This 'belief' is fundamentally the same as the unconscious instinctive 'belief' without which we could not live, or move, or perceive. Religious belief differs from our most basic and primitive motor and perceptual skills not in kind, but only in degree – in the quality and mode of its operation.

At this level we might fairly describe imagination as an 'analogy' of belief. But since belief is also, at every level, an act

[1] Ibid. p. 314.   [2] Ibid. p. 314.

of the illative imagination, the relationship is not merely one of analogy, but of interdependence. At a perceptual level, the imagination 'half-creates' the world around us in whose reality we instinctively believe, just as, at a religious level, the father-hood of God becomes for us a living reality through our imaginations. The illative imagination makes sense of our world at every level, from the simplest certainties to the most complex mystical vision, but whereas belief in our senses needs no 'proof' (even though our senses may be deceived), Christianity is both imagination *and* revelation, bearing witness to itself by the poetic creativity of its utterances. Not merely does its teaching embody revealed truth, the poetry of that truth draws from us the inward witness, 'the testimony borne to truth by the mind itself'.[1] 'Nor need reason come first and faith second,' declares Newman, '...but one and the same teaching is in different aspects both object and proof, and elicits one complex act both of inference and assent.'[2] Though Newman's view of scripture and of the teaching of the Church is very different from that of Coleridge, we can say, in this sense, that the *Grammar of Assent* is the culmination and completion of the 'poetic' mode of scriptural interpretation begun by Coleridge.

Yet to be in the tradition of Coleridge is not necessarily to be like him in all respects. Take, for instance, a passage such as the one we have just been discussing where Newman illustrates how real assent can arise from dogma:

'The Son is God.' What an illustration of the real assent which can be given to this proposition, and its power over our affections and emotions, is the first half of the first chapter of St. John's Gospel! or again the vision of our Lord in the first chapter of the Apocalypse! or the first chapter of St. John's first epistle! Again, how burning are St. Paul's words when he speaks of our Lord's crucifixion and death! what is the secret of that flame, but this same dogmatic sentence, 'The Son is God'. why should the death of the Son be more awful than any other death, except that He, though man, was God? And so, again, all through the Old Testament, what is it which gives an interpretation and a persuasive power to so many passages and portions, especially in the Psalms and the Prophets, but this same theological formula, 'The Messias is God', a proposition which never could thus vivify in the religious mind the letter of the sacred text, unless it appealed to the imagination, and could

[1] *Grammar of Assent*, p. 266.   [2] Ibid. p. 374.

be held with a much stronger assent than any that is merely notional.[1]

At such (relatively rare) lyrical points in the *Grammar of Assent* the reader can sense the compelling power of the scriptures, working in Newman as 'the living *educts* of the Imagination'. Yet it is also surely significant how rarely in the *Grammar* Newman's examples are taken from scripture. The opening of St John's Gospel is one of the few Biblical passages he makes use of, and few of us would find it a good instance of the kind of poetic and symbolic concreteness that he claims to find so typical of scripture as a whole. Moreover, what Newman is actually looking for here is not concreteness and particularity, but abstract propositional congruence. St John, St Paul, the Apocalypse, the Old Testament Psalms and Prophets all alike bear witness to the Divinity of Christ. To establish this point differences and ambiguities are ignored; unanimity is all. This curious contrast between Newman's idea of scripture and his actual use of it is not, I think, unfairly chosen. His exaltation of the 'poetry' of scripture everywhere goes hand-in-hand with a peculiar remoteness from the actual *feel* of the Bible. As here, the Biblical quotations in the final section of the *Grammar* on 'Revealed Religion' are given an abstract propositional flavour by their use as 'evidences' for a previously established point, rather than as 'living educts' in Coleridge's sense, working in the mind as poetry. There is no impression of struggle or difficulty, no shock of recognition or surprise as Newman engages with the complexities of the Biblical narrative. He knows what it is about in advance. One feels that he does not so much look at the language of the Gospels as look at 'propositions' about them. Can it be true, one wonders, that for all his claim to have renounced Locke and all his works, and the *ignis fatuus* of empiricist metaphysics, Newman's newly-found 'empiricism' is still strangely abstract and remote from the immediacy of Biblical religious experience? So, at least, Maurice thought.

He puts his finger at once on this peculiar remoteness that seems to run so counter to Newman's own thesis, and which so many readers of the *Grammar*, then as now, must dimly have sensed. Newman, Maurice claims in his review, fails to distinguish between 'assent' and 'belief', everywhere taking it for granted that 'belief' arises directly from 'real assent'. In fact, says Maurice, there is a fundamental difference. 'Assents, he [Newman] tells us again and again...belong strictly and exclusively to *propositions*. Do propositions, then, embrace the universe? Is there no region behind them or before them?'[1] But Newman, declares Maurice, is not to be blamed for this confusion: it is one into which he has been forced by his original premises. He does in fact with his talk of 'life' and 'imagination' desire to break free and draw just such a distinction; indeed, 'He has the most intense desire to breathe the open air – to live among facts, not among formulas. But he sees no way of escape.'[2] Ironically, it is Locke, whom Newman thought he had so effectively overthrown, who still holds him in thrall. Newman, cannot escape Locke's terminology, using the words 'principle' and 'proposition' synonymously, and so is trapped into believing that 'there is no time when facts may be observed without reference to propositions, no time when the principles which are indicated by facts may be contemplated out of the fetters of propositions'.[3] Thus the unfortunate Newman is always constrained to pour his life and imagination into assent to propositions, and to call *that* 'belief'. This, says Maurice, is un-Biblical. The essence of his critique of Newman can, he says, be found in a single sentence. According to Newman, 'Devotion must have its objects; these objects, as being supernatural, when not represented to our senses by material symbols, must be set before the mind in propositions.' Maurice retorts devastatingly, 'The devotion of the Jews was neither represented in material symbols, nor set before the mind in propositions.'[4] Biblical thought does not rest on assent to the proposition 'Hear O Israel: the Lord thy God is one Lord', but on the *belief* 'in an actual personal deliverer' who acts in history and changes things.[5]

Maurice's review of the *Grammar of Assent* is not of the same length and penetration as his earlier review of the *Essay on the Development of Christian Doctrine*. By 1870 he was a tired old man, within two years of his death. He does not always give the impression of having read Newman closely enough to do justice to the subtlety and movement of thought. For instance, he does

[1] Review of Dr Newman's *Grammar of Assent*, *Contemporary Review*, XIV (May 1870), p. 152.
[2] Ibid. p. 153.   [3] Ibid. p. 152.   [4] Ibid. p. 163.   [5] Ibid. p. 160.

not seem to grasp the degree to which Newman's argument rests on the recognition of the conceptual artificiality of the very propositions he is discussing; 'our most natural mode of reasoning,' Newman says, 'is, not from propositions to propositions, but from things to things, from concrete to concrete, from wholes to wholes'.[1] The implicit analogy always at the back of his mind seems to be with visual perception:

Whether the consequents, at which we arrive from the antecedents with which we start, lead us to assent or only towards assent, those antecedents commonly are not recognised by us as subjects for analysis; nay, often are only indirectly recognised as antecedents at all. Not only is the inference with its process ignored, but the antecedent also. To the mind itself the reasoning is a simple divination or prediction; as it literally is in the instance of enthusiasts, who mistake their own thoughts for inspirations.[2]

Just as Locke's mistake was to suppose that the mind was like a 'watcher' looking out through the mechanism of the eye, so we would be mistaken in supposing certainty to be the conscious rational conclusion from detailed logical propositions and the cumulation of probabilities. We see by a creative leap of the visual imagination; we believe by a corresponding leap of the illative imagination that transcends, and is unconscious of, its own mechanisms. The analysis of propositions and logical inference is like the image on the retina in visual perception: they are there, they are essential, but they are below the threshold of consciousness because they are a part of the mechanism by which consciousness is achieved.

Nevertheless, Maurice's distinction between 'assent' and 'belief' raises questions about Newman that cannot be ducked. Nowhere in the Bible, as Maurice points out, do we find 'poetic' or 'imaginative' responses of this kind being given to *propositions*; they are given to the God who commands personal obedience, or to the message of the prophets who proclaim his commands: not 'God is Love' or 'The Son is God', but 'Thus saith the Lord', or 'I desire mercy and not sacrifices...' As Newman himself recognises, the language of the Bible is everywhere concrete and not abstract; metaphorical, anecdotal and symbolic, not propositional. Even the opening of St John's Gospel is, if we look at it,

[1] *Grammar of Assent*, p. 251.   [2] Ibid. p. 251.

compressed, allusive, and highly metaphorical. The difference between 'assent' and 'belief' for Maurice is the difference between how one accepts a proposition, and how one accepts a person.[1] His criticism of Newman is basically not that he is mistaken about the imaginative and creative nature of belief,[2] but that humanly and psychologically speaking, he is looking for the springs of belief in barren ground. Newman is implicitly still governed by Lockeian models: the image on the retina cannot be the imaginative basis of vision – it is a blind alley. God is not set before the mind in propositions any more than the objects of sight are set before the mind *by* the image on the retina. Just as sight relies on the progressive modification of visual schemata drawn from previous experience, so religious perception is the product of previous experience: the tradition of the Bible and the Church, and a personal trust in the God so revealed. The development of religious perception is not a propositional process, but a *mythical* one.

It is, I think, in his approach to this 'poetic' or 'mythic' quality that Maurice finds Newman so deeply puzzling and paradoxical. Newman had developed the Romantic theological tradition of Wordsworth and Coleridge with sensitivity, skill, and brilliant reasoning. He is the theological climax of the fiduciary tradition. There is a ratiocinative power in his writing that Coleridge and Wordsworth, for all their insights, never possessed. Yet we are always conscious that they were poets in a sense that he was not. One only has to read *The Dream of Gerontius* to see the difference. They had a gift that Newman so often seemed to lack: a myth-making capacity to create metaphors and images that contained and yet went far beyond sequential argument. There is a deeply ambiguous quality in Newman's writing that troubles Maurice: it is as if in the *Grammar* he wishes simultaneously to affirm and deny this 'poetic' or 'mythic' basis of belief, which is why he always tends to identify belief with assent. One feels he wishes to argue that the 'poetic' is really a quality of propositions rather than of poetry.

This is a problem that others, beside Maurice, had observed. Thomas Mozley's notion of 'imagination' is a weak and entirely

---

[1] Review of *Grammar of Assent*, p. 156.

[2] 'Neither the imagination nor the intellect can surely be treated with indifference by any who think that God has made men in his own image' (p. 166).

conventional one, but he is nevertheless aware of Newman as 'a man well read in all the best works of imagination as in those of history or philosophy',[1] and who reached towards a synthesis in which 'this immense visionary world' is harnessed in apprehension of religious truth. 'Forty years ago,' continues Mozley, looking back at the Oxford Movement of his youth, 'we had arrived at the question, Was the Church alone to be shut out of this fairyland?'[2] Was there any meeting except in the victory of German philology? It was a question that Newman had faced then, and he continues to face it in the *Grammar of Assent*. He stands as it were with one foot in a world of empirical logic, the other in one where the Church itself is perceived not as an institution, a political settlement of the seventeenth century, or the repository of formulae, but with the concrete 'reality' of a work of art. Both poles were real. Yet, as we shall see in the next chapter, the answer to Mozley's question lay not as he believed, with Newman, but in a direction altogether different and unperceived.

Perhaps for Newman the only way we can make sense of this paradox is to recall his stress on the life of the whole giving meaning to the parts, and apply it not merely to his writing, but, like all his ideas, to himself. His gift is to tell his own story. The Newman myth is the story of his life. The *Grammar of Assent* is in this sense, the story that the *Apologia* could not reveal – the story that, Keble-like, had to be told secretly and under tension. Apart from the *Letter to the Duke of Norfolk* it is his last work.[3]

During the final decade of his life Newman was at work revising and republishing all his early Anglican works – as if the *Grammar* was, for him, the key to his whole life's work, enabling him to return to his early writing and re-arrange it within a new wider pattern. It occupies a very special place in Newman's vision of his own life. All his other works, he observed, had been written from the exigencies of some particular situation, 'works done in some office I held or engagement I had made...or has been from some especial call, or invitation, or necessity, or emergency...The Essay on Assent is nearly the only exception ...I had felt it on my conscience for years, that it would not do

---

[1] *Reminiscences*, II, 373.   [2] Ibid. 374.
[3] Though perhaps the 1877 Preface to the third edition of the *Via Media* deserves this title better.

to quit the world without doing it.'[1] Newman's theology, like Wordsworth's poetry, is part of the story of his life in that it is a gigantic effort at self-understanding – a coming to terms with the complex and ever-fascinating mental processes of John Henry Newman. It is, by a paradox that he himself was at least partly aware of, the very honesty of that egotistical sublime that gives his theology its enduring value *as theology*. The great event of Maurice's spiritual life was his rejection of the clear unequivocal propositions of Unitarianism for a Saviour whose dual nature confounded the cool logic of metaphysics; the drama of Newman's life was his movement from Oxford to Rome. His was not a struggle over the divinity of Christ, but over the legitimacy of certain propositions about the nature of the Church. The man who in silence had stumbled in agony of soul for the last time from Oxford to Littlemore wetting his companion's hand with his tears all the way knew well enough the cost of real assent to propositions. 'A locomotive engine could not move without steam, but still, under whatever number of forces, it certainly does start from Birmingham and does arrive in London.'[2]

[1] C. S. Dessain, *John Henry Newman* (Nelson, 1966), p. 148.

[2] Taking, we imagine, as Newman so often did, not the direct route from New Street to Euston, but the line from Birmingham Snow Hill station to Paddington which goes via Oxford.

process by which human spiritual desires and needs were worked into an explanatory framework and projected upon the external universe: Christianity was a system of anthropological fairy stories to be treated with disdain or sympathy according to the standpoint of the critic. On the other hand, this same 'myth' of 'two worlds' was to become an increasingly potent literary and poetic image that was to assume a multitude of shapes and forms as writers struggled to re-create a satisfactory language to describe man's spiritual experiences. Part of the importance of Coleridge to the minority of Victorians prepared to try and wrestle with him, was that he had already felt this bifurcation as a *polarisation* in which each pole necessarily implied the existence of the other. His Biblical criticism, derivative as much of it was, showed that he understood better than any of his English contemporaries the function of myth in scriptural narrative; conversely, the *Ancient Mariner* showed no less clearly that he understood the creative rôle of myth in the poetic symbolising of the human condition. The emphasis upon the nature of religious language (and therefore institutions) as 'poetic' by, as we have seen, an increasing number of nineteenth-century theologians is a recognition of the inherent *polarity* of mythological thought. Its precarious ambiguity is shown by the deeply divided reactions of writers: if for Maurice and Newman this polarity was to be welcomed as a new access of theological insight, for Carlyle and Matthew Arnold it was rather a new insight into the capacity of man to externalise his moral problems and create a God in his own image. We can see this ambiguity most clearly if we contrast two Victorian writers, both in their own ways strongly moulded by the Coleridgean tradition: Matthew Arnold, and George MacDonald.

Matthew Arnold was a product of the world of Keble and Newman. As a child he had spent long hours talking to Wordsworth, whose home at Rydal Mount was close to the Arnolds' holiday residence at Fox How, in the Lake District. His educational ethos was that of Anglican High Church Oxford at its zenith: an Oxford of rigorous piety and high literary culture. It was a world that Arnold did his best to keep at arm's length – affecting the manners and dress of a dandy, and refusing to read seriously. Nevertheless, his interests, poetry and theology, were those of his Oxford, and they remained the two great preoccupations of his life. The son of the great Dr Thomas Arnold of

Rugby, and the godson of Keble (in happier days before their doctrinal estrangement), Matthew Arnold was elected to a fellowship at Oriel in 1845 – the year that Newman finally resigned his Fellowship to be received into the Roman Catholic Church. Keble was then in the middle of his tenure as Professor of Poetry. Though Arnold had graduated the year before from Balliol with only a second-class degree – the result of his refusal to take work seriously – he was already recognised as one of the most brilliant and sensitive minds of his generation. At the age of twenty-three his reputation as a poet was already assured. His Rugby prize poem, *Alaric at Rome*, had been published in 1840, and in 1843 he had triumphantly carried off the highest poetic honour that Oxford could bestow on an undergraduate: the Newdigate Prize. In 1857 he was to become Professor of Poetry.

The title of Arnold's best-known theological work, *Literature and Dogma*, sounds as if it is about the superiority of literature over dogma. In fact it turns out to be about the superiority of dogma over literature. What he calls by the German word *Aberglaube*, or 'extra-belief', is simply the incrustation of miraculous legend, superstition, and fairy tale that he believed had grown up around the basic moral truths of Christianity, and which were in danger of strangling it.

'*Aberglaube* is the poetry of life.' That men should, by help of their imagination, take short cuts to what they ardently desire, whether the triumph of Israel or the triumph of Christianity, should tell themselves fairy-tales about it, should make these fairy-tales the basis for what is far more sure and solid than the fairy-tales, the desire itself – all this has in it, we repeat, nothing which is not natural, nothing blameable . . . In religion, above all, *extra-belief* is in itself no matter, assuredly, for blame. The object of religion is conduct; and if a man helps himself in his conduct by taking an object of hope and presentiment as if it were an object of certainty, he may even be said to gain thereby an advantage.

And yet there is always a drawback to man's advantage in thus treating, when he deals with religion and conduct, what is extra-belief and not certain as if it were a matter of certainty, and in making it his ground of action. *He pays for it*. The time comes when he discovers that it is *not* certain; and then the whole certainty of religion seems discredited, and the basis of conduct gone.[1]

[1] *Literature and Dogma*, pp. 80–1.

What makes George MacDonald such an interesting comparison for our purposes is that he is hailed not merely by the twentieth century but also by his

Arnold's position – as briefly set out here – is the essential foil to the 'poetic' theological tradition of Wordsworth and Coleridge, and his persistent and thoughtful attempts to demythologise religious belief illustrate better than anything else the ambiguous part played in this tradition by 'myth', or what he chose to call more colloquially 'fairy stories'. For Arnold it is obvious that 'the object of religion is conduct'.[1] 'Religion is ethics heightened, enkindled, lit up by feeling; the passage from morality to religion is made when to morality is applied emotion.'[2] It is *feeling* that makes the abstractions of a moral code come alive, and feeling – 'poetic feeling' – is therefore an essential element in morality. But the age of fairy stories is past, and modern man, if he is to survive as a 'spiritual' being, must learn to demythologise his belief. He must separate the kernel of abstract truth from its poetic husk. Behind the vivid poetic personifications of primitive Hebrew thought there lives, Arnold believed, a depth of insight that is fundamentally this-worldly, human, and moral.

own contemporaries as the prime creator of the very genre which Matthew Arnold felt could no longer be seriously entertained by an educated man, fairy stories; in particular, fairy stories of a specifically religious bias. The essential difference, of course, is that whereas MacDonald's fairy stories, *Phantastes*, the *Princess* books, *At the Back of the North Wind*, *The Golden Key*, *Lilith*, etc., were written *as* fairy stories, without claiming any historical truth, the Bible stories do. But this distinction is the less clear the more we are inclined to accept Arnold's own argument about the 'poetic' and 'imaginative' nature of the scriptures. If the Bible is myth with a profound moral import, then so are MacDonald's stories. Yet how far would we consider it a fruitful exercise to demythologise MacDonald's fairy stories? Interestingly enough, we do have one major attempt on record. Robert Lee Wolff has attempted this feat using Freud as his 'golden key'. His results have this in common with Arnold's attempts at demythologising the Bible: both reflect the initial beliefs and prejudices of the demythologisers with an astonishing accuracy. To those engaged upon the enterprise this is clearly highly satisfactory; to the uncommitted, the way in which the text bears out the critics' own ideas looks distinctly fishy. In short, Arnold's whole concept of 'demythologising' lacks credibility when we see that it is apparently based on naive epistemological assumptions about the text 'as it really is'. 'We seek,' he says, 'not to produce a complete work of ingenious criticism on the Bible...but to help readers, sick of popular and conventional theology, and resolved to take the Bible for nothing but what it really is – to help such readers to see what the Bible really is, and how very much, seen as it really is, it concerns them...'.The trouble with this straightforward 'plain man's approach' is that Arnold himself is apparently taken in by his own rhetoric, and is unable to see that the Bible 'as it really is' depends almost entirely on the set of mental pre-suppositions *he* brings to it, just as helping readers 'to see what the Bible really is' involves modifying *their* mental sets. He cannot see, for example, that his certainty that the Resurrection could not have happened is not a conclusion, but a premise.

[1] *Literature and Dogma*, p. 11.   [2] Ibid. p. 15.

'*God*, or *Eternal* is here really, at bottom, nothing but a deeply moved way of saying "the power which makes for conduct or righteousness".'[1] The poetry of religion is the vehicle of moral truth. The genius of Jesus in the New Testament is in his realisation that religion was not to be seen merely as a matter of rules of conduct between people, but, if these were to be effective and sincere, it concerned 'the inward feeling and disposition of the individual himself'.[2] 'While the Old Testament says: *Attend to conduct!* the New Testament says: *Attend to the feelings and dispositions whence conduct proceeds*'.[3]

For Arnold, Keble's phrase 'two worlds' had taken on a new and more urgent temporal meaning. He felt himself to be standing between the world of conventional Christendom whose epitome was the Oxford he knew and loved with its ethos of 'sweetness and light', and the aggressive confident world of nineteenth-century industrial 'progress', materialistic and 'philistine', degrading those involved as much by the brash vulgarity of its successes as the hideous poverty of its failures. Each world needed the other. By 1873, when *Literature and Dogma* was first published, Arnold had been both an Oxford don, and an inspector of state schools, and he knew both worlds and their weaknesses with an intimacy that few outside the Christian Socialist movement could rival. Writing the year after Maurice's death, he has abated none of his intellectual contempt for Maurice, perhaps just because in this respect his aims are so close to those of the older Cambridge man. 'This is what everyone sees to constitute the special moral feature of our times;' writes Arnold, '*the masses* are losing the Bible and its religion.'[4] If 'the masses' in the sense of the industrial proletariat had ever *had* the Bible – a question open to some doubt – it was certainly true, as Arnold clearly saw,that if the Bible was to speak to industrial Victorian England it would not be with the voice of the Oxford Movement, or even that of the Birmingham Oratory. 'At the present moment,' wrote Arnold in his Preface to *God and the Bible* in 1875, 'two things about the Christian religion must surely be clear to anybody with eyes in his head. One is, that men cannot do without it: the other they cannot do with it as it is.'[5]

[1] Ibid. p. 35.   [2] Ibid. p. 62.   [3] Ibid. p. 68.   [4] Ibid. p. 175.
[5] *The Complete Prose Works of Matthew Arnold*, vol. VII, *God and the Bible*, ed. R. H. Super (Michigan U. P., 1970), p. 378.

The remark, like the quest for the solution, is typical of Arnold. In his *Stanzas from the Grand Chartreuse* he describes himself, in an inversion of Keble's lines, as

> Wandering between two worlds, one dead,
> The other powerless to be born.

With a peculiar irony, the image is perhaps even more true of Matthew Arnold than he himself realised. His sense of Victorian England as two worlds, hostile and misunderstanding, led him not towards 'polarisation' in Coleridge's sense, but towards what was to prove its opposite, an attempt at *reconciliation*. Arnold was a 'Naturalist' in a far more thoroughgoing sense than ever Wordsworth was. He did not believe that there could be more than *one* world. For him, values must ultimately be deduced from the same material world as science and technology, because there was and could be no other.

To achieve such a reconciliation, the bases of religious belief must be made accessible to the same modes of verification as science.

...the great danger to the Bible at present arises from the assumption that whoever receives the Bible must set out with admitting certain propositions, such as the existence of a personal God, the consubstantiality of Jesus Christ with this personal God who is his Father, the miraculous birth, resurrection, and ascension of Jesus. Now, the nature of these propositions is such that we cannot possibly verify them. It seemed to us that with the uninstructed or ill-instructed masses of our people this obstacle to the Bible's reception, which for a long time was an obstacle not existent for them at all, is, as things now stand, an obstacle almost insuperable. Therefore we sought and seek to show that the Bible is really based upon propositions which all can verify.[1]

These 'propositions which all can verify' are revealed by an examination of the 'poetic' nature of the scriptures which can be demythologised to a few simple moral notions. In effect, Arnold stands the whole poetic tradition of the Romantics on its head. As we have seen, the argument of *Literature and Dogma* rests on two basic principles.[2] The first is that the Bible requires nothing for its understanding except what can be verified. 'For us, the God of popular religion is a legend, a fairy-tale; learned theology has simply taken this fairy-tale and dressed it metaphysically.'[3]

[1] *God and the Bible*, p. 144.   [2] Ibid. p. 155.   [3] Ibid. p. 151.

As a *moral* principle, what he calls 'the not ourselves which makes for righteousness'[1] can be verified by all with open minds. The second principle is that 'the language of the Bible is not scientific, but *literary*'.[2] The first principle, we observe, rests on the second. At first sight it would appear that any discussion of 'God' cannot rest on normal principles of verification, but this is to misunderstand the 'poetic' nature of Biblical thought, declares Arnold.'It is the language of poetry and emotion, approximate language thrown out, as it were, at certain great objects which the human mind augurs and feels after, and thrown out by men very liable ...to delusion and error.'[3] For him, 'poetry' is 'language not professing to be exact at all, and we are free to use it or not to use it as our sense of public propriety may dictate'.[4]

Now two things strike the reader very quickly about this kind or argument. The first is how much it appears to owe to what we might call 'anthropological' criticism – the approach of the German Historical Method. Arnold is using the word 'poetry' as almost synonymous with the anthropological use of the word 'myth'. 'Poetry' is not, as in the classical literary sense of Sidney or Johnson, a deliberate fiction created by an author with a moral or didactic intent to 'instruct through pleasing', or to utter a higher truth than mere historical veracity; nor is it used in its more Romantic Wordsworthian sense of 'the spontaneous overflow of powerful feelings'. Arnold does not anywhere display what has been called the Romantic tendency 'to pose and answer aesthetic questions in terms of the relation of art to the artist....'.[5] His Biblical Author is a kind of Jungian racial unconscious. The second thing that strikes the reader is nearly the converse of the first: that Arnold's argument starts from very *different* premises from those of the German Historical Method. He himself is at some pains to repudiate what he considers to be many of the excesses of the German critics:

Among German critics of the Bible, a sort of criticism which we may best, perhaps, describe as a *mechanical* criticism, is very rife. For negative purposes this criticism is particularly useful. It takes for granted that things are naturally all of a piece and follow one uniform rule; and that to know that this is so, and to judge things by the light of this knowledge, is the secret for sure criticism. People do not vary; people

[1] *Literature and Dogma*, p. 38.   [2] *God and the Bible*, p. 155.   [3] Ibid. p. 155.
[4] Ibid. pp. 156–7.   [5] Abrams, *The Mirror and the Lamp*, p. 3.

do not contradict themselves; people do not have under-currents of meaning; people do not divine...Things, too, like persons, must be rigidly consistent, must show no conflicting aspects, must have no flux and reflux, must not follow a slow, hesitating, often obscure line of growth...[1]

From this position it is clear how far Arnold remains within the Anglican tradition of Butler and of Coleridge – indeed his descriptions of 'poetry' as a language of 'emotion' as it were 'thrown out' after 'great objects' is strongly reminiscent of Keble. He is writing of 'the Germans' for an English audience which, as we have seen, knew surprisingly little about their thought, and though he wishes to propagate many of their ideas, he is anxious – not just for tactical reasons – not to be too closely identified with them. He is, seemingly, always conscious of the English minority tradition from which he has sprung and from which he cannot fully shake himself free. Indeed, he does not wish to. It is necessary to his purpose to try and retain the didacticism of a Sidney or a Johnson, and to add to this the no less didactic 'spontaneous' emotional outpouring of a Wordsworth or a Keble. It is, ironically, the very *success* of his attempt at reconciling two fundamentally polarised lines of thought that gives his writing such a curiously self-contradictory style. One is constantly dogged by the feeling that he is trying to have his cake and eat it. No one who has read Arnold's theological criticism can fail to be struck by the way in which he labours his points, for ever repeating himself, back-tracking and tucking in loose ends of his argument as if to demonstrate the seamless web of his humanistic reconciliation. To some extent the way in which he leans on the very tradition he wishes to repudiate is conscious policy: a demonstration of the 'catholicity' of his undertaking. His arguments, he stresses, stem as surely as those of the Oxford Movement from the ideas of Butler:

the greatness of Butler...is in his clear perception and powerful use of a 'course of life marked out for man by nature, whatever that nature may be.' His embarrassment and failure is in his attempt to establish a perception as clear, and a use as powerful, of the popular theology. But from Butler, and from his treatment of *nature* in connexion with religion, the idea of following out that treatment frankly and fully,

[1] *God and the Bible*, p. 203.

which is the design of *Literature and Dogma,* first, as I am proud to acknowledge, came to me.[1]

It is Butler's appeal to 'nature', not his double-vision but his single vision – his 'naturalism' – that, characteristically, Arnold hails as his significant contribution. From Butler, he can claim a theory of development of doctrine that reads like a mischievous parody of Newman. The unfolding of Christian doctrine, according to this view, is one of progressive demythologising. The vengeful God of the Old Testament is gradually seen as an ever more humanistic and moral Deity, moving from thunderclouds on Sinai to Incarnation, and finally to absorption with the 'spirit of man' – or even the 'poetic imagination'. Moreover, and this is very important for Arnold, such a progressive development of religious insight can be seen as 'natural' in Butler's sense. It corresponds to a process with which we are familiar in all areas of human knowledge. Science, for instance, began as mythology, or even animism, in which natural events are explained in terms of arbitrary and personal causes: the cow dies because it has been given the 'evil-eye' or because its owner has offended a local spirit. Gradually, with the advent of monotheism, men come to see that one God implies uniformity of nature, and even rationality; finally we discard the unnecessary hypothesis of a God, and we are left with scientific laws as a sufficient and final cause. Conveniently, such a developmental argument can also be used to detect error. The idea of 'Being', for example, that favourite stamping-ground of the metaphysicians Arnold so abhorred, he demonstrates to have been based upon a crude semantic confusion that became built into the language.[2]

But Arnold's dependence on the 'poetic' theological tradition of Wordsworth, Coleridge, and Keble, is ultimately fatal to the cause of demythologising. In the last resort, Arnold must deny the very concept on which the idea of the 'poetic' interpretation of scripture rested, that is, that poetry is the expression in words of something that can be put in no other way. For the tradition we have been tracing, that of Wordsworth, Coleridge, and Keble, form and content were essentially indivisible. It was not possible to describe the 'meaning' of the *Ancient Mariner* in other terms than those of the poem – just as it was not possible for Kierkegaard

[1] Ibid. p. 233.   [2] Ibid. pp. 184–9.

in *Fear and Trembling* that the story of Abraham and Isaac could be told in other words than those of *Genesis*. Though it is possible to find in myth and symbol new and, perhaps, progressively greater richness of meaning, a poetic or religious symbol could not (they believed) be paraphrased or adequately expressed in philosophical or abstract language. Behind this assumption is a view of man as an essentially story-telling animal. The human mind, they believed, works not primarily in terms of rational argument, but in myth and symbol as its basic mode.[1] This is a view that Arnold is committed to opposing – with the result that he constantly finds himself in the position of surreptitiously attributing to poetry an importance and a 'life' that his theory demands should be attached to the abstract concepts themselves. Arnold's vision of himself, 'between two worlds', is peculiarly poignant: if the former, in which he was nurtured, is now dead, the latter is no more than a critical method, which, in explaining everything, explains nothing and lacks the life and vitality of the poetry it has 'explained' – forever powerless to be born. As John Sterling and George Eliot had found, the 'method' of Strauss' *Life of Jesus* could destroy faith, but was powerless to replace it.[2]

Thus Arnold's limbo is not merely a limbo of faith, it is also an *aesthetic* one. His attempt to substitute reconciliation for polarity has drastically altered and weakened the value of poetry itself. For a poet, we have already seen how curiously 'anthropological' Arnold's use of the word 'poetry' tends to be. It always seems closer to a primitive mode of thought than a form of artistic creation. Nearly all the Victorian critics tend to use the word in two senses, a 'broad' sense meaning something very close to our concept of 'myth', and a 'narrow' sense for conscious artistic organisation. In Arnold's case, the broad sense seems almost to have obliterated the narrow. Take, for instance, the following passage:

We have to renounce impossible attempts to receive the legendary and

---

[1] See my *Coleridge and Wordsworth*, ch. 7.

[2] 'It will work deep and far, in such a time as ours. When so many minds are distracted about the history, or rather genesis of the Gospel, it is a great thing for partisans on the one side to have, what the other never wanted, a Book of which they can say, this is our Creed and Code – or rather Anti-creed and Anti-code... It seems admitted that the orthodox theologians have failed to give any sufficient answer.' Carlyle, *Life of Sterling*, p. 347.

miraculous matter of Scripture as grave historical and scientific fact. We have to accustom ourselves to regard henceforth all this part as poetry and legend. In the Old Testament, as an immense poetry growing round and investing an immortal truth, 'the secret of the Eternal:' *Righteousness is salvation.* In the New, as an immense poetry growing round and investing an immortal truth, the secret of Jesus: *He that will save his life shall lose it, he that will lose his life shall save it.*[1]

This kind of statement – and there are many such – reveals very clearly Arnold's dilemma between two worlds. He is not saying, as he might appear to be, that 'poetry' is simply a decorative fiction that is 'untrue' because he is also committed to the view that poetry can and often does embody the most profound truths. The very strength of its emotion brings those truths to life in men's hearts and minds. But...in the last resort 'poetry' and 'truth' are divisible; they must be separated. There is something that lies behind poetry and can be distilled from it; the kernel can be broken from out of the shell. Poetry is by no means a useless embellishment. It is – to continue the image of a nut – the husk that protects the seed, carries it safely to its destination, and provides for its safe arrival and acceptance. But in order that the seed of truth may grow, the husk must be dispensed with. If, at an earlier stage, poetry brings new truths 'to life', at a later stage of man's development it can be a source of confusion, misunderstanding, 'delusion and error'. If poetry is not itself 'untrue' it is because it is not itself concerned with ideas at all; it is merely a *mode* of expression. Here Arnold attempts to invoke the aid of Wordsworth:

For the power of Christianity has been in the immense emotion which it has excited; in its engaging, for the government of man's conduct, the mighty forces of love, reverence, gratitude, hope, pity, and awe – all that host of allies which Wordsworth includes under the one name of *imagination*, when he says that in the uprooting of old thoughts and old rules we must still always ask: –

> Survives *imagination*, to the change
> Superior? Help to virtue does she give?
> If not, O mortals, better cease to live!

Popular Christianity has enjoyed abundantly and with profit this help from the imagination to virtue and conduct. I have always thought,

---

[1] *God and the Bible*, p. 370.

therefore, that merely to destroy the illusions of popular Christianity was indefensible. Time, besides, was sure to do it; but when it is done, the whole work of again cementing the alliance between the imagination and conduct remains to be effected. To those who effect nothing for the new alliance but only dissolve the old, we take once more our text from Wordsworth, and we say: –

> Why with such earnest pains dost thou provoke
> The years to bring the inevitable yoke,
> Thus blindly with man's blessedness at strife?
> Full soon his soul will have its earthly freight; –

soon enough will the illusions which charmed and aided man's inexperience be gone; what have you to give him in the place of them?[1]

That, in essence, is Arnold's dilemma. He cannot even fall back on a creed of aestheticism, since he has burned his boats and denied that the imagination can create or bring to light truths which cannot be better put in 'scientific' prose. If *all* that Wordsworth meant by 'imagination' is the – admittedly 'mighty' – forces of love, reverence, etc. then these will, of course, remain extraneous to the basic truths of man's existence as Arnold appears to conceive them. That Wordsworth may have meant by 'imagination' an active and originating power of the mind, a 'symbolising' capacity, is ignored – as it has to be. That love, reverence, gratitude etc. were seen by Wordsworth as *themselves* basic truths is also ignored. The 'two worlds' of Plato seem ironically endemic of the human mind, and though we expel them with a pitchfork yet they will creep surreptitiously back under the fence. Wordsworth, in a sense, has his revenge. What Arnold calls the 'concrete' world of poetry and of religious language[2] finally becomes a mere visible manifestation of an abstract 'reality', encompassed by scientific laws and non-figurative philosophic language. The emotion and imagination of poetry have no corresponding 'ideal form' in this world of shadowy abstractions, and the very qualities that make human life worth living are ultimately in doubt.

> The sea of faith
> Was once, too, at the full, and round earth's shore
> Lay like the folds of a bright girdle furl'd;
> But now I only hear

---

[1] *God and the Bible*, p. 378.   [2] Ibid. p. 396.

Its melancholy, long, withdrawing roar,
Retreating to the breath
Of the night-wind down the vast edges drear
And naked shingles of the world.

Ah, love, let us be true
To one another! for the world, which seems
To lie before us like a land of dreams,
So various, so beautiful, so new,
Hath really neither joy, nor love, nor light,
Nor certitude, nor peace, nor help for pain . . . [1]

In 1845, the year that Matthew Arnold was elected to his Oriel Fellowship, George MacDonald received his M.A. in Chemistry and Natural Philosophy (as physics was called) at the University of Aberdeen. He was two years younger than Arnold, having been born at Huntly, in Aberdeenshire, in 1824. Whereas Arnold's career at Rugby and Oxford had been one of privilege and financial security, MacDonald's education was dogged by poverty. Though he had entered university on a bursary, he quickly ran out of money, and was forced to leave temporarily in 1842 to earn more. It is possible that his penury was helped by overindulgence in alcohol and the city's brothels.[2] Among other jobs in 1843 he seems to have spent some time in an unidentified castle in northern Scotland cataloguing a neglected library – whether or not it was the scene of a traumatically unhappy love-affair, as Wolff deduces from scanty evidence,[3] it is a setting that plays an important part in several of his novels, including *Lilith*. But the biggest difference between Arnold and MacDonald is nationality. The rest of our tradition have been English, not merely by birth, but, far more important, by culture and educa-tion products of Oxford or Cambridge. MacDonald was a poor Scot, the product of a very different educational system – more like that of France or Germany than England – and a scientist by training. His grandfather had been a Gaelic-speaking Catholic Highlander. His boyhood in Aberdeenshire had been spent, as one critic vividly puts it, 'in a traditional rural atmosphere,

[1] *Dover Beach*, lines 21–34.
[2] What evidence there is for this comes from the largely autobiographical *Alec Forbes of Howglen* (1865), see Richard Reis, *George MacDonald* (Twayne, 1972), p. 21.
[3] Robert Lee Wolff, *The Golden Key* (Yale U.P., 1961), pp. 16–17.

compounded of Calvinist hellfire, oatcakes, horsemanship, agri-
cultural virtues, and exploration of neighbourhood ruins and
wildernesses'.[1] It was a background very far removed from the
Barchester world of the Anglican establishment.

After some kind of spiritual crisis in 1847 or 1848 MacDonald
decided to become a minister, and in 1848 he entered Highbury
College, a Congregational theological college in London. We do
not know much about his inner life during this period, except for
some hints at a growing nature-mysticism – partly under the
influence of Turner's painting.[2] Certainly a strongly mystical
streak in his character was further developed by his reading of
German and English Romantics, including both Blake and
Novalis. Much of our conjecture about him at this period comes
from parallels and autobiographical suggestions in his novels –
the source, also, of the notion of a mis-spent youth in the fleshpots
of Aberdeen. What is certain is that comparatively early marriage
for both MacDonald and Arnold brought with it corresponding
financial responsibilities. It was impending marriage that forced
Arnold to accept the uncongenial post of inspector of schools in
1849. With the offer of a first church at Arundel, in Sussex,
MacDonald felt able to marry – but their security was short-
lived. Just before the move to Sussex, in 1850, he suffered a bad
attack of tuberculosis – the first of many. It was the family
disease. His father and two brothers had all died of various forms
of tubercular infections, and four of his eleven children were to
die of it. But to ill health was added an even more serious financial
threat. In May 1853, after a long struggle, he was forced to
resign from his church in Arundel as a result of charges of heresy
brought against him by the deacons. He was arraigned on two
counts: firstly, for having preached the possibility of life after
death for the heathen, and, secondly, for being tainted with
'German theology'.[3] From 1853 until his death in 1905 MacDonald
was a preacher without a pulpit. For the rest of his life he was
forced to support his family by writing: novels, poems, journal-
ism, criticism, and whatever literary hack-work came his way –
reviewing, editing a children's magazine for a short period, and by

[1] Reis, *MacDonald*, p. 20.
[2] Greville MacDonald, *George MacDonald and his Wife* (hereafter *Life*), (Allen
& Unwin, 1924), pp. 122–4.
[3] *Life*, p. 178.

religious plays acted (not always willingly) by the whole family.

The development of MacDonald's literary career was slow and painful. He had few contacts with the London literary scene, but, by chance, they centred on the minority religious tradition that is the subject of this study. His brother James had for years been a surgeon in Hackney, and had known Coleridge – on occasions risking a breach of friendship by refusing to supply him with opium. James Powell, MacDonald's father-in-law had also known Coleridge, and was fond of quoting him.[1] Even by 1850 we find hints that the young Congregationalist minister was prepared to look more favourably on the Church of England than heretofore: 'I am surprised to find so many of my notions in Dr. Arnold's letters,' he wrote to his fiancée, '– only so much enlarged and verified beyond my shelled-chicken-peepings...I wish the Church were better. I think I could almost go into it.'[2] Maurice, too, was clearly congenial to the way in which his thought was already developing. To his father he wrote in 1851:

The word *doctrine*, as used in the Bible, means teaching of duty, not theory...We are far too anxious to be definite and to have finished, well-polished, sharp-edged *systems* – forgetting that the more perfect a theory about the infinite, the surer it is to be wrong, the more impossible it is to be right...To no system would I subscribe...[3]

Through his friendship with A. J. Scott, the first Principle of Owens College, Manchester (later to become Manchester University), MacDonald was soon to meet Maurice, and acquaintance rapidly ripened into friendship. MacDonald, now living for a short time in Manchester, was present at Maurice's inaugural address at the Manchester Working Men's College, and one of his first paid jobs after leaving Arundel was as a lecturer there – at a salary of £30 a year. MacDonald's first prose book, and first of the symbolic fantasies, *Phantastes*, was read in manuscript by F. D. Maurice who helped him to find a publisher.[4] In 1865, after their move to London, the MacDonalds started attending Maurice's church in Vere Street, and as a result of his influence eventually became members of the Church of England. Through Scott at this time MacDonald also met a man who had been a major influence on Maurice, Thomas Erskine, and who, with Maurice, is the target for some of Arnold's most bitter personal

[1] Ibid. p. 137.   [2] Ibid. p. 149.   [3] Ibid. p. 155.   [4] Ibid. p. 290.

attacks. In the same circle also, he became friends with Ruskin, and made the acquaintance of both Hare and Carlyle.

With his first successful literary publication, the poem *Within and Without*, in 1855, MacDonald began to attract favourable attention. It was highly recommended by a sister of Sydney Smith.[1] Charles Kingsley wrote to him and Lady Byron, the poet's widow, who was a religious philanthropist, became a friend and unofficial patron of the struggling writer and his family. It was her gifts of money and a rent-free house at Hastings that actually kept the family from starving in these early days.[2] Other literary friendships quickly followed: that of Matthew Arnold himself, William de Morgan, and the Rossettis. Crabb Robinson, the veteran diarist and friend of almost all the first-generation Romantics, including Blake, Wordsworth, Coleridge, Keats, and Shelley, was sufficiently impressed by MacDonald's talents (and need) to leave him a legacy of £300 when he died in 1867.[3] Lewis Carroll knew the MacDonald family intimately enough to try out the completed manuscript of *Alice in Wonderland* on the children before publication.[4] By the 1860s George MacDonald seemed to know everyone, and to be a kind of establishment in himself. He was Ruskin's confidant over his love-affair with the youthful Rose LaTouche – and we must presume that the secrets of Ruskin's sex life perished with him. MacDonald's referees for his (unsuccessful) application for the Chair of Rhetoric and Belles Lettres at Edinburgh in 1865 included Ruskin, Maurice, Lord Houghton, Charles Kingsley, and Dean Stanley.[5] At a party at the MacDonald's house Ruskin led off a 'Sir Roger de Coverley' with Octavia Hill.[6] Tennyson borrowed his Gaelic copy of Ossian. Through the Leigh-Smiths (one of whose daughters, Madame Bodichon, founded Girton) MacDonald entered militant feminist circles. He dined regularly with Thackeray, Leigh Hunt, H. G. Lewes (George Eliot's lover), and George Smith (of Smith Elder, the publishers). A photograph of this period shows MacDonald with a group of other famous writers: Dickens, Thackeray, Wilkie Collins, Trollope, Bulwer-Lytton, Carlyle, Froude, and Macaulay.[7] In

---

[1] *Life*, p. 209.   [2] Ibid. pp. 300–13.   [3] Ibid. p. 310.   [4] Ibid. pp. 342–3.
[5] Wolff, *The Golden Key*, p. 5.   [6] Ibid. p. 5.
[7] Reproduced by Wolff, who suspects it is pre-1859 (*The Golden Key*, p. 5). It is in fact, clearly a 'fake' composed of a number of famous photographs of the period.

1872, on a triumphant tour of the U.S.A. MacDonald was warmly received by Emerson, Longfellow, and Whittier; a Fifth Avenue church begged him to become their minister at the then awesome salary of $20,000 a year. Mark Twain became a visitor to their London house. It is clear that MacDonald possessed a strong personal charisma: many seem to have regarded him as a prophet and saint, and he had a well-attested St Francis-like power over animals.[1]

Yet, for all this success in his own time, today MacDonald has, rightly, been called a forgotten novelist.[2] During his forty-six years as an active writer, from 1851 to 1897, he wrote well over fifty books. Twenty-five are novels. They have long been out of print, and, on the whole, deservedly so. What George Mac-Donald is remembered for is primarily as a writer of the genre that Arnold declared modern man had no need of: fairy stories.

Tributes to his genius come from the most unexpected as well as the more obvious directions. The *Times Literary Supplement* in 1924 on the centenary of his birth ran a leading article on him:

The author of *David Elginbrod* and *Robert Falconer* and *Alec Forbes* was a good novelist. The poet of the *Poems* and *The Diary of an Old Soul* was a true poet. The author of *The Golden Key* and of *Lilith* had a touch of genius... not yet has he been recognised as the man who did one sort of work better than anyone else has ever done it... the writing of what are commonly called his fairy stories.[3]

Charles Williams, J. R. R. Tolkein, and C. S. Lewis have all been influenced by, and borrowed from, him. Lewis has freely acknowledged his debt, and in an anthology of MacDonald's prose described his work like this:

What he does best is fantasy – fantasy that hovers between the allegorical and the mythopoeic. And this, in my opinion, he does better than any man... MacDonald is the greatest genius of this kind whom I know... The great works are *Phantastes*, the *Curdie* books, *The Golden Key*, *The Wise Woman*, and *Lilith*.[4]

Auden, in his introduction to the 1954 reprint of *Phantastes* and *Lilith* echoes this analysis:

[1] *Life*, p. 370.   [2] Wolff, *The Golden Key*, p. 4.
[3] 29 May 1924, pp. 328–9. Article by Harold Child.
[4] *George MacDonald: An Anthology* (Bles, 1946).

George MacDonald is pre-eminently a mythopoeic writer...In his power...to project his inner life into images, events, beings, landscapes which are valid for all, he is one of the most remarkable writers of the nineteenth century: *The Princess and the Goblins* [*sic*] is, in my opinion, the only English children's book in the same class as the Alice books, and *Lilith* is equal if not superior to the best of Poe.[1]

For our purposes, G. K. Chesterton's opinion of MacDonald's mythopoeic powers is more significant than those of later writers, since he is not reviving, but commenting on a near-contemporary. In *The Victorian Age in Literature* he pays tribute to

...George MacDonald, a Scot of genius as genuine as Carlyle's; he could write fairy-tales that made all experience a fairy-tale. He could give the real sense that everyone had the end of an elfin thread that must at last lead them into Paradise. It was a sort of optimist Calvinism. But such really significant fairy-tales were accidents of genius.[2]

In his excellent introduction to Greville MacDonald's not very perceptive Life of his father, Chesterton is more specific.

But in a certain rather special sense I for one can really testify to a book that has made a difference to my whole existence, which helped me to see things in a certain way from the start; a vision of things which even so real a revolution as a change of religious allegiance has substantially only crowned and confirmed. Of all the stories I have read ...it remains the most real, the most realistic, in the exact sense of the phrase the most like life. It is called *The Princess and the Goblin*...[3]

What is even more interesting and significant is that Chesterton, the writer of *Orthodoxy*, and later a champion of Catholicism, should have hailed MacDonald as the creator of an 'alternative theology' of genius, whose roots go back into pre-Reformation emotions.[4] MacDonald, he says, stands for an 'important turning-point in the history of Christendom': he is one of 'the morning stars of the Reunion'.[5] Coming from one of the most original minds of his age, these are strong words, and it is a mark of how pervasive the contrary 'Arnoldian' view of theology has become, that they should sound at first like a Chestertonian exaggeration. But I suspect that for Chesterton the point is an important one.

---

[1] *The Visionary Novels of George MacDonald*, ed. Freemantle (Noonday Press, 1954).

[2] *The Victorian Age in Literature* (Williams and Norgate, 1913), p. 152.

[3] *Life*, p. 9.   [4] Ibid. p. 12.   [5] Ibid. p. 13.

Our first observation must be that whatever Chesterton means by 'alternative', he does not mean 'heterodox' or 'heretical'. Heterodoxy for Chesterton was simply error. Neither of MacDonald's 'heresies' for which he was expelled by the good Congregationalists of Arundel would have been unacceptable perhaps even then to a more theologically minded community. To deny possible redemption to the heathen would be to set limits on the uncovenanted mercies of God – a step at which all but the most literal-minded of Calvinists have tended to hesitate. As for the 'taint' of German theology, it is more than likely that the Arundel deacons were thinking of Novalis, rather than 'theology' in its narrower sense. But, as we have seen, Germany was in any case the great catalyst in the development of English theology in the nineteenth century. The German Historical Method, so far from destroying native godliness and piety in England's green and pleasant land, enabled Coleridge, Hare, Pusey, Maurice, and even Newman himself to evolve in response to it an 'alternative' theology that was simultaneously dynamic and historical; one that was capable of coming to terms with the Bible as literature – and transforming, as it did so, our understanding of literature. If the Arundel charges suggest anything, they suggest how firmly wedded MacDonald was even at that stage to the tradition of Coleridge, and to the view that the Bible had all the depth and richness of a 'poetic' and symbolic narrative.

MacDonald, like Arnold, was widely read in German – though his references suggest he was more influenced by the poets than theologians. The first of his published works is a translation of *Twelve Spiritual Songs* of Novalis, and it is again a quotation from his favourite German poet that is the motto for *Phantastes*.[1] Evidence for the influence of Coleridge underlies almost every part of his critical essays. The conception of *England's Antiphon*, one of the best anthologies of devotional verse of its century, is clearly in the 'common tradition':

But we must not forget that, although the individual song springs from the heart of the individual, the song of a country is not merely cumulative: it is vital in its growth, and therefore composed of historically dependent members. No man would sing as he has sung, had not others

---

[1] In the first edition it contained two important misprints which have been faithfully copied by all subsequent editions! (Wolff, *The Golden Key*, pp. 42–4)

sung before him... The religious song of the country, I say again, is a growth rooted deep in all its story.[1]

Yet the influences of German historical critics, of Novalis, or even of the critical and religious tradition of Coleridge are hardly sufficient grounds for Chesterton's enthusiasm for Mac-Donald as an 'alternative' theologian. For Chesterton, the foil to MacDonald is Carlyle – his faith in a transcendent God destroyed by the 'Germans', yet unable to throw off the gloomy trappings of Calvinism. MacDonald offered Chesterton something that he needed and could not find in Carlyle. Chesterton, like both the Scots, was a poet, novelist, critic, *and* theologian, and it is this diversity of rôles with a single theological focus that provides us with a clue to what he found in MacDonald's fairy stories – that is, the possibility and even the growing need for this kind of writing in a demythologised England. MacDonald, I believe, showed Chesterton that imaginative literature need not merely illustrate theological insights, but could *create* new ones. He demonstrated that theology was of its nature a fundamentally poetic and mythopoeic activity, and that the growing divorce between theology and literature (which, paradoxically, had been aided by Arnold) was, in the long run, as damaging to literature as it was to theology. As Newman had seen so clearly, dogmatic abstract theology does not stand by itself, it grows out of a linguistic and mythic community. It was the decay of that community as an organic national entity that MacDonald, the half-deracinated Scot, could see so clearly in his own time – in many ways *more* clearly than his English friends. As he observes in his Preface to *England's Antiphon*, poetry is the cream of a people's thought, and an indication of the history of its religious feeling. For MacDonald, the English tradition, rightly under-stood, implies unity. His aim in the anthology is to demonstrate the interrelation of English society and the English Church, and thus 'to throw a pebble at that great Sabbath-breaker *Schism*'. The rôle of the theologian is essentially poetic (in the Cole-ridgean sense) in that it is his task to create the symbols by which an age or a people may find itself.

George MacDonald's conception of a symbol begins where Coleridge's left off. 'To him,' says Greville MacDonald, 'a

[1] *England's Antiphon*, p. 3.

symbol was far more than an arbitrary outward and visible sign of an abstract conception: its high virtue lay in a common *substance* with the idea presented. Perhaps this accounts for certain Roman Catholics claiming that he was never really outside the pale of the Church.'[1] In view of Chesterton's enthusiasm for MacDonald, it is interesting that this direct paraphrase of Coleridge should be discovered as orthodox Catholic doctrine. MacDonald's close adherence to Coleridge on the nature of a symbol is crucial, for what Coleridge's theory pre-supposes is the essential *polarity* of human experience: the existence of 'two worlds'.

Structurally, all George MacDonald's fantasy writing involves this confluence and tension between two physical worlds. 'The faculty of bi-local existing' as his son calls it forms the central action of the plot of his two adult fairy stories, *Phantastes* and *Lilith*. Anodos' entry into Fairyland in *Phantastes* is a simple enough technical device, but its *effect* depends on the layer upon layer of symbolic reference that MacDonald can so effortlessly bring to bear:

While these strange events were passing through my mind, I suddenly, as one awakes to the consciousness that the sea has been moaning by him for hours, or that the storm has been howling about his window all night, became aware of the sound of running water near me; and looking out of bed, I saw that a large green marble basin, in which I was wont to wash, and which stood on a low pedestal of the same material in a corner of my room, was overflowing like a spring; and that a stream of clear water was running over the carpet, all the length of the room, finding its outlet I knew not where. And, stranger still, where this carpet, which I had myself designed to imitate a field of grass and daisies, bordered the course of the little stream, the grass-blades and daisies seemed to wave in a tiny breeze that followed the water's flow; while under the rivulet they bent and swayed with every motion of the changeful current, as if they were about to dissolve with it, and, forsaking their fixed form, became as fluent as the waters.

My dressing table was an old fashioned piece of furniture of black oak, with drawers all down the front. These were elaborately carved in foliage, of which ivy formed the chief part. The nearer end of this table remained just as it had been, but on the further end a singular change had commenced. I happened to fix my eye on a little cluster of ivy-leaves. The first of these was evidently the work of the carver; the

[1] *Life*, pp. 481–2.

next looked curious; the third was unmistakably ivy; and just beyond it a tendril of clematis had twined itself about the gilt handle of one of the drawers. Hearing a slight motion above me, I looked up, and saw that the branches and leaves designed upon the curtains of my bed were slightly in motion. Not knowing what change might follow next, I thought it high time to get up; and, springing from the bed, my bare feet alighted upon a cool green sward; and although I dressed in all haste, I found myself completing my toilet under the boughs of a great tree...[1]

What in many writers would remain merely a clever set piece becomes in MacDonald's hands a *symbolic* event. The movement from 'imitation' nature in the carpet or carvings to 'real' nature suggests that this Fairyland is in some sense to be apprehended as more 'real' than the world in which Anodos has hitherto been brought up. What is artifice in our world is natural in the other. The stream from his overflowing basin has become the river of life in the most literal sense: as it flows across his carpet it *brings it to life*. The imitation is liberated into reality. Clearly, it also does the same to Anodos. It is the morning of his twenty-first birthday, and his next action, having dressed himself, is to wash in the stream on whose banks he finds himself. MacDonald is engaging archetypal levels – it is as if we have all of us entertained fantasies of this kind in one shape or another in our childhood.[2] But this combination of dream-sequence with a highly formalised wealth of explicit symbolism has another, unexpected, effect. We *see* the room that is vanishing with a peculiar intensity of detail. The result of transforming it before our eyes into another symbolic world by making it 'come alive' is to give us again a glimpse of a mid-Victorian bedroom replete with flower-patterns and vegetation motifs but with the shock of seeing the familiar for the first time. MacDonald, we realise, has actually looked at the befoliaged luxuriance of fashionable bedroom decoration with its clichés of natural forms in a way that had not been done before. The sudden impingement of the 'other' world shows us our own with new clarity.

The Fairyland of *Phantastes*, however, is not quite co-extensive with our own world in that it has a different time-scheme.

---

[1] *Phantastes and Lilith*, with an Introduction by C. S. Lewis (Eerdmans Press, 1964), pp. 19–20.

[2] In the Salem witch-trials one of the phenomena attested to by the girls was that certain witches had made plants spring out of the patterns in the carpet.

So far as we can tell – for some sequences do not have definite duration – Anodos spends many months in his other world, yet when he is finally returned to his 'more limited... bodily and earthly life' he finds that he has only been gone for twenty-one days.[1] Clearly, there is a symbolic correspondence between the twenty-one years of his own earlier life and the incidents in Fairyland, but it is not the one-for-one of conventional allegory. What looks at first sight much more like this kind of allegorical correspondence occurs in *Lilith*, where the two worlds are actually found to co-exist in time and space. Mr Raven (who is also the bird of that name) exclaims to Vane: 'if you could but hear the music! Those great long heads of wild hyacinth are inside the piano, among the strings of it, and give that peculiar sweetness to her playing! – Pardon me: I forgot your deafness!'[2] This is apparently a one-for-one allegorical correspondence, yet ...which level is which? Does the music of our world 'mean' hyacinths in the other, or hyacinths in the other 'mean' music in ours? What happens to the hyacinths when the music stops? This is not a world of phenomena versus a world of ideal 'reality', it is, rather, two parallel worlds each mysteriously impinging on the other, which is not the stuff of allegory as we normally expect it. Yet there is certainly a wider symbolic significance which MacDonald takes care to point out, but not explain:

'Two objects,' I said, 'cannot exist in the same place at the same time!'

'Can they not? I did not know – I remember now they do teach that with you...No man of the universe, only a man of the world could have said so!'[3]

Lilith implies a detailed system of 'correspondences' that looks back to Keble's symbolism of nature, and before that, to the Great Chain of Being. Mr Raven explains his dual nature as both bird *and* man like this:

Upon occasion...it is more convenient to put one's bird-self in front. Every one, as you ought to know, has a beast-self – and a bird-self, and a stupid fish-self, ay, and a creeping serpent-self too – which it takes a great deal of crushing to kill! In truth he has also a tree-self and a crystal-self, and I don't know how many selves more – all to get into

---

[1] *Phantastes and Lilith*, p. 181.   [2] Ibid. pp. 203–4.   [3] Ibid. p. 204.

harmony. You can tell what sort a man is by his creature that comes oftenest to the front.[1]

Clearly, some of these correspondences are moral, but not all: there is no suggestion of Mr Raven's bird-self being in any way different morally from his human self – which is a change from MacDonald's use of the same device in the earlier *Princess and Curdie*, where the animal self is a clue to the moral nature of the person. This is a good example of MacDonald's developing use of symbol: though it may rest on carefully schematised one-for-one correspondences, no sooner have we grasped them than they (Raven-like) change into a proliferation of further forms and suggestions that make it impossible to trace the story in one world as an analogue of events in the other. Each world has a 'real' life of its own.

'Once, forty years ago,' writes Greville MacDonald in 1924, 'I held conversation with my father on the laws of symbolism.'

He would allow that the algebraic symbol, which concerns only the three dimensioned, has no *substantial* relation to the unknown quantity; not the 'tree where it falleth' to the man unredeemed, the comparison being false. But the rose, when it gives some glimmer of the freedom for which a man hungers, does so because of its *substantial* unity with the man, each in degree being a signature of God's immanence. To a spriitual pilgrim the flower no longer seems a mere pretty design of the veil, 'the cloak and cloud that shadows me from Thee'; for see! she opens her wicket into the land of poetic reality, and he, passing through and looking gratefully back, then knows her for his sister the Rose, of spiritual substance one with himself. So may even a gem, giving from its heart reflections of Heavenly glory, awaken like memory in ourselves and send our eyes upwards. So also may we find co-substance between the stairs of a cathedral-spire and our own 'secret stair' up to the wider vision – the faculty of defying the 'plumb-line of gravity.'[2]

To Coleridge's idea of symbolism as 'bi-focal' or 'stereoscopic' vision has been superadded a system of 'correspondences' – not as some mechanical formula taken out of context from the early Fathers, but as an expression of his own mystical experience. Whereas Coleridge, one feels, would have agreed with Dante that the rose was a symbol of heaven – its beauty indicating a 'substantial unity' with a Platonic ideal of 'Beauty' – MacDonald

[1] *Phantastes and Lilith*, pp. 210–11.   [2] *Life*, p. 482.

insists that its spiritual unity is with man. Both reflect alike the glory of God. The two worlds are not hierarchically arranged, but parallel, each illuminating aspects of the other. So Mr Raven happily metamorphoses as man or bird in either world, yet in this world he is also a librarian, in the other he is also Adam, and a sexton.

I saw no raven, but the librarian – the same slender elderly man, in a rusty black coat, large in the body and long in the tails. I had seen only his back before; now for the first time I saw his face. It was so thin that it showed the shape of the bones under it, suggesting the skulls his last-claimed profession must have made him familiar with. But in truth I had never before seen a face so alive, or a look so keen or so friendly as that in his pale blue eyes, which yet had a haze about them as if they had done much weeping.

'You knew I was not a raven!' he said with a smile.

'I knew you were Mr. Raven,' I replied; 'but somehow I thought you a bird too!'

'What made you think me a bird?'

'You looked a raven, and I saw you dig worms out of the earth with your beak.'

'And then?'

'Toss them in the air.'

'And then?'

'They grew butterflies, and flew away.'

'Did you ever see a raven do that? I told you I was a sexton!'

'Does a sexton toss worms in the air, and turn them into butterflies?'

'Yes.'

'I never saw one do it!'

'You saw me do it! – But I am still librarian in your house, for I never was dismissed, and never gave up the office. Now I am librarian here as well.'

'But you have just told me you were sexton here!'

'So I am. It is much the same profession. Except you are a true sexton, books are but dead bodies to you, and a library nothing but a catacomb!'[1]

Much of this web of symbols can be disentangled: just as the raven transforms worms into butterflies, so the sexton buries sinful men and they are raised spiritual men; just as in the old Adam all die, so in Christ, the New Adam, all are made alive, as St Paul says; only he that will lose his life will save it; those who

---

[1] *Phantastes and Lilith*, p. 210.

treat book-learning as an end in itself, find books but dead bodies. We could go on – but the point is surely clear. Any one of these rôles can be read as allegorical but together, and presented to us in this disconcerting juxtaposition, we are prevented from simple equations. The combination is greater than the sum of its parts: the linking of Adam with a sexton changes our appreciation of both. What Gombrich calls in the sometimes no-less mystifying context of impressionist painting 'the beholder's share' is vital. We are faced with a poetic symbol, not a range of mechanical correspondences.

The relationship of the two worlds in *Lilith* is further clarified by a manuscript Mr Vane discovers in which his father describes a very similar conversation with his mysterious librarian:

'You would have me then understand, Mr. Raven,' I said, 'that you go through my house into another world, heedless of disparting space?'

'That I go through it is an incontrovertible acknowledgement of space,' returned the old librarian.

'Please do not quibble, Mr. Raven,' I rejoined. 'Please to take my question as you know I mean it.'

'There is in your house a door, one step through which carries me into a world very much another than this.'

'A better?'

'Not throughout; but so much another that most of its physical, and many of its mental laws are different from those of this world. As for moral laws, they must everywhere be fundamentally the same.'[1]

One is here very tempted to interpret 'house' in its mediaeval allegorised sense of 'the body'.[2] The 'incontrovertible acknowledgement of space' can, similarly, be seen as central to an incarnational theology. Yet we are brought up short by the explicit reminder that this other world is neither one of Platonic absolutes nor of unequivocal religious insight. If we were forced to try and classify it (a dangerous game) we should surely have to use some phrase like Greville MacDonald's 'land of poetic reality'. In the imagination the physical laws may be given a direct symbolic moral significance – Mr Vane, for instance, has to restore water to a parched land; a theme closely reminiscent of

[1] *Phantastes and Lilith*, p. 220.

[2] Similarly, the image of the mind as a castle is suggested by the very title of *Phantastes*, which is an allusion to the personification of Fancie, as the second of the three councillors who control the castle of the mind, in Phineas Fletcher's *Purple Island*.

MacDonald's friend Ruskin's *King of the Golden River*. The moral laws, however, are everywhere 'fundamentally the same'.

The suggestion of the body as a house occurs in the earlier *The Princess and the Goblin* (1872) where the co-existence of the two worlds is, perhaps, the most cleverly achieved of all. For Chesterton it was MacDonald's masterwork: all his other fairy stories were 'illustrations and even disguises of that one'.[1] In it, the little Princess, Irene, finds in the attics of the castle a very old and very beautiful lady whose name is *also* Irene, and who tells her that she is her great-great grandmother. Later we learn that she is in fact getting on for two thousand years old.[2] She lives on the eggs of white doves, and sits spinning in her room. Not surprisingly, the Princess Irene's nurse doesn't believe a word of this story when she is told about it, and the Princess discovers that the old lady can prove remarkably elusive. The next time she ventures up to the attics there is no trace of her great-great grandmother. On a subsequent successful visit the grandmother takes her into her bedroom where there is an enormous moon-like light that never goes out. Like the grandmother, however, the light is not always to be found: among other curious properties, we later discover, it is often easier to see from a distance than close to. The old lady tells the Princess 'a secret' that 'if that light were to go out you would fancy yourself lying in a bare garret, on a heap of old straw'.[3] This is later confirmed by Curdie, the miner's son, who at first cannot see either the grandmother or her wonderful possessions: 'I see a big, bare, garret-room....', he says, 'a tub, and a heap of musty straw, and a withered apple, and a ray of sunlight coming through a hole in the middle of the roof and shining on your head, and making all the place look a curious dusky brown.'[4] Only having undergone certain ordeals is Curdie able (or permitted) to see the grandmother and her world.

Some of the grandmother's attributes, such as her age, her name ('Peace'), and her being fed by doves, suggest that she is an allegory of the Church – and her rôle as guardian and seer would seem to confirm this. But we have to set against this view the evidence that she is apparently accessible only to very few chosen people, and that even by these she is not always easy to

[1] *Life*, p. 11.   [2] (Penguin, 1964) p. 109.   [3] Ibid. p. 85.
[4] Ibid. p. 155.

find. Her light is only intermittently visible – and then often most clearly at a distance. This may well reflect MacDonald's own experience of 'the Church'. The word has two meanings: the outer one, of the visible ecclesiastical organisation, and the inner one of mystical communion. Yet are we to conclude that the mystical communion of the Church is open only to a tiny élite of 'the elect' – the spiritual blood royal? MacDonald's rejection of Calvinism was too absolute, surely; by 1872 he was a member of Maurice's Vere Street congregation, confirmed in his vision of the Kingdom of Christ that was for all. Were it not that the grandmother is *fed* by doves, we might be tempted to see in her an analogue of the Holy Spirit. On the other hand, merely to describe her in terms of a 'mystical vision' would seem too private and personal. She is *potentially* real to everyone in the story. To be more than just arbitrary, as Newman saw, there must be assurance that inner certainty corresponds with some universal truth.

We should, perhaps, bear in mind George MacDonald's remark about *Phantastes* in a letter to Mrs Scott: 'I hope Mr. Scott will like my fairy-tale. I don't see what right the *Athenaeum* has to call it an allegory and judge or misjudge it accordingly – as if nothing but an allegory could have two meanings.'[1] In an essay he expands this point: 'A fairytale is not an allegory. There may be allegory in it, but it is not an allegory. He must be an artist indeed who can, in any mode, produce a strict allegory that is not a weariness to the spirit.'[2] MacDonald is not against *all* allegory: as we shall see, he reserved a very high place for Dante. The distinction he wishes to make is between allegory and what he means by 'fairy-tale', which uses allegory as one among a number of symbolic modes of narration. In *Lilith*, Mr Vane is dogged by the feeling that the events surrounding him have a dual meaning – or even a multiplicity of meanings:

A single thing would sometimes seem to be and mean many things, with an uncertain identity at the heart of them, which kept constantly altering their look... While without a doubt, for instance, that I was actually regarding a scene of activity, I might be, at the same moment, in my consciousness aware that I was perusing a metaphysical argument.[3]

This feeling of 'allegory-plus' is of the essence of what Mac-

[1] *Life*, p. 297.　　[2] *A Dish of Orts*, p. 317.　　[3] *Phantastes and Lilith*, p. 227.

Donald meant by fairy tale. I think it would be a mistake, however, to suppose that this was solely a property of the 'other'
world. The purpose of the other world is ultimately to reveal to
us *this* one in a new light. It is thus that Mr Raven defends his
rôle as librarian:

'A book,' he said louder, 'is a door in, and therefore a door out. – I
see old Sir Up'ard,' he went on, closing his eyes, 'and my heart swells
with love to him: – what world is he in?'
'The world of your heart!' I replied; '– that is, the idea of him is
there.'
'There is one world then at least on which your hall-door does not
open?'
'I grant you so much; but the things in that world are not things to
have and to hold.'
'Think a little farther,' he rejoined: 'did anything ever become yours,
except by getting into that world? – The thought is beyond you, however, at the present! – I tell you there are many more worlds, and more
doors to them, than you will think of in many years!'[1]

In short, Mr Raven is advancing a similar argument to Newman's in the *Grammar of Assent*. It is only by real assent ('The
world of your heart...') that we actually *possess* anything – and
real assent, we recall, is not to the abstract or theoretical, but to
what Newman calls 'the concrete'. For MacDonald, the fairy
tale is a reminder that we live our normal lives in touch with
different and separate worlds.

In *Phantastes*, when Anodos is reading in the magic library,
his reading seems to be pointing to *our* experience of reading
about him:

I was trying to find the root of a manifestation, the spiritual truth
whence a material vision sprang; or to combine two propositions, both
apparently true, either at once or in different remembered moods, and
to find the point in which their invisible converging lines would unite
in one, revealing a truth higher than either, and differing from both,
though so far from being opposed to either, it was whence each derived
its life and power.[2]

Symbols are themselves instruments of dialectic, drawing their
vitality from a Platonic synthesis that may lie beyond our

[1] *Phantastes and Lilith*, p. 221.   [2] Ibid. p. 81.

apprehension. A paradox may be the nearest we can approach to such a synthesis, for the imagination reaches beyond the frontiers of ratiocinative thought. We frequently say more than we can consciously mean in poetic symbolism: the twentieth-century 'intentional fallacy' is solved by MacDonald's Platonism. 'The fact that there is always more in a work of art – which is the highest human result of the embodying imagination – than the producer himself perceived while he produced it, seems to us a strong reason for attributing to it a larger origin than the man alone – for saying at the last, that the inspiration of the Almighty shaped its ends.'[1]

At this point we are confronted by something that makes MacDonald very different from the other writers in this tradition: his mysticism. When Coleridge says, 'the lowest depth that the light of our Consciousness can visit even with a doubtful Glimmering, is still at an unknown distance from the Ground', he is making an observation that is primarily psychological. When MacDonald writes of Vaughan's poetry, 'We must not forget that the deepest man can utter, will be but the type or symbol of something deeper yet, of which he can perceive only a doubtful glimmer',[2] whether or not he has Coleridge in mind, he is making an assertion of an utterly different nature. For Newman, the haunting question was, 'how can I know that my intuitions of God are true?' The apparatus of the *Grammar of Assent* was the result. We cannot say more of MacDonald's mysticism than that for him this kind of question seems to have been unnecessary. 'There is not a form that lives in the world,' he writes of Wordsworth, 'but is a window cloven through the blank darkness of nothingness, to let us look into the heart, and feeling, and nature of God.'[3] We are reminded more of Blake than of Wordsworth. 'Nature,' MacDonald claims, 'is brimful of symbolic and analogical parallels to the goings and comings, the growth and changes in the highest nature of man.'[4] 'The Lord puts things in subdefined, suggestive shapes, yielding no satisfactory meaning to the mere intellect... According as the new creation, that of reality, advances in him, the man becomes able to understand the words, the symbols, the parables of the Lord.'[5]

---

[1] *A Dish of Orts*, pp. 316–17.   [2] *England's Antiphon*, p. 257.
[3] *A Dish of Orts*, p. 258.   [4] *Miracles of Our Lord* (1870), p. 153.
[5] *Unspoken Sermons*, second series (Longman, 1885), pp. 49–50.

In his essay on 'The Imagination' (1867) MacDonald claims
that the world around man

...is an outward figuration of the condition of his mind; an inexhaustible storehouse of forms whence he may choose exponents – the
crystal pitchers that shall protect his thought and not need to be broken
that the light may break forth. The meanings are in those forms already,
else there could be no garment of unveiling...The man has but to
light the lamp within the form: his imagination is the light, it is not the
form.[1]

The imagination is the prime instrument of all religious perception – but, one feels, in a sense one stage on from Coleridge and
Newman. Richard Reis has pointed out the striking similarity of
such statements as these to utterances of Swedenborg, Boehme,
and Law, but adds, with salutary caution, '...the existence of a
single such agreement between MacDonald and any other
mystic proves nothing by itself; the important point is that *all*
mystics exhibit *many* psychological attributes and metaphysical
ideas in common.'[2]

What, then, *is* the relationship between the 'two worlds' in
George MacDonald's fairy tales? Why are they, for him, such a
peculiarly valuable medium of religious and mystical expression?
The strength of this kind of 'symbolism', as we have seen also in
Coleridge, is that it sees the world in terms of *archetypes* rather
than individuals. This does not mean that it is simplistic: one
only has to compare MacDonald's stories with C. S. Lewis'
more mechanically schematised Narnia to see MacDonald's
complexity – but the complexity is a philosophic one, rather than
one of personal idiosyncrasy. As Kierkegaard saw, the relationship between the moral and the religious is one of infinite paradox and mystery. It is this discrepancy which appears to interest
MacDonald – and to which his two worlds seem most often to be
related. In his essay on 'The Fantastic Imagination' he stresses
the importance of consistency in the laws of the two worlds:

The natural world has its laws, and no man must interfere with them
in the way of presentiment any more than in the way of use; but they
themselves may suggest laws of other kinds, and man may, if he pleases,
invent a little world of his own, with its own laws...

[1] *A Dish of Orts*, p. 5.
[2] Reis, *MacDonald*, p. 38. Evelyn Underhill's *Mysticism* (Methuen, 1960), he
points out, has many similar examples.

His world once invented, the highest law that comes into play is, that there shall be harmony between the laws by which the new world has begun to exist; and in the process of his creation, the inventor must hold by those laws...

It were no offence to suppose a world in which everything repelled instead of attracted the things around it; it would be wicked to write a tale representing a man it called good as always doing bad things.

...In physical things a man may invent; in moral things he must obey – and take their laws with him into his invented world as well.[1]

MacDonald's stories never suggest that morality may be overruled by a higher law as Kierkegaard does, but the main course of the action in *Lilith* is made to hinge upon the fact that the highest morality is *obedience*. Mr Vane – his name is clearly allegorical – wishes to help the children, but is told categorically by Mr Raven that in order to do so he must first sleep at his house – an invitation that clearly implies some kind of 'death'. In refusing, partly through fear and partly because he is unable to see what good it will do, Mr Vane finds that his genuine desire to do good is corrupted by his highly fallible judgement. Nevertheless, even in disobedience he learns and develops until he reaches the point where he chooses to accept Mr Raven's invitation voluntarily. However precarious our appreciation of morality may be, its demands remain absolute.

Such a view of the absoluteness of morality may come as a surprise to those reared in a world of anthropological relativity, but MacDonald's 'morality' is not a social creed, but, as it were, a two-dimensional projection of a three-dimensional world mystically perceived. The fact that Mercator's projection, for instance, produces some bad distortions near its edges, and alters the relative size of areas, does not mean that there is no real world, or globe, to which the map does, for some practical purposes, correspond better than any other. But, of course, we need other map projections as well. Like old maps, some will be better, some worse – and some will be fanciful or downright lying. For example, the portrait of Gwyntystorm in *The Princess and Curdie* is one such essay in relative commercial morality – as is the city of Bulika in *Lilith*. The England of capitalism and commerce seemed to MacDonald one of the most hideous moral distortions the world had known. 'One may readily conclude

---

[1] *A Dish of Orts*, pp. 314–16.

how poorly God thinks of riches when we see the sort of people he sends them to!' he once remarked to a wealthy Glasgow congregation;[1] more explicitly elsewhere he declares, 'Riches indubitably favour stupidity, poverty mental and moral development.'[2]

The idea of development is central to MacDonald's notion of morality. He saw life as a progressive enlightenment in which man climbs a kind of ladder, or scale of spiritual being. Not surprisingly, he found Darwin an immediate ally, but, as his son points out, ethical evolution was implied throughout his work long before Darwin published anything – and, moreover, however some Victorians may have interpreted him[3] 'ethical' evolution is not implied by Darwin's theory. In *The Princess and Curdie* we find a process of reverse evolution whereby the courtiers and people of Gwyntystorm become more and more like the animals they resemble: Curdie is given the power to detect what sort of animal they are devolving into by the feel of paw or hoof as they shake hands. MacDonald, of course, would have differed from such modern exponents of ethical evolution as Teilhard de Chardin in that, for him, the moral is prior to the scientific (in theory as well as fact) rather than vice versa. Evolution, for MacDonald, is primarily a *symbolic* process. 'All that moves in the mind is symbolized in Nature. Or, to use another more philosophical, and certainly not less poetic figure, the world is a sensuous analysis of humanity, and hence an inexhaustible wardrobe for the clothing of human thought.'[4] It is obvious how this kind of vision of life as a symbolic process of development within a God-filled universe of infinite variety, finds better and more natural expression within MacDonald's kind of fantasy or fairy tale than it would within the constraints of realistic fiction. Fantasy is more like poetry than the novel in its freedom to be openly symbolic.

Richard Reis, in what is by far the best book on George MacDonald so far, argues that the movement from one world to another signifies 'promotion' in the ethical ladder.[5] Now there is some evidence to support this idea. When Irene, in *The Princess*

---

[1] *Life*, p. 157.   [2] Ibid. 156.

[3] For opposing moral interpretations of evolution, see Stephen Toulmin, *Metaphysical Beliefs*, ed. Alastair MacIntyre (S.C.M., 1970).

[4] *A Dish of Orts*, p. 9.   [5] *MacDonald*, p. 127.

and the Goblin, asks about her grandmother's lamp, she is told:

'When I please I can make the lamp shine through the walls – shine so strong that it melts them away from before the sight, and shows itself as you saw it. But, as I told you, it is not everybody that can see it.'

'How is it that I can, then? I'm sure I don't know.'

'It is a gift born with you. And one day I hope everybody will have it.'[1]

Curdie's initiation clearly *is* some kind of promotion. On the other hand, as Reis also admits,[2] none of MacDonald's protagonists does achieve his goal. In the cases of Anodos and Mr Vane, they are returned to this world again filled with unsatisfied longings, 'no longer at ease here, in the old dispensation'. The ending of *The Princess and Curdie* is even more ambiguous: Irene and Curdie die childless, and after their death greed once again envelopes Gwyntystorm and causes its final and complete annihilation.[3] Life remains fundamentally tragic; insight is temporary and fleeting. The powers of mystical apprehension are slowly evolving in man, but at the moment are only the possession of a tiny minority. It might be best put theologically by saying that entry into the other worlds is by 'election' in the Augustinian rather than in the Calvinist sense. The other worlds are by no means exclusive, but the reasons for some rather than others being able to enter are not revealed at this stage of our development. Moreover, it is never clear that the Princess is *morally* any better than Curdie – indeed, most of the costly acts of courage and sacrifice come from Curdie, whose surname, lest we forget, is Peterson. Similarly, Mr Vane's behaviour in both worlds is regarded as misguided and often dangerous to all concerned. Nor in the two adult fairy stories are the other worlds morally superior places; both contain things of intense evil. Though the world of the grandmother in the two *Princess* books *is* entirely good, this is counterbalanced by a second level of symbolic structure which is morally retrogressive and partially evil – that of the goblins.

The Princess and the Goblin is about a three-storey universe. In the middle of the old house, 'half house, half castle', live the Princess Irene and the servants. Above, in the attics is the grandmother; below, tunnelling through the mountain, and,

---

[1] P. 104.   [2] *MacDonald,* p. 128.   [3] P. 219.

finally, into the cellars of the house, are the goblins. The frame-work is familiar in mediaeval allegory: the three-storey universe of Heaven, Earth, and Hell. The house or castle is the 'body'; the Princess is the 'soul', and her servants, the 'senses' – ignorant of any other world beyond their dimension, and therefore denying its existence. Though MacDonald was, as we have seen, opposed to any suggestion that his books were allegorical in any mechani-cal sense, we have also seen how deeply he believed in learning to interpret 'the language of correspondences by which God has given man clues to his meaning'.[1] 'The world,' says MacDonald, 'is the human being turned inside out'. He was familiar with mediaeval allegory at least in Dante – and he speaks of Dante as poet and mystic with unqualified reverence. When, in *At the Back of the North Wind*, the little boy, Diamond, actually goes to 'the back of the North Wind' we are told that one of the very few who have been there before him 'was a great Italian of noble family, who died more than five hundred years ago'.[2] His name, we are told, was Durante, 'and it means lasting, for his books will last as long as there are enough men in the world worthy of having them'. The description that follows makes it clear that location of 'the back of the North Wind' is the Earthly Paradise (*Purgatorio*, XXVIII–XXXIII). In other words, it seems plain that at this point, at any rate, MacDonald is announcing that his symbolism is to be identifiably linked with one of the world's great 'allegories' – and to be read as such. He couples this, how-ever, with one of his clearest statements on the nature of symbolic language.

I have now come to the most difficult part of my story. And why? Because I do not know enough about it. . . Things there are so different from things here! The people there do not speak the same language for one thing. Indeed, Diamond insisted that there they do not speak at all. I do not think he was right, but it may well have appeared so to Diamond. The fact is, we have different reports of the place from the most trustworthy people. Therefore we are bound to believe that it appears somewhat different to different people. All, however, agree in a general way about it.[3]

In spite of discrepancies, there *is* a reality – a potentially common reality – to which these various symbolic accounts of 'other

---

[1] Reis, *MacDonald*, p. 125.   [2] (Airmont, 1966), p. 87.
[3] *At the Back of the North Wind*, p. 87.

worlds' refer. The references to Dante, and others, are a way of insisting that MacDonald's symbolism, though personal, is *not* private.

But it is important to notice that the 'allegory' of *The Princess and the Goblin* is capable of more than one interpretation. It has been remarked that Freud is one of the best literary critics of his century, and this is one of several places in nineteenth-century fiction where a proto-'Freudian' psychological structure can be discerned. The Princess is, as it were, the Ego, guided by her Super-ego grandmother, but threatened by the goblins from underground – who, we are told explicitly, have been repressed and driven underground to become degenerate and the more dangerous because hardly ever visible.[1] Both the theological and the psychological seem too well developed for them not to be, in some sense,[2] intentional, but, as in Dante, it is the vitality and individuality of the 'surface' narrative that holds our attention, and prevents the story from being 'allegorical' in any simple sense. Bunyan, it is true, manages to give Christian the qualities of both archetype and individual, but Christian as an allegorical figure is still a whole person, and not a 'faculty' or facet of the personality as we must suppose MacDonald's characters to be. Moreover, if we do take Irene, for instance, to be an allegory of the 'soul' or 'psyche' we find that she, as a character, has herself senses, good and bad inclinations, and so on, with the result that we are caught up in the infinite regress that always threatens this kind of literature. MacDonald's denial that he is writing allegory in any mechanical sense implies that he was aware of precisely this kind of danger. His comment that a fairy tale may include levels of allegorical illustration without itself being allegorical is important. As in the *Ancient Mariner* we find that the religious and psychological levels in MacDonald conflict, co-exist, and are in some sense dependent upon each other while in no way being exhaustive. In *At the Back of the North Wind* we find Diamond's preternatural goodness – his 'other-worldliness' – instead of arousing respect or gratitude in those he has helped, causes contempt. He *is* a prig. There is, here at any rate, no easy

[1] This is not, of course, to imply that Freud was likely to have read MacDonald – merely that such schemes exist in a wide variety of forms in the nineteenth century.

[2] It does not matter, for the sake of this argument, whether MacDonald was or was not 'conscious' of what he was creating. I only wish to suggest that it is not random or fortuitous.

reconciliation of the two worlds: in human experience they remain, as they appear, polar opposites.

Parallels with the *Ancient Mariner*, as it has been one of the purposes of this study to show, are not out of place. It is significant that many of the links George MacDonald is quick to stress in his essays are with Wordsworth and Coleridge.[1] There may well be good reason for this. MacDonald *needed* the tradition of these two poets in a way that he did not need that of even the other mystics on whom he so plainly and unashamedly drew – such as Blake. C. S. Lewis has commented how:

A dominant form tends to attract to itself writers whose talents would have fitted them much better for work of some other kind. Thus the retiring Cowper writes satire in the eighteenth century; or in the nineteenth century a mystic and natural symbolist like George Mac-Donald is seduced into writing novels.[2]

This seems to me a very profound observation. Reis has amply demonstrated the way in which 'symbolism was for MacDonald a habitual language', and classes him as a writer with such authors as Blake, Shelley, and Kafka in his capacity to work 'not in words, but in images'.[3] Now MacDonald was living in the middle of the great age of the realistic novel: the world of Thackeray, George Eliot, and Trollope. Given his immediate circle of literary friends and acquaintances, and the need to earn money fast, it is hardly surprising that the bulk of his output is 'realistic' novels. Given the kind of sensibility with which Mac-Donald was endowed, it is hardly surprising that posterity should not find these novels 'realistic' in any lasting sense, but merely a mixture of acutely observed local colour and stylised plot dominated by heavy poetic moralising. To quote Reis yet again: 'Everything about George MacDonald's character, life, philosophy, and cast of mind seems, in the glare of hindsight, to have fitted him for the writing of symbolic fantasy and to have pre-destined him to mediocrity as a realistic novelist.'[4] His adult fairy stories, it is true, earned the praise of the discriminating.

[1] See, for instance, 'Wordsworth's Poetry', 'The Imagination' (Platonised Coleridge), 'A Sketch of Individual Development' (which could be either based on autobiographical experience, or on Wordsworth, or, most likely, both), as well as *England's Antiphon*.

[2] *The Allegory of Love* (Oxford, 1936), p. 232; Reis, *MacDonald*, p. 30.

[3] Reis, *MacDonald*, p. 112.   [4] Ibid. p. 106.

Dickens liked *Phantastes*; H. G. Wells, interestingly, was a great admirer of *Lilith*. As we have seen, Chesterton was influenced by his children's fantasies, and assigned a unique place to *The Princess and the Goblin*. Yet, by and large, MacDonald's own time was not on the same wavelength as his non-realistic books and classified his children's stories merely as moral entertainment, with very little idea of what they were trying to do.

George MacDonald was a pioneer with very few models to work from, but he did have at least one work of a similar nature to go on: the *Ancient Mariner*. Critics from Mrs Barbauld onwards have always had with the *Ancient Mariner* a problem of classification. It too seems to be possessed of overlapping worlds that impinge upon and influence each other in a relationship that is symbiotic rather than straightforwardly allegorical; it too works in terms of symbols rather than ideas; it too is arbitrary and yet moral. Above all, it stoutly resists demythologising – as Coleridge emphasised in his famous reply to Mrs Barbauld. Whatever its moral may be, two things about the poem are certain: one is that it *has* a moral; the second is that the moral cannot be extracted and adequately re-stated. It inheres *in* the myth as an inseparable element of the poetry. Similarly, in MacDonald's fairy stories it is precisely this element that makes him so powerful and satisfying a myth-maker, and which differentiates his fantasies so sharply from his more 'externally' moralised realistic novels. Moreover – and this is the true test of a 'tradition' in T. S. Eliot's sense[1] – part of George MacDonald's importance is that he enables us to understand better what Coleridge was doing in the *Ancient Mariner*. If MacDonald's fairy stories were undervalued by the Victorian age, it is no less true that the *Ancient Mariner* was undervalued for similar reasons – or admired merely for its creation of a 'dream-like' atmosphere, which was the Platonic revenge the Victorian psyche exacted for the normative emphasis on realism in fiction. MacDonald shows us how, like certain other great innovative works (*Tristram Shandy*, perhaps), the *Ancient Mariner* is better understood through its descendants than its forbears.

[1] 'Tradition and the Individual Talent', *Selected Essays*. It is hard to believe that Eliot, in producing his famous definition, had not been reading Thomas Arnold: 'it is most natural...that the past and present and future should be linked together in a chain...that in every age the dead should still, in a manner be present among the living' ('Sermon on Wills', *Sermons* (1845), VI, 325–6).

9

Summary: Tradition and the Church

The White Queen only looked at her in a helpless frightened sort of way, and kept repeating something in a whisper to herself that sounded like 'Bread-and-butter, bread-and-butter,' and Alice felt that if there was to be any conversation at all, she must manage it herself.[1]

If we accept the interpretation of those who see in *Alice Through the Looking Glass* a satire of the Victorian Church (and it is as plausible as most 'interpretations' of *Alice*) the Red Queen is commonly taken to be the Church of Rome and the White Queen the Church of England.[2] The White Queen is vague and amiable, and boasts of being able to 'read words of one letter'. When she was terrified by a great thunderstorm (suspiciously like the monstrous crow of Disestablishment which ended the battle of Tweedledum and Tweedledee, the High and Low Church parties) she confesses she couldn't remember her own name. Nevertheless she appears to know on which side her bread is buttered. Her rewards are curiously deferred on the famous principle of 'jam tomorrow and jam yesterday – but never jam today' – a state of organisation which is apparently made easier by living backwards, so that she can howl before she is hurt rather than after. Nor are matters spiritual neglected: she even manages to believe 'as many as six impossible things before breakfast'. It is difficult not to be reminded of Newman's scornful satires on the Anglican Church's state of consciousness in his *Lectures on Certain Difficulties felt by Anglicans*. Certainly the White Queen's characteristics have something strangely in

[1] Lewis Carroll, *Alice's Adventures in Wonderland and Through the Looking-Glass* (Macmillan, 1887), pp. 84–5.

[2] See *Aspects of Alice*, ed. Robert Phillips (Gollancz, 1972), in particular Alexander Taylor's article 'Through the Looking-Glass'. It is only fair to add that Shane Leslie, in 'Lewis Carroll and the Oxford Movement', disagrees with the usual interpretations, holding that the White Queen is Newman and the Red Queen Manning.

common with some aspects of the Church of England as we have observed them in this study.

What has been unfolded in the course of this book is a debate, at a variety of levels, about the nature of the Church: initially, the Church of England, but, inevitably as events progressed, about 'the Church' as a whole. It came to its head in the early middle years of the nineteenth century in a crisis that the Church of England was slow to recognise and even more reluctant to face. Too much was at stake. As an organisation it had lent itself to the support of a social order and an associated world-view based on privilege without responsibility. A contemporary article in the *Edinburgh Review* declares,

The thermometer of the Church of England sank to its lowest point in the first thirty years of George III. Unbelieving bishops and a slothful clergy, had succeeded in driving from the Church the faith and zeal of Methodism which Wesley had organized within her pale. The spirit was expelled, and the dregs remained. That was the age when jobbery and corruption, long supreme in the State, had triumphed over the virtue of the Church; when the money-changers not only entered the temple, but drove out the worshippers; when ecclesiastical revenues were monopolized by wealthy pluralists; when the name of curate lost its legal meaning, and, instead of denoting the incumbent of a living, came to signify the deputy of an absentee.[1]

Only a few years later Thomas Mozley describes a Church where 'thousands of livings were without parsonages, and with incomes so small as not to admit of building or even renting'. Consequently, 'non-residence was almost the rule in some districts, and...even the pastoral duties of which all clergymen are capable and which are always welcome, were discharged intermittingly and cursorily'. 'Church fabrics fell into disorder and even decay...bishops and dignitaries made fortunes, and used their patronage for private purposes.'[2] In its inward life the Anglican Church was, if anything, in even worse decay:

Forty years ago the negative side of the Church of England...was rapidly increasing. The state of things just as they were did not seem a sufficient basis for defence against the general dissolution of faith threatening the Church...This growing indifference was the great fact of that day. It was a public fact, a social fact, an academic fact, a domestic

[1] Lady Holland, *Memoir of the Rev. Sydney Smith* (London, 1855), I, 61–2.
[2] *Reminiscences*, I, 184.

fact. A man might avow any phase of unbelief, and any contempt of religion, without loss of character, in the service of the state, in society, at Oxford, and at home. It was expected of every young man in 'the world'. . . . For everything short of fanatical and intolerant atheism, there was not only condonance, but a certain degree of admiration.[1]

The result in the late 1820s and early 30s was that the old certainties were increasingly threatened not by ecclesiastical, but by *political* reform. In 1828 the acts barring dissenters from municipal office were finally repealed; in 1829 came Peel's Catholic Emancipation Act; and 1833 saw the suppression of ten redundant Irish bishoprics – with a clear warning to the remaining bishops to set their own house in order.[2] As so often happens with the collapse of conventional assumptions, certainties far wider than the original points at issue were suddenly seen to be called in question. To many, Catholic Emancipation in 1829 seemed no more than rudimentary natural justice, long overdue – as indeed it was. Those who, like Keble and Coleridge, opposed it, found themselves in an absurd and manifestly impossible moral position. Yet Keble and Coleridge had seen, as Peel had not, that in the wake of it men must begin to ask fundamental and awkward questions about the nature of the Church of England that had not been broached since the seventeenth century.

In his 1833 Assize Sermon on the 'National Apostasy' Keble doubted how the faithful could possibly continue 'their communion with the Church Established. . . without acquiring any taint of those Erastian principles on which she is now avowedly to be governed'.[3] Keble's most recent biographer, Georgina Battiscombe, comments,

The phrase strikes strangely on modern ears for we have been brought up to believe that the Erastianism which Keble regarded as a new and alarming danger was in fact the most notable characteristic of the Church of England in the eighteenth century. The term is often used as implying a Church connected with the state, but Keble is using it in the correct dictionary meaning of a Church subjected to the state. The eighteenth century church was not Erastian in the strict sense of the word. So long as full civic rights could only be enjoyed by members of the Church so long could Church and State be fairly described as two aspects of the same entity. Whilst that remained true the Church could

---

[1] Ibid. ii, 384–5.   [2] Storr, *English Theology*, p. 250.
[3] Battiscombe, *Keble*, p. 154.

not, accurately speaking, be described as Erastian, since nothing can be
subject to itself.[1]

What, then, *was* the Church of England? It was to this highly
topical question that Coleridge addressed himself so urgently in
1829–30. But in the short term the impact of *Church and State*
was slight compared with Keble's answer that thundered forth in
his Assize Sermon of 1833 and inaugurated what Oxford men
called the 'movement of 1833' and the rest of the country called
the 'Oxford Movement'. His answer was clear. To quote Miss
Battiscombe again,

The Anglican Church is the representative in England of the whole
Church Catholic and Apostolic, a society to use the biblical phrase,
'built upon the Apostles and prophets, Jesus Christ Himself being the
chief corner-stone.' Its authority is the authority of Christ, handed on
by Him to the Apostles and their successors. This Apostolic Church is
a greater thing than the Church of England, although the Church of
England is assuredly a true part of it, and it is to this Church that a
man's loyalty is ultimately due.[2]

But perhaps this was a less clear answer than those who met
afterwards at Hadleigh rectory to discuss more concrete action
originally supposed. Keble himself was absent from this initial
gathering of the Movement; so was Newman. It was the latter's
answer, slow and agonising in its terrible sincerity and relentless
personal logic that was to break the Oxford Movement as a
party. His logic, as we have seen, was peculiarly his own, yet
owing more to Coleridge than to Keble. Barchester, while it
might not entirely approve of some of Mr Arabin's Oxford
principles, could still enfold him into its comfortable establishment with a minimum of inconvenience to Mrs Proudie.[3] In the
last resort, Keble would not rock the boat; Newman was fully
prepared to walk on the water. To many contemporaries, the
Tractarians were a backward-looking and conservative movement, and as such they were a nuisance that could, fretfully, be
tolerated. But Newman, however much he might dream of the
early Fathers, was moved by a vision not of the past, but of the
Coleridgean 'idea' of the Church – and such radicalism was in the

---

[1] Battiscombe, *Keble*, p. 154.   [2] Ibid. pp. 155–6.
[3] Anthony Trollope, *Barchester Towers* (1857).

end intolerable to Anglican and Roman alike in the nineteenth century.

Thus if the first tremors had occurred in the shape of political reforms, the earthquake when it came was from the very theological and intellectual centre of the Church of England. Thomas Arnold's desire to substitute morality for religion, and his son's attempt to express this in terms of German historical criticism were in many ways more acceptable to the spiritual comfort of the English Church than the vision of the wider unity of the Body of Christ that inspired in different ways both Newman and Maurice. England was prepared neither for a universal spiritual society, if it really meant including Quakers and Dissenters, nor for the Church Holy and Apostolic, if it also meant being international and Roman; yet after 1845 it was no longer possible for the least theologically-minded to pretend that nothing had happened. The ground beneath the Church's feet might or might not be a via media, but it was certainly breaking up. To the Evangelicals the institution was less important than the state of the individual before God; their theology and to a large extent their literature was already formed. They were, as a group, profoundly anti-intellectual and anti-aesthetic, and, in spite of the 'socialism' of men like Kingsley, to that degree less dangerous to the structure of the social and political establishment.[1] For

[1] Evangelicalism, in its origin, was a reaction against the High-Church 'evidences'; the insurrection of the heart and conscience of man against an arid orthodoxy. It insisted on a 'vital Christianity', as against the Christianity of books. Its instinct was from the first against intelligence. No text found more favour with it than 'Not many wise, not many learned'.

Newman, 'Learning in the Church of England' (1863), *Essays*, ed. Nettleship (Oxford, 1889), II, 268. Newman's argument finds corroboration in Kingsley:

We may think too much! There is such a thing as mystifying one's self! Mystifying one's self is thinking a dozen thoughts in order to get to a conclusion, to which one might arrive by thinking one; getting at ideas by an unnecessarily subtle and circuitous path; then, because one has been through many steps, one fancies one has gone deep. This is one form of want of simplicity. This is not like being a little child, any more than analysing one's own feelings. A child goes straight to its point, and it hardly knows why...remember that habit, more than reason, will cure one of mystifying subtlety and morbid fear...Feed on Nature, and do not try to understand it...Think little and read less! Never give way to reveries...Distrust every idea which you cannot put into words; or rather distrust your own conception of it...

Charles Kingsley: His Letters and Memories of his Life, ed. by his wife, 7th edn (1877), I, 87–90)

For another similar view of the Evangelicals of the 1820s and 30s see Mozley, *Reminiscences*, ch XXIX.

those who cared for the Church as a divine institution, or for those for whom the Church as an earthly institution cared so well – like the rich clergy of Barchester – the twin challenges of Maurice and Newman were ultimately more dangerous than the attacks of the Benthamites and the *Westminster Review*. Leaving the wineskins innocuously intact, they threatened instead to turn the old wine into new.

Wordsworth's part in the dissolution of the old order was more obvious than Coleridge's in the 1830s and 40s even if it was in the long run less far-reaching. Both H. J. Rose and F. W. Faber were received warmly by him when they visited the Lake District.[1] He had become the unofficial poet laureate of the Oxford Movement, and he approved of its aims although he refused to be publicly more closely associated with it. In 1833 he had even agreed to a request from Benjamin Bailey (better known as Keats' friend and confidant) for his *Ecclesiastical Sonnets* to be printed 'as a book of devotion in verse to accompany Keble's *Christian Year*'.[2] In 1844 he permitted Faber to include one of his poems in the Life of St Berga which the former was contributing to Newman's *Lives of the English Saints*. Nevertheless, his hesitations indicate the degree to which he recognised the differences between himself and the Tractarians. When, in 1842, one of their number named Wilkinson invited Wordsworth to write in their support, he declined saying that 'It would seem to enroll me as a partisan, and the support which I might otherwise give to Catholic truth would, I fear, in numerous quarters, be impaired accordingly.'[3] In fact his difference with the Oxford Movement is crucial. As his comments to Crabb Robinson at this time suggest, he regarded orthodox Christian dogma as primarily metaphorical and symbolic whereas for the majority of the Oxford men a monolithic literalism still held sway over what were regarded as the revealed truths of Christianity. To Robinson, for instance, he commented that 'The Atonement is a doctrine which has its foundation in that consciousness of unworthiness and guilt which arises from an upright self-examination – as all orthodox doctrines are warranted by a humble spirit and all that is best in our moral nature.'[4] The

---

[1] Moorman, *Wordsworth, The Later Years*, pp. 478–83.
[2] Ibid. pp. 479–80. (Nothing more is known of this particular scheme.)
[3] Moorman, *Wordsworth, The Later Years*, p. 482.   [4] Ibid.

Athanasian Creed was a 'needless and mischievous' attempt at explaining what should not be explained; it was 'an unhappy excrescence'.[1] It is in their view of the Church and its doctrines as metaphors and symbols of a greater reality that Wordsworth and Coleridge remain at their closest in the 1830s.

If, as Coulson and Willey have both claimed, Coleridge's critical and aesthetic thought stems from fundamental religious preoccupations,[2] it is also characteristic of the unity of his mental processes that his religious thought should be closely shaped by the development of his critical and aesthetic ideas. We can see this clearly in *Church and State*. His vision was of harmonious symbolic counterpoint between the Church of England and the unreformed and therefore Anglican parliament. To this extent it was a defence of the old order, already breached and breaking up, rather than a reconstruction of a new. As so often happens, the finest statement of the eighteenth-century ideal occurs after it was irretrievably doomed. But this essentially conservative document rested upon foundations that were an implicit challenge to the very way of thinking it was apparently trying to uphold. Coleridge does not attempt to base his defence upon either ecclesiastical polity or upon the simple 'theological' premises most easily understood by his age – which would have meant recourse to 'evidences' and Natural Law. His argument for the status quo is grounded explicitly in *aesthetics*. The Church of England was *symbolic* in function. On the one hand it co-existed as a counterpoise or polarity of the civil power within the State; on the other, it contained within itself the polarity between the National Church and the Church of Christ. At each level, for Coleridge, it was sustained by a *metaphorical* tension. Thus at one level, just as the civil pole of the State could not properly be understood without seeing the ecclesiastical pole, so the ecclesiastical pole could not be understood without the civil. The Church's relation to parliament was not Erastian subservience, but dialectical unity. The organic unity of this symbolic tension was demonstrated by its repetition at every level: political, ecclesiastical, theological. The Church of England is like the miracles of Our Lord in that it is an *acted metaphor*. The tension between the National Church and the Church of Christ finds its paradigm in Christ himself: by the final definition of Nicaea,

[1] Ibid.   [2] See above, p. 10.

wholly Man and wholly God; fully human, yet 'of one substance with the Father'. A long tradition of speculative and systematic theology lies behind such an argument by analogy – much of it far more tenuous and far-fetched – but it was not in the main living tradition of the Church of England in the 1820s. Coleridge's argument for the existing state of affairs was revolutionary. Mediaeval and seventeenth-century metaphysics had been sealed off from English theological thinking by a century of rationalism and 'Paleyite' natural apologetic. Butler's great analogy for religion is from 'nature' as perceived by science; to structure the political and socio-ecclesiastical framework by means of analogy from revelation and dogmatic theology was to stand the accepted order on its head. It was only possible for Coleridge to do so because of the existence of a parallel tradition in literary criticism that was accustomed to thinking symbolically, and which, while it was ultimately derived from the earlier methods of theological analogy, existed at the beginning of the nineteenth century as an independent and autonomous way of thinking.

What Coleridge did, in effect, was to re-introduce to the Church of England a mode of thought which had originally flourished there and then died out. The result was not dissimilar to the kind of far-reaching ecological change brought about by the re-introduction of the horse to South America. The ground for this shift of thought in England had been well prepared. A. W. Schlegel's literary criticism had been translated in 1815 and even without Coleridge's lectures of 1818 the currents of German critical thought were beginning to seep into English consciousness in a way that German theology had yet to do. The years 1820–40 were a period of intense intellectual excitement and activity in the English universities – and Germany was the catalyst. We have already mentioned Pusey's visit in 1823; in 1831 Robert Wilberforce had followed to investigate for himself the work of Schleiermacher, Neander, Tholuck, and Freytag.[1] In 1825 Connop Thirlwall published his translation of Schliermacher's *Critical Essay on the Gospel of St Luke* with an introduction of his own. It was immediately read and annotated by Coleridge. Between 1828 and 1832 we recall that Hare and Thirlwall were at work publishing their translation of Niebuhr's *History of Rome*, complete with notes of their own. Milman's

[1] Newsome, *Parting of Friends*, p. 78.

Professorship of Poetry at Oxford from 1821–31 had helped to disseminate German ideas of myth and history there,[1] and such was the pace of intellectual change even in Oxford that by 1835 Mark Pattison found that honours men were expected 'to know something of Niebuhr's views'.[2] Clearly it was not in fact proving possible to separate theology from the developments in literary criticism and the historical method. Yet the way in which England tended to absorb the new ideas from Germany is characteristic. In 1796 Kant had attacked his fellow philosopher Friedrich Heinrich Jacobi in an article entitled 'On a Certain Genteel Tone which has of late appeared in Philosophy'.[3] The main weight of his charge was that Jacobi had dispensed with the hard work of philosophy by substituting an emphasis on intuition and feeling, dangerously embellished with aesthetic and analogical turns of phrase. The fact is, declared Kant, 'philosophy is fundamentally prosaic; and to attempt to philosophize poetically is very much as if a merchant should undertake to make up his account-books not in prose but in verse'. In England, however, it was widely assumed (with some justification) that Kant and Jacobi were saying much the same thing about the distinction between 'Reason' and 'Understanding' – the issue on which they had fallen out. Coleridge, Carlyle, and, in America, Emerson took over from Kant a 'philosophy' assumed to be almost identical to that of Jacobi. Carlyle describes the Kantian 'Reason' thus:

Not by logic or argument does it work; yet surely and clearly may it be taught to work; and its domain lies in that higher region whither logic and argument cannot reach; in that holier region where Poetry and Virtue and Divinity abide, in whose presence Understanding wavers and recoils, dazzled into utter darkness by that 'sea of light', at once the fountain and the termination of true knowledge.[4]

The phrases may be Carlyle's, but the spirit of this 'poetic' enthusiasm for the ineffable certainties of Reason was fully shared by Coleridge in *Aids to Reflection* – and, for all Newman's avowed lack of acquaintance with the Germans, there are similarities

---

[1] Forbes, *The Liberal Anglican Idea of History*, p. 34.   [2] *Memoirs*, p. 151.

[3] A. O. Lovejoy, *The Reason, the Understanding, and Time* (Johns Hopkins, 1961), p. 11.

[4] *The State of German Literature, Critical and Miscellaneous Essays*, I (Chapman & Hall 1869), 96.

with his 'illative sense'. In becoming Anglicised, Kant had become poeticised.

Moreover, it is significant that the people in whom this 'poeticising' tendency was most marked were also among the best able to judge the quality and tone of the German sources. Carlyle is by no means always scholarly in his approach to the German philosophers,[1] but he does seem to have known something of the dispute between Kant and Jacobi,[2] and his 1829 essay on Novalis suggests that his claim for the 'poetic' status of Reason is made as a conscious act of interpretation.[3] Much more powerful evidence, however, comes from Julius Hare who, as we have seen, was a key figure in the dissemination of German ideas and was arguably the finest German scholar in England of his day. In *Guesses at Truth*, a *Friend*-like compendium of politics, philosophy, and criticism, which he published jointly with his brother Augustus in 1827, we find him comparing the Reason and the Understanding to the sun and moon respectively in an extended poetic conceit.

> ...when the calculating, expediential Understanding has superseded the Conscience and the Reason, the Senses soon rush out from their dens, and sweep away everything before them. If there be nothing brighter than the reflected light of the moon, the wild beasts will not keep in their lair. And when that moon, after having reached a moment of apparent glory, by looking full at the sun, fancies it may turn away from the sun, and still have light in itself, it straightway begins to wane, and ere long goes out altogether, leaving its worshippers in the darkness, which it had vainly dreamt it would enlighten.[4]

Behind such a complex Coleridgean metaphor is a conscious theory of the relationship of poetry to philosophy that was to engender a whole tradition of Victorian thought. 'Poetry is to philosophy', declares Hare, 'what the sabbath is to the rest of the week.'[5] If German authorisation for this kind of analogy were needed, he had only to ignore Kant and the philosophers and turn, as Carlyle did, to Novalis. Hare knew, for instance, the aphorisms very similar in tone in the *Thoughts on Religion* –

---

[1] See, for instance, his cavalier comment that Novalis' metaphysics appear 'synonymous with what little we understand of Fichte's, and might indeed...be classed under the head of Kantianism, or German metaphysics generally' ('Novalis', *Critical and Miscellaneous Essays*, II, 273).

[2] Ibid. p. 278.   [3] Ibid. p. 279.   [4] *Guesses at Truth*, p. 80.   [5] Ibid. p. 11.

which could even have served as another model for *Guesses at Truth*.[1] 'Poetry is among the feelings what Philosophy is in relation to thoughts,' writes Novalis, and again, 'Among the ancients Religion was already in a certain measure what it has become with us, namely, practical poesy.'[2] But Hare was prepared, at least in conversation, to press such analogies to their extreme conclusion. In an argument with Whewell, an old college friend, later to be Master of Trinity, Hare was accused of adopting the philosophy of certain writers because he admired their poetry. He replied, emphasising every word, 'But poetry is philosophy, and philosophy is poetry.' *Guesses at Truth* contains the (unattributed) rider to this, with echoes also of Novalis, 'In simpler ages the two things went together; and then Poetry and Philosophy were united. But that universal solvent, Civilization, which pulverizes to cement, and splits to fagot, has divided them; and they are now far as the Poles assunder.'[3] Since the second edition of *Guesses at Truth* was dedicated to Wordsworth we need no clues as to the 'certain writers' whose philosophy Hare believed to be co-extensive with their poetry – nor to the sources of this kind of intellectual synaesthesia and primitivism. If restoration of the original unity of poetry and philosophy were possible in the destructive ethos of nineteenth-century civilisation, then it was to Wordsworth and Coleridge that the clerisy must turn. In his dedication of 1838 Hare writes, 'You and he [Coleridge] came forward together in a shallow, hard, worldly age, – an age alien and almost averse from the higher and more strenuous exercises of imagination and thought – as the purifiers and regenerators of poetry and philosophy.' For Hare, Wordsworth and Coleridge were final evidence of the inseparability of aesthetic theory from theology and philosophy.

Whilst over certain theological issues the Tractarians reacted fiercely against Coleridge and the 'Germanising' influences, it is also clear how much they owed to contemporary movements in

---

[1] *Guesses at Truth*, p. 295. Hare takes Novalis's as an example of an aphoristic style.

[2] *Hymns and Thoughts on Religion*, trans. W. Hastie (1888), p. 83.

It was this collection of Novalis that made such an impact on George Mac-Donald. His first published work (1851) was a translation of twelve of the *Spiritual Songs* (*Life*, p. 159). *Phantastes*, his first novel, opens with quotations from the *Thoughts*, and *Lilith*, his last, closes with one.

[3] *Guesses at Truth*, p. 185.

aesthetic theory which were derived ultimately from the same source. Pattison, we may remember, attributed Newman's support for his unsuccessful attempt at an Oriel Fellowship to the fact that he had recently developed a passion for Coleridge's ideas.[1] The way in which Coleridge affects Keble is even more striking. The Kebles' home at Fairford was one of the few where the old assumptions of High Tory Anglicanism had been kept alive, and the young John Keble did not need Coleridge to point him back to the Caroline divines. Nevertheless, when he began to assert the new-found self-consciousness of the Church of England he did so not in the traditional language of seventeenth-century polemic, but in the metaphors that, via Coleridge, had come to dominate the whole debate: those of the Church as 'poetic' – as a *work of art*. The distinctive 'tradition' of Coleridge, and, to a lesser but significant extent, of Wordsworth can be traced in this use of a common language drawn in the first place from aesthetics.

The complex relationship between Maurice and the Oxford Movement, for instance, can be seen in the framework of assumptions they shared about the nature of the Church. For Keble, the Church was 'poetic' in that it offered not merely divine illumination, but also 'soothing' catharsis. It was God's Work of Art in which man was invited to participate. This was as true for Maurice as it was for Keble. But for Maurice the divine Work of Art – at one level present in the universal bounty of the Creation itself – could not be limited and confined by esoteric initiation into an organisation. The New Creation if finite in form, was infinite in scope. Just as for Wordsworth and Coleridge the whole idea of Art was essentially anti-élitist, speaking to all men, so, for Maurice, universality was a fundamental attribute of the Church of God. Maurice believed in the formal structure of the Church as passionately as Keble himself (witness his zeal to defend Subscription to the Thirty-Nine Articles as a test of admission to Oxford[2]) but he saw it not as a means of exclusion, but as the framework on which the Kingdom of Christ was to be built: not spiritual in character if it was not also universal; not universal in appeal if it was not also spiritual.

Newman apparently cast the debate into other terms, yet, as

---

[1] *Memoirs*, pp. 164–5.
[2] *Subscription no Bondage* (Parker, 1835).

we have seen, his thought is no less permeated than Keble's or Maurice's by the same aesthetic imagery. The Church as a work of art is at the root of his conception of an 'idea' in the *Development of Christian Doctrine*. Less obviously, it also underlies his quest for authority. The Church does not command assent by force, nor even by the threat of Hell-fire; she attracts, woos, confronts, and elicits from the believer a total and unified response of his whole being that is 'poetic'. Her authority is not to be challenged at the rational level alone, we experience it with that immediacy and compulsion we feel when confronted by the really great work of art. Contemporary aesthetics provided a theory of the 'unconscious' that eighteenth-century theology conspicuously lacked. Newman's 'illative sense' like Maurice's 'feeling' for Platonic truth rested on a psychology that saw man as much more than a merely rational creature.[1] Just as assent to religious propositions is not of a different kind from material ones, so art and religious experience are part of a continuum of human sensibility, the lower giving us clues towards the understanding of the higher. Yet it was left perhaps to MacDonald, more than to any of the 'professional' theologians, to explore the implications of such aesthetic imagery applied to the nature of the Church. Newman and Maurice had both in their own ways followed Butler in denying the separation of religious and secular experience; MacDonald saw perhaps more clearly than any of his contemporaries that religious experience is, of its very nature, metaphorical and mythological – that it is bound up with the 'poetic' structure of language itself.

It is always interesting to try and see when and why people stop thinking about a subject in one set of terms and start to do so in another. But does such a change in religious sensibility haue a wider meaning than merely a change in intellectual and

---

1 If any reflecting mind be surprised that the aids of the Divine Spirit should be deeper than our Consciousness can reach, it must arise from the not having attended sufficiently to the nature and necessary limits of human Consciousness. For the same impossibility exists as to the first acts and movements of our will – the farthest back our recollection can follow the traces, never leads to the first footmark – the lowest depth that the light of our Consciousness can visit even with a doubtful Glimmering, is still at an unknown distance from the Ground: and so, indeed, must it be with all Truths, and all modes of being that can neither be counted, coloured, or delineated.
Coleridge, *Aids to Reflection*, p. 60. See also my *Coleridge and Wordsworth*, pp. 195–7.

emotional reflexes? The answer, it seems,is yes. We have compared this revival of aesthetic language with the re-introduction of the horse to South America – transforming at once the ecological and social structure of the continent. Something dimly analogous did happen in the Victorian Church, and we can trace its effect by looking at what distinguishes the tradition of Coleridge from the great bulk of Anglican thinking. The nineteenth-century crisis of faith over the historical accuracy of the Bible which had begun in England as early as the 1820s was, in fact, a conflict between two attitudes of mind which were both relatively new. Both depended upon what we may loosely call the 'modern' idea of history. Only with the rise of a concept of 'history' as a verifiable (and therefore 'objective') record of human events do we get the corresponding attempt to treat the Biblical narrative as an 'inspired' record of such events. A sixteenth-century divine would have taken it for granted that the scriptures were 'inspired', but if pressed it would have become clear that what he meant by this was that they were charged with divine meaning – to be interpreted by means of allegory, correspondences, and the most complex of symbolism. Questions of 'historical accuracy' would not have been meaningful except in these terms. That was what 'history' was about. Biblical literalism in its nineteenth- or twentieth-century sense is a relatively new phenomenon born of the scientific revolution and the development of a historical consciousness. Archbishop's Ussher's famous attempt at producing an accurate Biblical chronology in the seventeenth century can be seen as an activity in this sense parallel to the foundation of the Royal Society. Significantly, his collected works were not published until the 1840s – for a generation already shaken by the suggestion of Mantell and Lyell that the geological age of the earth and its fossil record did not correspond to the account given in Genesis.[1] Similarly, it comes as a shock to discover that the Council of King's College under Principal Jelf should dismiss Maurice for 'heretical' views on eternity when identical ideas can be found in seventeenth-century poetry,[2] or even in Augustine. On Tuesday, 11 April 1848, the Theological Examiners at Cambridge asked candidates: '1. Give the date of the deluge.'

[1] See, for instance, Tennyson's *In Memoriam*, LV.

[2] For instance, one of George MacDonald's favourite poems, Herrick's *Eternity*.

The proper and correct answer was '2348 B.C. and 1656 after the creation of the world.'[1] The Tractarians were no less opposed to 'liberal' theology than these Cambridge examiners. Newman would not read the German critics for fear it might damage his faith; Pusey was more tough-minded, but no more inclined to give ground. But through the new language and corresponding sensibility they had inherited via Keble and through the common tradition of the English Romantic poets, they were able to think of scriptural inspiration in quite other terms from the Evangelicals and literalists. It is surely remarkable that neither Newman nor Maurice was deeply disturbed by Darwin's *Origin of Species* when it was published in 1859. As their letters make clear, they were intrigued by it speculatively as laymen, as they might by any other bold new scientific hypothesis.[2] But the shift in theological sensibility betokened by the new aesthetic imagery is far wider and more far-reaching than the question of accepting or rejecting the methods of the German historical critics or of the new scientific discoveries – important as these were. The literary idea of the 'poetic' gave a framework for thinking about myth that was independent both of philological criticism and science. As their disinterested reaction to Darwin suggests, it enabled Maurice and Newman to take up a position that was not primarily defensive at all. An Evangelical message that is rejected is one that has failed; there is nothing left but shake the dust from the heels and invoke the sanctions of Hell upon the ungodly. A work of art that is rejected is not thereby diminished; it stands in judgement over its critics, confident that it will outlive them. Behind the change of sensibility that we call English Romanticism there lies a new kind of confidence. It is a confidence that we see in Newman accepting the process of historical change as evidence for the dynamic power of the unfolding 'idea' of the Church; a confidence that allows Maurice to proclaim that, against all appearances, the Kingdom of Christ is universal – and already here.

In this sense, therefore, this book has been about a 'tradition' of religious thought – provided we do not seek to interpret the word too narrowly. To begin with, Coleridge himself was not a

[1] David Pailin, *The Way to Faith* (Epworth, 1969), p. 25; W. H. Pinnock, *An Analysis of Scripture History* (Cambridge, 1848), pp. 17 and 248.
[2] Pailin, *The Way to Faith*, p. 65; Maurice, *Life*, II, 608.

systematic thinker, and, notably, neither were the other members of the 'tradition'. All were men possessed of and by a vision of the Church that was primarily 'poetic'. It was not a vision confined to these men alone, or to the nineteenth century, but it was a vision to be found particularly in men whose training and habits of thought were still *both* theological *and* literary. The more specialised training of the twentieth century has produced Biblical scholars, men of prophetic social and ecumenical vision, and great practical wisdom; whether the English Church has produced theologians of the stature of Maurice and Newman is more questionable. It is significant that the one man who, in many ways, comes nearest to their status was a layman and a poet who like Maurice was reared as a Unitarian outside the Anglican tradition: T. S. Eliot. In his famous definition of 'tradition' we find the final development of the union of aesthetic and theological thought that we have been following. He describes it not in terms of continuity and repetition, but of discontinuity and change. 'To conform merely,' he writes, 'would be for the new work not really to conform at all; it would not be new, and would not therefore be a work of art.'[1] Great art – like genuine theology – changes our understanding of all that has preceded and led up to it. In modifying our sense of the present it modifies our awareness of the past. 'Tradition' is not an exploration and development of one man's ideas, it is a series of great and original innovators building on each other, or on a common source. Such a view of artistic development (and it is not peculiar to Eliot) has roots in Coleridge's *Essay on Method*[2] as surely as does Newman's development of doctrine – but behind that lie two millennia of Christian thought, itself the product of the Old Testament prophetic tradition.

This brings us to the final point of our conclusion: the need to establish some kind of a perspective from which to make sense of the complex web of influences and ideas that we have been tracing in the relations of Coleridge and Wordsworth with the Victorian Church. Coleridge was a highly original thinker, and an eclectic one, but he was not an eccentric or heterodox one. Eliot, we recall, always used the word 'tradition' in the singular

[1] 'Tradition and the Individual Talent', *Selected Essays*, p. 12.
[2] For a further discussion of this Theory in relation to Coleridge see my *Coleridge and Wordsworth* pp. 116–19.

and not in the plural. Coleridge stands in a long line of poets and theologians extending back over three thousand years of history who have enabled the people of God (whether Jew or Christian) to understand and re-formulate their position in times of change and crisis by a radical shift in the prevailing religious metaphors by which they thought and felt. In so doing they were able to fire their own and succeeding ages with a vision that transcended the philosophy of a particular period, even while making use of it. Behind Coleridge and his nineteenth-century successors are poets like Donne, Herbert, and Dante, or theologians like Andrewes, Aquinas, and Augustine who were prepared to hold to their vision and yet see it in all the complexity of its social and political implications. The problem – if there is a problem – in recognising this quality in Coleridge lies partly in the fact that, unlike so many of his kind, he was not a transparently 'holy' man. It is not merely that he lacked (for most people) the immediate charisma of many of those mentioned above, or, for that matter, of Keble, Maurice, Newman, or MacDonald; he was less secure in his own relationships and, therefore perhaps, less straightforward – he *was* inclined to fabricate and plagiarise; he was for some of his life a drug-addict. Nevertheless, it is possible to say without exaggeration that it was he, a man of such obvious and, to many, such contemptible failings, who did more than any other to save the Church of England in the next few generations.[1] He gave it what it most needed: not merely a new set of conceptual tools, but a new climate of thought and feeling in which to apply them.

'If it be right,' wrote J. S. Mill in 1840, '. . . that a knowledge of the speculative opinions of the men between twenty and thirty years of age is the great source of political prophecy, the exist-ence of Coleridge will show itself by no slight or ambiguous traces in the coming history of our country: for no one has contributed more to shape the opinions of those among its younger men, who can be said to have opinions at all.'[2] Ironically, Mill was the first, outside the circle of Hare and Maurice, to recognise Coleridge's importance to the Victorian age. His prophetic essay on Coleridge was written, appropriately, as a review of *Church and State*.

[1] For a slightly different, but essentially complementary view, see Basil Willey's *Nineteenth Century Studies*, pp. 39–40.
[2] *Bentham and Coleridge*; p. 99.

ROMANTICISM AND RELIGION

The influence of Coleridge, like that of Bentham, extends far beyond
those who share in the peculiarities of his religious or philosophical
creed. He has been the great awakener in this country of the spirit of
philosophy, within the bounds of traditional opinions. He has been,
almost as truly as Bentham, 'the great questioner of things established;'
for a questioner needs not necessarily be an enemy. By Bentham, beyond
all others, men have been led to ask themselves, in regard to any
ancient or received opinion, is it true? and by Coleridge, What is the
meaning of it? The one took his stand *outside* the received opinion, and
surveyed it as an entire stranger to it; the other looked at it from within,
and endeavoured to see it with the eyes of a believer in it; to discover
by what apparent facts it was at first suggested, and by what appearances it has ever since been rendered continually credible – has seemed,
to a succession of persons, to be a faithful interpretation of their
experience.[1]

This tribute from Mill, an outsider to the Church (though one of
its most acute observers) can be balanced against what was, again
outside the circle of Hare and Maurice, one of the most influential
assessments from within: F. J. A. Hort's essay in the *Cambridge
Essays* of 1856. Two characteristics of Coleridge stand out above
all else for Hort: the polarity of his thought, and its Platonism.
Though he very shrewdly observes how Coleridge's idea of
Imagination is rooted in his determination to unravel the mystery
of Wordsworth's greatness as a poet, he goes on at once to
assert its essentially Platonic origins. Writing from the opposite
point of view, as a theologian, Hort was as concerned as Mill
to stress the unity of Coleridge's thinking. 'For with him, as with
every one to whom truth is more than a subject for speculation,
there is no line of separation between the different subjects of his
thoughts, still less between his thoughts and his life.'[2] His poetry,
his philosophy, his theology, and his social thought could only be
understood as a single organic unity rooted in the experiences of
his life. The problems of Wordsworth's idiosyncratic poetics
could not be separated from fundamental principles of aesthetics
and their philosophical and theological implications. As Hort
memorably puts it:

The felt necessity of discovering what it was in Wordsworth's mind
which made him so truly a poet, and yet so wanting in the recognised
marks and badges of a poet, drove him into a partly psychological

[1] *Bentham and Coleridge*, pp. 99–100.   [2] Coleridge, *Cambridge Essays*, p. 294.

266

inquiry, and revealed to him the essential diversity of imagination and fancy...The question was of far greater importance than appears on the surface; for the answer involved a complete revolution in the theory and recognition of poetry and art in England, perhaps with even wider and deeper results than the parallel work accomplished chiefly by Lessing and Goethe in Germany.[1]

But, Hort at once goes on to argue, this new critical structure 'cannot be acquitted of philosophy, and even theology'. The idea of the Imagination is a 'doctrine'.

Coleridge undoubtedly believed that the outward world of sense is but the appropriate clothing and manifestation of an invisible and spiritual world; and that true poetry deals on the one hand only with the world of sense, and on the other hand with it and its manifold contents only so far as they are symbols of corresponding realities in the world of spirit.[2]

In language strongly reminiscent of Keble he goes on to link Coleridge's notion of a symbol with irony and paradox in a structure that is at once aesthetic and theological.[3] For Hort, the process that was to bring the old Anglican order with its static frame of theological reference crashing down a generation later was already begun in the *Lyrical Ballads*. For him, no less than for Mill and Newman, Coleridge was above all the man who had made trial of his age, and changed it beyond recall by showing it what it already was; who showed it that the deepest needs of Church and society were primarily 'poetic'.

Through Coleridge, and through the radical shift in religious sensibility that he helped to bring about, Maurice was able to create a vision of the English Church, at once spiritual and social, that Anglicans have yet to assimilate. Through Coleridge and Wordsworth the Oxford Movement was able to re-assert both the independence of the Church, and its interdependence with society. Through Coleridge and Maurice, MacDonald was able to discover something in the Church wider and more spiritual than could be found among the Congregationalists of Arundel or the moral precepts of Arnold. Perhaps most ironic of all, through Newman, the Anglican tradition of Coleridge has become part of the heritage of the Roman Catholic Church itself.

[1] Ibid. p. 304.   [2] Ibid. p. 305.   [3] Ibid. pp. 306–7.

Appendix:
Wordsworth and Kierkegaard

The best way to show up the parallels between Wordsworth and Kierkegaard is to look at some examples in detail. The famous 'spots of time' passage from book xi (1805) is one of the key sections of *The Prelude* where Wordsworth tries to state some of the basic principles of his poetry:

> There are in our existence spots of time,
> Which with distinct pre-eminence retain
> A vivifying virtue, whence, depressed
> By false opinion and contentious thought,
> Or ought of heavier or more deadly weight,
> In trivial occupations, and the round
> Of ordinary intercourse, our minds
> Are nourished and invisibly repaired;   (258–65)

He continues, by way of illustration, to tell the story of how as a child he had been separated from the servant supposed to be accompanying him when they were out riding, and so came by himself on the spot where there had once been a gibbet. Someone had carved in the turf the name of the murderer. The little boy must clearly have been terrified, but Wordsworth doesn't *say* this. Instead he describes how he left the spot again and caught sight of a girl with a pitcher on her head battling her way against the strong wind. Now at last, and only now, is he prepared to describe to us his emotions:

>   . . . It was, in truth,
> An ordinary sight; but I should need
> Colours and words that are unknown to man,
> To paint the visionary dreariness
> Which, while I looked all round for my lost guide,
> Did at that time invest the naked pool,
> The beacon on the lonely eminence,

The woman and her garments vexed and tossed
By the strong wind.   (308–16)

Clearly much of the emotional pressure behind this 'visionary dreariness' comes from the discovery of the gibbet, rather than the girl, and Wordsworth's honest inarticulateness in showing us the transference of the boy's emotion from an area where he could not talk about it, to where he could, is peculiarly effective. It is, moreover, clear that 'visionary dreariness' is one of the mainsprings of Wordsworth's poetic Imagination.[1] Nevertheless, even after this degree of self-analysis, the next lines still strike the attentive reader with considerable shock. When he became engaged to Mary Hutchinson, he tells us, he felt impelled to bring her and his sister Dorothy back to this very spot – now endowed with a 'pleasure' and even a 'radiance' because of their former associations of childish inarticulate terror.

> When, in a blessed season,
> With those two dear ones, to my heart so dear,
> When in the blessed time of early love,
> Long afterwards, I roamed about
> In daily presence of this very scene,
> Upon the naked pool and dreary crags,
> And on the melancholy beacon, fell
> The spirit of pleasure and youth's golden gleam;
> And think ye not with radiance more divine
> From these remembrances, and from the power
> They left behind? So feeling comes in aid
> Of feeling, and diversity of strength
> Attends us, if but once we have been strong.
> Oh! mystery of man, from what a depth
> Proceed thy honours. I am lost, but see
> In simple childhood something of the base
> On which thy greatness stands; but this I feel
> That from thyself it is that thou must give,
> Else never canst receive. The days gone by
> Come back upon me from the dawn almost
> Of life: the hiding-places of my power
> Seem open; I approach, and then they close;
> I see by glimpses now; when age comes on,
> May scarcely see at all, and I would give,

---

[1] See, for instance, D. G. James, 'Wordsworth and Tennyson', *Proceedings of the British Academy*, XXXVI (1950), 119.

While yet we may, as far as words can give,
A substance and a life to what I feel:
I would enshrine the spirit of the past
For future restoration.   (316–43)

In conventional terms it is very hard to be sure what Words-worth is saying here – and the confession in lines 329–31 sug-gests that he too is having some difficulty. *Why* is what he so vividly calls 'visionary dreariness' as important to his poetic development as he clearly knows it to be? *Why* was it so essential that he should return to the scene of these 'remembrances' with his future wife? *Why* is this whole lengthy confession of failing, or at best intermittent, powers of recall affirmed with such con-fidence as a source of strength? – a claim which is repeated a few lines later after the incident he connected with the death of his father: 'All these were spectacles and sounds to which/I often would repair, and thence would drink/As at a fountain.' The 1850 version leaves these lines unaltered. Wordsworth is clearly very much involved with Nature not merely as a thing part-created by the 'ennobling interchange' of sense perception, but also as a historical thing – created and organised by the memory. It is not difficult to see in these passages a continuation of and commentary on the section of Book I which so offended and puzzled Blake. If, in the earlier passage it is never clear how far the 'Wisdom and Spirit of the universe' is inherent *in* Nature, and how far it shines *through* Nature to nurture and draw out the affections of the growing boy, here it is clear that Wordsworth is no longer preoccupied with the same questions. The focus now is not so much on the incidents themselves – the 'spots of time', of which the earlier passage was one – as on a certain complexity of reaction in the poet when contemplating these moments '. . .in which/We have had deepest feeling that the mind/Is lord and master. . .'. There has been a subtle shift in emphasis. We no longer find ourselves asking, as in the earlier examples, 'is this Naturalism?' We find ourselves asking instead the much more pertinent further question in Kierkegaard's terms: 'is Words-worth now seeking "recollection" or "repetition"?'

Kierkegaard's distinction between what he calls 'recollection' and 'repetition' offers us, it seems to me, a way of looking at the 'spots of time' theory that is very closely parallel to that of Wordsworth. As we have seen, *The Prelude* moves from feeling that the memories of these moments stand in Wordsworth's life as permanent affirmations of value, to a much more complex process of questioning *what* is actually happening as he recalls them. We can actually see his centre of interest shifting while he is at work on *The Prelude* if we compare the treatment of incidents from his boyhood in books I and II with book XI, where the moments in question date from exactly the same period of his early life as those in the opening books. Set this against the opening of Kierkegaard's *Repetition*. He begins like this:

Inasmuch as for a long time I have been engaged, at least occasionally, with the problem whether a repetition is possible and what significance it has, whether a thing gains or loses by being repeated, it suddenly occurred to me, 'Thou canst take a trip to Berlin, where thou hast been before, and convince thyself now whether a repetition is possible and what significance it may have.'....Say what one will, it is sure to play a very important rôle in modern philosophy: for *repetition* is a decisive expression for what 'recollection' was for the Greeks. Just as they taught that all knowledge is a recollection, so will modern philosophy teach that the whole of life is a repetition...Repetition and recollection are the same movement, only in opposite directions; for what is recollected has been, is repeated backwards, whereas repetition properly so called is recollected forwards. Therefore repetition, if it is possible, makes a man happy, whereas recollection makes him unhappy – provided he gives himself time to live and does not at once, in the very moment of birth, try to find a pretext for stealing out of life, alleging, for example, that he has forgotten something.

The love of recollection is the only happy love, an author has said. In that he is perfectly right, too – if one will only remember that it first makes a man unhappy. In truth, the love of repetition is the only happy love. Like that of recollection it has not the disquietude of hope, the anxious adventuresomeness of discoverers, nor the sadness of recollection; it has the blessed certainty of the instant. Hope is a new garment, starched and stiff and glittering, yet one has never had it on, and hence one does not know how it will become one and how it fits. Recollection is a discarded garment, which beautiful as it may be, does not fit, for one has outgrown it. Repetition is an imperishable garment, which fits snugly and comfortably, neither too tight nor too loose. Hope is a charming maiden but slips through the fingers, recollection is a beautiful old woman but of no use at the instant, repetition is a beloved wife of whom one never tires.[1]

[1] *Repetition: An Essay in Experimental Psychology*, trans. Walter Lowrie (Harper Torchbooks, 1964), pp. 33–4.

For all its colloquial clarity, or perhaps even because of it, such an introduction to the subject was likely to be misunderstood – and it was. One of his earliest reviews – a very favourable one – by Professor J. L. Heiberg in a book called *Urania* praised *Repetition* for its significance in 'the natural category' and contrasts this with the 'spiritual sphere'. Now Kierkegaard says nothing at all about repetition in nature, nor does he talk about the 'spiritual' in the Hegelian sense that Heiberg uses it – which comprises the objects of such disinterested contemplation as the philosophy of history. Kierkegaard, like Wordsworth, is thinking of 'repetition' in the personal history of the individual, which to the individual he recognises as of absolute interest.[1] He was so incensed by Heiberg that he wrote a letter to 'the real reader of the book' in which he tells us that 'like Clement Alexandrinus I have tried to write in such a way that the heretics could not understand it'.[2] However, he is then provoked into describing his concept of repetition in much clearer detail:

The concept Repetition, when it is employed in the sphere of individual freedom, has a history, in the fact that freedom passes through several stages in order to attain itself. (A) Freedom is first defined as pleasure or in pleasure. What it now fears is repetition, because it is as if repetition possessed a magic power to hold freedom captive when once it had contrived to get it under its influence. But in spite of all the inventiveness of pleasure repetition makes its appearance. Then freedom in pleasure falls into despair. The same instant freedom makes its appearance in a higher form. (B) Freedom defined as shrewdness. Freedom is still in a finite relation to its object and is itself only ambiguously defined aesthetically. Repetition is assumed to exist, but it is the task of freedom to see constantly a new side of repetition... However, since freedom defined as shrewdness is only finitely characterised, repetition must again make its appearance, that is repetition of the trick by which shrewdness wants to delude repetition and make it something else. Then shrewdness falls into despair. (C) Now freedom breaks forth in its highest form, which is defined in relation to itself. Here everything is inverted, and the opposite of the first standpoint is in evidence. Now the highest interest of freedom is to bring about repetition, and it fears only lest change might have the power to alter its eternal nature. Here the problem emerges: *Is repetition possible?*[3]

[1] *Repetition*, Editor's Introduction, p. 10.
[2] Ibid. p. 11.
[3] Ibid. pp. 11–12.

The first stage is that of simple 'pleasure', when constant novelty and variety is necessary to prevent repetition and so boredom; the second stage, which arises from the first when it is recognised that repetition cannot be avoided, is that of the 'aesthetic'. Here, as in a work of art, the novelty is found (or sought) in the many artistic or aesthetic possibilities of repetition. (The fugue in music might be an example of this.) The final stage, that of the 'religious', *contains* the first two, but cannot be known from them. It does not seem to be a 'stage' like the others, but consists rather in a movement, a constant questioning of the first two stages.

The example to which most of *Repetition* is devoted is, at first sight, typically bizarre. In stage (A) Kierkegaard falls in love with a girl called Regina; in the second stage, (B), he becomes so enamoured of the *idea* of *being in love* that he realises that he is in danger of losing sight of Regina as anything more than the object of his love; in the final stage (C) he sacrifices his 'love' by convincing Regina that he is unfaithful, and so losing her – in his despair at what he has now done, finding that his love is not, as he had hoped, being 'repeated' to him, he discovers new levels in himself, simultaneously immediate, aesthetic, and spiritual: he has *become* a poet. The 'poetic' achievement in this case, we notice, lies not in any completed artefact (not even the book, *Repetition*, itself) but in the constant questioning, '*is repetition possible?*' In Kierkegaard's own case this has an added poignancy because of the tragi-comedy of his personal situation. It is clear that when he began to write *Repetition* it was partly with the model of Job in mind: he expected that Regina would in the end be restored to him. Only when he heard of her engagement to another man did the unknowability of the final stage in relation to the first two become apparent.

Clearly, Kierkegaard's predicament is not the same as that of Wordsworth, but he does offer us a model in trying to understand something as radically new and different as the latter appears to have been attempting to find in the 'language of Nature'. Let us turn to *Tintern Abbey*.

> . . . I cannot paint
> What then I was. The sounding cataract
> Haunted me like a passion; the tall rock,
> The mountain, and the deep and gloomy wood,
> Their colours and their forms, were then to me

An appetite; a feeling and a love,
That had no need of a remoter charm,
By thought supplied, nor any interest
Unborrowed from the eye. – That time is past,
And all its aching joys are now no more,
And all its dizzy raptures. Not for this
Faint I, nor mourn nor murmur; other gifts
Have followed; for such loss, I would believe,
Abundant recompense. For I have learned
To look on nature, not as in the hour
Of thoughtless youth; but hearing oftentimes
The still, sad music of humanity... (75–91)

Wordsworth, it seems to me, is struggling to describe his changed relationship with Nature in terms curiously parallel to those of Kierkegaard. The whole poem is explicitly about the possibility of 'repetition'. In revisiting Tintern Abbey in July 1798 Wordsworth is returning to the place where in 1793 he had reached perhaps his nadir of despair – some have even suggested that he was contemplating suicide. He had returned to England in the Spring of 1793, penniless, fleeing from the reign of terror, and leaving behind him an illegitimate child – the result of his affair with Annette Vallon. His hopes for the French Revolution, and with them his hopes for a new dawn for mankind had collapsed in ruins. Many of his friends had been guillotined, or had themselves fled into exile. His attempt to force the hand of Annette's parents into allowing her marriage had failed even more ignominiously – she and the child had simply been removed beyond his reach. In the late summer of 1793 he had set out on 'a tour of the West' with his friend Raisley Calvert, but while crossing Salisbury Plain their conveyance, a 'whiskey', had been overturned and smashed beyond immediate repair. Calvert had taken his horse, and ridden off northwards to his home, and Wordsworth, in the most solitary walk of his life, had continued alone into Wales on foot. This second visit described now in *Tintern Abbey* is like the places in book XI of *The Prelude* to which he felt a compulsive need to return for restoration and new strength. As in those cases, Wordsworth makes no attempt to allude directly to his own previous state of mind, but like them, this is a memory not of past happiness, but of misery and loss of faith. It is the anguish of that moral crisis that separates what now

he is from those boyish days of 'glad animal movements'. His
original unreflective faith in human goodness as 'natural' could
not survive his despair in the French Revolution; it is *through*
that despair he claims to have reached a more enduring wisdom.
He now no longer accepts simple values *in* Nature, but sees it
instead as *symbolic* of an unseen moral world that he can find in no
other way. He seeks now not for new experiences, but, by
returning to Tintern with his sister Dorothy, to repeat that first
coming *as a poem*, and as an affirmation of Nature's healing
power. The repetition, we notice, is at *two* levels. On the narrative level he is revisiting a spot where in the past he experienced
despair and was solaced by the beauty of nature. The fact that he
can still be deeply moved by this – that he can 'repeat' the
experience in memory – is proof that 'repetition is possible'. At
the aesthetic level (here not to be confused with Kierkegaard's
'aesthetic' category) he is seeking *in the poem* to recreate, or
repeat, the experience of repetition as a work of art. He is seeking in the poem *Tintern Abbey* to 'enshrine the spirit of the past
for future restoration'.[1] The irony here is the very closeness of
the tragic parallel with Kierkegaard. Just as Kierkegaard began
to write *Repetition* with the conviction that Regina would still be
restored to him, so Wordsworth hopes for Dorothy that

> . . . Nature never did betray
> The heart that loved her. (122–3)

In 1829 the 'wild-eyed' Dorothy who had brought William
through his own spiritual crisis, and taught him to love Nature,

---

[1] Stuart M. Sperry has distinguished between two characteristic kinds of
'memory' in Wordsworth: what he calls the 'reconstitutive' memory of *Tintern
Abbey*, and the 'negative' or 'premonitory' memory of the *Immortality Ode*. In the
former, argues Sperry, he is trying to recapture a vividness of apprehension that he
once possessed, and can still recall in his poetry; in the latter he is unable to – all he
can remember is that he once possessed a 'visionary gleam'. Kenneth Johnston,
following Sperry, claims that the paradox of the *Immortality Ode* is that this 'negative'
memory – essentially no more than a dimly recalled 'mode of being' – is ultimately
more sustaining than the actual memories of *Tintern Abbey*. This seems to me a useful
approach provided that one sees both kinds as successive stages in a single process
of deepening ambiguity – a process which, as Sperry and Johnston both show,
is most fully exemplified in *The Prelude*. See my own discussion of 'Memory and
Perception' in Wordsworth in chapter 5 of *Coleridge and Wordsworth*.

(Stuart M. Sperry Jr, 'From *Tintern Abbey* to the *Intimations Ode*: Wordsworth
and the Function of Memory', *The Wordsworth Circle*, vol. I, no. 2 (Spring 1970);
Kenneth R. Johnston, 'Recollecting Forgetting: Forcing Paradox to the Limit in
the *Intimations Ode*', *The Wordsworth Circle*, vol. II, no. 2 (Spring 1971).)

herself had a far more serious breakdown from which she never recovered. The last twenty-five years of her life were passed in a state of partial or complete insanity.

The achievement of *Tintern Abbey* is not in a position gained or a future assured, but a moment won. Repetition was possible *then*: for the future, the question is always open. Such moments of repetition are essentially *meta-stable* – fleeting, transient, and tantalising, even as they are concrete and specific in time and place. They cannot be made moments of 'blessed assurance', for the question 'Is repetition possible?' can never take it for granted that the answer will be affirmative. Precisely this tension is always present in the Biblical tradition of typology on which both Wordsworth and Kierkegaard are drawing in their own ways. 'When, in discussing typology,' Charity writes, 'one speaks, as one must, of "repetition", one is using this term of God's acts and it therefore has to do justice both to steadfastness and to newness.'[1] Here, as in Kierkegaard, be it noted, repetition is *sought*: what is desired is consistency 'between the "new" events of the gospel and the divine acts in the past which are received as fundamental to her own existence by Israel. It is an argument which leads not to the formula, Q.E.D., but to the question mark.'[2] In this tension and questioning of the events of the past and their mysterious echoes in the present Wordsworth and Kierkegaard reveal common roots in a far older way of looking at history. What was once asked of the history of a people, is now asked of the biography of an individual. In *The Prelude* the events of childhood are revisited with a constant dual reference: What did they once hold? What do they now mean? Is repetition possible?

> The days gone by
> Come back upon me from the dawn almost
> Of life: the hiding places of my power
> Seem open; I approach, and then they close;
> I see by glimpses now; when age comes on,
> May scarcely see at all...

For Wordsworth, the central crisis of *The Prelude*, most representative because most extreme, is over the failure of the French Revolution and his loss of faith in man – the same crisis that lies

[1] A. C. Charity, *Events and their Afterlife* (Cambridge, 1966), p. 33.
[2] Ibid. p. 100.

at the heart of *Tintern Abbey*, completed a few years before. What has changed is the *feeling*. He still affirms the healing and moral power of his intercourse with Nature, but the quality of the confidence has subtly changed. Whether or not we use specific-ally Kierkegaardian terms to describe the process of disconfirma-tion and re-discovery that Wordsworth finds in the spots of time, it has long been recognised – by Coleridge, Arnold, MacDonald, even by Blake – that what he affirms through these experiences is a unity or 'wholeness' that is immediately apprehended as *religious* in quality. What he shares with Kierkegaard is not a particular schematised structure or theory of repetition (though the similarities are striking enough to suggest the degree of common ground) but this quality of religious awareness. Both feel the 'religious' as a new unity arising from the *failure* of spontaneous pleasure and aesthetic repetition, but utterly dif-ferent in kind from them in that it questions the possibility of its own achievement. This vision of wholeness involves both con-firming *and* denying at the same time; it is a unity constantly under tension. Nature is, for the poet Wordsworth, simultane-ously security and insecurity. Being a poet *means* to live danger-ously. If we compare the spots of time passages in *The Prelude* (especially those in the later books) with *Tintern Abbey* we find in the former a 'fear and trembling', a sense of the precariousness and struggle that underlies the easy cliché about Nature or our moral growth. It is this tension, this quality of feeling, that is of primary interest to Wordsworth – not the 'philosophical' schema that would justify it. His sense of the religious as a *feeling* of unity and harmony under tension is, I believe, what links Words-worth with the Victorians (here, including Kierkegaard) and separates him from his own near-contemporaries, Coleridge and Blake.

Moreover, it is only with something approaching a Kierke-gaardian sense of paradox that we can begin to see how the inherent dichotomies in Wordsworth that were noticed by Blake and Coleridge between 'Naturalism' and 'Platonism', or between an immanent and transcendent sense of God in nature, are to be satisfactorily resolved. Only then, I suspect, do we begin to understand how the foundations of Wordsworth's peculiar emotional strength can lie not in certainties, but in uncertainty and contradiction. He puts his finger, as it were, on the point

Bibliography

Place of publication is London, except where otherwise stated.

Abrams, M. H. 'Coleridge and the Romantic Vision of the World', *Coleridge's Variety*, ed. Beer. Macmillan, 1974.
> *The Mirror and the Lamp*. Oxford, New York, 1953. Reprinted Norton, New York, 1958.

Adams, Maurianne. *Coleridge and the Victorians*. Unpublished Ph.D. thesis, University of Indiana, 1967.

Allchin, A. M. *F. D. Maurice as Theologian*. Unpublished paper.
> ed. (with John Coulson). *The Rediscovery of Newman: An Oxford Symposium*. Sheed & Ward/S.P.C.K., 1967.

Anon. 'Nature Development and Theology', *Contemporary Review*, vol. XIV. May 1870.

Appleyard, J. A. *Coleridge's Philosophy of Literature*. Harvard, Mass., 1965.

Armour, R. W. and Howes, R. F. *Coleridge the Talker*. Cornell U.P., New York, 1940. Reprinted Johnson Reprint Corp., 1969.

Arnold, Matthew. *God and the Bible*, ed. R. H. Super. Michigan U.P., 1970.
> *Literature and Dogma*. 1873. Popular edn. Smith Elder, 1895.
> *Poetical Works*. Macmillan, 1890.
> 'Wordsworth', *Essays in Criticism: Second Series*. Macmillan, 1888.

Arnold, Thomas. 'Sermon on Wills', *Sermons*, vol. VI. 1845.

Augustine, St. *Confessions*, trans. E. B. Pusey. Everyman, 1907. Reprinted 1966.

Barfield, Owen. *What Coleridge Thought*. Oxford, 1972.

Baring-Gould, S. *The Vicar of Morwenstow*. 3rd edn. Methuen, 1906.

Barth, Robert. *Coleridge and Christian Doctrine*. Harvard, Mass., 1969.

Battiscombe, Georgina. *John Keble*. Constable, 1963.

Beek, W. J. A. *John Keble's Literary and Religious Contribution to the Oxford Movement*. Nijmegen, 1959.

Beer, John. *Coleridge the Visionary*. Chatto, 1959.
> 'Ice and Spring: Coleridge's Imaginative Education', *Coleridge's Variety*, ed. Beer. Macmillan, 1974.

Berger, Peter L. *A Rumour of Angels*. Pelican, 1970.

Blake, William. *The Complete Writings of William Blake*, ed. G. Keynes. Oxford, 1966.

Boulger, James D. *Coleridge as Religious Thinker*. Yale, New Haven, Conn., 1961.

Burns, Robert. *David Hume and Miracles in Historical Perspective*. Unpublished Ph.D. thesis, University of Princeton, 1971.

Burrow, John. *Evolution and Society*. Cambridge, 1966.

Burtt, E. A. *Metaphysical Foundations of Modern Science*. Routledge, 1932.

Butler, Joseph. *The Analogy of Religion*. Everyman, 1906.

Campbell, J. D. *Samuel Taylor Coleridge*. 1894.

Capes, J. M. 'A Parallel and a Contrast', *The Gentleman's Magazine*, IX, 33–44. 1872.

Carlyle, Thomas. *Critical and Miscellaneous Essays*. 7 vols. Chapman & Hall, 1869.

    Life of John Sterling. Chelsea Edition, Chapman & Hall, 1893.

    New Letters of Thomas Carlyle, ed. A. Carlyle. Bodley Head, 1904.

    Sartor Resartus. Chapman & Hall, 1888.

Carroll, Lewis. *Alice's Adventures in Wonderland and Through the Looking-Glass*. Macmillan, 1887.

Chadwick, Owen. *From Bossuet to Newman: the Idea of Doctrinal Development*. Cambridge, 1957.

    The Mind of the Oxford Movement. Black, Edinburgh, 1960.

    The Victorian Church. Black, Edinburgh, 1966.

Charity, A. C. *Events and their Afterlife*. Cambridge, 1966.

Chesterton, G. K. *The Victorian Age in Literature*. Williams and Norgate, 1913.

Church, Mary, ed. *Life and Letters of Dean Church*. Macmillan, 1895.

Church, R. W. 'William Wordsworth', *Dante and Other Essays*. Macmillan, 1888.

Coleridge, J. T. *Memoir of the Rev. John Keble*. 1869.

Coleridge, S. T. *Aids to Reflection*. ed. T. Fenby. Grant, Edinburgh, 1905.

    Anima Poetae, ed. E. H. Coleridge. Heinemann, 1895.

    Biographia Literaria, ed. J. Shawcross. Oxford, 1907.

    Church and State. 2nd edn, ed. H. N. Coleridge, 1839.

    Confessions of an Inquiring Spirit. 2nd edn, ed. H. N. Coleridge. 1849.

    The Friend, ed. Barbara Rooke. Routledge, 1969.

    Lay Sermons, ed. R. J. White. Routledge, 1972.

    Collected Letters, ed. E. L. Griggs. Oxford, 1956–9.

    Literary Remains, ed. H. N. Coleridge, 1836–8.

Notebooks, ed. K. Coburn. Routledge, 1957–62.

Notebooks, nos. 36–42. Unpublished: British Museum Manuscript Room, Add. Ms. 47, 531–47, 537.

Philosophical Lectures, ed. K. Coburn. Routledge, 1949.

Poems, ed. E. H. Coleridge. Oxford, 1912.

Shakespeare Criticism, ed. T. M. Raysor. 2nd edn. Everyman, 1960.

Table Talk, ed. H. N. Coleridge. Murray, 1852.

'The Theory of Life', *Misc. Aesthetic and Literary*. Bohn/Bell, 1892.

Collingwood, R. G. *The Idea of History*. Clarendon, Oxford, 1946.

Coulson, John. *Adjectives for God, or Bottom's Dream*. Unpublished paper.

'Belief and Imagination', *Downside Review*, vol. 90, no. 298. January 1972.

Maurice, Newman, and the Problem of Religious Subscription. Unpublished paper.

Newman and the Common Tradition. Clarendon, Oxford, 1970.

ed. (with A. M. Allchin). *The Rediscovery of Newman: An Oxford Symposium*. Sheed & Ward/S.P.C.K., 1967.

Creed, J. M. *The Divinity of Jesus Christ*. Cambridge, 1938.

Crowther, M. A. *The Church Embattled*. David and Charles, 1970.

De Quincey, Thomas. 'German Studies and Kant in Particular', *The Collected Writings of Thomas De Quincey*, vol. ii, ed. Masson. A. & C. Black, 1896.

Reminiscences of the English Lake Poets. Everyman, 1961.

Derham, William. *Physico-Theology*. 1713.

Astro-Theology. 1715.

Dessain, C. S. *John Henry Newman*. Nelson, 1966.

Eichorn, Johann Gottfried. *Einleitung in das Alte Testament*. Leipzig, 1780–3.

Eliot, T. S. *Notes Towards a Definition of Culture*. Faber, 1947.

Introduction to Simone Weil's *The Need for Roots*. Routledge, 1952.

'Tradition and the Individual Talent', *Selected Essays*. 3rd edn. Faber, 1951.

Emerson, Ralph Waldo. *English Traits*. Riverside Edition. Routledge, 1883.

Emmet, Dorothy. 'Coleridge on the Growth of the Mind', *Bulletin of the John Rylands Library*, vol. 34, no. 2. Manchester, March 1952.

'Coleridge on Powers in Mind and Nature', *Coleridge's Variety*. Macmillan, 1974.

Review of Stephen Prickett's *Coleridge and Wordsworth*, *Review of English Studies*. August 1971.

Escher, M. C. *The Graphic Work of M. C. Escher*. Oldbourne Press, 1961.

Faber, F. W. *Faber: Poet and Priest*. Selected Letters by Frederick William Faber, 1833–63, ed. Raleigh Addington. D. Brown & Sons, Cowbridge and Bridgend, Glamorgan, 1974.

Faber, Geoffrey. *Oxford Apostles*. Faber, 1933.

Fairweather, E. R., ed. *The Oxford Movement*. Oxford, New York, 1964.

Ferry, David. *The Limits of Mortality*. Middletown, Conn., 1959.

Forbes, Duncan. *The Liberal Anglican Idea of History*. Cambridge, 1952.

Fruman, Norman. *Coleridge: The Damaged Archangel*. Allen & Unwin, 1972.

Gillman, James. *The Life of Samuel Taylor Coleridge*. 1838.

Gombrich, E. H. *Art and Illusion*. Phaidon, 1960.

Green, J. H. *Spiritual Philosophy: founded on the teaching of the late Samuel Taylor Coleridge*. 1865.

Harding, A. J. *Coleridge and the Idea of Love*. Cambridge, 1975.

Harding, D. W. 'The Theme of the *Ancient Mariner*', *Scrutiny*, ix. 1941.

Hare, Augustus J. C. *Memorials of a Quiet Life*, George Allen, 1872.

Hare, Julius Charles. *Charges to the Clergy of the Archdeaconry of Lewes*. Macmillan, 1856.

  Guesses at Truth. 3rd edn. Macmillan, 1866.

  'Memoir of the Life of Sterling', *Essays and Tales of John Sterling*. 1848.

  Mission of the Comforter. 1846.

Hanson, Lawrence. *The Life of Samuel Taylor Coleridge*, Allen & Unwin, 1938.

Hartley, David. *Observations on Man, his Frame, his Duties, and his Expectations*. 1749.

Hartman, Geoffrey. *Wordsworth's Poetry, 1787–1814*. Yale, New Haven, Conn., 1964.

Haywood, Bruce. *Novalis: The Veil of Imagery*. Mouton, The Hague, 1959.

Higham, Florence. *Frederick Denison Maurice*. S.C.M., 1947.

Holland, Lady. *Memoir of the Rev. Sydney Smith*. 3rd edn. 1855.

Hopkins, Gerard Manley. *The Correspondence of G. M. Hopkins and R. W. Dixon*, ed. Abbot. Oxford, 1935.

  Poems. 4th edn, ed. W. H. Gardner and N. H. Mackenzie. Oxford, 1967.

Hort, F. J. A. 'Coleridge', *Cambridge Essays*, vol. ii. Parker, 1856.

Hough, Graham. 'Coleridge and the Victorians', *The English Mind*. Cambridge, 1964.

Houghton, Walter E. *The Victorian Frame of Mind*, Yale, New Haven, Conn., 1957.

Hume, David. *A Treatise of Human Nature*, Everyman, 1911.

'*Of Miracles*', *Works of David Hume*, vol. I, *Essays Moral, Political, and Literary*. World's Classics. Oxford, 1903.

Jackson, R. R. de J. *Method and Imagination in Coleridge's Criticism*. Routledge, 1969.

James, D. G. *Scepticism and Poetry*. Allen & Unwin, 1937.

'Wordsworth and Tennyson', *Proceedings of the British Academy*, vol. XXXVI. 1950.

Johnston, Kenneth R. 'Recollecting Forgetting: Forcing Paradox to the Limit in the *Intimations Ode*', *The Wordsworth Circle*, vol. II, no. 2. Spring 1971.

Kearney, Hugh. *Scholars and Gentlemen*. Faber, 1970.

Keats, John. *The Letters of John Keats*, ed. M. Buxton Forman. 4th edn. Oxford, 1952.

Keble, John. *The Christian Year*. 43rd edn. Parker, 1853.

Lectures on Poetry, trans. E. K. Francis. Oxford, 1912.

Kierkegaard, Søren. *Fear and Trembling*, trans. Walter Lowrie. Princeton, N. J., 1968.

Repetition: An Essay in Experimental Psychology, trans. Walter Lowrie. Harper Torchbooks, New York, 1964.

King, William. *An Essay on the Origin of Evil*, trans. Edmund Law. 3rd edn. Cambridge, 1734.

Kingsley, Charles. *Charles Kingsley: His Letters and Memories of his Life*, ed. by his wife. 7th edn. 1877.

Knights, L. C. 'Idea and Symbol: Some Hints from Coleridge', *Further Explorations*. Chatto, 1965.

'Taming the Albatross' (Review of J. A. Appleyard's *Coleridge's Philosophy of Literature*), *New York Review of Books*. 26 May 1966.

Lewis, C. S. *The Allegory of Love*. Oxford, 1936.

George MacDonald: An Anthology. Bles, 1946.

Locke, John. *An Essay Concerning Human Understanding*, ed. J. W. Yolton. Everyman, 1961.

Lovejoy, A. O. *Essays in the History of Ideas*. Johns Hopkins, Baltimore, 1948.

The Great Chain of Being. Harvard, Cambridge, Mass., 1936.

The Reason, the Understanding, and Time. Johns Hopkins, Baltimore, 1961.

McClain, Frank Mauldin. *Maurice: Man and Moralist*. S.P.C.K., 1972.

MacDonald, George. *Alec Forbes of Howglen*. 1865.

A Dish of Orts. Sampson Low, 1893.

At the Back of the North Wind. Airmont, New York, 1966.

England's Antiphon. Macmillan, 1868.

Miracles of Our Lord. 1870.

The Princess and the Goblin. Puffin, Penguin, 1964.

The Princess and Curdie. Puffin, Penguin, 1964.

The Visionary Novels of George MacDonald, with an Introduction by W. H. Auden, ed. Freemantle. Noonday Press, New York, 1954.

Phantastes and Lilith, with an Introduction by C. S. Lewis. Eerdmans Press, Grand Rapids, Michigan, 1964.

Short Stories. Blackie, 1928.

Unspoken Sermons. Second series. Longman, 1885.

MacDonald, Greville. *George MacDonald and his Wife*. Allen & Unwin, 1924.

McFarland, Thomas. 'Coleridge's Anxiety', *Coleridge's Variety*, Macmillan, 1974.

Coleridge and the Pantheist Tradition. Clarendon, Oxford, 1969.

MacKinnon, D. M. 'Coleridge and Kant', *Coleridge's Variety*, ed. J. Beer. Macmillan, 1974.

Mansel, Henry Longueville. *An Examination of the Rev. F. D. Maurice's Strictures on the Bampton Lectures of 1858*. 1859.

The Limits of Religious Thought. 2nd edn. 1858.

Martin, B. W. *John Keble: Priest, Professor, and Poet*. Unpublished Ph.D. thesis, Bodley Library, Oxford 1972.

Martineau, James. *Essays, Reviews and Addresses*. Longman, 1890.

Maurice, Frederick Denison. 'Introduction' to J. C. Hare's *Charges*. 1856.

Lectures on Ecclesiastical History of the First and Second Centuries. Macmillan, 1854.

Review of Froude's *History*, vols. v and vi, *Macmillan's Magazine*, vol. ii. August 1860.

Review of Dr Newman's *Grammar of Assent*, *Contemporary Review*, vol. xiv. May 1870.

Sequel to the Inquiry 'What is Revelation'? 1860.

Subscription No Bondage, by 'Rusticus'. Parker, Oxford, 1835.

The Doctrine of Sacrifice. Macmillan, 1864.

The Friendship of Books, ed. and with a Preface by Thomas Hughes. 2nd edn. Macmillan, 1874.

The Kingdom of Christ. 4th edn. Macmillan, 1891.

The Life of Frederick Denison Maurice...Chiefly told in his own Letters, ed. Frederick Maurice. 4th edn. Macmillan, 1885.

Theological Essays. Macmillan, 1853.

Three Lectures on the Epistle to the Hebrews, with a Preface containing a Review of Dr Newman's Theory of Development. 1846.

What is Revelation? 1859.

Mill, John Stuart. *Autobiography*. World's Classics. Oxford, 1924.

Bentham and Coleridge, Introduction by F. R. Leavis. Chatto, 1950.

Essays on Literature and Society, ed. Schneewind. Collier-Macmillan, New York, 1965.

Montaigne, Michel de. 'Apologie de Raimond Sebond', *Les Essais de Michel de Montaigne*, ed. Pierre Villey, tome II, Paris, 1922.

Moorman, Mary. *William Wordsworth, The Early Years 1770–1803*. Oxford, 1957.

William Wordsworth, The Later Years 1803–1850. Oxford, 1965.

Mozley, Thomas. *Reminiscences, Chiefly of Oriel College and the Oxford Movement*. Longman, 1882.

Muirhead, J. H. *Coleridge as Philosopher*. Allen & Unwin. 1930.

Newman, John Henry. *Apologia Pro Vita Sua*, ed. M. J. Svaglic. Oxford, 1967.

Essays, ed. Nettleship. Oxford, 1889.

Essays Critical and Historical. Longman, 1846. 9th edn. 1890.

Essay on the Development of Christian Doctrine. 1st edn. 1845.

ibid. 3rd edn. New Ark Library. Sheed & Ward, 1960.

A Grammar of Assent, ed. C. F. Harrold. New edn. Longman, 1957.

The Idea of a University. Longman, 1910.

Lectures on Certain Difficulties felt by Anglicans in Submitting to the Catholic Church. 2nd edn. 1850.

Letter to the Duke of Norfolk. 1875.

Letters and Diaries, ed. C. S. Dessain. Oxford, 1961– (in progress).

Loss and Gain. 1848.

University Sketches, ed. George Sampson. 1902.

Verses on Various Occasions. Burns, Oates & Co., 1874.

Via Media. 3rd edn. 1877.

Newsome, David. *The Parting of Friends*. Murray, 1966.

Two Classes of Men. Murray, 1974.

Nicolson, Marjorie Hope. *Newton Demands the Muse*. Archon Books, Hamden, Conn., 1963.

Niebuhr, G. B. *History of Rome*, trans. J. C. Hare and Connop Thirlwall. 1828–32.

Novalis. *Hymns and Thoughts on Religion*, trans. W. Hastie, T. and T. Clark. Edinburgh, 1888.

Nuttall, A. D. *A Common Sky*. Sussex University Press, Chatto, 1974.

'Did Mersault Mean to Kill the Arab? The Intentional Fallacy Fallacy', *The Critical Quarterly*. Spring 1968.

Two Concepts of Allegory. Routledge, 1967.

Orsini, G. N. G. *Coleridge and German Idealism*. Southern Illinois University Press, Carbondale and Edwardsville, 1969.

Pailin, David. *The Way to Faith; An Examination of Newman's 'Grammar of Assent' as a Response to the Search for Certainty in Faith*. Epworth, 1969.

Paley, William. *A View of the Evidences of Christianity*, 2nd edn. 1794.
Natural Theology, 3rd edn. 1803.

Palmer, Tony. *Belief and Will*. Unpublished paper.
Objectivity, Unpublished paper.

Pattison, Mark. *Memoirs*. Macmillan, 1885.

Peacock, Thomas Love. *Melincourt*. 1817.

Phillips, Robert, ed. *Aspects of Alice*. Gollancz, 1972.

Pinnock, W. H. *An Analysis of Scripture History*. Cambridge, 1848.

Plato, *The Republic*, trans. H. D. P. Lee. Penguin, 1955.
The Symposium, trans. W. Hamilton. Penguin, 1951.

Pope, Alexander. *Essay on Man*. 1733.

Prickett, Stephen. *Coleridge and Wordsworth. The Poetry of Growth*. Cambridge, 1970.
'Dante, Beatrice, and M. C. Escher: Disconfirmation as a Metaphor', *Journal of European Studies*, no. 2. 1972.

Rader, Melvin. *Wordsworth: A Philosophical Approach*. Oxford, 1967.

Ramsey, A. M. *F. D. Maurice and the Conflicts of Modern Theology*. Cambridge, 1951.

Ray, John. *Wisdom of God in the Creation*. 1701.

Reardon, B. M. G. *From Coleridge to Gore*. Longman, 1971.
Religious Thought in the Nineteenth Century. Cambridge, 1966.

Reckitt, Maurice B. *Maurice to Temple*. Faber, 1947.

Reis, Richard. *George MacDonald*. Twayne, New York, 1972.

Richards, I. A. *Coleridge on Imagination*. Kegan Paul, 1934.

Robertson, F. W. *Lectures on the Influence of Poetry and Wordsworth*. Reprinted 1906.
Sermons on Religion and Life. Everyman, 1906.

Robinson, Henry Crabb. *Henry Crabb Robinson on Books and their Writers*, ed. E. J. Morely. Dent, 1938.

Rousseau, Jean-Jacques. *Confessions*. Penguin, 1953.

Rowntree, J. S. 'Notes on *The Christian Year*'. Reprint Bodley Library, 1927.

Russell, Bertrand. *Freedom and Organization 1814–1914*. Allen & Unwin, 1934.

Sanders, C. R. *Coleridge and the Broad Church Movement*. Duke University Press. N. Carolina, 1942.

Sanderson, David. 'Coleridge's Political "Sermons": Discursive Language and the Voice of God', *The Journal of Modern Philology*, vol. 70, no. 4. May 1973.

Schelling, Friedrich Wilhelm Joseph von. *Entwurf eines Systems der Naturphilosophie*. Jena, 1799.
Philosophie der Mythologie. Berlin, 1857.
System des transcendentalen Idealismus. Tübingen, 1800.

Schlegel, August Wilhelm von. *Lectures on Dramatic Art and Literature*, trans. Black. 1815.

Shafer, Robert. *Christianity and Naturalism*. Yale, New Haven, Conn., 1926.

Shaffer, E. S. *'Kubla Khan' and 'The Fall of Jerusalem'*. Cambridge, 1975.

Shawcross, J. 'Introduction' to *Biographia Literaria*. Oxford, 1907.

Snyder, Alice. *Coleridge on Logic and Learning*, Yale, New Haven, Conn., 1929.

Sperry, Stuart M., Jr. 'From *Tintern Abbey* to the *Intimations Ode*: Wordsworth and the Function of Memory', *The Wordsworth Circle*, vol. I, no. 2. Spring 1970.

Sterling, John. *Essays and Tales of John Sterling*. 1848.

Stewart, Dugald. *Philosophical Essays*. Edinburgh, 1810.

Storr, V. F. *The Development of English Theology in the Nineteenth Century, 1800–1860*. Longman, 1913.

Strachey, Lytton. 'Life of Cardinal Manning', *Eminent Victorians*. Chatto, 1918.

Tillich, Paul. *Theology of Culture*. Oxford, New York, 1959.

Tindal, M. *Christianity as Old as the Creation or The Gospel a Republication of the Religion of Nature*. 1730.

Toulmin, Stephen. *Metaphysical Beliefs*, ed. Alastair MacIntyre. S.C.M., 1970.

Trail, H. D. *Coleridge*. Macmillan, 1884.

Trollope, Anthony. *The Warden*. 1855.

Barchester Towers. 1857.

The Last Chronicle of Barset. 1867.

Underhill, Evelyn. *Mysticism*. University Paperbacks. Methuen, 1960.

Vargish, Thomas. *Newman: The Contemplation of Mind*. Oxford, 1970.

Vidler, Alec R. *F. D. Maurice and Company*. S.C.M., 1966.

The Church in an Age of Revolution. The Pelican History of the Church, vol. v. Penguin, 1961.

Ward, Wilfred. *The Life of John Henry Cardinal Newman*. Longman, 1912.

Warren, Robert Penn. 'A Poem of Pure Imagination', *Selected Essays*. Eyre & Spottiswoode, 1964.

Wellek, René. *Immanuel Kant in England*. Princeton, New Jersey, 1931.

Wesley, John. *Sermons on Several Occasions*, First series, 4th edn. 1787.

Willey, Basil. *Nineteenth Century Studies*. Peregrine, 1964.

The Eighteenth Century Background. Chatto, 1940.

Samuel Taylor Coleridge. Chatto, 1972.

Williams, Isaac. Tracts *Eighty* and *Eighty Seven*, 'On Reserve in

Communicating Religious Knowledge', *The Oxford Movement*, ed. Fairweather. Oxford, New York, 1964.

Wittgenstein, Ludwig. *Philosophical Investigations*. Blackwell, Oxford, 1953.

Wolff, Robert Lee. *The Golden Key*. Yale U.P., New Haven, Conn., 1961.

Wood, E. F. L. 'John Keble', *Leaders of the Church 1800–1900*, ed. G. W. E. Russell. Mowbray, 1909.

Wood, H. G. *Frederick Denison Maurice*. Cambridge, 1950.

Wordsworth, William. *Poetical Works*, ed. E. De Selincourt, 5 vols. Oxford, 1940–9.

'Preface', *Lyrical Ballads*, ed. R. L. Brett and A. R. Jones. Methuen, 1965.

The Prose Works of William Wordsworth, ed. Grosart. Moxon, 1876.

Index